Contract Law

We work with leading authors to develop the strongest educational materials in law, bringing cutting-edge thinking and best learning practice to a global market.

Under a range of well-known imprints, including Longman, we craft high quality print and electronic publications which help readers to understand and apply their content, whether studying or at work.

To find out about the complete range of our publishing please visit us on the World Wide Web at: **www.pearsoneduc.com**

Contract Law

Fourth Edition

Catherine Elliott and
Frances Quinn

An imprint of **Pearson Education**

Harlow, England • London • New York • Boston • San Francisco • Toronto
Sydney • Tokyo • Singapore • Hong Kong • Seoul • Taipei • New Delhi
Cape Town • Madrid • Mexico City • Amsterdam • Munich • Paris • Milan

Pearson Education Limited

Edinburgh Gate
Harlow
Essex CM20 2JE
England

and Associated Companies throughout the world

Visit us on the World Wide Web at:
www.pearsoneduc.com

First published in Great Britain 1996
Second edition published 1999
Third edition published 2001
Fourth edition 2003

ISBN 0 582 47330 6

British Library Cataloguing-in-Publication Data
A catalogue record for this book is available from the British Library

10 9 8 7 6 5 4 3 2 1
08 07 06 05 04 03

Typeset in 10.5/12pt Baskerville by 35
Printed and bound by Henry Ling Limited, at the Dorset Press, Dorchester, DT1 1HD

The publisher's policy is to use paper manufactured from sustainable forests.

Contents

Preface *ix*
Acknowledgements *x*
Table of cases *xi*
Table of statutes *xxi*
Table of statutory instruments *xxiv*
Table of EC legislation *xxv*

▶ **Introduction** *1*

Why do we need contract law? *1*
The origins of contract law *2*
Freedom of contract *4*
Contract and fairness *4*
The objective approach *5*

Part I
THE FORMATION OF A CONTRACT

▶ **1 Offer and acceptance** *9*

Unilateral and bilateral contracts *9*
Offer *10*
Invitations to treat *10*
How long does an offer last? *14*
Acceptance *18*
Acceptance must be communicated *24*
Exceptions to the communication rule *24*
Ignorance of the offer *28*
Cross offers *29*
Time of the formation of the contract *30*
Offer and acceptance implied by the court *30*

Auctions, tenders and the sale of land *31*
How important are offer and acceptance? *36*
Problems with offer and acceptance *37*

Answering questions *39*

▶ **2 Certainty** *42*

Provision for clarification *42*
Terms implied by statute *43*
Previous course of dealing *43*
Reasonableness *44*
Custom *44*
The 'officious bystander' *44*
Removing minor uncertain terms *44*

Answering questions *45*

▶ **3 Intention to create legal relations** *46*

Social and domestic agreements *46*
Commercial agreements *48*
How important is intention to create legal relations? *51*

Answering questions *52*

▶ **4 Capacity** *53*

Minors *53*
Mental incapacity *58*
Corporations *60*

Answering questions *61*

▶ **5 Formalities** *63*

Contracts which must be made by
deed *63*
Contracts which must be in writing *63*
Contracts which must be evidenced
in writing *64*
Contracts made through the internet
and by e-mail *64*

Answering questions *65*

▶ **6 Consideration** *66*

What is consideration? *66*
Performance of an existing duty *73*
Waiver and promissory estoppel *80*
Agreement by deed *85*
Consideration and conditional gifts *85*
Problems with consideration *86*
The future of consideration *88*
Reform *89*

Answering questions *90*

Part 2
THE CONTENTS OF A
CONTRACT

▶ **7 Terms of the contract** *95*

Express terms *95*
Oral statements *95*
Written terms *99*
Collateral contracts *101*
Entire agreement clauses *101*
Oral and written statements *102*
Construction of express terms *102*

Implied terms *105*
Terms implied in fact *105*
Terms implied in law *108*
Terms implied by custom *110*
Terms implied by trade usage *110*

The relative importance of contractual
terms *110*
Conditions *110*
Warranties *111*
Innominate terms *112*

Answering questions *114*

▶ **8 Unfair contract terms** *117*

Exemption clauses *117*
Common law controls *118*
Statutory controls *127*

Unfair terms *132*
Unfair Terms in Consumer Contracts
Regulations 1999 *132*
Comparison between the 1999
Regulations and UCTA *138*
Other legislative controls *138*

Answering questions *139*

Part 3
VITIATING FACTORS

▶ **9 Misrepresentation** *145*

What is misrepresentation? *145*
Types of misrepresentation *150*
Remedies for misrepresentation *153*
Misrepresentation and terms *159*
Exemption clauses and
misrepresentation *159*

Answering questions *159*

▶ **10 Mistake** *162*

General principles *162*
Common mistake at common
law *165*
Cross-purposes mistake at common
law *170*
Equity and cross-purposes
mistake *176*

Mistakes relating to documents *176*
Criticism and reform *178*

Answering questions *180*

11 Illegality *182*

Introduction *182*
Violation of legal rules and public
   policy *183*
The contract is against public
   policy *187*
The effect of an illegal contract *190*
Criticism *193*
Reform *195*

Answering questions *195*

12 Duress and undue influence *197*

Duress *197*
Undue influence *200*
Inequality of bargaining power *207*

Answering questions *208*

Part 4
THE RIGHTS AND LIABILITIES OF THIRD PARTIES

13 Third parties *213*

The privity rule *213*
Reform *213*
Contractual rights conferred on third
   parties *214*
Statutory rights *215*
Common law exceptions *218*
Exceptions in equity *225*
Arguments for the privity rule *226*
Arguments against the privity
   rule *228*

Answering questions *230*

Part 5
DISCHARGE AND REMEDIES

14 Discharge of contract *235*

Performance *235*
The entire performance rule *235*
Mitigation of the entire performance
   rule *236*
Vicarious performance *239*

Frustration *240*
What will amount to frustration? *240*
Time of frustrating event *243*
Limits to frustration *243*
Legal consequences of frustration *245*
The theory of frustration *248*

Breach *249*
Actual breach *249*
Anticipatory breach *250*
Lawful excuse *250*
Effect of breach *251*
Choice to affirm or discharge *253*

Agreement *255*
Consideration *256*
Formalities *256*

Answering questions *257*

15 Remedies *263*

Common law remedies *263*
Damages *263*
Action for an agreed sum *282*
Restitution *283*
Quantum meruit *286*

Equitable remedies *288*
Specific performance *288*
Injunction *291*

Remedies agreed by the parties *293*
Liquidated damages *293*
Penalty clauses *293*

Extinction of remedies 294
The statutory time limits 294
Problems with remedies 296

Answering questions 298

Part 6
CONSUMER PROTECTION

▶ **16 Consumer contracts** 307

History 307
Contracts for the sale of goods 308
Contracts for the supply of services 315
Hire contracts 316
Manufacturers' liability 316

Consumer protection by the criminal
    law 320
Unsolicited goods 322
Consumer credit 323
Contract law and consumer
    protection 324
Reform 324

Answering questions 327

▶ **Appendix** 331

Answering examination questions 331
Essay questions 333
Problem questions 335

Glossary 337
Index 342

Preface

The fourth edition of this book aims to build on the strengths that have led to the success and popularity of the previous editions, which have been extremely well received by both teachers and students alike. It incorporates all the important legal developments that have taken place since the publication of the third edition. As with our previous editions, our aim has been to provide a clear explanation of the law of contract. As well as setting out the law itself, we look at the principles behind it, and discuss some of the issues and debates arising from contract law. We hope that the material will allow you to enter into some of that debate and develop your own views as to how the law should develop.

One of our priorities in writing this book has been to explain the material clearly, so that it is easy to understand, without lowering the quality of the content. Too often, law is avoided as a difficult subject, when the real difficulty is the vocabulary and style of legal textbooks. For that reason, we have aimed to use 'plain English' as far as possible, and explain the more complex legal terminology where it arises. There is also a glossary explaining common terms at the back of the book. In addition, chapters are structured so that material is in a systematic order for the purposes of both learning and revision, and clear subheadings make specific points easy to locate.

Although we hope that many readers will use this book to satisfy a general interest in the law, we recognize that the majority will be those who have to sit an examination in the subject. Therefore, each chapter features typical examination questions, with detailed guidance on answering them, using the material in the book. This is obviously useful at revision time, but we recommend that, when first reading the book, you take the opportunity offered by the questions sections to think through the material that you have just read and look at it from different angles. This will help you both to understand and remember it. You will also find that the Appendix at the end of the book gives useful general advice on answering examination questions on contract law.

This book is part of a series that has been produced by the authors. The other books in the series are *English Legal System, AS Law, Criminal Law* and *Tort Law.*

We have endeavoured to state the law as at 1 January 2003.

Catherine Elliott and Frances Quinn
London 2003

Acknowledgements

We are grateful to the following for permission to reproduce the following copyright material:

The Department of Trade and Industry for permission to reproduce Figure 16.1, 'DTI Guidance Flow Chart', from their website http://www.dti.gov.uk.

We are indebted to the following examination boards for permission to reproduce questions that have appeared in their examination papers:

Assessment and Qualifications Alliance (AQA)
Edexcel Foundation
Oxford Cambridge and RSA Examinations Board (OCR)
Welsh Joint Education Committee (WJEC)

The examination boards are not responsible for any suggested answers to the questions.

In some instances we have been unable to trace the owners of copyright material and we would appreciate any information that would enable us to do so.

Table of cases

Adams v Lindsell (1818) 1 B & Ald 68 25
Addis v Gramophone Co Ltd [1909] AC
  488 264, 265, 298, 299
Ailsa Craig Fishing Co Ltd v Malvern
  Fishing Co Ltd (The Strathallan)
  [1983] 1 WLR 964 124
Alderslade v Hendon Laundry Ltd
  [1945] KB 189 125
Alfred McAlpine Construction Ltd v
  Panatown Ltd (No 1) [2001] 1 AC
  518 223
Alliance Bank Ltd v Broom (1864) 2 Dr
  & Sm 289 72
Allied Maples Group Ltd v Simmons &
  Simmons [1995] 1 WLR 1602 279
Alpenstow Ltd v Regalian Properties plc
  [1985] 1 WLR 721 35
Alpha Trading Ltd v Dunnshaw-Patten
  Ltd [1981] QB 290 106
Amalgamated Investment & Property Co
  v John Walker & Sons [1977] 1 WLR
  164 163, 243
Anderson Ltd v Daniel [1924] 1 KB 138
  182
Anglia Television Ltd v Reed [1972] 1
  QB 60 274, 275
Applegate v Moss [1971] 1 QB 406 295
Archbolds (Freightage) Ltd v S
  Spanglett Ltd [1961] 1 QB 374 192
Armhouse Lee Ltd v Chappell *The
  Times*, August 7, 1996 188
Ashmore Benson Pease & Co Ltd v AV
  Dawson Ltd [1973] 1 WLR 828 192
Ashton v Turner [1981] QB 137 190
Associated Japanese Bank
  (International) Ltd v Credit du Nord
  SA [1989] 1 WLR 255 167
Atlas Express Ltd v Kafco (Importers
  and Distributors) Ltd [1989] QB 833
  199, 209, 210

Attorney General v Blake [2001] 1 AC
  268 280
Avery v Bowden (1856) 6 E & B 953
  250

Bailey v Bullock [1950] 2 All ER 1167
  267
Baird Textile Holdings Ltd v Marks &
  Spencer plc [2001] EWCA Civ 274
  30, 42, 84
Balfour v Balfour [1919] 2 KB 571 46,
  47, 52
Balfour Beatty Construction (Scotland)
  Ltd v Scottish Power 1994 SLT 807
  272
Bank of Credit and Commerce
  International SA v Aboody [1990] 1
  QB 923 203
Bank of Credit and Commerce
  International SA (In Liquidation) v
  Ali (No 1) [2001] UKHL 8 103
Bannerman v White (1861) 10 CBNS
  844 96
Barclays Bank plc v O'Brien [1994] 1
  AC 180 204, 205, 208, 209
Barclays Bank plc v Schwartz *The Times*,
  August 2, 1995 59
Barry v Davies (t/a Heathcote Ball &
  Co) [2000] 1 WLR 1962 32
Barton (Alexander) v Armstrong
  (Alexander Ewan) [1976] AC 104
  199
Beale v Taylor [1967] 1 WLR 1193 309
Bell v Lever Bros Ltd [1932] AC 161
  167, 168, 169, 180
Bennett v Bennett [1952] 1 KB 249
  189
Beswick v Beswick [1968] AC 58 213,
  226, 229, 288
Bisset v Wilkinson [1927] AC 177 147

Blackpool and Fylde Aero Club v
Blackpool BC [1990] 1 WLR 1195 32
Bland v Sparkes *The Times*, December
17, 1999 257
Bolton v Mahadeva [1972] 1 WLR 1009
236
Boone v Eyre (1779) 1 Hy Bl 273n
236
Bowerman v Association of British
Travel Agents Ltd [1996] CLC 451
11
Bowmakers Ltd v Barnet Instruments
Ltd [1945] KB 65 191
Bowman v Secular Society Ltd [1917]
AC 406 188
BP Exploration Co (Libya) Ltd v Hunt
(No 2) [1979] 1 WLR 783 247
Brace v Calder [1895] 2 QB 253 273
Bradbury v Morgan (1862) 1 H & C 249
16
Brimnes, The *see* Tenax Steamship Co v
Owners of the Motor Vessel Brimnes
Brinkibon v Stahag Stahl und
Stahlwarenhandels GmbH [1983] 2
AC 3 28, 40
British Crane Hire Corp Ltd v Ipswich
Plant Hire Ltd [1975] QB 303 110
British Road Services Ltd v Arthur v
Crutchley & Co Ltd (No 1) [1968] 1
All ER 811 20
British Steel Corp v Cleveland Bridge &
Engineering Co Ltd [1984] 1 All ER
504 286
British Transport Commission v Gourley
[1956] AC 185 279
British Westinghouse Electric &
Manufacturing Co Ltd v
Underground Electric Railways Co
of London Ltd (No 2) [1912] AC
673 273
Brogden v Metropolitan Rail Co (1877)
2 App Cas 666 19
Brown v KMR Services Ltd [1995] 4 All
ER 598 271
Bunge Corp v Tradax Export SA [1981]
1 WLR 711 110, 303
Butler Machine Tool Co v Ex-cell-o
Corp (England) [1979] 1 WLR 401
20, 41

Byrne & Co v Leon Van Tien Hoven &
Co (1879–80) LR 5 CPD 344 16, 17,
27, 300

C&P Haulage v Middleton [1983] 1
WLR 1461 275
Car and Universal Finance Co Ltd v
Caldwell [1965] 1 QB 525 153
Carlill v Carbolic Smoke Ball Co [1893]
1 QB 256 10, 11, 25, 41, 49, 115,
226, 317
Casey's Patents, Steward v Casey, Re
[1892] 1 Ch 104 70
Cehave NV v Bremer Handels GmbH
(The Hansa Nord) [1976] QB 44
114
Central London Property Trust v High
Trees House Ltd [1947] KB 130 81,
82, 83, 85, 88, 90
Centrovincial Estates v Merchant
Investors Assurance Co [1983] Com
LR 158 171
Chapelton v Barry Urban DC [1940] 1
KB 532 120
Chaplin v Hicks [1911] 2 KB 786 278
Chappell & Co Ltd v Nestle Co Ltd
[1960] AC 87 71, 329
Chapple v Cooper (1844) 13 M & W
252 54, 62
Charles Rickards Ltd v Oppenheim
[1950] 1 KB 616 80, 239
Charter v Sullivan [1957] 2 QB 117
277
Cheese v Thomas [1994] 1 WLR 129
203
China-Pacific SA v Food Corp of India
(The Winson) [1981] QB 403 82
CIBC Mortgages plc v Pitt [1994] 1 AC
200 203
City and Westminster Properties (1934)
Ltd v Mudd [1959] Ch 129 101
Clarke v Earl of Dunraven (The
Satanita) [1897] AC 59 36, 41
Clay v Yates (1856) 1 H & N 73 193
Clea Shipping Corp v Bulk Oil
International (The Alaskan Trader)
(No 2) [1984] 1 All ER 129 255, 258
Clements v London and North Western
Railway Co (1894) 2 QB 482 55, 61

Collen v Wright (1857) 8 E & B 647 220

Collins v Godefroy (1831) 1 B & Ad 950 73

Combe v Combe [1951] 2 KB 215 72, 84, 88, 92

Commission of the European Communities v United Kingdom (C300/95) [1997] All ER (EC) 481 320

Cooper v Parker (1885) 15 CB 822 78

Cooper v Phibbs (1867) LR 2 HL 149 167

Cooperative Insurance Society Ltd v Argyll Stores (Holdings) Ltd [1998] AC 1 290

Cope v Rowlands (1836) 2 M & W 149 185

Corpe v Overton (1833) 10 Bing 252 56

Couchman v Hill [1947] KB 554 100

Couldery v Bartrum (1881) 19 Ch D 394 87

County Ltd v Girozentrale Securities [1996] 1 BCLC 653 268

Couturier v Hastie (1856) 5 HL Cas 673 166

Cowan v Milbourn (1866–67) LR 2 Ex 230 187, 193

Cowan v O'Connor (1888) LR 20 QBD 640 26

Cowern v Nield (1912) 2 KB 419 55, 62

Craddock Bros Ltd v Hunt [1923] 2 Ch 136 178

Craven Ellis v Canons Ltd [1936] 2 KB 403 287, 288

CTN Cash and Carry Ltd v Gallaher Ltd [1994] 4 All ER 714 199, 209

Cundy v Lindsay (1878) 3 App Cas 459 172, 173

Curtis v Chemical Cleaning & Dyeing Co [1951] 1 KB 805 118, 126

Cutter v Powell (1795) 6 Term Rep 320 235, 237

D&C Builders Ltd v Rees [1966] 2 QB 617 83, 87

Davies v Taylor (1974)AC 207 279

Daniels v White & Sons Ltd [1938] 4 All ER 258 318

Darlington BC v Wiltshier Northern Ltd [1995] 1 WLR 68 223, 229

Daulia Ltd v Four Millbank Nominees Ltd [1978] Ch 231 22

Davies v Collins [1945] 1 All ER 247 239

Davis Contractors v Fareham Urban DC [1956] AC 696 241, 249, 258

De Francesco v Barnum (1890) 45 Ch D 430 55, 61

Denton v GN Railway (1856) 5 E & B 860 13

Derry v Peek (1889) LR 14 App Cas 337 150, 159, 261

Dick Bentley Productions Ltd v Harold Smith (Motors) Ltd [1965] 1 WLR 623 96

Dickinson v Dodds (1875–76) LR 2 Ch D 463 17, 40

Diesen v Samson 1971 SLT (Sh Ct) 49 265

Dimmock v Hallett (1866–67) LR 2 Ch App 21 147, 148

Director General of Fair Trading v First National Bank plc [2001] UKHL 52 133, 135

DO Ferguson Associates v Sohl 62 BLR 95 285

Donoghue v Stevenson [1932] AC 562 317

Doyle v Olby (Ironmongers) Ltd [1969] 2 QB 158 157

Doyle v White City Stadium Ltd [1935] 1 KB 110 55, 61

Duffy v Newcastle United Football Co Ltd The Times, July 7, 2000 98

Dunlop Pneumatic Tyre Co Ltd v New Garage & Motor Co Ltd [1915] AC 79 293

Dunlop Pneumatic Tyre Co Ltd v Selfridge & Co [1915] AC 847 66

Dunmore v Alexander (1830) 9 Shaw (Ct of Sess) 190 28

Eastwood v Kenyon (1840) 11 Ad & El 438 86

Ecay v Godfrey (1947) 80 Ll L Rep 286 98

Eccles v Bryant [1948] Ch 93 36

Edgington v Fitzmaurice (1885) LR 29
Ch D 459   147, 148, 149
Edwards v Skyways [1964] 1 WLR 349
50
Entores Ltd v Miles Far East Corp
[1955] 2 QB 327   24, 25, 27, 40
Equitable Life Assurance Society v
Hyman [2000] 2 WLR 798   108
Erlanger v New Sombrero Phosphate
Co (1877–78) LR 3 App Cas 1218
155
Errington v Errington and Woods
[1952] 1 KB 290   22, 52, 89
Esso Petroleum Co Ltd v Customs and
Excise Commissioners [1976] 1 WLR
1   48
Esso Petroleum Co Ltd v Harper's
Garage (Stourport) Ltd [1968] AC
269   184
Esso Petroleum Co Ltd v Mardon
[1976] QB 801   151
Eurymedon, The see New Zealand
Shipping Co Ltd v AM Satterthwaite
& Co Ltd (The Eurymedon)
Everet v Williams (1725) Lindley on
Partnerships, 11th Edn p123   183

Farley v Skinner (No 2) [2001] UKHL
49   266, 267
Fawcett v Smethurst (1914) 84 LJKB
473   54
Felthouse v Bindley (1862) 6 LT 157
19, 23, 24, 25, 39, 116, 302, 322
Fibrosa Spolka Akcyjna v Fairbairn
Lawson Combe Barbour Ltd [1943]
AC 32   242, 245, 246, 284
Financings v Stimson [1962] 1 WLR
1184   14
Fisher v Bell [1961] 1 QB 394   12, 332
Fitch v Snedaker (1868) 38 NY 248   29
Fletcher v Krell (1873) 42 LJ QB 55
145
Foakes v Beer (1883–84) LR 9 App Cas
605   77, 87, 90
Foley v Classique Coaches Ltd [1934] 2
KB 1   43
Ford Motor Co Ltd v Amalgamated
Union of Engineering and Foundry
Workers [1969] 2 QB 303   51

Forman & Co Proprietary Ltd v
Liddesdale, The [1900] AC 190   286
Foster v Driscoll [1929] 1 KB 470   189
Frost v Knight (1871–72) LR 7 Ex 111
250, 251

Gallie v Lee see Saunders (Executrix of
the Estate of Rose Maud Gallie) v
Anglia Building Society (formerly
Northampton Town and County
Building Society)
Gamerco SA v ICM/Fair Warning
(Agency) Ltd [1995] 1 WLR 1126
248
George Mitchell (Chesterhall) Ltd v
Finney Lock Seeds Ltd [1983] 2 AC
803   131, 141
Gibbons v Proctor (1891) 64 LT 594
29
Gibson v Manchester City Council
[1979] 1 WLR 294   10, 37, 302
Gilbert & Partners v Knight [1968] 2 All
ER 248   287
Glasbrook Bros Ltd v Glamorgan CC
[1925] AC 270   41, 73, 74
Goldsoll v Goldman [1915] 1 Ch 292
193
Grainger & Son v Gough (Surveyor of
Taxes) [1896] AC 325   12
Great Northern Railway Co v Witham
(1873–74) LR 9 CP 16   9, 34
Great Peace Shipping Ltd v Tsavliris
Salvage (International) Ltd (2001)
151 NLJ 1696   170
Green v Russell, McCarthy (Third
Party) [1959] 2 QB 226   226
Griffiths v Peter Conway Ltd [1939] 1
All ER 685   311

Hadley v Baxendale (1854) 9 Ex 341
268, 269, 270, 271, 298
Hadley v Kemp [1999] EMLR 589   63
Harris v Nickerson (1872–73) LR 8 QB
286   31
Harris v Sheffield United Football Club
[1988] QB 77   41, 74
Harrison & Jones v Bunten & Lancaster
[1953] 1 QB 646   168
Hart v O'Connor [1985] AC 1000   58

Hartley v Ponsonby (1857) 7 E & B 872
75

Hartog v Colin and Shields [1939] 3 All
ER 566 171

Harvela Investments Ltd v Royal Trust
Co of Canada (CI) Ltd [1986] AC
207 32, 33

Harvey v Facey [1893] AC 552 35, 302

Hayes v James & Charles Dodd (A
Firm) [1990] 2 All ER 815 264

Hedley Byrne & Co Ltd v Heller &
Partners Ltd [1964] AC 465 96, 150,
151, 153, 158, 159

Henderson v Arthur [1907] 1 KB 10 99

Henthorn v Fraser [1892] 2 Ch 27 26,
27

Hermann v Charlesworth [1905] 2 KB
123 188

Herne Bay Steam Boat Co v Hutton
[1903] 2 KB 683 243

Heron II, The see Koufos v C Czarnikow
Ltd (The Heron II)

Heyman v Darwins Ltd [1942] AC 356
253

Heywood v Wellers (A Firm) [1976] QB
446 265

Hickman v Haynes (1874–75) LR 10 CP
598 80

Hillas (WN)& Co Ltd v Arcos Ltd
(1932) 43 Ll L Rep 359 42, 43, 44,
45

Hirachand Punamchand v Temple
[1911] 2 KB 330 78

Hochster v De La Tour (1853) 2 El &
Bl 678 250

Hoenig v Isaacs [1952] 2 All ER 176
236

Hollier v Rambler Motors [1972] 2 QB
71 123, 140

Holman v Johnson (1775) 1 Cowp 341
194

Holwell Securities Ltd v Hughes [1974]
1 WLR 155 27

Hongkong Fir Shipping Co Ltd v
Kawasaki Kisen Kaisha Ltd (The
Hongkong Fir) [1962] 2 QB 26 112,
113

Houghton v Trafalgar Insurance Co Ltd
[1954] 1 QB 247 123, 133

Household Fire & Carriage Accident
Insurance Co Ltd v Grant (1878–79)
LR 4 Ex D 216 26

Howard Marine & Dredging Co Ltd v A
Ogden & Sons (Excavations) Ltd
[1978] QB 574 152, 160

Hughes v Metropolitan Railway Co
(1877) 2 App Cas 439 80, 81, 82, 83

Hunt v Silk (1804) 5 East 449 285

Hyde v Wrench (1840) 3 Beav 334 15

Ingram v Little [1961] 1 QB 31 174,
181

Inland Revenue Commissioners v Fry
[2001] STC 1715 23

Interfoto Picture Library Ltd v Stiletto
Visual Programmes Ltd [1989] QB
433 121, 122, 135

Investors Compensation Scheme Ltd v
West Bromwich Building Society
(No 1) [1998] 1 WLR 896 102, 103,
329

J Evans & Son (Portsmouth) Ltd v
Andrea Merzario Ltd [1976] 1 WLR
1078 48, 102

Jackson v Horizon Holidays Ltd [1975]
1 WLR 1468 221, 226, 231, 265, 298

Jacobs & Young v Kent (US) (1921) 129
NE 889 278

Jarvis v Swans Tours Ltd [1973] QB 233
264, 265

Jones v Padavatton [1969] 1 WLR 328
47, 68

Jones v Vernon's Pools [1938] 2 All ER
626 50

King's Norton Metal Co v Edridge,
Merrett & Co Ltd (1897) 14 TLR 98
172, 173

Kleinwort Benson Ltd v Lincoln City
Council [1999] 2 AC 349 164, 165,
284

Koufos v C Czarnikow Ltd (The Heron
II) [1969] 1 AC 350 269, 270, 298

Krell v Henry [1903] 2 KB 740 243, 261

Lampleigh v Brathwait (1615) Hob 105
69

Lauritzen (J) A/S *v* Wijsmuller BV
(The Super Servant Two) [1990] 1
Lloyd's Rep 1 245, 258
Lazenby Garages *v* Wright [1976] 1
WLR 459 277
Leaf *v* International Galleries [1950] 2
KB 86 155, 161
Les Affreteurs Reunis SA *v* Leopold
Walford (London) Ltd [1919] AC 801
225
Leslie (R) Ltd *v* Sheill [1914] 2 KB 607
57
L'Estrange *v* F Graucob Ltd [1934] 2
KB 394 6, 118, 176, 196
Levy *v* Yates (1838) 8 Ad & El 129 182
Lewis *v* Averay (No 1) [1972] 1 QB 198
173, 181
Linden Gardens Trust Ltd *v* Lenesta
Sludge Disposals Ltd [1994] 1 AC 85
222, 223
Liverpool City Council *v* Irwin [1977]
AC 239 108
Lloyds Bank Ltd *v* Bundy [1975] QB
326 201, 202, 203, 207, 208, 209, 210
Lockett *v* A & M Charles Ltd [1938] 4
All ER 170 315
Loftus *v* Roberts (1902) 18 TLR 532 42
Luxor (Eastbourne) Ltd *v* Cooper
[1941] AC 108 22, 107

McArdle, Re [1951] Ch 669 69
McRae *v* Commonwealth Disposals
Commission (1951) 84 CLR 377 166,
180, 275
Mahkutai, The [1996] AC 650 224
Mahmoud and Ispahani, Re [1921] 2
KB 716 190
Malik *v* Bank of Credit and Commerce
International SA (In Liquidation)
[1998] AC 20 104, 109
Mannai Investment Co Ltd *v* Eagle Star
Life Assurance Co Ltd [1997] AC 749
103
Maredelanto Compania Naviera
SA *v* Bergbau-Handel GmbH
(The Mihalis Angelos) [1971]
1 QB 164 111, 114
Maritime National Fish Ltd *v* Ocean
Trawlers Ltd [1935] AC 524 244

Martinez *v* Ellesse International SpA
CHANI 98/0855/3 104
Martin-Smith *v* Williams [1999] EMLR
571 252
Mason *v* Provident Clothing & Supply
Co Ltd [1913] 1 KB 65 184
Mendelssohn *v* Normand [1970] 1 QB
177 126
Merritt *v* Merritt (1969) 119 NLJ 484
47, 52
Middleton *v* Wiggins (1995) 123
Miles *v* New Zealand Alford Estate Co
(1886) 32 Ch D 266 72
Miles *v* Wakefield MDC [1987] AC 539
287
Modahl *v* British Athletic Federation Ltd
(No 1) *The Times*, July 23, 1999 249
Mohamed *v* Alaga & Co [1998] 2 All
ER 720 194
Moorcock, The (1889) LR 14 PD 64 106
Moore & Co Ltd and Landauer & Co
Re [1921] 2 KB 519 235, 310
Morone *v* Morone (1980) (unreported)
US 47
Morris *v* Baron & Co [1918] AC 1 256
Muirhead *v* Industrial Tank Specialities
Ltd [1986] QB 507 318

Nash *v* Inman [1908] 2 KB 1 54, 62
National Westminster Bank plc *v*
Morgan [1985] AC 686 202, 203,
208, 209, 210
New Zealand Shipping Co Ltd *v* AM
Satterthwaite & Co Ltd (The
Eurymedon) [1975] AC 154 80, 86,
126, 224, 225, 229
Nicholson and Venn *v* Smith-Marriott
(1947) 177 LT 189 168
Nickoll & Knight *v* Ashton Edridge &
Co [1901] 2 KB 126 241
Nicolene Ltd *v* Simmonds [1953] 1 QB
543 44, 45
Nordenfelt *v* Maxim Nordenfelt Guns &
Ammunition Co Ltd [1894] AC 535
184, 196
North Ocean Shipping Co *v* Hyundai
Construction Co (The Atlantic
Baron) [1979] QB 705 198, 200, 209,
210

Nurdin & Peacock plc *v* DB Ramsden & Co Ltd [1999] 1 WLR 1249 164

Nutt *v* Read (2000) 32 HLR 761 168, 170

O'Brien *v* MGN Ltd [2001] EWCA Civ 1279 122

Occidental Worldwide Investment Corp *v* Skibs A/S Avanti (The Siboen and The Sibotre) [1976] 1 Lloyd's Rep 293 280

Olley *v* Marlborough Court Ltd [1949] 1 KB 532 119, 329

Oscar Chess *v* Williams [1957] 1 WLR 370 96

Overseas Tankship (UK) Ltd *v* Miller Steamship Co Pty Ltd (The Wagon Mound) [1967] 1 AC 617 158

Page One Records, Ltd *v* Britton [1968] 1 WLR 157 292

Pao On *v* Lau Yiu Long [1980] AC 614 80, 198, 209

Parker *v* South Eastern Railway Co (1876–77) LR 2 CPD 416 119

Parkinson *v* College of Ambulance Ltd [1925] 2 KB 1 189, 191

Partridge *v* Crittenden [1968] 1 WLR 1204 12, 115

Patel *v* Ali [1984] Ch 283 289

Payne *v* Cave (1789) 100 ER 502 16

Pearce *v* Brookes [1861–73] All ER Rep 102 188, 192

Peck *v* Lateu (1973) 117 SJ 185 48

Penn *v* Bristol and West Building Society [1997] 1 WLR 1356 220

Percival *v* London County Council Asylums and Mental Deficiency Committee (1918) 87 LJKB 677 34

Perry *v* Sidney Phillips & Son [1982] 1 WLR 1297 267

Pharmaceutical Society of Great Britain *v* Boots Cash Chemists (Southern) Ltd [1953] 1 QB 401 12

Phillips *v* Brooks Ltd [1919] 2 KB 243 174, 181

Phillips Products *v* Hyland [1987] 1 WLR 659 131

Photo Production Ltd *v* Securicor Transport Ltd [1980] AC 827 125

Pilbrow *v* Pearless de Rougemont & Co [1999] 3 All ER 355 249, 252

Pilkington *v* Wood [1953] Ch 770 272

Pinnel's Case (1602) 76, 77, 78, 83, 87, 90

Planche *v* Colburn (1831) 8 Bing 14 238, 287

Pollard *v* Clayton (1855) 1 K & J 462 296

Posner *v* Scott-Lewis [1987] Ch 25 290

Preist *v* Last [1903] 2 KB 148 311

Pym *v* Campbell (1856) 6 E & B 370 100

Quinn *v* Burch Bros (Builders) Ltd [1966] 2 QB 370 268

R *v* Clarke (1927) 40 CLR 227 29

R *v* Oldham MBC Ex p Garlick [1993] AC 509 58

R *v* Rusby 170 ER 241 3

R&B Customs Brokers Co Ltd *v* United Dominions Trust Ltd [1988] 1 WLR 321 127

Raineri *v* Miles [1981] AC 1050 238

Ramsgate Victoria Hotel *v* Montefiore (1866) LR 1 Exch 109 14

Reardon Smith Line Ltd *v* Hansen-Tangen (The Diana Prosperity) [1976] 1 WLR 989 113, 114

Redgrave *v* Hurd (1881–82) LR 20 Ch D 1 149

Regalian Properties plc *v* London Docklands Development Corp [1995] 1 WLR 212 286

Reigate *v* Union Manufacturing Co (Ramsbottom) Ltd [1918] 1 KB 592 106

Robinson *v* Davison (1871) LR 6 Exch 269 241

Robinson *v* Graves [1935] 1 KB 579 315

Roscorla *v* Thomas (1842) 3 QB 234 69, 92

Rose & Frank Co *v* JR Crompton & Bros Ltd [1923] 2 KB 261 49

Rose (Frederick E) (London) Ltd *v* Pim (William H) Junior & Co Ltd [1953] 2 QB 450 178

Routledge *v* Grant (1828) 4 Bing 653 16, 331

Routledge *v* McKay, Nugent (Third Party), Ashgrove (Fourth Party), Mawson (Fifth Party) [1954] 1 WLR 615 97

Royal Bank of Scotland plc *v* Etridge (No 2) [2001] UKHL 44 200, 202, 204, 205, 207, 259

Royal Boskalis Westminster NV *v* Mountain [1999] QB 674 189

Royscot Trust Ltd *v* Rogerson [1991] 2 QB 297 158

Russell *v* Fulling *The Times*, June 23, 1999 187

Ruxley Electronics and Construction Ltd *v* Forsyth [1996] AC 344 266, 278

Ryan *v* Mutual Tontine Westminster Chambers Association [1893] 1 Ch 116 290

Sapwell *v* Bass [1910] 2 KB 486 276

Satef-Huttenes Alberns SpA *v* Paloma Tercera Shipping Co SA (The Pegase) [1981] 1 Lloyd's Rep 175 271, 303

Saunders (Executrix of the Estate of Rose Maud Gallie) *v* Anglia Building Society (formerly Northampton Town and County Building Society) [1971] AC 1004 177, 210

Scammell (G) and Nephew Ltd *v* Ouston (HC&JG) [1941] AC 251 42

Schawel *v* Reade (1913) 46 ILT 281, HL 97, 99

Schuler AG *v* Wickman Machine Tool Sales Ltd [1974] AC 235 111, 112, 114

Scotson *v* Pegg (1861) 6 H & N 295 79

Scott *v* Coulson [1903] 2 Ch 249 165

Scriven Bros & Co *v* Hindley & Co [1913] 3 KB 564 171

Scruttons Ltd *v* Midland Silicones Ltd [1962] AC 446 126

Seaman *v* Fonereau (1743) 2 Stra 1183 146

Selectmove, Re [1995] 1 WLR 474 19, 77, 83, 87, 90, 302

Shadwell *v* Shadwell (1860) 9 CBNS 159 79, 86

Shanklin Pier Ltd *v* Detel Products Ltd [1951] 2 KB 854 224, 229

Shirlaw *v* Southern Foundries (1926) Ltd [1939] 2 KB 206 105

Shogun Finance Ltd *v* Hudson [2001] EWCA Civ 1000 175, 176, 181

Shuey *v* United States (1875) 92 US 73 18

Simpkins *v* Pays [1955] 1 WLR 975 48

Sinochem International Oil (London) Co Ltd *v* Mobil Sales and Supply Corp (No 1) [2000] 1 All ER (Comm) 474 103

Sir Lindsay Parkinson & Co *v* Commissioners of Works and Public Buildings [1949] 2 KB 632 286

Small *v* Attwood (1838) 3 Y & C Ex 150 149

Smith New Court Securities Ltd *v* Citibank *see* Smith New Court Securities Ltd *v* Scrimgeour Vickers (Asset Management) Ltd

Smith *v* Eric S Bush (A Firm) [1990] 1 AC 831 131

Smith *v* Hughes (1870–71) LR 6 QB 597 6, 162

Smith *v* Land & House Property Corp (1885) LR 28 Ch D 7 148

Smith *v* Wilson (1832) 3 B & Ad 728 101, 110

Smith New Court Securities Ltd *v* Scrimgeour Vickers (Asset Management) Ltd [1997] AC 254 157, 158

Solle *v* Butcher [1950] 1 KB 671 169, 180

Spencer *v* Harding (1869–70) LR 5 CP 561 32

Spice Girls Ltd *v* Aprilia World Service BV [2002] EWCA Civ 15 152

Spring *v* Guardian Assurance plc [1995] 2 AC 296 109

Spring *v* National Amalgamated Stevedores and Dockers Society (No 2) [1956] 1 WLR 585 107

Spurling Ltd v Bradshaw [1956] 1 WLR
461 122, 140
St John Shipping Corp v Joseph Rank
Ltd [1957] 1 QB 267 192
Startup v Macdonald (1843) 6 Man & G
593 238
Steinburg v Scala (Leeds) Ltd [1923] 2
Ch 452 56, 62
Stevenson v Rogers [1999] QB 1028
128, 308
Stevenson Jaques & Co v McLean
(1879–80) LR 5 QBD 346 15
Stewart v Reavell's Garage [1952] 2 QB
545 240
Stilk v Myrick (1809) 2 Camp 317 75
Stocznia Gdanska SA v Latvian Shipping
Co [1998] 1 WLR 574 284
Sudbrook Trading Estate Ltd v Eggleton
[1983] 1 AC 444 44, 45
Sugar v LMS Railway Co [1941] 1 All
ER 172 120
Suisse Atlantique Societe d'Armement
SA v NV Rotterdamsche Kolen
Centrale [1967] 1 AC 361 125
Sumpter v Hedges [1898] 1 QB 673
237
Super Servant Two see Lauritzen (J)
A/S v Wijsmuller BV (The Super
Servant Two)
Surrey CC and Mole DC v Bredero
Homes Ltd [1993] 1 WLR 1361 280

Taylor v Caldwell (1863) 32 LJ QB 164
240, 243, 248
Tenax Steamship Co v Owners of the
Motor Vessel Brimnes (The Brimnes)
[1975] QB 929 18, 25
Thomas v Thomas (1842) 2 QB 851
70, 71
Thompson Ltd v Robinson
(Gunmakers) Ltd [1955] Ch 177 277
Thornton v Shoe Lane Parking [1971]
2 QB 163 13, 119, 121, 133,
140, 141, 329
Timeload Ltd v British
Telecommunications plc [1995]
EMLR 459 129
Tinn v Hoffman (1873) 29 LT 271 20,
23, 30

Tinsley v Milligan [1994] 1 AC 340
191, 194
Tiverton Estates Ltd v Wearwell Ltd
[1975] Ch 146 35
Trollope & Colls Ltd v North West
Metropolitan Regional Hospital Board
[1973] 1 WLR 601 106
Tsakiroglou & Co Ltd v Noblee Thorl
GmbH [1962] AC 93 241, 258
Tulk v Moxhay (1848) 2 Ph 774 226
Tungsten Electric Co Ltd v Tool Metal
Manufacturing Co Ltd (No 3) [1955]
1 WLR 761 83, 84, 90
Tweddle v Atkinson (1861) 1 B & S 393
213, 214, 227

United Scientific Holdings v Burnley BC
[1978] AC 904 239
Universe Tankships Inc of Monrovia v
International Transport Workers
Federation (The Universe Sentinel)
[1983] 1 AC 366 200

Vacwell Engineering Co Ltd v BDH
Chemicals Ltd [1971] 1 QB 111 271,
318
Vaswani v Italian Motors (Sales and
Services) Ltd [1996] 1 WLR 270 251
Victoria Laundry (Windsor) v Newman
Industries [1949] 2 KB 528 269, 270,
298
Vigers v Pike (1842) 8 ER 220 155
Vitol SA v Norelf Ltd (The Santa Clara)
[1996] AC 800 253

Walker v Boyle [1982] 1 WLR 495 159
Walters v Morgan (1861) 3 De GF & J
718 289
Ward v Byham [1956] 1 WLR 496 74, 86
Warlow v Harrison (1858) 1 El & El 295
31, 32
Warner Bros Pictures Inc v Nelson
[1937] 1 KB 209 292
Warren v Mendy [1989] 1 WLR 853
292
Waugh v HB Clifford & Sons Ltd
[1982] Ch 374 219
Weeks v Tybald (1604) Noy 11 49
White v Bluett (1853) 23 LJ Ex 36 71

White v John Warwick & Co [1953] 1
WLR 1285 124
White & Carter (Councils) Ltd v
McGregor [1962] AC 413 254, 255,
258
Whittington v Seale-Hayne (1900) 82
LT 49 154, 160
Wilkie v London Passenger Transport
Board [1947] 1 All ER 258 13
Williams v Carwardine (1833) 4 B & Ad
621 29
Williams v Roffey Bros & Nicholls
(Contractors) Ltd [1991] 1 QB 1 75,
76, 77, 87, 88, 90, 91
Wilson v Rickett Cockerell & Co Ltd
[1954] 1 QB 598 311

With v O'Flanagan [1936] Ch 575 146
Wood v Scarth (1855) 2 K & J 33 170
Woodar Investment Development Ltd v
Wimpey Construction UK Ltd [1980]
1 WLR 277 214, 222, 251
Woodman v Photo Trade Processing
May 7, 1981, unreported 132
Wroth v Tyler [1974] Ch 30 271

Yates Building Co Ltd v RJ Pulleyn &
Sons (York) Ltd (1975) 237 EG 183
23

Zanzibar v British Aerospace
(Lancaster House) Ltd [2000] 1
WLR 2333 156

Table of statutes

Arbitration Act 1889 43
Arbitration Act 1996 43

Betting, Gaming and Lotteries Act 1963
.... 186
Bills of Exchange Act 1882 .... 64, 218
  s 27 70

Companies Act 1985 .... 60, 64, 340
Companies Act 1989 60
Competition Act 1998 .... 185, 186
Consumer Credit Act 1974
.... 307, 323, 324
  s 60 64
Consumer Protection Act 1961
.... 307
Consumer Protection Act 1987
.... 301, 317, 320
  Pt I 138
  Pt II 138, 321
  Pt III 321, 322
  s 1(1) 319
  s 2(1) 319
  s 2(2) 319
  s 3(1) 319
  s 5(1) 319
  s 5(2) 319
  s 5(4) 319
  s 7 .... 138, 319
  s 10 321
Consumer Safety Act 1978 307
Consumer Safety (Amendment) Act
  1978 307
Contracts (Rights of Third Parties) Act
  1999 .... 73, 126, 214, 227, 230
  s 1 216
  s 1(1)(a) 215
  s 1(1)(b) 215
  s 1(2) 215
  s 1(3) 216

s 1(5) 217
s 1(6) 215
s 2 216
s 2(3) 216
s 2(4) 216
s 2(6) 216
s 3 217
s 5 217
s 6 .... 218, 221

Electronic Communications Act 2000
  Pt II 65
  s 8 .... 63, 65
  s 11 30

Fair Trading Act 1973
.... 307, 313, 321
Family Law Reform Act 1969 53
Financial Services Act 1986 190

Gaming Act 1845
  s 18 186

Hire Purchase Act 1964 175

Infants Relief Act 1874 53

Late Payment of Commercial Debts
  (Interest) Act 1998 109
Latent Damage Act 1986 .... 294, 295
Law of Property Act 1925
.... 63, 92, 256
  s 41 239
  s 56(1) 217, 218
Law of Property (Miscellaneous
  Provisions) Act 1989 64
  s 1 85
Law Reform (Frustrated Contracts) Act
  1943 .... 259, 284, 288
  s 1(1) 246

s 1(2) 246, 261
s 1(3) 246
Limitation Act 1980 294
s 29 295
s 30 295
s 32 295
s 36(1) 295

Married Women's Property Act 1882
.... 217
Mental Health Act 1983 59
Minors' Contracts Act 1987 53
s 2 .... 57, 62
s 3 .... 57, 63
Misrepresentation Act 1967 .... 160, 161
s 1 159
s 2(1) 151, 152, 153, 157, 158, 159
s 2(2) 158, 159
s 3 159

Occupiers' Liability Act 1957 128
Official Secrets Act 1911 281

Protection of Birds Act 1954 12

Rehabilitation of Offenders Act 1974
.... 146

Sale and Supply of Goods Act 1994
.... 300, 307, 308,
310, 312, 313, 328
Sale of Goods Act 1893 307
s 6 166
Sale of Goods Act 1979
.... 45, 54, 109, 111, 114,
116, 129, 139, 236, 301,
307, 314, 315, 318, 328, 330
s 2(1) 308
s 3 59
s 3(2) 53, 62
s 6 166
s 8(2) 43
s 11 313
s 12(1) 309
ss 12–15 316
s 13 .... 113, 300, 310, 325
s 13(1) 309
s 13(3) 309

ss 13–15 312
s 14 .... 309, 325
s 14(2) 300, 308, 310
s 14(3) 300, 311
s 15 .... 312, 327
s 15A 312
s 29(5) 238
s 50 .... 276, 277
s 51 276
s 57(2) 31
s 61 111
Sale of Goods (Amendment) Act 1995
.... 314
Solicitors Act 1974 194
Supply of Goods and Services Act 1982
.... 301, 307, 308, 326, 328, 330
s 2–5 316
s 6 316
ss 6–10 316
s 7 316
s 13 315
s 14(1) 315
s 15(1) 316
Supply of Goods (Implied Terms) Act
1973 326

Third Parties (Right Against Insurers)
Act 1930 217
Trade Union and Labour Relations
(Consolidation) Act 1992 51
Trades Descriptions Act 1968
.... 13, 307, 321

Unfair Contract Terms Act 1977
.... 4, 109, 116, 117, 119, 124,
125, 137, 138, 139, 140, 151,
159, 301, 307, 316, 327, 328
s 1 128
s 2 .... 128, 131, 139
s 2(1) 128, 141
s 2(2) 128, 141
s 3 129
s 4 129
s 5 .... 129, 317
s 6 .... 129, 130, 131, 139, 313, 330
s 7 .... 130, 131
s 8 130
s 11(1) 130

s 11(2) 130
s 11(4) 130
s 11(5) 130
s 12 .... 127, 130
s 13 139

ss 13–15 130
Sched 2 130
Unsolicited Goods and Services Act
  1971 322
  s 2 323

Table of statutory instruments

Consumer Transactions (Restrictions
on Statements) Order 1976 (SI No
1813) 313, 327

Sale and supply of Goods to Consumer
Regulations [not yet in force] 325

Unfair Terms in Consumer Contracts
Regulations 1994 (SI No 3159)
.... 132, 134, 136, 137, 313
Unfair Terms in Consumer Contracts
Regulations 1999 (SI No 2083) 116,

117, 135, 136, 137, 140, 141, 209, 301,
327, 328, 330
reg 132
reg 3(2) 138
reg 4(1) 132
reg 5 141
reg 5(1) 134
reg 5(3) 133
reg 6 134
reg 6(2) 133, 141
Sched 2 .... 134, 141

Table of EC legislation

Directive 85/374 Defective Products
Liability OJ 1985 L210
.... 319, 320
Directive on Sale of Consumer Goods
and Associated Guarantees 1999/44/
EC 325, 327
Directive 93/13 Unfair Terms in
Consumer Contracts OJ 1993 L95/29
.... 132, 133, 134
Art 11 141

European Electronic Commerce
Directive 2000/31/EC
Art 9 65
Art 10 64

Treaty of Rome (EC Treaty) 1957
Art 85 .... 185, 186
Art 85(1) 185
Treaty on European Union 1993
(Maastricht Treaty) 132

Introduction

A sk most people to describe a contract, and they will talk about a piece of paper – the documents you sign when you start a job, buy a house or hire a television, for example. While it is certainly true that these documents are often contracts, in law the term has a wider meaning, covering any legally binding agreement, written or unwritten. In order to be legally binding, an agreement must satisfy certain requirements, which will be discussed in Part 1, but with a few exceptions, being in writing is not one of those requirements. We make contracts when we buy goods at the supermarket, when we get on a bus or train, and when we put money into a machine to buy chocolate or drinks – all without a word being written down, or sometimes even spoken.

Why do we need contract law?

The obvious answer is because promises should be binding, but in fact the law only enforces certain types of promise, essentially those which involve some form of exchange. A promise for which nothing is given in return is called a gratuitous promise, and is not usually enforceable in law (the exception is where such a promise is put into a formal document called a deed).

Why then do we need laws specifically designed to enforce promises involving an exchange? The major reason appears to be the kind of society we live in, which is called a market capitalist society. In such a society, people buy and sell fairly freely, making their own bargains, both on the small scale of ordinary shoppers in supermarkets, and on the much bigger one of a project such as the construction of the Channel Tunnel, which involved many different parties, each buying and selling goods and services. Although, as we shall see, there are areas in which government intervenes, in general we choose what we want to buy, who from, and to some extent at least, at what price.

It would be impossible to run a society on this basis if promises were not binding. Long-term projects show this very clearly – contractors working on the Channel Tunnel, for example, would have been very reluctant to invest time and money on the project if they knew that the British and

French Governments could suddenly decide that they did not want a tunnel after all, and not be expected to compensate the contractors. On a smaller scale, who would book a package holiday if the tour operator was free to decide not to fly you home at the end of it? How would manufacturers run their businesses if customers could simply withdraw orders, even though the goods had been made specially for them? A market economy call only work efficiently if its members can plan their business activities, and they can only do this if they know that they can rely on promises made to them.

In fact, contract law rarely forces a party to fulfil contractual promises, but what it does do is try to compensate innocent parties financially, usually by attempting to put them in the position they would have been in if the contract had been performed as agreed. This has the double function of helping parties to know what they can expect if the contract is not performed, and encouraging performance by ensuring that those who fail to perform cannot simply get away with their breach.

▶ The origins of contract law

In order to understand the rationale underlying contract law, it helps to know a little about its history. Although some principles of contract law go back three centuries, the majority of contract rules were established in the early nineteenth century. Before that, contract hardly existed as a separate branch of law, and took up very few pages in textbooks. Yet today, it is one of the core subjects which lawyers must study, and affects many areas of daily life. What caused the change?

The answer lies in the transformation of our society which occurred during the late eighteenth and early nineteenth centuries, a transformation which has been described as a move from status to contract. Today, we are very used to the important role that 'the market' plays in our society. We take it for granted that, for example, the price of food should generally be set by the manufacturer or retailer, with the customer choosing to take it or leave it. We may not actually negotiate a bargain in many areas of ordinary life, but we see the operation of the market in the fact that manufacturers have to set prices at which people will buy. We would be rather surprised if Parliament suddenly made it illegal to charge more than 50p for a loaf of bread.

Before the nineteenth century, however, there were many areas of life where free negotiation and bargaining were simply not an issue. An example is the market for what were regarded as essential foodstuffs, which included wheat, bread and beer. Although bakers and millers were entitled to make a profit, that did not mean they could sell at whatever price people would pay. Prices and quality standards for bread were fixed, according to the price the baker had had to pay for the wheat, so limiting their profits, and ensuring that they could not take advantage of shortages.

Activities such as buying goods and then selling them in the same market at a higher price, buying up supplies before they reached the market, and cornering the market by buying huge stocks of a particular commodity are all seen as good business practice now, but in the eighteenth century market for essential foodstuffs, they were criminal offences, called regrating, forestalling and engrossing respectively. The basis for this approach was explained by Kenyon J in **R** *v* **Rusby**: 'Though in a status society some may have greater luxuries and comfort than others, all should have the necessaries of life.' In other words, there was a basic right to a reasonable standard of living, and nobody was expected to negotiate that standard for themselves.

A similar, though less humane, approach was taken to relationships between employer and employee – or master and servant, as they were called then. These days, we expect to have an employment contract detailing our hours of work, duties and pay, even though the amount of control we actually have in negotiating those areas may be negligible. In a status society, employment obligations were simply derived from whether you were a master or a servant; masters were entitled to ask servants to do more or less anything, and criminal sanctions could be used against an employee who disobeyed. Employers had obligations too (though rather less onerous than those of employees), which sometimes included supplying food or medical care. Both sets of obligations were seen as fixed for everyone who was either an employee or an employer, and not a matter for individual negotiation. Even wages were often set by local magistrates.

All this began to change in the eighteenth and nineteenth centuries. Society itself was undergoing huge changes, moving from an agricultural to an industrial economy, and with that came political changes, and changes in the way people saw society. With the rise of an economic doctrine called *laissez-faire* came a view that society was no more than a collection of self-interested individuals, each of whom was the best judge of their own interests, and should, as far as possible, be left alone to pursue those interests. If we apply this view to the market for bread, for example, it would suggest that bakers would sell bread for the highest price they could get, while consumers shopped around for the lowest, and the result should be a bargain suitable to both. The market would consist of hundreds and hundreds of similar transactions, with the result that everyone would be able to secure their own best interests, and the state would not need to intervene to do this for them – in fact it should not do so, because the parties should be left alone to decide what was best for them.

This *laissez-faire* approach carved out a very important place for con-tracts. As we have seen, where people make their own transactions, unregulated by the state, it is important that they keep their promises, and as a result, contract law became an increasingly important way of enforcing obligations.

▶ Freedom of contract

Its origins in the *laissez-faire* doctrine of the nineteenth century have had enormous influence on the development of contract law. Perhaps the most striking reflection of this is the importance traditionally placed on freedom of contract. This doctrine promotes the idea that since parties are the best judges of their own interests, they should be free to make contracts on any terms they choose – on the assumption that nobody would choose unfavourable terms. Once this choice is made, the job of the courts is simply to act as an umpire, holding the parties to their promises; it is not the courts' role to ask whether the bargain made was a fair one.

Some academics, notably Professor Atiyah (*The Rise and Fall of Freedom of Contract*, 1985), have suggested that this extreme position lasted only a short time, and that the courts were always concerned to establish some concept of fairness. His view has been challenged, but in any case, it is clear that over the last century, the courts have moved away from their reluctance to intervene, sometimes of their own accord, sometimes under the guidance of Parliament through legislation such as the Unfair Contract Terms Act 1977. However, as the basic principle still holds, decisions which actually have their basis in notions of fairness may be disguised behind more technical issues.

▶ Contract and fairness

Traditional contract law lays down rules which are designed to apply in any contractual situation, regardless of who the parties are, their relationship to each other, and the subject matter of a contract. This means that the law uses basically the same rules to analyse the contract that arises when you go into a supermarket to buy a tin of beans as it does to analyse the contract to build the Channel Tunnel.

The basis for this approach is derived from the *laissez-faire* belief that parties should be left alone to make their own bargains. This, it was thought, required the law simply to provide a framework, allowing parties to know what they had to do to make their agreements binding. This framework was intended to treat everybody equally, since to make different rules for one type of contracting party than for another would be to intervene in the fairness of the bargain. As a result, the same rules were applied to contracts in which both parties had equal bargaining power (between two businesses, for example) as to those where one party had significantly less economic power, or legal or technical knowledge, such as a consumer contract.

This approach, often called procedural fairness, or formal justice, was judged to be fair because it treats everybody equally, favouring no one. The problem with it is that if people are unequal to begin with, treating them equally simply maintains the inequality. This has obvious repercussions in contract law. Take, for example, an employment contract stating that if either party is dissatisfied with the other's performance, the dissatisfied party can terminate the contract at any time. This clearly amounts to treating both parties in exactly the same way, making them play by the same rules. But in doing so, it gives the more powerful employer the useful opportunity to sack the employee at any time, while the corresponding 'benefit' to the less powerful employee will in many cases amount to no more than the chance to become unemployed.

Over the last century the law has to some extent moved away from simple procedural fairness, and an element of what is called substantive fairness, or distributive justice, has developed. Substantive fairness aims to redress the balance of power between unequal parties, giving protection to the weaker one. So, for example, terms are now implied by law into employment contracts so that employers cannot simply dismiss employees without reasonable grounds for doing so. Similar protections have been given to tenants and to consumers, and in these three areas (and some others), traditional contract rules are overlaid with special rules applying only to particular types of contract. You can see the way in which this approach operates in Chapter 16.

The balance between substantive and procedural fairness in contract law is always an uneasy one, but major academics such as Treitel (*The Law of Contract*, 1999) and Atiyah believe that there has been, as Atiyah puts it, 'a move from principle to pragmatism'. He suggests that in modern cases, the courts have been less concerned with laying down general rules, and more with producing justice in individual cases. In fact, an examination of the cases, especially those between businesses, where bargaining power is assumed to be equal, shows that although the courts are often attempting to secure substantive justice, they still tend to hide that attempt behind what appears to be an application of the traditional rules. The cases on innominate terms (p. 112 below), and on reasonable notice, particularly **Interfoto** (see p. 121 below), have been seen as examples of this.

▶ The objective approach

Contract law claims to be about enforcing obligations which the parties have voluntarily assumed. Bearing in mind that contracts do not have to be in writing, and that even where they are, important points may be left out, it is clear that contract law faces a problem: how to find out what – or even whether – the parties agreed. For example, if I promise to clean your car, meaning that I will wash the outside, and you promise to give me £10 in return, assuming that I will vacuum the inside as well, what have we agreed?

Contract law's approach to this problem is to look for the appearance of consent. If my words and/or actions would suggest to a reasonable person that I was agreeing to clean the inside of your car as well as the outside, then that is what I will have to do before I get my £10. This approach was explained by Blackburn J in **Smith** *v* **Hughes** (1871): 'If, whatever a man's real intention may be, he so conducts himself that a reasonable man would believe he was assenting to the terms proposed by the other party, and that other party upon that belief enters into the contract with him, the man thus conducting himself would be equally bound as if he had intended to agree to the other party's terms.'

In some cases, the basis for this approach is obvious. If you get into a taxi and simply state your destination, it is perfectly reasonable for the driver to assume you are agreeing to pay for the ride; it would not be right to allow you to claim at the end that although your behaviour might have suggested that, you had no such intention in your mind, and so are not obliged to pay. In practice, the principle has led to some potentially harsh results, such as the rule, established in a case called **L'Estrange** *v* **Graucob** (1934), that a person who signs a contractual document is bound by it, even though they may not have understood or even read it.

Part 1

The formation of a contract

There are five basic requirements that need to be satisfied in order to make a contract:

- **An agreement** between the parties (which is usually shown by the fact that one has made an offer and the other has accepted it).
- **An intention** to be legally bound by that agreement (often called intent to create legal relations).
- **Certainty** as to the terms of the agreement.
- **Capacity** to contract.
- **Consideration** provided by each of the parties – put simply, this means that there must be some kind of exchange between the parties. If I say I will give you my car, and you simply agree to have it, I have voluntarily made you a promise (often called a gratuitous promise), which you cannot enforce in law if I change my mind. If, however, I promise to hand over my car and you promise to pay me a sum of money in return, we have each provided consideration.

In addition, in some cases, the parties must comply with certain formalities. Remember that, with a few exceptions, it is **not** necessary for a contract to be in writing – a contract is an agreement, not a piece of paper.

In this part of the book we will consider these different requirements for the creation of a contract.

1 Offer and acceptance

For a contract to exist, usually one party must have made an offer, and the other must have accepted it. Once acceptance takes effect, a contract will usually be binding on both parties, and the rules of offer and acceptance are typically used to pinpoint when a series of negotiations has passed that point, in order to decide whether the parties are obliged to fulfil their promises. There is generally no halfway house – negotiations have either crystallized into a binding contract, or they are not binding at all.

Unilateral and bilateral contracts

In order to understand the law on offer and acceptance, you need to understand the concepts of unilateral and bilateral contracts. Most contracts are bilateral. This means that each party takes on an obligation, usually by promising the other something – for example, Ann promises to sell something and Ben to buy it. (Although contracts where there are mutual obligations are always called bilateral, there may in fact be more than two parties to such a contract.)

By contrast, a unilateral contract arises where only one party assumes an obligation under the contract. Examples might be promising to give your mother £50 if she gives up smoking for a year, or to pay a £100 reward to anyone who finds your lost purse, or, as the court suggested in **Great Northern Railway Co** *v* **Witham** (1873), to pay someone £100 to walk from London to York. What makes these situations unilateral contracts is that only one party has assumed an obligation – you are obliged to pay your mother if she gives up smoking, but she has not promised in turn to give up smoking. Similarly, you are obliged to pay the reward to anyone who finds your purse, but nobody need actually have undertaken to do so.

A common example of a unilateral contract is that between estate agents and people trying to sell their houses – the seller promises to pay a specified percentage of the house price to the estate agent if the house is sold, but the estate agent is not required to promise in return to sell the house, or even to try to do so.

▶ Offer

The person making an offer is called the offeror, and the person to whom the offer is made is called the offeree. A communication will be treated as an offer if it indicates the terms on which the offeror is prepared to make a contract (such as the price of the goods for sale), and gives a clear indication that the offeror intends to be bound by those terms if they are accepted by the offeree.

An offer may be express, as when Ann tells Ben that she will sell her CD player for £200, but it can also be implied from conduct – a common example is taking goods to the cash desk in a supermarket, which is an implied offer to buy those goods.

Offers to the public at large

In most cases, an offer will be made to a specified person – as when Ann offers to sell her computer to Ben. However, offers can be addressed to a group of people, or even to the general public. For example, a student may offer to sell her old textbooks to anyone in the year below, or the owner of a lost dog may offer a reward to anyone who finds it.

In **Carlill** *v* **Carbolic Smoke Ball Co** (1893) the defendants were the manufacturers of 'smokeballs' which they claimed could prevent flu. They published advertisements stating that if anyone used their smokeball for a specified time and still caught flu, they would pay that person £100, and that to prove they were serious about the claim, they had deposited £1,000 with their bankers.

Mrs Carlill bought and used a smokeball, but nevertheless ended up with flu. She therefore claimed the £100, which the company refused to pay. They argued that their advertisement could not give rise to a contract, since it was impossible to make a contract with the whole world, and that therefore they were not legally bound to pay the money. This argument was rejected by the court, which held that the advertisement did constitute an offer to the world at large, which became a contract when it was accepted by Mrs Carlill using the smokeball and getting flu. She was therefore entitled to the £100.

A contract arising from an offer to the public at large, like that in **Carlill**, is usually a unilateral contract.

▶ Invitations to treat

Some kinds of transaction involve a preliminary stage in which one party invites the other to make an offer. This stage is called an invitation to treat. In **Gibson** *v* **Manchester City Council** (1979) a council tenant was interested in buying his house. He completed an application form and received a letter from the Council stating that it 'may be prepared to sell the house to you' for £2,180. Mr Gibson initially queried the purchase price, pointing out that the path to the house was in a bad condition. The Council refused to change the price, saying that the price had been fixed taking into account the condition of the property. Mr Gibson then wrote on 18 March 1971 asking the Council to 'carry on with the purchase as per my application'. Following a change in political control of the Council in May 1971, it decided to stop selling Council houses to tenants, and Mr Gibson was informed that the Council would not proceed with the sale of the house. Mr Gibson brought legal proceedings claiming that the letter he had received stating the purchase price was an offer which he had accepted on 18 March 1971. The House of Lords, however, ruled that the Council had not made an offer; the letter giving the purchase price was merely one step in the negotiations for a contract and amounted only to an invitation to treat. Its purpose was simply to invite the making of a 'formal application', amounting to an offer, from the tenant.

Confusion can sometimes arise when what would appear, in the everyday sense of the word, to be an offer, is held by the law to be only an invitation to treat. This issue arises particularly in the following areas.

Advertisements

A distinction is generally made between advertisements for a unilateral contract, and those for a bilateral contract.

Advertisements for unilateral contracts

These include advertisements such as the one in **Carlill** *v* **Carbolic Smoke Ball Co,** or those offering rewards for the return of lost property, or for information leading to the arrest or conviction of a criminal. They are usually treated as offers, on the basis that the contract can normally be accepted without any need for further negotiations between the parties, and the person making the advertisement intends to be bound by it. A recent illustration is provided by the Court of Appeal in **Bowerman** *v* **Association of British Travel Agents Ltd** (1996). A school had booked a skiing holiday with a tour operator which was a member of the Association of British Travel Agents (ABTA). All members of this association display a notice provided by ABTA which states:

> Where holidays or other travel arrangements have not yet commenced at the time of failure [of the tour operator], ABTA arranges for you to be reimbursed the money you have paid in respect of your holiday arrangements.

The tour operator became insolvent and cancelled the skiing holiday. The school was refunded the money they had paid for the holiday, but not the cost of the wasted travel insurance. The plaintiff brought an action against ABTA to seek reimbursement of the cost of this insurance.

He argued, and the Court of Appeal agreed, that the ABTA notice constituted an offer which the customer accepted by contracting with an ABTA member.

● *Advertisements for a bilateral contract*
These are the type of advertisements which advertise specified goods at a certain price, such as those found at the back of newspapers and magazines. They are usually considered invitations to treat, on the grounds that they may lead to further bargaining – potential buyers might want to negotiate about the price, for example – and that since stocks could run out, it would be unreasonable to expect the advertisers to sell to everybody who applied.

In **Partridge** *v* **Crittenden** (1968), an advertisement in a magazine stated 'Bramblefinch cocks and hens, 25s each'. As the Bramblefinch was a protected species, the person who placed the advertisement was charged with unlawfully offering for sale a wild bird contrary to the Protection of Birds Act 1954, but his conviction was quashed on the grounds that the advertisement was not an offer but an invitation to treat.

It was held in **Grainger & Sons** *v* **Gough** (1896) that the circulation of a price-list by a wine merchant was not an offer to sell at those prices but merely an invitation to treat.

Shopping

Price-marked goods on display on the shelves or in the windows of shops are generally regarded as invitations to treat, rather than offers to sell goods at that price. In **Fisher** *v* **Bell** (1960) the defendant had displayed flick knives in his shop window, and was convicted of the criminal offence of offering such knives for sale. On appeal, Lord Parker CJ stated that the display of an article with a price on it in a shop window was only an invitation to treat and not an offer, and the conviction was overturned.

Where goods are sold on a self-service basis, the customer makes an offer to buy when presenting the goods at the cash desk, and the shopkeeper may accept or reject that offer. In **Pharmaceutical Society of Great Britain** *v* **Boots Cash Chemists (Southern) Ltd** (1953) Boots were charged with an offence concerning the sale of certain medicines which could only be sold by or under the supervision of a qualified pharmacist. Two customers in a self-service shop selected the medicines, which were price-marked, from the open shelves, and placed them in the shop's wire baskets. The shelves were not supervised by a pharmacist, but a pharmacist had been instructed to supervise the transaction at the cash desk. The issue was therefore whether the sale had taken place at the shelves or at the cash desk.

The Court of Appeal decided the shelf display was like an advertisement for a bilateral contract, and was therefore merely an invitation to treat.

The offer was made by the customer when medicines were placed in the basket, and was only accepted when the goods were presented at the cash desk. Since a pharmacist was supervising at that point no offence had been committed.

There are two main practical consequences of this principle. First, shops do not have to sell goods at the marked price – so if a shop assistant wrongly marks a CD at £2.99 rather than £12.99, for example, you cannot insist on buying it at that price (though the shop may be committing an offence under the Trade Descriptions Act 1968 – see Chapter 16 on consumer contracts). Secondly, a customer cannot insist on buying a particular item on display – so you cannot make a shopkeeper sell you the sweater in the window even if there are none left inside the shop. Displaying the goods is not an offer, so a customer cannot accept it and thereby make a binding contract.

Timetables and tickets for transport

The legal position here is rather unclear. Is a bus timetable an offer to run services at those times, or just an invitation to treat? Does the bus pulling up at a stop constitute an offer to carry you, which you accept by boarding the bus? Or, again, is even this stage just an invitation to treat, so that the offer is actually made by you getting on the bus or by handing over money for the ticket? These points may seem academic, but they become important when something goes wrong. If, for example, the bus crashes and you are injured, your ability to sue for breach of contract will depend on whether the contract had actually been completed when the accident occurred.

Although there have been many cases in this area, no single reliable rule has emerged, and it seems that the exact point at which a contract is made depends in each case on the particular facts. For example, in **Denton v GN Railway** (1856) it was said that railway company advertisements detailing the times at and conditions under which trains would run were offers. But in **Wilkie v London Passenger Transport Board** (1947) Lord Greene thought that a contract between bus company and passenger was made when a person intending to travel 'puts himself either on the platform or inside the bus'. The opinion was *obiter* but, if correct, it implies that the company makes an offer of carriage by running the bus or train and the passenger accepts when he or she gets properly on board, completing the contract. Therefore if the bus crashed, an injured passenger could have a claim against the bus company for breach of contract despite not having yet paid the fare or been given a ticket.

However, in **Thornton v Shoe Lane Parking Ltd** (1971) it was suggested that the contract may be formed rather later. If the legal principles laid down in **Thornton** are applied to this factual situation, it would appear that passengers asking for a ticket to their destination are making an invitation to treat. The bus company makes an offer by issuing the tickets, and the passengers accept the offer by keeping the tickets without objection. Fortunately, these questions are not governed solely by the law of contract as some legislation relevant to the field of public transport has since been passed.

There are other less common situations in which the courts will have to decide whether a communication is an offer or merely an invitation to treat. The test used is whether a person watching the proceedings would have thought the party concerned was making an offer or not (the objective approach discussed at p. 5).

How long does an offer last?

An offer may cease to exist under any of the following circumstances.

Specified time

Where an offeror states that an offer will remain open for a specific length of time, it lapses when that time is up (though it can be revoked before that – see p. 16 below).

Reasonable length of time

Where the offeror has not specified how long the offer will remain open, it will lapse after a reasonable length of time has passed. Exactly how long this is will depend upon whether the means of communicating the offer were fast or slow and on its subject matter – for example, offers to buy perishable goods, or a commodity whose price fluctuates daily, will lapse quite quickly. Offers to buy shares on the stock market may last only seconds.

In **Ramsgate Victoria Hotel** *v* **Montefiore** (1866) the defendant applied for shares in the plaintiff company, paying a deposit into their bank. After hearing nothing from them for five months, he was then informed that the shares had been allotted to him, and asked to pay the balance due on them. He refused to do so, and the court upheld his argument that five months was not a reasonable length of time for acceptance of an offer to buy shares, which are a commodity with a rapidly fluctuating price. Therefore the offer had lapsed before the company tried to accept it, and there was no contract between them.

Failure of a precondition

Some offers are made subject to certain conditions, and if such conditions are not in place, the offer may lapse. For example, a person might offer to sell their bike for £50 if they manage to buy a car at the weekend. In **Financings Ltd** *v* **Stimson** (1962) the defendant saw a car for sale at £350 by a second-hand car dealer on 16 March. He decided to buy it on hire-purchase terms. The way that hire-purchase works in such cases is that the finance company buys the car outright from the dealer, and then sells it to the buyer, who pays in instalments. The defendant would therefore be buying the car from the finance company (the plaintiffs), rather than from the dealer. The defendant signed the plaintiff's form, which stated that the agreement would be binding on the finance company only when signed on its behalf. The car dealer did not have the authority to do this, so it had to be sent to the plaintiffs for signing. On 18 March the defendant paid the first instalment of £70. On 24 March the car was stolen from the dealer's premises. It was later found, badly damaged and the defendant no longer wanted to buy it. Not knowing this, on 25 March the plaintiffs signed the written 'agreement'. They subsequently sued the defendant for failure to pay the instalments. The Court of Appeal ruled in favour of the defendant, as the so-called 'agreement' was really an offer to make a contract with the plaintiffs, which was subject to the implied condition that the car remained in much the same state as it was in when the offer was made, until that offer was accepted. The plaintiffs were claiming that they had accepted the offer by signing the document on 24 March. As the implied condition had been broken by then, the offer was no longer open so no contract had been concluded.

Rejection

An offer lapses when the offeree rejects it. If Ann offers to sell Ben her car on Tuesday, and Ben says no, Ben cannot come back on Wednesday and insist on accepting the offer.

Counter offer

A counter offer terminates the original offer. In **Hyde** _v_ **Wrench** (1840) the defendant offered to sell his farm for £1,000, and the plaintiff responded by offering to buy it at £950 – this is called making a counter offer. The farm owner refused to sell at that price, and when the plaintiff later tried to accept the offer to buy at £1,000, it was held that this offer was no longer available; it had been terminated by the counter offer. In this situation the offeror can make a new offer on exactly the same terms, but is not obliged to do so.

Requests for information

A request for information about an offer (such as whether delivery could be earlier than suggested) does not amount to a counter offer, so the original offer remains open. In **Stevenson** _v_ **McLean** (1880) the defendant made an offer on a Saturday to sell iron to the plaintiffs at a cash on delivery price of 40 shillings, and stated that the offer would remain available until the following Monday. The plaintiffs replied by asking if they could buy the goods on credit. They received no answer. On Monday afternoon they contacted the defendant to accept the offer, but the iron had already been sold to someone else.

When the plaintiffs sued for breach of contract, it was held that their reply to the offer had been merely a request for information, not a counter offer, so the original offer still stood and there was a binding contract.

Death of the offeror

The position is not entirely clear, but it appears that if the offeree knows that the offeror has died, the offer will lapse; if the offeree is unaware of the offeror's death, it probably will not (**Bradbury** *v* **Morgan** (1862)). So if, for example, A promises to sell her video recorder to B, then dies soon after, and B writes to accept the offer not knowing that A is dead, it seems that the people responsible for A's affairs after death would be obliged to sell the video recorder to B and B would be obliged to pay the price to the executors.

However, where an offer requires personal performance by the offeror (such as painting a picture, or appearing in a film) it will usually lapse on the offeror's death.

Death of the offeree

There is no English case on this point, but it seems probable that the offer lapses and cannot be accepted after the offeree's death by the offeree's representatives.

Withdrawal of offer

The old case of **Payne** *v* **Cave** (1789) establishes the principle that an offer may be withdrawn at any time up until it is accepted. This is frequently described by lawyers as a 'revocation'. In **Routledge** *v* **Grant** (1828) the defendant made a provisional offer to buy the plaintiff's house at a specified price, 'a definite answer to be given within six weeks from date'. It was held that, regardless of this provision, the defendant still had the right to withdraw the offer at any moment before acceptance, even though the time limit had not expired.

There are a number of rules about revocation.

Revocation must be communicated
It is not enough for offerors simply to change their mind about an offer; they must notify the offeree that it is being revoked. In **Byrne** *v* **Van**

Tienhoven (1880) the defendants, a Cardiff company, had, on 1 October, posted a letter to New York offering to sell the plaintiffs 1,000 boxes of tinplates. On receiving the letter on 11 October, the plaintiffs immediately accepted by telegram. Acceptances sent by telegram take effect as soon as they are sent (see p. 25 below for details of the postal rule).

In the meantime, on 8 October, the defendants had written to revoke their offer, and this letter reached the defendants on 20 October. It was held that there was a binding contract, because revocation could only take effect on communication, but the acceptance by telegram took effect as soon as it was sent – in this case nine days before the revocation was received. By the time the second letter reached the plaintiffs, a contract had already been made.

Revocation of an offer does not have to be communicated by the offeror; the communication can be made by some other reliable source. In **Dickinson** *v* **Dodds** (1876) the defendant offered to sell a house to the plaintiff, the offer 'to be left open until Friday, June 12, 9 am'. On 11 June the defendant sold the house to a third party, Allan, and the plaintiff heard about the sale through a fourth man. Before 9 am on 12 June, the plaintiff handed the defendant a letter in which he said he was accepting the offer. It was held by the Court of Appeal that the offer had already been revoked by the communication from the fourth man, so there was no contract. By hearing the news from the fourth man, Dickinson 'knew that Dodds was no longer minded to sell the property to him as plainly and clearly as if Dodds had told him in so many words'.

An offeror who promises to keep an offer open for a specified period may still revoke that offer at any time before it is accepted, unless the promise to keep it open is supported by some consideration from the other party (by providing consideration the parties make a separate contract called an option).

In certain office situations, a great deal of mail may be received daily. Because of the volume, mail does not go directly to the person whose name is on the envelope, but is received, opened and sorted by clerical staff and then distributed to the relevant people. In these situations there may be some difficulty in pinpointing when the information in the letter can be said to be communicated: is it when the letter is received within the company, when it is opened, or when it is actually read by the relevant member of staff? There is no authority on the point but the approach would probably be that communication occurred when the letter was opened, even though there may in those circumstances be no true communication.

There are two main exceptions to the rule that the withdrawal must be communicated to the offeree. First, if an offeree moves to a new address without notifying the offeror, a withdrawal which was delivered to the offeree's last known address will be effective on delivery there. In the same way, where a withdrawal reaches the offeree, but the offeree simply

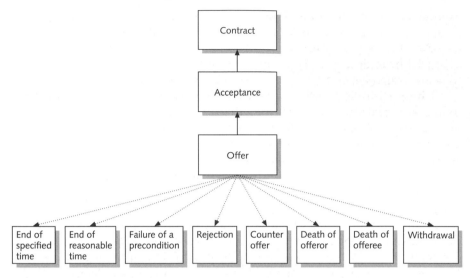

Figure 1.1 Termination of an offer

fails to read it, it probably still takes effect on reaching them (see *The Brimnes* (1975) p. 25 below). This would be the position where a withdrawal by telex or fax reached the offeror's office during normal business hours but was not actually seen or read by the offeree or by any of their staff until some time afterwards.

Second, where a unilateral offer is made to the world at large, to be accepted by conduct, it can probably be revoked without the need for communication if the revocation takes place before performance has begun. For example, if you place a newspaper advertisement offering a reward for the return of something you have lost, and then decide you might actually be better off spending that money on replacing the item, it would probably be impossible for you to make sure that everyone who knew about the offer knows you are withdrawing it – even if you place a notice of withdrawal in the newspaper, you cannot guarantee that everyone concerned will see it. It seems to be enough for an offeror to take reasonable steps to bring the withdrawal to the attention of such persons, even though it may not be possible to ensure that they all know about it. Thus, in the US case of **Shuey** (1875) it was held that an offer made by advertisements in a newspaper could be revoked by a similar advertisement, even though the second advertisement was not read by all the offerees.

Acceptance

Acceptance of an offer means unconditional agreement to all the terms of that offer. Acceptance will often be oral or in writing, but in some cases an offeree may accept an offer by doing something, such as delivering goods in response to an offer to buy. The courts will only interpret conduct as indicating acceptance if it seems reasonable to infer that the offeree acted with the intention of accepting the offer.

In **Brogden** *v* **Metropolitan Rail Co** (1877) Brogden had supplied the railway company with coal for several years without any formal agreement. The parties then decided to make things official, so the rail company sent Brogden a draft agreement, which left a blank space for Brogden to insert the name of an arbitrator. After doing so and signing the document, Brogden returned it, marked 'approved'.

The company's employee put the draft away in a desk drawer, where it stayed for the next two years, without any further steps being taken regarding it. Brogden continued to supply coal under the terms of the contract, and the railway company to pay for it. Eventually a dispute arose between them, and Brogden denied that any binding contract existed.

The courts held that by inserting the arbitrator's name, Brogden added a new term to the potential contract, and therefore, in returning it to the railway company, he was offering (in fact counter offering) to supply coal under the contract. But when was that offer accepted? The House of Lords decided that an acceptance by conduct could be inferred from the parties' behaviour, and a valid contract was completed either when the company first ordered coal after receiving the draft agreement from Brogden, or at the latest when he supplied the first lot of coal.

Merely remaining silent cannot amount to an acceptance, unless it is absolutely clear that acceptance was intended. In **Felthouse** *v* **Bindley** (1862) an uncle and his nephew had talked about the possible sale of the nephew's horse to the uncle, but there had been some confusion about the price. The uncle subsequently wrote to the nephew, offering to pay £30 and 15 shillings and saying, 'If I hear no more about him, I consider the horse mine at that price.' The nephew was on the point of selling off some of his property in an auction. He did not reply to the uncle's letter, but did tell the auctioneer to keep the horse out of the sale. The auctioneer forgot to do this, and the horse was sold. It was held that there was no contract between the uncle and the nephew. The court felt that the nephew's conduct in trying to keep the horse out of the sale did not necessarily imply that he intended to accept his uncle's offer – even though the nephew actually wrote afterwards to apologize for the mistake – and so it was not clear that his silence in response to the offer was intended to constitute acceptance. This can be criticized in that it is hard to see how there could have been clearer evidence that the nephew did actually intend to sell, but, on the other hand, there are many situations in which it would be undesirable and confusing for silence to amount to acceptance.

It has been pointed out by the Court of Appeal in **Re Selectmove Ltd** (1995) that an acceptance by silence could be sufficient if it was the offeree who suggested that their silence would be sufficient. Thus in **Felthouse**, if the nephew had been the one to say that if his uncle heard nothing more he could treat the offer as accepted, there would have been a contract.

Unilateral contracts are usually accepted by conduct. If I offer £100 to anyone who finds my lost dog, finding the dog will be acceptance of the offer, making my promise binding – it is not necessary for anyone to contact me and say that they intend to take up my offer and find the dog.

Acceptance must be unconditional

An acceptance must accept the precise terms of an offer. In **Tinn** *v* **Hoffman** (1873) one party offered to sell the other 1,200 tons of iron. It was held that the other party's order for 800 tons was not an acceptance.

Negotiation and the 'battle of the forms'

Where parties carry on a long process of negotiation, it may be difficult to pinpoint exactly when an offer has been made and accepted. In such cases the courts will look at the whole course of negotiations to decide whether the parties have in fact reached agreement at all and, if so, when.

This process can be particularly difficult where the so-called 'battle of the forms' arises. Rather than negotiating terms each time a contract is made, many businesses try to save time and money by contracting on standard terms, which will be printed on company stationery such as order forms and delivery notes. The 'battle of the forms' occurs where one party sends a form stating that the contract is on their standard terms of business, and the other party responds by returning their own form and stating that the contract is on **their** terms.

The general rule in such cases is that the 'last shot' wins the battle. Each new form issued is treated as a counter offer, so that when one party performs its obligation under the contract (by delivering goods for example), that action will be seen as acceptance by conduct of the offer in the last form. In **British Road Services** *v* **Crutchley (Arthur V) Ltd** (1968) the plaintiffs delivered some whisky to the defendants for storage. The BRS driver handed the defendants a delivery note, which listed his company's 'conditions of carriage'. Crutchley's employee stamped the note 'Received under [our] conditions' and handed it back to the driver. The court held that stamping the delivery note in this way amounted to a counter offer, which BRS accepted by handing over the goods. The contract therefore incorporated Crutchley's conditions, rather than those of BRS.

However, a more recent case shows that the 'last shot' will not always succeed. In **Butler Machine Tool Ltd** *v* **Ex-Cell-O Corp** (1979) the defendants wanted to buy a machine from the plaintiffs, to be delivered ten months after the order. The plaintiffs supplied a quotation (which was taken to be an offer), and on this document were printed their standard terms, including a clause allowing them to increase the price of the goods if the costs had risen by the date of delivery (known as a price-variation clause). The document also stated that their terms would prevail over any terms and conditions in the buyers' order. The buyers responded by placing an order, which was stated to be on their own terms and conditions, and these were listed on the order form. These terms did not contain a price-variation clause. The order form included a tear-off acknowledgement slip, which contained the words: 'we accept your order on the terms and conditions thereon' (referring to the order form). The sellers duly returned the acknowledgement slip to the buyers, with a letter stating that the order was being accepted in accordance with the earlier quotation. The acknowledgement slip and accompanying letter were the last forms issued before delivery.

When the ten months were up, the machine was delivered and the sellers claimed an extra £2,892, under the provisions of the price-variation clause. The buyers refused to pay the extra amount, so the sellers sued them for it. The Court of Appeal held that the buyers' reply to the quotation was not an unconditional acceptance, and therefore constituted a counter offer. The sellers had accepted that counter offer by returning the acknowledgement slip, which referred back to the buyers' conditions. The sellers pointed out that they had stated in their accompanying letter that the order was booked in accordance with the earlier quotation, but this was interpreted by the Court of Appeal as referring back to the type and price of the machine tool, rather than to the terms listed on the back of the sellers' document. It merely confirmed that the machine in question was the one originally quoted for, and did not modify the conditions of the contract. The contract was therefore made under the buyers' conditions.

The Court of Appeal also contemplated what the legal position would have been if the slip had not been returned by the sellers. The majority thought that the usual rules of offer and counter offer would have to be applied, which in many cases would mean that there was no contract until the goods were delivered and accepted by the buyer, with either party being free to withdraw before that. Lord Denning MR, on the other hand, suggested that the courts should take a much less rigid approach and decide whether the parties thought they had made a binding contract, and if it appeared that they did, the court should go on to examine the documents as a whole to find out what the content of their agreement might be. This approach has not been adopted by the courts.

Acceptance of unilateral offers

It has generally been assumed that there is no acceptance until the act has been completely performed – so if Ann says to Ben that she will give Ben £5 if Ben washes her car, Ben would not be entitled to the money until the job is finished, and could not wash half the car and ask for

£2.50. What then is the position if your teacher offers a prize for the best essay on contract, and then revokes the offer after the students have started work but before any essays are handed in? Unfortunately, the law gives no clear answer.

In **Luxor (Eastbourne) Ltd** *v* **Cooper** (1941) an owner of land had promised to pay an estate agent £10,000 in commission if the agent was able to find a buyer willing to pay £175,000 for the land. The arrangement was on the terms that are usual between estate agents and their clients, whereby the agent is paid commission if a buyer is found, and nothing if not. The House of Lords held that the owner in the case could revoke his promise at any time before the sale was completed, even after the estate agents had made extensive efforts to find a buyer, just as the estate agent could decide not to try to find a buyer, or to stop trying to do so. Although this decision might appear to support the view that offers of unilateral contracts are freely revocable until performance is complete, it may be more accurately seen as an approach specific to such estate agency arrangements.

In **Daulia Ltd** *v* **Four Millbank Nominees Ltd** (1978) the Court of Appeal stated decisively that once an offeree had started to perform on a unilateral contract, it was too late for the offeror to revoke the offer. It should be noted that this statement was *obiter*, since the court found that the offeree in the case had in fact completed his performance before the supposed revocation.

It now appears that there are some circumstances in which part-performance may amount to acceptance. In **Errington** *v* **Errington** (1952) a father bought a house in his own name for £750, borrowing £500 of the price by means of a mortgage from a building society. He bought the house for his son and daughter-in-law to live in, and told them that if they met the mortgage repayments, the house would be signed over to them once the mortgage was paid off. The couple moved in, and began to pay the mortgage instalments, but they never in fact made a promise to continue with the payments until the mortgage was paid off, which meant that the contract was unilateral.

When the father later died, the people in charge of his affairs sought to withdraw the offer. The Court of Appeal held that it was too late to do this. The part performance by the son and daughter-in-law constituted an acceptance of the contract and the father (or, after his death, his representatives) was bound by the resulting contract unless the son and daughter-in-law ceased to make the payments, in which case the offer was no longer binding.

Specified methods of acceptance

If an offeror states that his or her offer must be accepted in a particular way, then only acceptance by that method or an equally effective one will be binding. To be considered equally effective, a mode of acceptance should not be slower than the method specified in the offer, nor have any disadvantages for the offeror. It was stated in **Tinn** *v* **Hoffman** (1873) that where the offeree was asked to reply 'by return of post', any method which would arrive before return of post would be sufficient.

Where a specified method of acceptance has been included for the offeree's own benefit, however, the offeree is not obliged to accept in that way. In **Yates Building Co Ltd** *v* **J Pulleyn & Sons (York) Ltd** (1975) the sellers stated that the option they were offering should be accepted by 'notice in writing . . . to be sent registered or recorded delivery'. The purchaser sent his acceptance by ordinary letter post, but the court held that the acceptance was still effective. The requirement of registered or recorded delivery was for the benefit of the offeree rather than the offeror (as it ensured that their acceptance was received and that they had proof of their acceptance) and was not therefore mandatory.

The case of **Felthouse** *v* **Bindley** (see p. 19 above) shows that, although the offeror can stipulate how the acceptance is to be made, he or she cannot stipulate that silence shall amount to acceptance. In the same way, if the offeror states that the performance of certain acts by the offeree will amount to an acceptance, and the offeree performs those acts, there will only be an acceptance if the offeree was aware of the terms of the offer and objectively intended their acts to amount to an acceptance. In **Inland Revenue Commissioners** *v* **Fry** (2001) the Inland Revenue claimed over £100,000 of unpaid tax from Mrs Fry. Following negotiations, Mrs Fry wrote to the Inland Revenue enclosing a cheque for £10,000. In her letter she said that if the Inland Revenue accepted her offer of £10,000 in full and final settlement, it should present the cheque for payment. The Inland Revenue cashed the cheque but subsequently informed Mrs Fry that her offer was unacceptable. The High Court held that the Inland Revenue was entitled to the full amount of tax which it had claimed. The court explained that it was fundamental to the existence of a binding contract that there was a meeting of minds. An offer prescribing a mode of acceptance could be accepted by an offeree acting in accordance with that mode of acceptance. However, the Inland Revenue received thousands of cheques each day and there was no evidence that, when it cashed the cheque from Mrs Fry, it knew of the offer. The cashing of the cheque gave rise to no more than a rebuttable presumption of acceptance of the terms of the offer in the accompanying letter. On the evidence, that presumption had been rebutted, as a reasonable observer would not have assumed that the cheque was banked with the intention of accepting the offer in the letter.

An offeror who has requested the offeree to use a particular method of acceptance can always waive the right to insist on that method.

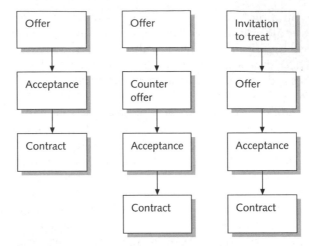

Figure 1.2 Three examples of how a contract can be made

Acceptance must be communicated

An acceptance does not usually take effect until it is communicated to the offeror. As Lord Denning explained in **Entores Ltd v Miles Far East Corporation** (1955), if A shouts an offer to B across a river, but just as B yells back an acceptance, a noisy aircraft flies over, preventing A from hearing B's reply, no contract has been made. A must be able to hear B's acceptance before it can take effect. The same would apply if the contract was made by telephone, and A failed to catch what B said because of interference on the line; there is no contract until A knows that B is accepting the offer. The principal reason for this rule is that, without it, people might be bound by a contract without knowing that their offers had been accepted, which could obviously create difficulties in all kinds of situations.

Where parties negotiate face to face, communication of the acceptance is unlikely to be a problem; any difficulties tend to arise where the parties are communicating at a distance, for example by post, telephone, telegram, telex, fax or messenger.

Exceptions to the communication rule

There are some circumstances in which an acceptance may take effect without being communicated to the offeror.

Terms of the offer

An offer may state or imply that acceptance need not be communicated to the offeror, although, as **Felthouse v Bindley** shows, it is not possible to state that the offeree will be bound unless he or she indicates that the offer is not accepted (in other words that silence will be taken as acceptance). This means that offerors are free to expose themselves to the risk of unknowingly incurring an obligation, but may not impose that risk on someone else. It seems to follow from this that if the horse in **Felthouse** *v* **Bindley** had been kept out of the sale for the uncle, and the uncle had then refused to buy it, the nephew could have sued his uncle, who would have been unable to rely on the fact that acceptance was not communicated to him.

Unilateral contracts do not usually require acceptance to be communicated to the offeror. In **Carlill** *v* **Carbolic Smoke Ball Co** (1893) the defendants argued that the plaintiff should have notified them that she was accepting their offer, but the court held that such a unilateral offer implied that performance of the terms of the offer would be enough to amount to acceptance.

Conduct of the offeror

An offeror who fails to receive an acceptance through their own fault may be prevented from claiming that the non-communication means they should not be bound by the contract. In the **Entores** case (1955) it was suggested that this principle could apply where an offer was accepted by telephone, and the offeror did not catch the words of acceptance, but failed to ask for them to be repeated; and in *The Brimnes* (1975), where the acceptance is sent by telex during business hours, but is simply not read by anyone in the offeror's office.

The postal rule

The general rule for acceptances by post is that they take effect when they are posted, rather than when they are communicated. The main reason for this rule is historical, since it dates from a time when communication through the post was even slower and less reliable than it is today. Even now, there is some practical purpose for the rule, in that it is easier to prove that a letter has been posted than to prove that it has been received or brought to the attention of the offeror.

The postal rule was laid down in **Adams** *v* **Lindsell** (1818). On 2 September 1817, the defendants wrote to the plaintiffs, who processed wool, offering to sell them a quantity of sheep fleeces, and stating that they required an answer 'in course of post'. Unfortunately, the defendants did not address the letter correctly, and as a result it did not reach the plaintiffs until the evening of 5 September. The plaintiffs posted their acceptance the same evening, and it reached the defendants on 9 September. It appeared that if the original letter had been correctly addressed, the plaintiffs could have expected a reply 'in course of post' by 7 September. That date came and went, and they had heard nothing from the plaintiffs, so on 8 September they sold the wool to a third party. The issue in the case was whether a contract had been made before the sale to the third party on 8 September. The court held that a contract was concluded as soon as the acceptance was posted, so that the defendants were bound from the evening of 5 September, and had therefore breached the contract by selling the wool to the third party. (Under current law there would have been a contract even without the postal rule, because the revocation of the offer could only take effect if it was communicated to the offeree – selling the wool to a third party without notifying the plaintiffs would not amount to revocation. However, in 1818 the rules on revocation were not fully developed, so the court may well have considered that the sale was sufficient to revoke the offer, which was why an effective acceptance would have to take place before 8 September.)

The postal rule was applied to acceptance by telegram in **Cowan** v **O'Connor** (1888), where it was held that an acceptance came into effect when the telegram was placed with the Post Office. These days the Post Office in England no longer offers a telegram service, but the same rule will apply to the telemessage service which replaced it. All the principles listed below concerning postal acceptances are also likely to apply to such telemessages.

Application of the postal rule
Use of the postal service must be reasonable. Only when it is reasonable to use the post to indicate acceptance can the postal rule apply. If the offer does not dictate a method of acceptance, appropriate methods can be inferred from the means used to make the offer. An offer made by post may generally be accepted by post, but it may be reasonable to accept by post even though the offer was delivered in some other way. In **Henthorn** v **Fraser** (1892) the defendant was based in Liverpool and the plaintiff lived in Birkenhead. The defendant gave the plaintiff in Liverpool a document containing an offer in Liverpool, and the plaintiff accepted it by posting a letter from Birkenhead. It was held that, despite the offer having been handed over in person, acceptance by post was reasonable because the parties were based in different towns.

Where an offer is made by an instant method of communication, such as telex, fax or telephone, an acceptance by post would not usually be reasonable.

Effect of the postal rule
The postal rule has two main practical consequences:

- A postal acceptance can take effect when it is posted, even if it gets lost in the post and never reaches the offeror. In **Household Fire Insurance** v **Grant** (1879) Grant had applied for (and therefore offered to buy) shares in the plaintiff company. The shares were allotted to him and his name was put on the register of shareholders. The company did write to say that the shares had been allotted to Grant, but the letter was lost in the post and he never received it. Some time later the company went into liquidation, and the liquidator claimed from Grant the balance owing on the price of his shares. It was held that Grant was bound to pay the balance, because the contract had been completed when the company's letter was posted.

It is likely that the same rule applies where the letter eventually arrives, but is delayed by postal problems.

* Where an acceptance is posted after the offeror posts a revocation of the offer, but before that revocation has been received, the acceptance will be binding (posted acceptances take effect on posting, posted revocations on communication). This point is illustrated by the cases of **Byrne** v **Van Tienhoven** (1880) and **Henthorn** v **Fraser** (1892).

Exceptions to the postal rule

Offers requiring communication of acceptance   An offeror may avoid the postal rule by making it a term of their offer that acceptance will only take effect when it is communicated to them. In **Holwell Securities** v **Hughes** (1974) the defendants offered to sell some freehold property to the plaintiffs but the offer stated that the acceptance had to be 'by notice in writing'. The plaintiffs posted their acceptance, but it never reached the defendants, despite being properly addressed. The court held that 'notice' meant communication, and therefore it would not be appropriate to apply the postal rule.

Instant methods of communication   When an acceptance is made by an instant mode of communication, such as telephone or telex, the postal rule does not apply. In such cases the acceptor will usually know at once that they have not managed to communicate with the offeror, and will need to try again.

In **Entores** v **Miles Far East Corporation** (1955) the plaintiffs were a London company and the defendants were an American corporation with agents in Amsterdam. Both the London company and the defendants' agents in Amsterdam had telex machines, which allow users to type in a message, and have it almost immediately received and printed out by the recipient's machine. The plaintiffs in London telexed the defendants' Amsterdam agents offering to buy goods from them, and the agents accepted, again by telex. The court case arose when the plaintiffs alleged that the defendant had broken their contract and wanted to bring an action against them. The rules of civil litigation stated that they could only bring this action in England if the contract had been made in England. The Court of Appeal held that because telex allows almost instant communication, the parties were in the same position as if they had negotiated in each other's presence or over the telephone, so the postal rule did not apply and an acceptance did not take effect until it had been received by the plaintiffs. Because the acceptance had been received in London, the contract was deemed to have been made there, and so the legal action could go ahead.

This approach was approved by the House of Lords in **Brinkibon** *v* **Stahag Stahl GmbH** (1983). The facts here were similar, except that the offer was made by telex from Vienna to London, and accepted by a telex from London to Vienna. The House of Lords held that the contract was therefore made in Vienna.

In both cases the telex machines were in the offices of the parties, and the messages were received inside normal working hours. In **Brinkibon** the House of Lords said that a telex message sent outside working hours would not be considered instantaneous, so the time and place in which the contract was completed would be determined by the intentions of the parties, standard business practice and, if possible, by analysing where the risk should most fairly lie.

There is no authority on when an acceptance by fax is binding, but as fax machines generally indicate whether or not a message has been successfully transmitted, the logical approach might be to treat an acceptance by fax as effective when sent, unless the sender is aware that the transmission was unsuccessful and was not received by the offeror. Even if the fax received is hard to read, the offeror will usually still know where it has come from, and has the opportunity to request clarification.

Misdirected acceptance Where a letter of acceptance is lost or delayed because the offeree has wrongly or incompletely addressed it through their own carelessness, it seems reasonable that the postal rule should not apply, although there is no precise authority to this effect. Treitel, a leading contract law academic, suggests that a better rule might be that if a badly addressed acceptance takes effect at all, it should do so at the time which is least advantageous to the party responsible for the misdirection.

Withdrawal of postal acceptance

Where the postal rule applies, it seems unlikely that an offeree could revoke a postal acceptance by phone (or some other instant means of communication) before it arrives, though there is no English case on the point. A Scottish case, **Dunmore** *v* **Alexander** (1830) does appear to allow such a revocation, but the court's views were only *obiter* on this point.

▶ Ignorance of the offer

It is generally thought that a person cannot accept an offer of which they are unaware, because in order to create a binding contract, the parties must reach agreement. If their wishes merely happen to coincide, that may be very convenient for both, but it does not constitute a contract and cannot legally bind them. Thus, if Ann advertises a reward for the return of a lost cat and Ben, not having seen or heard of the advertisement, comes across the cat, reads Ann's address on its collar and takes it back to Ann, is Ann bound to pay Ben the reward? No English case has clearly decided this point, and the cases abroad conflict with the main English case. On general principles Ben is probably unable to claim the reward.

In the American case of **Williams** *v* **Carwardine** (1833) the defendant offered a $20 reward for information leading to the discovery of the murderer of Walter Carwardine, and leaflets concerning the reward were distributed in the area where the plaintiff lived. The plaintiff apparently knew about the reward, but when she gave the information it was not in order to receive the money. She believed she had only a short time to live, and thought that giving the information might ease her conscience. The court held that she was entitled to the reward: she was aware of the offer and had complied with its terms, and her motive for doing so was irrelevant. A second US case, **Fitch** *v* **Snedaker** (1868), stated that a person who gives information without knowledge of the offer of a reward cannot claim the reward.

The main English case on this topic is **Gibbons** *v* **Proctor** (1891). A reward had been advertised for information leading to the arrest or conviction of the perpetrator of a particular crime and the plaintiff attempted to claim the reward, even though he had not originally known of the offer. He was allowed to receive the money, but the result does not shed much light on the problem because the plaintiff did know of the offer of reward by the time the information was given on his behalf to the person named in the advertisement.

Following the Australian case of **R** *v* **Clarke** (1927), it would appear that if the offeree knew of the offer in the past but has completely forgotten about it, they are treated as never having known about it. In that case a reward was offered by the Australian Government for information leading to the conviction of the murderers of two policemen. The Government also promised that an accomplice giving such information would receive a free pardon. Clarke was such an accomplice, who panicked and provided the information required in order to obtain the pardon, forgetting, at the time, about the reward. He remembered it later, but it was held that he was not entitled to the money.

▶ Cross offers

These present a similar problem. If Ann writes to Ben offering to sell her television for £50, and by coincidence Ben happens to write offering to buy the television for £50, the two letters crossing in the post, do the letters create a contract between them? On the principles of offer and acceptance it appears not, since the offeree does not know about the offer at the time of the potential acceptance. The point has never been decided in a case but there are *obiter dicta* in **Tinn** *v* **Hoffman** (1873) which suggest there would be no contract.

Time of the formation of the contract

Normally a contract is formed when an effective acceptance has been communicated to the offeree. An exception to this is the postal rule, where the contract is formed at the time the acceptance is posted and there is no need for communication. A further exception to the general rule has been created by s. 11 of the Electronic Communications Act 2000. This establishes the precise time at which an electronic contract is made. Electronic contracts are concluded when the customer has both:

- received an acknowledgement that their acceptance has been received, and
- confirmed their receipt of that acknowledgement.

These communications are taken to be effective when the receiving party is able to access them. Section 11 applies unless the parties agree otherwise. Thus electronic contracts will normally be formed at a later stage than other contracts.

Offer and acceptance implied by the court

Sometimes the parties may be in dispute as to whether a contract existed between them. They may never have signed any written agreement but one party may argue that the offer and acceptance had been made orally or through their conduct. Thus, in **Baird Textile Holdings Ltd** *v* **Marks & Spencer plc (2001)** Marks & Spencer had been in a business relationship with Baird Textile Holdings (BTH) for 30 years. BTH were based in the United Kingdom and had been a major supplier of clothes to Marks & Spencer over the years. In October 1999, Marks & Spencer advised BTH that it was ending all supply arrangements between them with effect from the end of the current production season. BTH brought a legal action against Marks & Spencer alleging that they had a contract with the company, and that a term of this contract had been breached by Marks & Spencer's terminating their supply arrangements in this way. The Court of Appeal held that there was no contract governing the relationship between the two litigants and that therefore Marks & Spencer were not in breach of a contract. It held that a contract should only be implied if it was necessary to do so 'to give business reality to a transaction and to create enforceable obligations between parties who are dealing with one another in circumstances in which one would expect that business reality and those enforceable obligations to exist'. It would not be necessary to imply such a contract if the parties might have acted in just the same way as they did without a contract. Marks & Spencer had preferred not to be bound by a contract so that they had maximum flexibility. For business reasons BTH had accepted this state of affairs.

> ## Auctions, tenders and the sale of land

The above rules of offer and acceptance apply to the sale of land and to sales by tender and auction, but it is useful to know how those rules apply in practice in these fairly common situations.

Auction sales

The parties to an auction sale are the bidder and the owner of the goods. The auctioneer simply provides a service, and is not a party to the contract between buyer and seller. Under the Sale of Goods Act 1979 (s. 57(2)), the general rule is that the auctioneer's request for bids is an invitation to treat, and each bid is an offer. Each bidder's offer lapses as soon as a higher bid is made, and an offer is accepted by the auctioneer (on behalf of the seller) on the fall of the hammer. Any bidder may therefore withdraw a bid before the hammer falls, and the auctioneer may also withdraw the goods on behalf of the seller before that point.

Advertisement of an auction
An advertisement that an auction is to take place at a certain time is a mere declaration of intention and is not an offer which those who attend at the specified time thereby accept. This was decided in **Harris** *v* **Nickerson** (1873), where the plaintiff failed to recover damages for travelling to an auction which was subsequently cancelled.

Auction 'without reserve'
In many cases, sellers at an auction specify reserve prices – the lowest prices they will accept for their goods. If nobody bids at least that amount, the goods are not sold. An auction 'without reserve', on the other hand, means that the goods will be sold to the highest bidder, however low their bid. We have seen that an advertisement announcing that an auction will be held is an invitation to treat and not an offer, but in **Warlow** *v* **Harrison** (1859) it was held that if such an advertisement includes the words 'without reserve', it becomes an offer, from the auctioneers to the public at large, that if the auction is held they will sell to the highest bidder (though it does not oblige the auctioneers to hold the sale in the first place). The offer is accepted when a person makes a bid and when doing so assumes that there is no reserve. That acceptance completes a contract, which is separate from any contract that might be made between the highest bidder and the owner of the property being sold. An auctioneer who then puts a reserve price on any of the lots breaches this separate contract.

In **Barry** *v* **Davies** (2000) the defendant auctioneers were instructed to sell two engine analysers, which were specialist machines used in the motor trade. The claimant had been told the sale would be 'without reserve'. New machines would cost £14,000 each. The auctioneer attempted to start the bidding at £5,000, then £3,000, but the claimant was the only person interested in the machines and placed a bid of just £200 for each machine. The auctioneer refused to accept that bid and withdrew the machines from the sale. The claimant sought damages for breach of contract and he was awarded £27,600. The defendants' appeal was dismissed and the case of **Warlow** *v* **Harrison** was followed. A contract existed between the auctioneer and the bidder that the auction would be without reserve, and that contract had been breached.

Tenders

When a large organization, such as a company, hospital, local council or government ministry, needs to find a supplier of goods or services, it will often advertise for tenders. Companies wishing to secure the business then reply to the advertisement, detailing the price at which they are willing to supply the goods or services, and the advertiser chooses whichever is the more favourable quotation. Tenders can also be invited for the sale of goods, in much the same way as bids are made at an auction.

As a general rule, a request for tenders is regarded as an invitation to treat (**Spencer** *v* **Harding** (1870)), so there is no obligation to accept any of the tenders put forward. The tenders themselves are offers, and a contract comes into existence when one of them is accepted.

In exceptional cases, however, an invitation for tenders may itself be an offer, and submission of a tender then becomes acceptance of that offer. The main example of this is where the invitation to tender makes it clear that the lowest tender (or the highest in the case of tenders to buy) will be accepted. In **Harvela Investments Ltd** *v* **Royal Trust Co of Canada (CI) Ltd** (1985) the defendants telexed two parties inviting them to submit tenders for the purchase of some shares, stating in the invitation 'we bind ourselves to accept the [highest] offer'. The House of Lords said that the telex was a unilateral offer to accept the highest bid, which would be followed by a bilateral contract with the highest bidder.

An invitation to tender may also be regarded as an offer to consider all tenders correctly submitted, even if it is not an undertaking actually to accept one. In **Blackpool and Fylde Aero Club Ltd** *v* **Blackpool Borough Council** (1990) the Council invited tenders from people wishing to operate leisure flights from the local airport. Those who wished to submit a tender were to reply to the Town Hall, in envelopes provided, by a certain deadline. The plaintiff returned his bid before the deadline was up, but the Council mistakenly thought it had arrived late. They therefore refused to consider it, and accepted one of the other tenders.

The plaintiff's claim for breach of contract was upheld by the Court of Appeal. Although the Council was not obliged to accept any of the tenders, the terms of their invitation to tender constituted an offer at least to consider any tender which was submitted in accordance with their rules. That offer was accepted by anyone who put forward a tender in the correct manner, and their acceptance would create a unilateral contract, obliging the Council to consider the tender. The Council was in breach of this unilateral contract.

In some cases a tenderer makes what is called a 'referential' tender, offering to top anyone else's bid by a specified amount. This occurred in **Harvela Investments Ltd** *v* **Royal Trust Co of Canada (CI) Ltd** (1985). Some shares were for sale, and the plaintiffs offered C\$2,175,000 for them. Another party offered to pay C\$2,100,000, or if this was not the highest bid, to pay C\$101,000 'in excess of any other offer'. The House of Lords made it clear that the type of 'referential' tender made by the second party was not legally an offer, and was not permissible in such a transaction. Therefore the first defendants were bound to accept the plaintiffs' bid. Their Lordships explained their decision on the grounds that the purpose of a sale by fixed bidding is to provoke the best price from purchasers regardless of what others might be prepared to pay, and that referential bids worked against this. Such bids would also present practical problems if allowed: if everyone made referential bids it would be impossible to define exactly what offer was being made, and if only some parties made bids in that way, the others would not have a valid opportunity to have their offers accepted.

Acceptance of tenders
The implications of choosing to accept a tender depend on what sort of tender is involved.

Specific tenders Where an invitation to tender specifies that a particular quantity of goods is required on a particular date, or between certain dates, agreeing to one of the tenders submitted will constitute acceptance of an offer (the tender), creating a contract. This is the case even if delivery is to be in instalments as and when requested. If a company tenders to supply 100 wheelchairs to a hospital between 1 January and 1 June, their contract is completed when the hospital chooses the company's tender, and delivery must be made between those dates.

Non-specific tenders Some invitations to tender are not specific, and may simply state that certain goods may be required, up to a particular maximum quantity, with deliveries to be made 'if and when' requested. For example, an invitation to tender made by a hospital may ask for tenders to supply up to 1,000 test tubes, 'if and when' required. In such a case, taking up one of the tenders submitted does not amount to acceptance of an offer in the contractual sense, and there is no contract. Once the tender is approved, it becomes what is called a standing offer. The hospital may order no test tubes at all, may spread delivery over several instalments, or may take the whole 1,000 test tubes at once. If the hospital does buy the test tubes or some of them, whether in instalments or all at once, then each time it places an order it accepts the test tube manufacturer's offer, and a separate contract for the amount required is made on each occasion. The result is that when the hospital places an order, the company is bound to supply within the terms of the offer as required, but the company can revoke the offer to supply at any time, and will then only be bound by orders already placed.

This kind of situation would not oblige the hospital to order its test tubes only from the company whose tender it approved. In **Percival** *v* **LCC** (1918) Percival submitted a tender to the LCC for the supply of certain goods 'in such quantities and at such times and in such manner' as the Committee required. The tender was approved, but the LCC eventually placed its orders with other suppliers. Percival claimed damages for breach of contract, but the court held that acceptance of the non-specific tender did not constitute a contract, and the LCC were not obliged to order goods – although Percival was obliged to supply goods which were ordered under the terms of the standing offer, so long as the offer had not been revoked.

The nature of a standing offer was considered in **Great Northern Railway Co** *v* **Witham** (1873). The plaintiffs had invited tenders for the supply of stores, and the defendant made a tender in these words: 'I undertake to supply the Company for twelve months with such quantities of [the specified articles] as the Company may order from time to time.' The railway company accepted this tender, and later placed some orders, which were met by the defendant. The court case arose when the railway company placed an order for goods within the scope of the tender, and the defendant refused to supply them. The court found that the supplying company was in breach of contract because the tender was a standing offer, which the railway company could accept each time it placed an order, thereby creating a contract each time. The standing offer could be revoked at any time, but the tenderer was bound by orders already made, since these were acceptances of his offer and thereby completed a contract.

Sale of land

The standard rules of contract apply to the sale of land (which includes the sale of buildings such as houses), but the courts apply those rules fairly strictly, tending to require very clear evidence of an intention to be bound before they will state that an offer has definitely been made. The main reason for this is simply that land is expensive, and specific areas of land are unique and irreplaceable; damages are therefore often inadequate as a remedy for breach of contract in a sale of land, and it is better to avoid problems beforehand than put them right after a contract is made.

In **Harvey** *v* **Facey** (1893) the plaintiffs sent the defendants a telegram asking: 'Will you sell us Bumper Hall Pen? Telegraph lowest cash price.' The reply arrived, stating: 'Lowest price for Bumper Hall Pen, £900.' The plaintiffs then sent a telegram back saying: 'We agree to buy Bumper Hall Pen for £900 asked by you. Please send us your title deeds.' On these facts, the Privy Council held that there was no contract. They regarded the telegram from the defendants as merely a statement of what the minimum price would be if the defendants eventually decided to sell. It was therefore not an offer which could be accepted by the third telegram.

In practice the normal procedure for sales involving land is as follows:

Sale 'subject to contract'

First, parties agree on the sale, often through an estate agent. At this stage their agreement may be described as 'subject to contract', and although the effect of these words depends on the intention of the parties, there is a strong presumption against there being a contract at this stage (**Tiverton Estates Ltd** *v* **Wearwell Ltd** (1975)). If the parties sign a document at this point, it will usually be an agreement to make a more formal contract in the future, rather than a contract to go through with the sale. It was held in **Alpenstow Ltd** *v* **Regalian Properties plc** (1985) that there were some circumstances in which the courts may infer that the parties intended to be legally bound when signing the original document, even though it was said to be 'subject to contract', but such cases would arise only rarely.

The idea of making an agreement 'subject to contract' is to allow the buyers to check thoroughly all the details of the land (to make sure, for example, that there are no plans to build a new airport just behind the house they are thinking of buying, or that the house is not affected by subsidence).

Exchange of contracts

The next stage is that the buyer and seller agree on the terms of the formal contract (usually through their solicitors, though there is no legal reason why the parties cannot make all the arrangements themselves). Both parties then sign a copy of the contract, and agree on a date on which the contracts will be exchanged, at which point the buyer usually pays a deposit of around 10 per cent of the sale price. Once the contracts are exchanged, a binding contract exists (though it is difficult to see this transaction in terms of offer and acceptance). However, if the contract is breached at this point the buyer can only claim damages – the buyer has no rights in the property itself.

After exchanging contracts, the parties may make further inquiries (checking, for example, that the seller really does own the property), and then the ownership of the land and house is transferred to the buyer, usually by means of a document known as a transfer. At this stage the buyer pays the balance of the purchase price to the seller. The buyer then has rights in the property – in the event of the seller breaching the contract, the buyer can have her property rights enforced in court, rather than just claiming damages.

These principles are illustrated by **Eccles** v **Bryant** (1947). After signing an agreement 'subject to contract', the parties consulted their solicitors, who agreed a draft contract. Each party signed the contract, and the buyer forwarded his copy to the seller's solicitor so that contracts could be exchanged. However, the seller changed his mind about the sale, and his solicitor informed the buyer's solicitor that the property had been sold to another buyer. The buyer tried to sue for breach of contract, but the Court of Appeal held that the negotiations were subject to formal contract, and the parties had not intended to be bound until they exchanged contracts. No binding obligations could arise before this took place. The court did not say when the exchange would be deemed to have taken place – that is, whether it was effective on posting of the contracts, or on receipt. In many cases a contract will specify when an exchange will be considered complete, by stating, for example, that the contract will be binding when the contracts are actually delivered.

▶ How important are offer and acceptance?

Although offer and acceptance can provide the courts with a useful technique for assessing at what point an agreement should be binding, what the courts are really looking to judge is whether the parties have come to an agreement, and there are some cases in which the rules on offer and acceptance give little help.

An example of this type of situation is **Clarke** v **Dunraven** (1897), which concerned two yacht owners who had entered for a yacht race. The paperwork they completed in order to enter included an undertaking to obey the club rules, and these rules contained an obligation to pay for 'all damages' caused by fouling. During the manoeuvring at the start of the race, one yacht, the *Satanita*, fouled another, the *Valkyrie*, which sank as a result. The owner of the *Valkyrie* sued the owner of the *Satanita* for the cost of the lost yacht, but the defendant claimed that he was under no obligation to pay the whole cost, and was only liable to pay the lesser damages laid down by a statute which limited liability to £8 for every ton of the yacht. The plaintiff claimed that entering the competition in accordance with the rules had created a contract between the competitors, and this contract obliged the defendant to pay 'all damages'.

Clearly it was difficult to see how there could be an offer by one competitor and acceptance by the other, since their relations had been with the yacht club and not with each other. There was obviously an offer and an acceptance between each competitor and the club, but was there a contract between the competitors? The House of Lords held that there was, on the basis that 'a contract is concluded when one party has communicated to another an offer and that other has accepted it or when the parties have united in a concurrent expression of intention to create a legal obligation'. Therefore responsibility for accidents was governed by the race rules, and the defendant had to pay the full cost of the yacht.

There are problems in analysing the contract between the entrants to the race in terms of offer and acceptance. It seems rather far-fetched to imagine that, on starting the race, each competitor was making an offer to all the other competitors and simultaneously accepting their offers – and in any case, since the offers and acceptances would all occur at the same moment, they would be cross offers and would technically not create a contract.

As we have seen, contracts for the sale of land are also examples of agreements that do not usually fall neatly into concepts of offer and acceptance. We will also see later that the problems arising from the offer and acceptance analysis are sometimes avoided by the courts using the device of collateral contracts (see p. 224 below).

Problems with offer and acceptance

Artificiality

Clearly there are situations in which the concepts of offer and acceptance have to be stretched, and interpreted rather artificially, even though it is obvious that the parties have reached an agreement. In **Gibson** *v* **Manchester City Council** (1979) Lord Denning made it clear that he was in favour of looking at negotiations as a whole, in order to determine whether there was a contract, rather than trying to impose offer and acceptance on the facts, but his method has largely been rejected by the courts as being too uncertain and allowing too wide a discretion.

Revocation of unilateral offers

The problem of whether a unilateral offer can be accepted by part-performance has caused difficulties for the courts. It can be argued that since the offeree has not promised to complete performance, they are free to stop at any time, so the offeror should be equally free to revoke the offer at any time. But this would mean, for example, that if A says to B, 'I'll pay you £100 if you paint my living room', A could withdraw the offer even though B had painted all but one square foot of the room, and pay nothing.

This is generally considered unjust, and various academics have expressed the view that in fact an offer cannot be withdrawn once there has been substantial performance. American academics have contended that the offeror can be seen as making two offers: the main offer that the price will be paid when the act is performed, and an implied accompanying offer that the main offer will not be revoked once performance has begun. On this assumption, the act of starting performance is both acceptance of the implied offer, and consideration for the secondary promise that the offer will not be withdrawn once performance begins. An offeror who does attempt to revoke the offer after performance has started may be sued for the breach of the secondary promise.

In England this approach has been considered rather artificial. Sir Frederick Pollock has reasoned that it might be more realistic to say that the main offer itself is accepted by beginning rather than completing performance, on the basis that acceptance simply means agreement to the terms of the offer, and there are many circumstances in which beginning performance will mean just that. Whether an act counts as beginning performance, and therefore accepting the offer, or whether it is just preparation for performing will depend on the facts of the case – so, for example, an offer of a reward for the return of lost property could still be revoked after someone had spent time looking for the property without success, but not after they had actually found it and taken steps towards returning it to the owner. This principle was adopted in 1937 by the Law Revision Committee.

Revocation of offers for specific periods

The rule that an offer can be revoked at any time before acceptance even if the offeror has said it will remain open for a specified time could be considered unfairly biased in favour of the offeror, and makes it difficult for the offeree to plan their affairs with certainty.

In a Working Paper published in 1975, the Law Commission recommended that where an offeror promises not to revoke the offer for a specified time, that promise should be binding, without the need for consideration, and if it is broken the offeree should be able to sue for damages.

An 'all or nothing' approach

The 'all or nothing' approach of offer and acceptance is not helpful in cases where there is clearly not a binding contract under that approach, and yet going back on agreements made would cause great hardship or inconvenience to one party. The problems associated with housebuying are well known – the buyer may go to all the expense of a survey and solicitor's fees, and may even have sold their own house, only to find that the seller withdraws the house from sale, sells it to someone else, or demands a higher price – generally known as 'gazumping'. So long as all this takes place before contracts are exchanged, the buyer has no remedy at all (though the Government is proposing to legislate to deal with some of these specific problems). Similarly, in a commercial situation, pressure of time may mean that a company starts work on a potential project before a contract is drawn up and signed. They will be at a disadvantage if in the end the other party decides not to contract.

Objectivity

The courts claim that they are concerned with following the intention of the parties in deciding whether there is a contract, yet they make it quite clear that they are not actually seeking to discover what **was** intended, but what, looking at the parties' behaviour, an 'officious bystander' might assume they intended. This can mean that even though the parties were actually in agreement, no contract results, as was the case in **Felthouse** *v* **Bindley** – the nephew had asked for the horse to be kept out of the sale because he was going to sell it to his uncle, but because he did not actually communicate his acceptance, there was no contract.

▶ ANSWERING QUESTIONS

1 At 9.00 am on Monday 13 August, Maurice, a car dealer, sends a telex to Austin offering to sell him a rare vintage car for £50,000. Austin receives the telex at 9.15 am and telexes his acceptance at 1.00 pm. Austin is aware that Maurice's office is closed for lunch between 1.00 and 2.00 pm. On his return to the office, Maurice does not bother to check whether he has received a telex from Austin and at 2.30 pm receives an offer for the car from Ford, which he accepts. At 4.00 pm Austin hears from another car dealer that Maurice has sold the car to Ford. He is advised that it will cost him an additional £2,000 to buy a similar car and he immediately sends Maurice another telex demanding that the original car be sold to him. Maurice receives this telex at 5.00 pm, at the same time as he reads the acceptance telex.

Advise Austin of his legal position and what remedies, if any, are open to him.
Oxford

Austin clearly wishes to establish that, at some point, he made a binding contract with Maurice; your task is to pinpoint when, if at all, that contract was made, using the rules of offer and acceptance. The clearest way to do this is to take each communication in turn, and consider its legal effect.

Maurice's first telex is clearly an offer; does Austin validly accept it? The general rule is that acceptance takes effect on communication; the application of this rule to telexed acceptances is contained in the cases of **Entores** and **Brinkibon**. Considering that the telex was sent outside working hours, when should it take effect, and considering the factors mentioned in **Brinkibon** – intentions of the parties, standard business practice – where should the risk lie? Obviously there is no clear answer, but in assessing where the risk should lie, you might take into account the fact that it seems reasonable for Austin to assume the telex would be read shortly after the lunch hour was finished, and to expect Maurice to check whether any reply had been received. This is relevant because in other cases on communication, the courts seem reluctant to bail out parties who fail to receive messages through their own fault (such as the requirement that telephone callers should ask for clarification if they cannot hear the other party – **Entores**). If Austin's telex acceptance is deemed to take effect when the telex is sent, a binding contract exists between them at that point, and this will take priority over the contract made with Ford. You should then consider the position if the rule that acceptance only takes effect on communication is strictly applied.

The next relevant communication is the other car dealer telling Austin that the car has been sold; **Dickinson v Dodds** makes it plain that information from a third party can amount to a revocation, and if this is the case, the offer ceases to be available and there is no contract between Austin and Maurice. However, in **Dickinson v Dodds** the message from the third party was such that the revocation was as clear as if the offeror had said it himself; if for any reason this was not the case here (if the dealer was known to be untrust-worthy, for example), there would be no revocation, and the offer would still be available for acceptance at 5 pm, at which point the contract would be made.

The issue of remedies is discussed fully in Chapter 15, but, assuming a contract was made, Austin is likely to be limited to claiming damages. Maurice could only be forced to sell the car if the courts granted specific performance, and this is only done when damages would be an inadequate way of putting the plaintiff in the position they should have enjoyed if the contract had been performed as agreed. Here this could be done by allowing Austin to claim the difference between the car's price and the cost of a replacement.

2 Peter's car has been stolen. He places an advertisement in the Morriston *Evening News* stating that a reward of £1,000 will be given to any person who provides information leading to the recovery of the car – provided the reward is claimed by 1 January. Andrew, a policeman, finds the car, which has suffered severe accident damage. His best friend Kelvin tells him about the reward and Andrew applies for it by a letter posted on 30 December. The letter arrives at Peter's house on 2 January.

Advise Andrew whether he has a contractual right to the reward. *WJEC*

This question concerns the issue of offer and acceptance and consideration in unilateral contracts. You first need to consider whether Peter's advertisement is an offer. It is worth pointing out that not all advertisements are seen as offers, although in this case the issue is fairly straightforward as there are several cases in which advertisements proposing unilateral contracts, and specifically involving rewards, have been recognized as offers.

The fact that Andrew did not see the advertisement but was told about it by a friend seems to raise the issue of whether an offer can be accepted by someone who does not know about it. The cases on this matter are inconclusive, but the fact that Andrew does know about the reward by the time he applies for it would seem to avoid the problem.

The next issue is whether Andrew applies for the reward in time. As you know, acceptance does not usually take effect until it is communicated, but acceptances sent by post may take effect on posting – the postal rule. The postal rule will apply so long as it is reasonable to submit the application by post, and here there seems no reason why it should not be. This means that the offer is accepted in time, even though the letter arrives after the specified closing date.

However, there is another important issue to examine: consideration (discussed in Chapter 6). Since Andrew is a policeman, it could be argued that finding the car and informing the owner of its whereabouts is no more than his public duty. In order to have provided consideration for the reward, he would need to have gone beyond this, as explained in cases such as **Glasbrook Brothers** v **Glamorgan County Council** and **Harris** v **Sheffield United** (see p. 73).

3 Critically evaluate what in law will amount to an 'offer'. *OCR*

Your introduction could start with a definition of an offer, which is stated at p. 10 to be a communication which indicates the terms on which the offeror is prepared to make a contract and gives a clear indication that the offeror intends to be bound by those terms if they are accepted by the offeree. Your introduction could also put the concept of an offer into the wider context of the principle of freedom of contract. Contract law's emphasis on the requirement of an offer is an example of the belief that the parties should be free to make contracts on any terms they choose.

You could then move on to distinguishing the concept of an offer from an invitation to treat. You might start by looking at bilateral contracts and examine the approach of the courts to the specific scenarios of advertisements, shopping, timetables and tickets for transport, tenders (p. 32), auctions (p. 31) and the sale of land (p. 34). Offers for unilateral contracts could then be considered, and in particular the case of **Carlill** v **Carbolic Smoke Ball Co**.

The next stage of your answer could contain an examination of how long an offer lasts (p. 14).

The question requires you to 'critically evaluate' and it will therefore not be enough to simply describe the law. One of the problem areas has been the 'battle of the forms' (p. 20), and you could look closely at cases such as **Butler Machine Tool Ltd** v **Ex-Cell-O Corp**. The case of **Clarke** v **Dunraven** (p. 36) provides an example of the type of scenario which does not fit comfortably within the concept of offer (and acceptance). Other criticisms of the law on offers can be found at p. 37 under the subheading 'Problems with offer and acceptance'.

2 Certainty

In order to be a binding contract, an agreement must be certain – that is, it should not be unduly vague, or obviously incomplete. For example, in **Loftus** *v* **Roberts** (1902) Roberts engaged an actress to appear in a play at 'a West End salary to be mutually arranged between us'. The court held that there was no binding contract between them because the provision concerning payment was too vague.

Similarly, in **Scammell** *v* **Ouston** (1941), Ouston agreed to buy a van from Scammell, providing his old lorry in part-exchange and paying the balance 'on hire-purchase terms' over two years. Before the precise nature of those terms could be negotiated, Scammell decided not to go ahead with the deal, and claimed there was no contract between the parties. The House of Lords agreed, pointing out that although the courts aimed to uphold an agreement if there really was one, the terms used were too vague to signify any true agreement. The phrase 'hire-purchase terms' could be used to describe many different arrangements: it left open such questions as whether payments would be made on a weekly, monthly or yearly basis; whether there would be an initial deposit; and what the interest rate would be. Consequently, the parties could not be said to have made a sufficiently certain agreement to constitute a contract.

In **Baird Textile Holdings Ltd** *v* **Marks & Spencer plc** (2001) (discussed on p. 84) Baird Textile Holdings argued that they had a contract with Marks & Spencer under which Marks & Spencer 'would acquire garments from BTH in quantities and at prices which in all the circumstances were reasonable'. The Court of Appeal held that these terms would be too uncertain to be part of a valid contract.

However, the courts will usually look to see if there is any way to make an apparently vague or incomplete agreement more certain; as Lord Tomlin observed in **Hillas** *v* **Arcos** (1932) (p. 43 below), they do not want to 'incur the reproach of being the destroyer of bargains'. The following are the main methods used.

Provision for clarification

In some circumstances prices and other factors affecting a contract are likely to fluctuate, and the parties to an agreement will therefore be reluctant to commit themselves to a rigid arrangement concerning those factors. In such cases, contracts may leave such details vague, but contain provisions stating how they are to be clarified (such as by independent arbitration).

In **Foley** *v* **Classique Coaches** (1934) the plaintiff was the owner of a petrol station and some land adjoining it. The defendants ran a coach business, and the plaintiff sold them the land, on condition that they entered into an agreement to buy all the petrol they needed for the coaches from him, 'at a price to be agreed by the parties in writing and from time to time'. This agreement went ahead, but the defendants broke it, and argued that it was incomplete, and therefore not a binding contract, because the term regarding price was too vague. In fact, the contract provided that any dispute should be referred to arbitration in accordance with the Arbitration Act 1889 (now the Arbitration Act 1996). The Court of Appeal interpreted this as meaning that there was an implied term that the petrol should be sold at a reasonable price, with the arbitration clause being intended to sort out any dispute as to whether a price was reasonable. This meant that the contract was more certain than it looked at first glance, and the court decided that it was sufficiently certain to be binding on the parties.

Terms implied by statute

In some cases, statutes provide that certain terms should be read into contracts of particular types, even though those terms have not actually been agreed between the parties. For example, under the Sale of Goods Act 1979 an agreement for the sale of goods can become binding as soon as the parties have agreed to buy and sell, with the details of the contract being laid down by law, or determined by the standard of reasonableness. In such a case, the parties do not even have to have agreed on a price – s. 8(2) of the Act provides that if the contract does not specify a price, the buyer is entitled to pay a reasonable price. We will look at terms implied by statute more fully in Chapter 7.

Previous course of dealing

Where two parties have had dealings in the past, their previous agreements may be used to clarify uncertain terms in a contract. In **Hillas** *v* **Arcos** (1932) Hillas had contracted to buy timber 'of fair specification' from Arcos in 1930. The agreement also included an option to purchase the following year, which did not detail the type or size of the wood to be bought. When Hillas tried to exercise the option, they discovered that Arcos had in fact already sold all the wood they had that year, and so Hillas sued for breach of contract. The House of Lords held that although the terms used were apparently unspecific, the parties were both very familiar with the way business was done in the timber industry, and had done a large amount of business with each other in the past. Consequently, the terms could be interpreted in the light of what they would usually mean in that industry and between those parties. They were therefore sufficiently certain to create a contract.

Reasonableness

Sometimes the courts will clarify vague terms by relying on the principle of reasonableness. In **Sudbrook Trading Estate Ltd** *v* **Eggleton** (1982) leaseholders had the option to buy the premises 'at such price as may be agreed upon by two valuers', the parties being able to nominate one each. The landlord refused to appoint a valuer, and claimed that the agreement was not a binding contract because there was no provision detailing how the price would be reached if the two valuers disagreed. The House of Lords disagreed, stating that the important point was that the price was to be set by professional valuers. Such individuals would be obliged to apply professional and, by implication, reasonable standards in setting the price, and therefore the option was actually a definite agreement to sell at a reasonable price. The condition that each party should appoint one of the valuers was merely 'subsidiary and inessential'.

Custom

Apparent vagueness can be resolved by custom – as we have seen, the customary way of dealing in the timber industry played a part in clarifying the terms in **Hillas** *v* **Arcos**, in combination with the parties' previous mutual dealings.

The 'officious bystander'

A term may be implied by applying the 'officious bystander' test. This test will be looked at in Chapter 7 at p. 105, but basically the court asks itself whether someone observing the making of a contract would have believed that a particular term was part of the contract. An example might be that if you heard your next door neighbour offer to buy someone's car for 'a thousand' you would, assuming you were in Britain, presume that she meant £1,000, rather than the same amount in dollars or pesetas, even though the form of currency had not been specified.

Removing minor uncertain terms

In extreme cases, a minor term may be not only vague but also meaningless. Providing it is sufficiently unimportant, it can be struck out, allowing the courts to enforce the rest of the contract. Thus in **Nicolene** *v* **Simmonds** (1953) Nicolene ordered some steel bars from Simmonds. The terms of the agreement to buy were quite clear, except that the transaction was stated to be subject to 'the usual conditions of acceptance'. The parties later disagreed about the quality of the metal delivered, at which point Simmonds contended that there was no enforceable contract because the words 'usual conditions of acceptance' were too uncertain. The court agreed that the words were uncertain, because there were in fact no 'usual conditions', but it held that as the problematic term only concerned a subsidiary matter, they could be ignored.

▶ ANSWERING QUESTIONS

1 Albert is an importer and distributor of tea. Two years ago he bought five tonnes of tea from Louise, at a cost of £25,000. Last Monday, Albert ordered from Louise ten tonnes of Indian tea of 'standard grade' at £40,000. The tea was to be packed according to the 'established hygienic procedures'. Louise agreed to deliver the tea, but then later refused to do so. She argued that no contract existed between herself and Albert because there was no precise agreement as to the quality of the tea and there were no established hygienic procedures for packing tea.

In order for there to be a binding contract between Albert and Louise, an agreement must be certain, that is it should not be unduly vague or obviously incomplete. There are two aspects of this agreement which appear uncertain: the type of tea that was to be delivered and the requirement that the tea should have been packed under the established hygienic procedures. In practice, the courts will usually look to see if there is any way to make an apparently vague agreement more certain. Under the Sale of Goods Act 1979 an agreement for the sale of goods (here we have an agreement for the sale of tea) can become binding as soon as the parties have agreed to buy and sell, with the details of the contract being determined by the standard of reasonableness. This principle of reasonableness will also be applied under common law: **Sudbrook Trading Estate Ltd** v **Eggleton**.

In addition, there is a previous course of dealing between Albert and Louise, so the courts can look at their earlier agreement to clarify the meaning of these uncertain terms: **Hillas** v **Arcos**. It may be that there are also relevant customs in the tea trade which can clarify the meaning of the agreement.

Applying the principle in **Nicolene** v **Simmonds**, the court might be prepared to delete the term as to the usual hygienic procedures on the basis that it is a minor term that is meaningless.

In the light of this discussion it is likely that, in the business context, a court will find this agreement sufficiently certain to be binding on Louise.

3 Intention to create legal relations

If two or more parties make an agreement without any intention of being legally bound by it, that agreement will not be regarded by the courts as a contract. It is important to remember with regard to this issue that the courts assess the parties' intentions objectively – so, if to onlookers their behaviour or words would suggest they intended to be bound, the fact that one secretly had reservations is irrelevant.

As far as intent to be legally bound is concerned, contracts can be divided into domestic and social agreements on the one hand and commercial transactions on the other. Where an agreement falls into the domestic and social category, there is a rebuttable presumption that the parties do not intend to create legal relations. The reverse applies in commercial agreements, where it is presumed that the parties do intend such agreements to be legally binding. Again, this principle can be rebutted if there is evidence that the parties did not intend their agreement to be legally enforceable.

Social and domestic agreements

Agreements between husband and wife

Where a husband and wife who are living together as one household make an agreement, courts will assume that they do not intend to be legally bound, unless there is evidence to the contrary. In **Balfour** *v* **Balfour** (1919) the defendant was a civil servant stationed in Ceylon (now Sri Lanka). While the couple were on leave in England, Mrs Balfour was taken ill, and it eventually became clear that her husband would have to return by himself. He promised to pay her a monthly maintenance allowance of £30. They later decided to separate, upon which the husband refused to make any more payments. The Court of Appeal decided he was not bound to pay the allowance because at the time when the agreement was made there was no intention to create legal relations. When this type of agreement was made between husband and wife, said Atkin LJ, it was a family matter in which the courts really had no place to interfere.

On its facts, **Balfour** might well be decided differently if it arose today; while the courts still seem reluctant to give effect to agreements made while spouses are still cohabiting, there have been a string of cases in which those who are separating or divorcing are treated as intending to create legal relations. In **Merritt** v **Merritt** (1969) Mr Merritt had left his wife to go and live with another woman, and subsequently met his spouse to resolve various financial arrangements. Sitting in Mr Merritt's car, they decided that he would pay his wife £40 a month, out of which she was to pay the outstanding mortgage payments on their house; he would transfer the house to her sole ownership when the mortgage was paid off. Mrs Merritt then refused to get out of the car until her husband put the agreement in writing. Eventually, he signed a piece of paper stating what they had agreed. The wife duly paid off the mortgage, but the husband then refused to transfer ownership of the house to her. The Court of Appeal upheld the wife's claim. Lord Denning pointed out that the presumption applied in **Balfour** v **Balfour**, that an agreement between husband and wife was 'a family arrangement', was not valid where the parties had separated or were about to do so. In such circumstances the parties 'do not rely on honourable understandings', but 'bargain keenly', and it could be safely presumed that any agreement between them was intended to be legally binding.

The US courts have shown themselves increasingly willing to give effect to domestic agreements, as shown by the case of **Morone** v **Morone** (1980), where an agreement between a cohabiting couple that the man would financially support the woman in return for her help in running their home and helping in his business was held to be binding.

Agreements between parent and child

Agreements of a domestic nature between parents and children are also presumed not to be intended to be binding, though again the presumption can be rebutted. In **Jones** v **Padavatton** (1969) the plaintiff was a resident of Trinidad. Her daughter had a secretarial job in Washington, but her mother wanted her to give it up and train to be a barrister in England. The mother therefore volunteered to give her daughter a monthly allowance for the duration of her Bar studies. The daughter accepted the offer and went to England. Later on, the pair made a second agreement, under which the mother bought a house for the daughter to live in, and in which she could rent out rooms in order to support herself, instead of receiving the allowance. Neither agreement was ever put in writing. The daughter persistently failed to pass her Bar examinations and, five years after the original bargain was made, they quarrelled, and her mother sought possession of the house. On the facts of the case, the majority of the Court of Appeal considered that neither agreement was intended to create legal relations: they were merely family arrangements in which both parties, who had been close at the time, were happy to trust each other to keep the bargain. The mother was therefore entitled to possession of the house.

Social agreements

The presumption that an agreement is not intended to be legally binding is also applied to social relationships between people who are not related. Again, it can be rebutted. In **Simpkins** *v* **Pays** (1955) the plaintiff enjoyed entering competitions run in Sunday newspapers. When he took lodgings in the defendant's house, she and her granddaughter began to do the competitions with him, sharing the cost of entry. The plaintiff filled in the forms in the name of the defendant, and she promised to share any winnings. Eventually one of the entries was successful, and the defendant won £750. The plaintiff claimed a third of the sum as his share of the prize, but the defendant refused, claiming that she had not intended to be legally bound by the agreement. The court upheld the plaintiff's claim, considering that they had all contributed to the competition with the expectation that any prize would be shared.

Similarly, in **Peck** *v* **Lateu** (1973) the court found an intention to create legal relations where two women had agreed to share any money won by either of them at bingo.

Commercial agreements

There is a strong presumption in commercial agreements that the parties intend to be legally bound, and, unless there is very clear contrary evidence, this presumption will not be rebutted. In **Esso Petroleum Ltd** *v* **Commissioners of Customs and Excise** (1976) Esso ran a sales promotion in which 'coins' showing members of the England football squad for the 1970 World Cup were to be given away free, one with every four gallons of petrol. The scheme was advertised on television and by posters at filling stations. The case arose when for tax purposes it became necessary to decide whether or not there was a contract of sale – did a motorist who bought four gallons of petrol have a contractual right to one of the coins? The House of Lords held, by a majority, that the coins were not being sold, and so were not liable for tax, but that there was intent to create legal relations. Lord Simon pointed out that 'the whole transaction took place in a setting of business relations', that it was undesirable to allow companies to make promises in advertisements that they were not bound to keep, and that Esso knew that despite the coins' negligible monetary value, they would be attractive to motorists and Esso would therefore derive considerable commercial benefit from the scheme.

In **J Evans & Son (Portsmouth) Ltd** *v* **Andrea Merzario Ltd** (1976) the plaintiffs were machinery importers, who had regularly used the defendants, a firm of forwarding agents, to arrange transport of their goods. The machinery was prone to rust if stored on deck, and so it had always been agreed that it would be carried below decks. In 1967, in the course of a 'courtesy call' to the plaintiffs, the defendants' representative put forward the idea of carrying the goods by container transport, assuring them that their containers would always be kept below decks because of the rust problem (many container ships are designed to have the containers stacked on deck). The plaintiffs agreed to the change. About a year later, a container with one of the plaintiffs' machines inside was carried on deck instead of below, and, not being properly secured, fell overboard as the ship left port and was lost. The plaintiffs sued, and the defendants argued that the promise to store the containers below decks was not intended to be legally binding since it was made in the course of a courtesy call, was not related to any particular transaction, and its future duration was not specified. The Court of Appeal rejected this argument, saying that the background to the promise meant that an intent to be contractually bound could be inferred: the parties had previously done business together, in which goods were always transported below decks, and the plaintiffs would not have agreed to the change in method if the promise had not been made.

The presumption that parties to a commercial agreement intend to create legal relations may be rebutted where the words of a contract, or an offer, suggest that legal relations were not intended. There are three main situations where this will occur.

'Mere puffs'

Where an offer is extremely vague, or clearly not intended to be taken seriously, the law will not give its acceptance contractual effect. In **Weeks _v_ Tybald** (1604) the defendant announced that he would give £100 to any suitable man who would marry his daughter, but it was held that his words were not intended to be taken seriously, and his promise was not legally binding.

This principle is sometimes applied to the extravagant language used in advertising and sales promotions, but only if there is no evidence of contractual intent. In **Carlill _v_ Carbolic Smoke Ball Co** (1893) (discussed at p. 10, above), the defendants argued that their statement was 'a mere puff', an advertising gimmick which was never intended to be taken seriously. This contention was rejected by the court, pointing out that the advertisement stated that the company had deposited £1,000 with their bankers 'to show their sincerity', which was strong evidence that they had intended to be legally bound.

Honour clauses

In **Rose and Frank _v_ Crompton Bros** (1923) the plaintiffs had been buying goods from the defendants for some time, and in 1913, the parties signed an agreement that this arrangement should continue for a specified period, with prices set for six months at a time. Though otherwise ordinary, the agreement contained one unusual term, the 'honourable pledge clause'. It stated: 'This agreement is not entered into . . . as a formal or legal agreement, and shall not be subject to legal jurisdiction in the law courts . . . but it is only a definite expression and record of the purpose and intention of the parties concerned, to which they each honourably pledge themselves.' In 1919, the defendants terminated the agreement without giving the specified notice. The plaintiffs sued, making two separate claims. The first was for breach of the agreement contained in the written document of July 1913, that the buying and selling arrangement would continue for the specified period. This claim was rejected by the court, which held that the wording of the agreement placed neither side under any obligation to go on giving or accepting orders. Scrutton LJ commented: 'I can see no reason why, even in business matters, the parties should not intend to rely on each other's good faith and honour, and to exclude all idea of settling disputes by an outside intervention . . .'

The second claim concerned non-delivery of goods, which the plaintiffs had ordered in accordance with the agreement, before it was terminated. This claim was upheld, on the basis that when each individual order was placed and accepted, it constituted a new and separate contract, which was enforceable in its own right, without reference to the original document.

Similarly, where a football pools coupon states that it is 'binding in honour only', the pools company cannot be sued for payment by a winner: **Jones** *v* **Vernon's Pools** (1938).

Agreement 'subject to contract'

Use of these words on an agreement is usually (though not always) taken to mean that the parties do not intend to be legally bound until formal contracts are exchanged (see p. 35 above).

Ambiguity

Where the words of a business agreement are ambiguous, the courts will favour the interpretation which suggests that the parties did intend to create legal relations, and therefore find that there is a contract. In **Edwards** *v* **Skyways Ltd** (1964) the plaintiff was a pilot employed by the defendants. As part of a redundancy agreement, Skyways promised to make an *ex gratia* payment of a specified amount in return for Mr Edwards not claiming his full pension rights. Later, the company refused to make the payment, claiming that the words '*ex gratia*' showed that there was no intention to create legal relations. The Court of Appeal rejected this argument, stating that this was a commercial agreement and there was therefore a strong presumption in favour of creating legal relations. The words '*ex gratia*' merely signified that the employers were not admitting any pre-existing liability to make the payment; it did not mean that they were not bound by the agreement.

Collective bargaining agreements

There is one exception to the rule that the parties to a commercial agreement are presumed to intend to be legally bound. Under a collective bargaining agreement, an employer negotiates pay and conditions with the workforce as a whole (usually represented by a trade union), rather than on an individual basis. Such agreements are binding in most countries, but in **Ford Motor Co Ltd** *v* **Amalgamated Union of Engineering and Foundry Workers** (1969) it was held that in English law such an agreement was not intended to be legally binding. A carefully worded written agreement had been drawn up between Ford and various trade unions, including a clause stating that the unions should not call a strike unless specified negotiating procedures had been carried out first. The union breached this clause, and the plaintiffs sought to prevent them calling the strike. The court, basing its decision on public policy, held that there was evidence that at the time, it was the general opinion in the industrial world that such agreements were not legally enforceable, and that both sides would have known this. Therefore they could not be said to have intended to be legally bound.

This approach is now contained in the Trade Union and Labour Relations (Consolidation) Act 1992, which states that collective agreements are conclusively presumed not to be intended to be legally binding unless they expressly state otherwise in writing. This presumption is rarely, if ever, displaced, and in the past few years has been relied upon by employers seeking to break agreements to negotiate with unions.

▶ How important is intention to create legal relations?

In practice, it is rare for contract cases to involve problems with the requirement of intention to create legal relations. This is largely because, in many of the situations in which the issue might be raised, particularly domestic and social ones, there is no consideration. The courts will only consider intent to create legal relations if offer and acceptance and consideration have already been established.

The US academic Professor Williston has suggested that in fact the common law does not demand any positive intention to create a legal obligation as an element of contract. In his view, the separate element of intention serves no purpose in our system, and is useful only in legal systems which do not have the test of consideration to help them to determine the boundaries of contract. He suggests that mere social arrangements will be enforced as contracts if the other requirements – offer and acceptance and consideration, for example – are present, and the issue of intention to be legally bound adds nothing to the decision of the court. But the case of **Balfour** *v* **Balfour** is an example of offer, acceptance and consideration existing but there still being no contract, and the only explanation for this lack of contract seems to be that there was no intention to be legally bound.

Feminists argue that the presumption against contractual intention in domestic agreements is in fact the law's way of saying that the work usually done by women is not to be regarded as important – it is seen as something done out of love for the family, rather than an economic contribution which ought to be paid for.

▶ ANSWERING QUESTIONS

1 Robert and Theresa are planning to divorce. They have spent their married life in a house which they bought in joint names, with the help of a mortgage which has six years still to run. Robert and Theresa agree that Robert will move out of the house, and if Theresa meets the mortgage repayments for the next six years, Robert will, at the end of that time, transfer sole ownership of the house to her. Theresa pays the mortgage for a year, at which point Robert says he has changed his mind, and does not intend to transfer his share of the house to her.

Advise Theresa. How, if it all, would your advice differ if Robert had changed his mind before Theresa had started paying the mortgage?

Here you first need to consider the question of intention to create legal relations, bearing in mind that this is a domestic agreement. Point out the presumption established in **Balfour**, and its rebuttal in **Merritt**, which seems to apply here. Assuming that there is intent to create legal relations, has there been an offer and an acceptance? It would seem that Robert made a unilateral offer, to be accepted by performance, in the form of Theresa repaying the mortgage, so the question arises of whether such an offer can be revoked once performance has started. As you know, the traditional assumption was that acceptance did not take effect until performance was complete, but the opposite conclusion was reached in **Errington v Errington**. This case seems to have clear application to the facts here, and suggests that Robert cannot revoke his offer unless Theresa stops paying the mortgage. However, if this is a unilateral offer, your advice might differ should Robert attempt to revoke before the payments start, since an offer can be revoked at any time before it is accepted, in this case by performance. If, on the other hand, the agreement was bilateral, and Theresa made a promise to pay the mortgage in return for Robert's promise to convey the house to her, that agreement would become binding when the promises were exchanged, and Robert's offer could not be revoked afterwards.

4 Capacity

There are some categories of people whose power to make contracts is limited by law. The main categories are minors, and people considered incapable of contracting due to mental disorders or drunkenness.

Contracts are of course not only made between individual people. In many cases, one or both parties will actually be groups of people, such as companies, local authorities and other organizations. Such groups are generally called corporations, and the contracting capacity of a corporation depends on what type of corporation it is.

Minors

Traditionally, anyone under 21 was regarded by the law as a minor (in fact the law usually called such people 'infants'). Their ability to make contracts was first limited by the common law, and then by the Infants Relief Act 1874, which introduced rather complicated provisions on the subject. In 1969, the Family Law Reform Act reduced the age of majority to 18, and replaced the term 'infant' with 'minor', and then in 1987, the Minors' Contracts Act repealed the Infants Relief Act 1874, and restored the common law, which still governs contracts made by minors today.

The basic common law rule is that contracts do not bind minors. There are, however, some types of contract which are binding on minors, or which are merely voidable.

Contracts binding on a minor

The only contracts which are binding on a minor are contracts for the supply of necessaries. 'Necessaries' are interpreted as not just including the supply of necessary goods and services, but also contracts of service for the minor's benefit.

Contracts for necessary goods and services

Under the Sale of Goods Act 1979, s. 3(2) 'necessaries' means 'goods suitable to the condition in life of the minor or other person concerned and to his actual requirements at the time of sale and delivery'. It therefore includes more than just such essentials as food, shelter and clothing, and in deciding the issue the courts can take into account the social status of the particular minor – items which might not be considered necessaries for a working-class child may nevertheless be necessaries for one from a wealthy background.

When deciding if a contract is one for necessaries, the courts first of all determine whether the goods or services are capable of amounting to necessaries in law, and then consider whether they are in fact necessaries as far as the minor before them is concerned. The tests are notoriously difficult to apply, but effectively mean that a minor will be bound by most consumer contracts, but usually not by commercial ones.

In **Nash** v **Inman** (1908) a Savile Row tailor supplied a Cambridge undergraduate with 'eleven fancy waistcoats at two guineas each'. When he sued for payment, it was claimed that the contract could not be enforced against the student, as he was a minor (at this time people were considered minors until the age of 21). The Court of Appeal held that although the goods were suitable to the young man's 'condition in life' (he was 'the son of an architect of good position'), they did not satisfy the second limb of the statutory definition. They could not be regarded as suitable to his actual requirements at the time, because his father had given uncontradicted evidence that he already had a sufficient wardrobe of clothes. Therefore the contract was not binding.

Under common law, a similar approach is taken to contracts for services as for goods. In **Chapple** v **Cooper** (1844) an undertaker sued a widow, who was a minor, for the cost of her husband's funeral. It was held that this was a necessary service, and so the young woman was obliged to pay. In discussing what kind of goods and services could be considered necessaries, the court said 'Articles of mere luxury are always excluded, though luxurious articles of utility are in some cases allowed.'

The Sale of Goods Act also provides that if necessaries are sold to a minor, but before receiving the goods the minor decides that they are no longer wanted, there is no obligation to accept and pay for them. Nor is a minor bound by a contract which contains oppressive or exceptionally onerous terms. Whether a term is sufficiently onerous to exclude liability will depend on the circumstances of each case. In **Fawcett** v **Smethurst** (1914) a minor was held not to be bound by a contract for the hire of a car, even though it was a necessary service in this case, because the contract included a term making him liable for damage to the car 'in any event' – that is, whether or not the damage was his fault.

Where there is a binding contract for necessaries, the minor is only bound to pay a reasonable price for them, which need not be the contract price.

Contracts of service for the minor's benefit
Minors are also bound by contracts of service, providing these are on the whole beneficial to them. In practice this generally means contracts

of employment under which a minor gains some training, experience or instruction for an occupation – an apprenticeship would be a common example. In **Clements v London and North Western Railway Co** (1894) a minor made an agreement under which he gave up his statutory right to personal injury benefit, but gained rights under an insurance scheme to which his employers would contribute. It was held that the rights gained were more beneficial than those given up, and so the contract was, on balance, for the minor's benefit and therefore binding.

In **De Francesco v Barnum** (1890) a 14-year-old girl entered into a stage-dancing apprenticeship with De Francesco, under an agreement which was considerably more favourable to De Francesco than to the girl. She was not to marry during the seven years of the apprenticeship, could not take on professional engagements without his written consent and was completely subject to De Francesco's commands. He, on the other hand, made no commitment to employ her, and stated that if he did do so it would be at a very low rate of pay. The agreement also allowed him to send her abroad, and to put an end to the agreement at any time. Fry LJ concluded: 'Those are stipulations of an extraordinary and unusual character, which throw, or appear to throw, an inordinate power into the hands of the master without any correlative obligation.' Consequently, the court held that the contract was not for the minor's benefit, and could not therefore be enforced against her.

In some cases the courts have widened the concept of a contract of service beyond the usual employment situations. In **Doyle v White City Stadium Ltd** (1935) the plaintiff was a minor who entered into an agreement with the British Boxing Board to secure a fighter's licence. One of the terms of such a licence was that if a boxer was disqualified for committing a foul, he would not receive the 'purse' (fee) for the fight, only his travelling expenses. Doyle was contracted to take part in a fight, for which the purse was £3,000, and the contract was subject to British Boxing Board rules. He was disqualified for hitting below the belt, but tried to claim the £3,000 from the promoters and the Board. The court looked at the contract, and held that although boxing was not an occupation in which an ordinary apprenticeship was possible, the type of contract made with the Board could be compared with a contract of apprenticeship. Looked at as a whole, the contract was beneficial to the minor, and even the clause which deprived him of £3,000 was one which was designed to encourage clean fighting and thereby protect young, inexperienced boxers. He was thus bound by the contract and could not claim the £3,000.

There is no general principle that a contract for the benefit of a minor is automatically binding on him or her. For example, trading contracts are never binding on minors, even where they are for their benefit. Thus, in **Cowern v Nield** (1912) a minor was in business selling hay and straw. It was held that he was not liable to repay the price of a consignment of hay that he failed to deliver.

Contracts voidable at common law

Apart from contracts for necessaries which bind the minor, the general rule at common law is that a minor's contracts are voidable. In other words, these contracts are not binding on the minor, but bind the other party. Thus, these contracts are valid when they are made, but can be terminated by a minor at any time before becoming 18 or within a reasonable time afterwards. This category covers contracts which involve a long-term interest in property such as land, shares or partnerships. If such a contract is terminated before any money is paid or obligations created, the position will be as if the contract had never been made in the first place, but problems can arise where obligations are incurred or money is paid, and then the minor terminates the contract. The law is somewhat unclear, but it seems likely that a minor would be liable to pay any debts arising before such a contract is terminated. Where a minor has already paid money under a contract, and then terminates it, whether that money can be recovered will depend on whether the minor got anything in return for it.

In **Corpe** v **Overton** (1833) a minor agreed to enter into a partnership, which was to be formed in the future. He paid a £100 deposit, knowing that he would lose it if he did not in the end go through with the partnership. Before the partnership was put into operation, the minor repudiated the agreement. The courts held that he was entitled to have his deposit back, because there was a total failure of consideration – at the time he terminated the contract, he had received nothing in return for it.

A contrasting case is **Steinberg** v **Scala (Leeds) Ltd** (1923). The plaintiff, a minor, bought shares in Scala. These shares were not fully paid up, which means that a company issuing such shares can subsequently demand from a shareholder payments up to the nominal value of the shares: for example, if a person pays £1 for a share which has a nominal value of £2.50, she can be asked to pay a further £1.50 at a later stage. Scala did make such a request, and Ms Steinberg paid a further £250. The court case arose because she later decided to reject the contract, and wanted her £250 back. Her claim failed: the court held that although terminating the contract meant she was free from any future obligation to make payment, she could not get the £250 back because there had not been a total failure of consideration. She had the shares, so she had got something in return for her money.

Remedies against minors

Clearly the rules on minors and contracts have the potential to create injustice – for example, where an adult is unaware that the other party to a contract is a minor. Consequently, the equitable remedy of restitution, which is used to make anyone who has been unjustly enriched give back their profit, has been applied to minors. If a minor fraudulently obtains goods and then keeps them, an order for restitution can be made to make the minor give them back to the claimant.

In practice, this equitable remedy has become less important in the light of the new power granted by s. 3 of the Minors' Contracts Act 1987. Under this Act, where an adult has entered into an unenforceable contract with a minor, or a contract which the minor has terminated, the courts may give any property acquired by the minor under the contract back to the adult, provided it is 'just and equitable' to do so. This provision goes further than the equitable remedy, in that it may be used even if the minor has not acted fraudulently. A young person who has already sold or exchanged the property may have to pay the cost of the goods, or give up any property received in exchange for them. However, a minor who no longer has the goods or any proceeds of their sale or exchange cannot be made to pay anything, as this would effectively enforce what is still an unenforceable agreement.

The equitable remedy of specific performance can never be used against a minor, nor can it be used by a minor, because the remedy requires mutuality between the parties (see p. 291 below).

If an adult realises that they are making a contract with a minor they may ask for a guarantee from an adult. Under s. 2 of the Minors' Contracts Act 1987, where a contract is unenforceable because it was made with a minor, a guarantee of that contract will be enforceable. Thus, the adult who provided that guarantee will have to compensate the other contracting party for their loss according to the terms of the guarantee. This arrangement is frequently used where loans are made to minors.

Minors and tort

Minors can usually be liable under tort law so long as they are old enough to know the nature of what they are doing, but this rule cannot be used as an indirect way of enforcing a contract which would otherwise not be binding on a minor. In **Leslie Ltd** v **Sheill** (1914) a minor borrowed money, having lied about his age. The contract for the loan was an unenforceable one. In deliberately misrepresenting his age, the minor committed the tort of deceit, and knowing that he could not sue the minor for breach of contract to recover the money, the moneylender brought an action for damages in tort. The action was unsuccessful because the court held that it was merely an attempt to enforce a contract on which the minor was not liable.

Very young children

The cases discussed so far generally concern older children. With very young children the courts may take the view that they lack the mental capacity to enter a contract, so that the rules on mental incapacity, discussed below, would apply. Thus, in **R** *v* **Oldham Metropolitan Borough Council,** *ex parte* **Garlick** (1993), the House of Lords considered that the laws on the validity of contracts made by minors could only apply if they were old enough to understand the nature of the transaction and the nature of any continuing obligations incurred. Thus, while a child well under the age of ten could buy sweets, a four-year-old could not contract for the occupation of residential premises.

Problems with the law on minors

The law on minors and contracts is widely thought to be out of step with modern society. Many of the cases arose more than 100 years ago, and often involved people between 18 and 21, who would now be considered adults. It is also strange that the age of full contractual capacity is 18, when an individual of 16 or 17 may legally be in full-time employment, married and even a parent. In addition, consumer protection laws may reduce the need for special protection for minors.

Reform

In 1982, the Law Commission proposed that all contracts should be binding on minors who are 16 years or over. Below that age, contracts should be enforceable by minors, but not against them. A minor who misrepresents their age in order to secure a contract should be liable in tort for deceit, but in other cases of fraud a minor under 16 should not be liable if the effect of that liability would be to allow the other party to enforce indirectly an otherwise unenforceable contract.

▶ Mental incapacity

This category covers people suffering from mental disability (which appears to include both mental illness and mental handicap), and those who are drunk when the contract is made. In general, contracts made with someone in either state will be valid, unless, at the time when the contract is made, that person is incapable of understanding the nature of the transaction and the other party knows this. In such circumstances the contract is voidable: the party suffering from mental disability or drunkenness can choose whether or not to terminate it.

Where one party is incapable, through drunkenness or mental disability, of understanding the nature of the transaction, but the other party does not realize this, the courts will ignore the incapacity. In **Hart** *v* **O'Connor** (1985) the Privy Council held that a person of unsound mind was bound

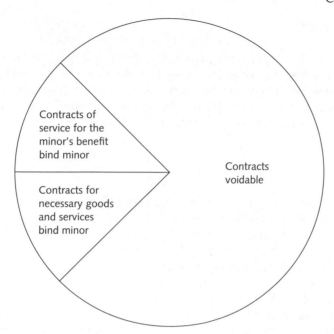

Figure 4.1 Contracts with minors

by his agreement to sell some land because, when the contract was made, the buyer did not realize that the seller had any mental incapacity.

The fact that a person has a poor understanding of the language in which the contract was made and is illiterate does not render them incapable of making a contract. The defendant in **Barclays Bank** *v* **Schwartz** (1995) was Romanian and had signed contracts rendering him liable for his company's debts of over £500,000. In an attempt to resist paying the money he argued that his poor English and illiteracy meant he lacked the capacity to make the contracts. This argument was rejected by the Court of Appeal, being described by the court as 'straight from the book of feeble excuses'. A person who was illiterate, or did not understand the language of a contract, was aware of this, and the obligation was on them to make sure that the contract was explained.

There are no specific rules governing contracts made for necessaries by mentally incapable parties; they are subject to the general rules above, and also to s. 3 of the Sale of Goods Act 1979, which, as for minors, states that only a reasonable price need be paid for necessaries (regardless of whether the other party was unaware of the disability). In some cases, the Mental Health Act 1983 puts the property of a mentally disordered person under the control of the courts. Contracts made by such individuals are void.

Corporations

A corporation is a legal entity, usually in fact a group of people, which is treated by the law as having a separate identity from the person or persons who constitute it. There are three main types of corporation: registered companies, corporations established by statute, and chartered corporations. Each has a different level of contracting ability.

Registered companies

These are companies registered under the Companies Act 1985 – in effect, most commercial companies. When registering, companies must supply a document called a memorandum of association, which carries information including an 'objects clause' laying down the range of activities in which that company will be allowed to engage. Before the Companies Act 1989 was passed, any contract that was outside a company's stated range of activities was invalid – it was said to be *ultra vires* (meaning outside the powers of the company). Under the 1989 Act, a company can be liable for a contract made outside its stated activities if the other party has acted in good faith. The reason for limiting the contractual capacity of registered companies is to provide shareholders and creditors with safeguards against directors who use company resources for their own unauthorized purposes.

Statutory corporations

These corporations are created for particular purposes by Acts of Parliament – the Independent Broadcasting Authority is an example, as are local authorities. The statute creating each corporation will specify the purposes for which that corporation may make contracts, and any contract entered into which is outside the powers can be declared *ultra vires* and therefore void.

Chartered corporations

These are corporations set up by Royal Charter, which means that their rights are officially granted by the Crown – examples are charities, and some universities and other educational institutions. They have the same contractual capacity as an adult human being of full capacity, and can enter into any kind of contract (although a charter may be withdrawn if such an institution becomes involved in activities which offend against the spirit of the charter).

▶ ANSWERING QUESTIONS

1 Nadine and Olivia, both aged 17, are keen on dancing and theatre and both decide to pursue a career in this field.

Nadine gains a place at stage school, and begins her course with enthusiasm. However, she soon becomes annoyed at some of the terms to which she finds she has agreed, in particular one which prevents her from taking part in any professional productions during the school vacation, without permission from the school, and another which obliges her to hand over 30 per cent of any earnings from such productions, during her time at the school. Nadine has been invited to take part in a professional play during the summer, and would now like to avoid these obligations.

Olivia's career takes a different course. She borrows money from Countrywide Bank to set up her own small but successful business, selling dance and stage clothing and equipment, the proceeds of which pay for singing and dancing lessons. After a few months, Olivia's main supplier finds out that she is only 17 and refuses to trade further with her. This leaves Olivia without enough business to pay for this month's lessons, and her teacher is pressing her to meet her obligations. She is also behind with the payments on her mobile telephone account, and has received a demand for payment.

Advise both Nadine and Olivia regarding the enforceability of any contracts which they may have made. *OCR*

This question is concerned with the capacity of minors in contract law. In your introduction you could point out that the basic common law rule is that contracts do not bind minors. There are, however, some types of contract which are binding on minors, or which are voidable.

You could structure your answer by dividing it into two parts looking first at the position of Nadine and then the position of Olivia. Looking first at Nadine, we are told that she is 17 years old and we need to consider her capacity to make a contract with the stage school. As she is under 18, she is treated as a minor for the purposes of contract law. Minors are bound by contracts of service for the minor's benefit (see p. 54 above). You would need to look at such cases as **Clements v London and North Western Railway Company**, **De Francesco v Barnum** and **Doyle v White City Stadium** to decide whether the contract with the stage school falls within this category. **De Francesco v Barnum** is most similar to the facts of this case, as it concerned a stage-dancing apprenticeship. In that case the contract was found to contain 'stipulations of an extraordinary and unusual character, which throw, or appear to throw, an inordinate power into the hands of the master without any correlative obligation'. The terms of this contract are not as extraordinary as those in **De Francesco** and it is not certain whether a court would find this contract to be for Nadine's benefit or not.

Turning now to Olivia, again she is 17 years old and treated as a minor for the purposes of contract law. She has made four contracts: a contract for a loan, a contract with a supplier of stage clothes and equipment, a contract for singing and dancing lessons and a contract for a mobile phone. Each contract needs to be considered separately. Looking first at the contract for a loan, this contract is voidable (p. 56). Olivia therefore has a right to terminate the contract if she decides she no longer wants the loan because she cannot make purchases from the supplier. On terminating the contract, she would probably have to return any money she had received under it. Olivia may have already paid interest on the loan and she is unlikely to be able to get this money back because she had the benefit of being able to buy stage clothes and equipment from her supplier with the money from the loan: **Steinberg** v **Scala (Leeds) Ltd**. If an adult had provided a guarantee for repayment of the loan, this guarantee will be enforceable under s. 2 of the Minors' Contracts Act 1987 (see p. 57).

The contract for the supply of stage clothes and equipment was not binding on Olivia because it was a trading contract (**Cowern** v **Nield**), but it was binding on the supplier. It will depend on the terms of the contract itself whether the supplier had a right to terminate supplies at the point in which he did, or whether he was in breach of contract. Any breach would give Olivia a right to damages, but she would not have a right to specific performance (see p. 57).

As regards the contract for the singing and dancing lessons, this is a contract of service for the minor's benefit and is therefore binding on Olivia. She will have to pay for the lessons.

The legal status of the contract for the mobile phone will depend on whether this is treated as a contract for a necessity under the Sale of Goods Act 1979, s. 3(2) in which case it would be binding (see p. 53). While owning a mobile phone is popular with young people, it is probably not a necessary item: **Nash** v **Inman**. The *dicta* in **Chapple** v **Cooper** could be considered where it was stated that 'Articles of mere luxury are always excluded, though luxurious articles of utility are in some cases allowed'. She could therefore terminate the contract for the mobile phone. Olivia will have to return the telephone, because under s. 3 of the Minors' Contracts Act 1987, where an adult has entered into an unenforceable contract with a minor, or a contract which the minor has terminated, the courts may give any property acquired by the minor under the contract back to the adult, provided it is 'just and equitable' to do so.

5 Formalities

As we have seen, the general rule of contract law is that an agreement does not have to take a specific written form in order to be deemed a binding contract. Often the contract will simply be oral. As it can be difficult to prove later what was said orally, there are practical advantages of putting a contract in writing, despite there being no legal requirements to do so. In **Hadley** v **Kemp** (1999) Gary Kemp was the songwriter in the pop group Spandau Ballet. He was sued by other members of the group for royalties received for the group's music. The basis of their claim was that there had been an oral agreement to share these royalties. They were unable to prove the existence of any oral agreement and so their action failed.

Of course most complex transactions are made in writing, and this clearly helps the parties prove their case if there is any disagreement, but usually lack of written formalities will not prevent a court from finding a contract. Following the Electronic Communications Act 2000, s. 8, legislation preventing the use of electronic communications for the formation of a contract can be removed by delegated legislation, and electronic signatures will be legally recognized. There are some types of contract which currently require certain formalities to be followed to make them enforceable. They fall into three groups: those which must be made by deed, those which must be in writing and those which have to be evidenced in writing.

Contracts which must be made by deed

Under the Law of Property Act 1925 a contract for a lease of three years or more must be made by deed, which basically means it must be put into a formal document, signed in front of witnesses. (A deed may also be used as a way of making binding what would otherwise be a gratuitous promise, without the need for consideration from the other party.)

Contracts which must be in writing

Some statutes lay down that certain types of contract must be in writing. Most contracts for the sale or disposition of an interest in land made since 27 September 1989 must be made in writing under the Law of Property (Miscellaneous Provisions) Act 1989. The document must be signed by each party or their representatives. Other contracts that need to be made in writing are those involving the transfer of shares in a limited company (Companies Act 1985); bills of exchange, cheques and promissory notes (Bills of Exchange Act 1882); and regulated consumer credit agreements, such as hire-purchase contracts (Consumer Credit Act 1974, s. 60).

Contracts which must be evidenced in writing

Contracts of guarantee (where one party guarantees the obligation of another, such as a parent guaranteeing a daughter's bank overdraft) are required by statute to be 'evidenced in writing'. Contracts for the sale or disposition of an interest in land made before 27 September 1989 are still covered by the old law prior to the Law of Property (Miscellaneous Provisions) Act 1989, and only have to be evidenced in writing.

'Evidenced in writing' essentially means that although the contract itself need not be a written one, there must be some written evidence of the transaction. The evidence must have existed before one party tried to enforce the contract against the other, and it must be signed by the party against whom the contract is to be enforced. If a note or memorandum containing the terms of a contract was signed only by one party to that contract, the contract could be enforced by the non-signer against the signer, but not *vice versa*. Such a note or memorandum does not have to have been created for the purpose of enforcing a contract, and in fact a string of documents can be added together to form evidence of a contract – if, for example, there is a document signed by the defendant which contains an express or implicit reference to another document, and that second document contains the terms of the contract.

Contracts made through the internet and by e-mail

Increasingly, contracts are being made over the internet. In particular, the internet is being used to order goods and services from suppliers. The European Union is keen to promote the development of a European internet industry. It has therefore passed the European Electronic Commerce Directive. The Directive lays down some specific formalities that will need to be followed in order to make binding contracts over the internet. Thus, article 10 imposes a general requirement on service providers to give a clear account, prior to the conclusion of a contract, of the steps which must be followed to ensure 'full and informed consent'. This part of the Directive has been brought into force by the Electronic Commerce (EC Directive) Regulations 2002. Under these Regulations companies must provide receipts for orders placed electronically without delay, allow customers to change an order easily before buying and provide information such as business email addresses. Businesses which do not comply with the regulations face having to pay statutory damages to customers or 'stop now' orders which will force them to change their procedures.

Article 9 of the Directive requires Member States to ensure that their legal systems allow contracts to be concluded by electronic means. There must be nothing in the law of the Member States to prevent or affect the validity of a contract concluded electronically just because it was so concluded. There is an exception to this in the case of contracts which require some act on the part of a notary or registration with a public authority for their validity. Contracts dealing with matters of succession or family law are also excluded.

The Electronic Communications Act 2000 has responded to this requirement. Section 8 of the Act contains a power to remove restrictions arising from legislation which currently prevent the use of electronic communications. Most contracts do not need to be made on paper and such contracts could already be made through electronic communications. But it has been seen that certain contracts require written documents. Under the 2000 Act, where necessary and desirable this legislation may be amended to allow for the use of electronic communications to make such contracts.

Part II of the Electronic Communications Act 2000 makes provision for the legal recognition of electronic signatures. For example, if in the future electronic conveyancing was introduced, then it would no longer be possible for individuals to physically sign the legal documents, but instead electronic signatures could be used. Different forms of electronic signatures are possible, but in practice the most useful is likely to be the digital signature. This uses cryptography technology to convert information into disguised data so that the message sent is unique from the person sending the message and cannot be copied, in the same way that a written signature is unique to each individual.

▶ ANSWERING QUESTIONS

It is rare for an examination question to be concerned purely with the issue of formalities. Question 4 at the end of Chapter 6 raises the issue of formalities along with some other issues.

6 Consideration

In English law, an agreement is not usually binding unless it is supported by what is called consideration. Put simply, this means that each party must give something in return for what is gained from the other party, so if you wish to enforce someone's promise to you, you must prove that you gave something in return for that promise.

Consideration may be a thing or a service – I give you my car and you give me £1,000, or you clean my windows and I pay you £5. It may also take the form of promises – I promise to work for you and you promise to pay me a salary. A promise not supported by consideration is called a gratuitous promise; for example, if I simply say I will give you my car, without requiring anything in return. This type of promise is not usually enforceable in law.

Although up to now we have been talking about the requirements for making a contract in the first place, it is important to note that many of the problems concerning consideration arise not when a contract is made, but when one or other party seeks to modify it – such as by paying a lower price than that agreed. A promise to accept such a modification was traditionally not binding unless supported by new consideration, but recent cases have changed the rules in such situations.

What is consideration?

Consideration is usually described as being something which represents either some benefit to the person making a promise (the promisor) or some detriment to the person to whom the promise is made (the promisee), or both.

In **Dunlop** *v* **Selfridge** (1915) the House of Lords explained consideration in terms of purchase and sale – the plaintiff must show that he or she has bought the defendant's promise, by doing, giving or promising something in return for it.

Atiyah has suggested that consideration can simply be seen as 'a reason for the enforcement of promises', with that reason being 'the justice of the case'.

Promisor and promisee

In most contracts, two promises will be exchanged, so each party is both a promisor and a promisee. In a contract case, the claimant will often be arguing that the defendant has broken the promise made to the claimant, and therefore the claimant will usually be the promisee, and the defendant will be the promisor. So if Ann contracts to paint Ben's bathroom and Ben promises to pay her £200 for doing it, there are two promises in this contract: Ann's promise to do the painting and Ben's promise to pay Ann £200. If Ann fails to paint the bathroom, Ben can sue her, and if the issue of consideration arises, Ben will seek to prove that his promise to pay £200 was consideration for Ann's promise to paint the bathroom. In that action, Ann will be the promisor, and Ben the promisee.

On the other hand, if Ann does the work but Ben does not pay the price, Ben can be sued by Ann, and if consideration is at issue, Ann will have to prove that her promise to paint the bathroom was consideration for Ben's promise to pay. In that action, Ann will be the promisee and Ben the promisor.

Ann's promise to paint the bathroom can be portrayed by the following diagram:

Ben's promise to pay £200 can be portrayed by the following diagram:

The contract between Ann and Ben can be portrayed by the following diagram:

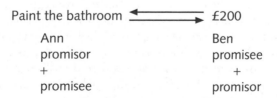

Consideration need not benefit the promisor

Consideration need not benefit the promisor – so there can be consideration where the promisee suffers some detriment at the promisor's request, but this gives no particular benefit to the promisor. For example, in **Jones** *v* **Padavatton** (see p. 47 above), the daughter's giving up her job would be consideration for the mother providing an allowance, even though it did not directly benefit the mother (though as we have seen, the mother's promise was not binding because there was no intention to create legal relations).

Another way in which consideration can be given by the promisee without benefiting the promisor is where contracts are made for the benefit of a third party – if, for example, Ann promises to pay Ben to give Ann's daughter driving lessons, Ben will be able to enforce this promise; although he has given no direct benefit to Ann, he has suffered some detriment in that he has provided the lessons.

'Executory' and 'executed' consideration

Consideration is often divided into two categories: executory and executed. Executory consideration is where something is to be done in the future after the contract has been formed. Executory consideration exists when the contracting parties make promises to each other because they are promising something for the future, after the contract has been made – on making the contract you promise to deliver some goods to me and I promise to pay for them when they arrive, for example. A bilateral contract usually involves executory consideration.

Executed consideration is where at the time of the formation of the contract the consideration has already been performed. If I promise to give £20 to anyone who finds my lost handbag, returning the bag is both acceptance of my offer (and thus the time when the contract is formed) and executed consideration for my promise. Executed consideration usually occurs in unilateral contracts.

Consideration must not be past

Lawyers often say that consideration must not be past, but this is slightly confusing because the emphasis is not really about the time that the consideration was given, but more about whether the consideration was given in exchange for the other party's consideration. Consideration must be given **in return** for the promise or act of the other party; something done, given or promised for another reason will not count as consideration. If one party has completed performance before the other offered consideration, then as a matter of fact it is unlikely that the earlier performance was done in return for that consideration. So, if Ann looks after Ben's dog while Ben is on holiday, and when Ben returns he promises to give Ann some money, Ann cannot enforce that promise because she did not look after the dog in return for it – she had already looked after the dog.

This issue arose in **Roscorla** *v* **Thomas** (1842). The defendant sold the plaintiff a horse. After the sale was completed, the defendant told the plaintiff that the animal was 'sound and free from any vice'. This turned out to be rather far from the truth, and the plaintiff sued. The court held that the defendant's promise was unenforceable, because it was made after the sale. If the promise about the horse's condition had been made before, the plaintiff would have provided consideration for it by buying the horse. As it was made after the sale, the consideration was past, for it had not been given in return for the promise.

Whether or not consideration is past is a question of fact, and the wording of an agreement will not necessarily be conclusive. In **Re McArdle** (1951) a widow had been left the family home in her husband's will. The will allowed her to live in it for the rest of her life, and on her death it was to be inherited by their five children equally. During the mother's lifetime, one of her sons and his wife lived with her in the house and the daughter-in-law paid for some home improvements. When these were finished, the other four children signed a document which promised to pay her £488 for the work, 'in consideration of [her] carrying out certain alterations and improvements to the property'.

After the mother died, the daughter-in-law tried to claim the money, but her husband's brothers and sisters refused to pay. The Court of Appeal held that although the wording of the document suggested that the payment related to work to be done in the future, the facts of the case made it clear that the promise was given in return for something already done; it was therefore past consideration, and the promise was not binding.

There are two exceptions to the rule that past consideration is no consideration. The first is where the past consideration was provided at the promisor's request, and it was understood that payment would be made. This exception can be traced back to the old case of **Lampleigh** *v* **Brathwait** (1615). Thomas Brathwait had been convicted of killing a man, and he asked Anthony Lampleigh to obtain a pardon for him from the King. After considerable trouble and expense, Lampleigh managed to do so. In the excitement of getting his pardon, Brathwait promised to pay Lampleigh £100, but later refused to hand over the money, so Lampleigh sued.

It might appear that Lampleigh's consideration was past, since he had secured the pardon before the promise to pay was made. In fact, the court upheld Lampleigh's claim. It reasoned that Lampleigh had obtained the pardon at Brathwait's own request, and this request carried with it the unspoken understanding that the service would be paid for. Lampleigh obtained the pardon after, and in return for, this implied promise to pay, and so obtaining the pardon was good consideration for the promise to pay. The later promise, specifying that £100 would be paid, was said to be merely confirmation of the original, unspoken one.

This reasoning seems less odd when we consider that today there are many requests which carry with them unsaid promises to pay – when we ask a taxi driver to take us somewhere, or ask the milkman to leave an extra pint, we do not actually say that we will pay for those goods and services, but clearly it is understood by both parties that we will. It may well be that requests to secure royal pardons had the same well-understood effect in 1615.

A (slightly) more recent case on this principle is **Re Casey's Patents** (1892). The defendants owned some patent rights, and the plaintiff worked for them. They wrote to him, saying that in consideration of his services as manager in relation to the patents, they were going to give him a one-third interest in them. They later claimed that as their promise was made in relation to services which the plaintiff had already given, it was past consideration and therefore the promise was not binding. The court held, however, that the plaintiff's services were clearly always meant to be paid for, and the promise was merely putting this expectation into the form of a specified amount.

The second exception to the rule on past consideration is the bill of exchange. Under s. 27 of the Bills of Exchange Act 1882 an 'antecedent debt or liability' may be consideration for receipt of a bill of exchange.

Consideration must be sufficient

Although consideration must provide some benefit to the promisor or detriment to the promisee, these do not have to amount to a great deal. This principle is usually described in the rather confusing phrase 'consideration must be sufficient but need not be adequate', which effectively means that the courts will not inquire into the adequacy of consideration, so long as there is some. Providing something is given in return for a promise, it does not matter that it is not much, or not what the promise would usually be considered to be worth. So if, for example, A promises to sell B her state-of-the-art CD player for £5, the consideration paid by B clearly provides very little benefit to A, and amounts to only a small loss to B, but nevertheless, the transaction will be binding because some consideration has been provided by both sides. It is often said that just one peppercorn can be good consideration – even if the promisee does not like pepper!

The reason for this rule is the old idea of freedom of contract, which required that the parties themselves should be allowed to make the bargains that suit them, without interference from the courts.

In **Thomas** v **Thomas** (1842) the plaintiff was a widow whose husband had stated that if he died before his wife, she should be allowed to live in his house for the rest of her life, after which it was to pass to his sons.

When the man died, the defendant, who was his executor, agreed that the widow could continue to occupy the house in return for a promise that she would pay £1 a year and keep the house in good repair. Despite this, some time later, the defendants tried to evict the widow, so she sued them for breach of contract. The defendants claimed that their promise was not binding due to lack of consideration. However, the court held that the widow's promise to pay £1 and keep up the repairs was sufficient consideration to make the owners' promise binding.

The same principle was applied in **Chappell** v **Nestlé** (1960). Nestlé ran a special offer involving a record of a song called 'Rockin' Shoes' – customers could get a copy of the record by sending in 1s 6d (about seven-and-a-half pence) and three wrappers from Nestlé's bars of chocolate. The copyright holders for the record brought an action against Nestlé, which among other things claimed that royalties should be paid on the price of the record.

To calculate the royalties due, it was necessary to establish what price Nestlé were charging for the record, and the copyright holder alleged that this price (which was the consideration for the promise to send the record) included the three wrappers. Nestlé, on the other hand, contended that the consideration was only the 1s 6d, and that they threw away the wrappers they received. The House of Lords held that the wrappers did form part of the consideration – the fact that they were of no real worth to Nestlé was irrelevant.

The interesting implication of this case is that if the fact that the wrappers were useless to Nestlé was irrelevant, presumably wrappers alone could have amounted to consideration – if, for example, Nestlé had just asked for three wrappers, and not requested money in addition.

Consideration must be of economic value

It is sometimes said that consideration must have some 'economic' value, though, as the Nestlé case shows, this economic value may be negligible. What this principle basically seems to mean is that there must be some physical value, rather than just an emotional or sentimental one. In **Thomas** v **Thomas** (discussed above), for example, the plaintiff suggested that following her husband's wishes was part of the consideration, but the court rejected this argument because they said the husband's wishes had no economic value (though in the event this did not alter the outcome of the case, as the widow's own promise was consideration).

Similarly, in **White** v **Bluett** (1853), a father promised not to make his son repay money he had borrowed, if the son promised not to keep boring him with complaints. The court held that the son's promise was not sufficient consideration to make his father's promise binding, because it had no economic value.

Consideration can be a promise not to sue

If one party has a possible civil claim against the other, a promise not to enforce that claim is good consideration for a promise given in return. If, for example, Ann crashes into Ben's car, Ben might agree that he will not sue Ann if Ann pays for the damage, and Ben's promise not to sue will be consideration for Ann's promise to pay.

In **Alliance Bank Ltd** *v* **Broom** (1864) Broom had an overdraft of £22,000 with the bank, and they asked him to provide some security. Mr Broom promised to do so, but never did, and as a result the bank sued him. Mr Broom argued that there was no consideration for his promise to provide security, but the court held that the consideration was provided by the bank's implied promise not to sue for a while, giving Mr Broom time to provide security, even though they did sue fairly shortly afterwards.

Where forbearing to enforce a legal claim is offered as consideration, there must have been some intention actually to bring proceedings. In **Miles** *v* **New Zealand Alford Estate Co** (1886) a company had bought some land which it was dissatisfied with. The seller later promised to make certain payments to the company, and the company alleged that it had provided consideration for this promise by not taking legal proceedings to rescind the contract when they found the problems with the land. This argument was rejected by the Court of Appeal, which held that there was no consideration for the vendor's promise, because there was no evidence that the buyers ever really intended to bring proceedings to rescind.

In the same case, it was pointed out that if the party who has the claim believes it to be legally valid, but it turns out not to be, the promise will still be good consideration if that party had honestly believed they had a valid claim – so in the car accident example above, even if it subsequently transpires that for some reason B could not have successfully sued A anyway, B's promise not to sue is still valid consideration, providing B honestly believes he has a claim against A.

One party's promise not to enforce an existing claim can only provide consideration if the promise given in return was actually induced by the promise not to enforce the claim. In **Combe** *v* **Combe** (1951) a husband and his wife were involved in divorce proceedings, during which he promised to pay her an annual allowance. She later brought an action to enforce this promise and argued, among other things, that she had given consideration for it by not exercising her right to apply to the court for a maintenance order. It was held that this could not be consideration because her husband had not asked her not to apply to the court, and therefore his promise had not been made in return for her promising not to do so.

This principle can be a difficult one to apply. In **Alliance Bank** *v* **Broom** the defendant did not ask the bank not to sue, yet the bank's forbearance to do so was held to constitute consideration. However, the decision has been explained on the basis that by promising to supply security, the debtor was by implication asking the bank not to sue.

Contracts (Rights of Third Parties) Act 1999

Following the Contracts (Rights of Third Parties) Act 1999, a term in a contract is sometimes enforceable by a third party. It is not necessary for consideration to have been given by the third party.

▶ Performance of an existing duty

Where a promisee already owes the promisor a legal duty, then in theory performing that duty should not in itself be consideration – if the promisee does nothing more than they are already obliged to do, they are suffering no detriment and the promisor is only getting a benefit to which he or she was already entitled. In most cases the courts have observed this principle, but as we shall see, in recent years they have discovered consideration in the performance of an existing duty, causing some controversy in the process.

Existing duties can be divided into three main categories: public duties; contractual duties to the promisor; and contractual duties to a third party.

Existing public duty

Where a person is merely carrying out duties they are legally obliged to perform – such as a police officer protecting citizens, or a juror listening to evidence – doing that alone will not be consideration. In **Collins** *v* **Godefroy** (1831) the plaintiff had been summoned to give evidence in a court action. The defendant promised to give him six guineas for doing so, but later refused to pay. The plaintiff tried to enforce the promise, but it was held that since he was legally obliged to give the evidence, doing so could not be considered consideration for the promise. Clearly there are public policy reasons, as well as technical legal ones, for this principle.

However, where a promisee is under a public duty, but does something which goes beyond what they are bound to do under that duty, that extra act can amount to consideration. In **Glasbrook Brothers** *v* **Glamorgan County Council** (1925) Glasbrook Brothers were the owners of a coal mine in South Wales. Their employees went on strike and Glasbrook Brothers asked the police to place a guard at the coal mine during the strike. The police refused to do this as they considered that regular checks by a mobile police patrol would be sufficient to protect the mine. The mine owners therefore offered to pay the police £2,200 to cover the extra cost of having the police stationed at the mine full time during the strike. When the strike was over the mine owners refused to pay. They argued that the police had an existing duty to protect the mine and therefore had provided no consideration for their promise to pay. The House of Lords held that the police had provided an extra service which did amount to consideration. The police were merely under a public duty to maintain law and order and could choose how they achieved this. Viscount Cave LC said:

> If in the judgement of the police authorities, formed reasonably and in good faith, the garrison was necessary for the protection of life and property, then they were not entitled to make a charge for it.

As on the facts this was not the case, they were entitled to charge for the extra service.

In the later case of **Harris** *v* **Sheffield United Football Club Ltd** (1988) the football club sought to rely on the above reasoning to argue that they should not have to pay for police officers attending their ground at home matches. They argued that a big police presence was necessary to maintain law and order. But the case was distinguished. In **Glasbrook Brothers** the coal mine owners could not call off the strike, so the threat to law and order was not their fault. But in the present case, the football club chose to hold football matches on Saturday afternoons to get maximum attendance. This created a bigger risk to law and order so the necessity for the large police presence was self-induced. As a result the police services had to be paid for.

The case of **Ward** *v* **Byham** (1956) illustrates the willingness of the courts to find evidence of some consideration where public policy reasons seem to demand that a promise be binding. Ms Ward and Mr Byham lived together from 1949 to 1954, and in 1950 had a daughter. In 1954 Mr Byham threw Ms Ward out of the house, but kept their daughter with him. Some months later Ms Ward asked to take the child to live with her, and Mr Byham wrote to say that she could do so, and he would pay £1 a week maintenance, provided that she could 'prove that [the daughter] will be well looked after and happy', and that the little girl was allowed to decide for herself whether or not she wanted to go and live with her mother. Ms Ward duly took their daughter. Mr Byham paid the maintenance as agreed for seven months, but stopped when Ms Ward married another man. She sued for the money. Mr Byham alleged that there was no consideration because as the mother of an illegitimate child, she was already under a statutory duty to maintain the little girl, so her promise to do so was not consideration. On the facts, the majority of the court held that there was a valid contract, because her promise to see that their daughter was happy, and to allow her to choose which parent she wanted to live with, went beyond her statutory duty, and could therefore be consideration for Mr Byham's promise to pay maintenance.

Existing contractual duty to the promisor

The position on contractual duties and consideration has changed in recent years, and the implications of the change are still rather unclear. In the past, the rule was that performance of an existing contractual duty owed to a promisor was not consideration, as illustrated by two nineteenth-century shipping cases. In **Stilk** v **Myrick** (1809) two sailors deserted a ship during a voyage and the captain was unable to find replacements for them. The eight remaining crew members were promised extra wages for sailing the ship back home short-handed, but when they arrived back in London, the captain refused to pay the extra money. The sailors sued for it, but the court held that there was no consideration for the captain's promise; the sailors had already contracted to sail to their destination and back, and that was all they had done.

In **Hartley** v **Ponsonby** (1857) half the crew deserted a ship, and the rest were promised extra money to carry on working the ship to Bombay. Again, at the end of the voyage the captain refused to pay the extra money and the plaintiff sued. In this case the court held that there was consideration, because the crew had become so small that the remainder of the voyage was more dangerous than it had been when they made their contracts. In agreeing to carry on, the plaintiff was taking on duties beyond those in his original contract, and had therefore provided consideration for the promise to pay extra. In the light of the Court of Appeal case of **Williams** v **Roffey** (1990) a distinction now has to be drawn between contractual duties to supply goods or services and con-tractual duties to pay debts.

Contractual duties to supply goods or services

In **Williams** v **Roffey** (1990) these principles were reconsidered by the Court of Appeal. Roffey were a building firm with a contract to refurbish a block of flats. They sub-contracted the carpentry work on the project to Williams, agreeing to pay him £20,000 for the work. But before the work was finished, it became obvious that Williams had financial problems, which would prevent him finishing the work on time. Roffey's agreement with the owners of the flats contained a penalty clause, which meant Roffey would lose out if the complete project was not finished on time. Roffey agreed that the original contract price had been too low, and their representative approached Williams, offering an extra £10,300 on top of the agreed price of £20,000 in return for finishing the job on schedule. The agreement also included changes to the working arrangements: instead of Williams working on several flats at once, he would finish one at a time, so allowing other contractors doing different work to come in after him. When the carpentry work was done, Roffey refused to honour their promise to pay the extra £10,300, so Williams sued for breach of contract. The Court of Appeal found that Roffey's promise to pay extra was supported by valuable consideration: in return for Williams finishing the job on time, Roffey would avoid losing money under the penalty clause in their contract with the building's owners, and the cost and inconvenience of finding another contractor to finish the job, and had also benefited from the altered working arrangements. Even though Williams was only doing what he had originally contracted to do, Roffey was receiving extra benefit.

As a result of **Williams** *v* **Roffey**, the law now seems to be that if one party's promise to perform an existing contractual duty to supply goods or services confers an additional practical benefit on the other party, then providing that no duress is involved, it will be sufficient consideration to make a promise given in return binding, even though in legal terms they are only agreeing to carry out their existing contractual duty. The case has caused much interest in the world of contract law, and some of its possible implications are discussed later in this chapter.

Contractual duties to pay debts

Special rules apply to contractual duties regarding debts. Where someone owes another money and cannot pay the full amount, they will sometimes offer to pay a smaller sum, on condition that the creditor promises to accept it as full settlement for the debt – in other words, agrees not to sue later for the full amount. Even if such an agreement is made, it is only binding if the debtor provides some consideration for it by adding some extra element.

In **Pinnel's Case** (1602) Pinnel sued Cole for £8 10s, which Cole owed on a bond (a promise under seal to pay money). The debt had become due on 11 November. Cole argued that at Pinnel's request, he had given him £5 2s 6d on 1 October, which Pinnel had accepted in full settlement of the debt. Pinnel actually won the case on a technicality, but the court made it clear that had it not been for that technicality, they would have found in favour of Cole, because of the fact that he had made payment earlier than the due date, and this amounted to fresh consideration for the promise to accept less than the full amount. The court stated: 'Payment of a lesser sum on the day in satisfaction of a greater cannot be any satisfaction for the whole but a change in time or mode of payment, or the addition by the debtor of a tomtit, or canary or the like will suffice to constitute consideration for the [creditor's promise to forgo his debt].' In other words, if the debtor pays early, or in a more convenient place, or gives something else as well as the part-payment, the creditor is receiving some benefit and the debtor some detriment, and this is fresh consideration for the creditor's new promise to accept part-payment and not insist on getting the whole amount. Suppose, for example, Ann lends Ben £100, and they agree that Ben will pay the money back in one month's time. If Ann arrives on the appointed date, to find that Ben only has £40, and will only hand over that amount if Ann agrees that it is in full settlement for the debt, Ann can agree to this, and still sue Ben for the other £60 later – Ben has given no consideration for Ann's promise to accept the part-payment, and so the promise is not binding. If, however, Ben pays the £40 before the month is up, or offers Ann £40 and a book, then if in either of these circumstances Ann agrees to accept the part-payment as full settlement, that promise will be binding because Ben has given consideration for it.

The rule was approved in **Foakes** *v* **Beer** (1884). Mrs Beer was owed £2,090 by Dr Foakes, on what is known as a judgment debt. She could have obtained a court order for the seizure and sale of his property to pay the debt, but instead she agreed that he could give her £500 immediately, and pay the rest in instalments. If he did this, she said, she would not take legal action. Interest is usually payable on a judgment debt, but their agreement did not mention this. However, when Dr Foakes had paid off the debt, Mrs Beer asked for the interest as well. Dr Foakes refused to pay it, relying on their agreement. Mrs Beer sued, claiming that there was no consideration for the agreement. The House of Lords upheld her claim by applying the rule in **Pinnel's Case**: payment of part of the debt did not in itself constitute consideration for Mrs Beer's promise to forgo the balance.

This approach was confirmed more recently by the Court of Appeal in **Re Selectmove Ltd** (1995). The case concerned an alleged arrangement between the Inland Revenue and Selectmove under which it was alleged that it had been agreed that Selectmove could pay off its tax liabilities by instalments. Despite this alleged arrangement, the Inland Revenue later demanded immediate payment in full, and on failure to receive this payment sought to have the company wound up due to its continuing tax debts. Selectmove resisted this action on the basis that the previous arrangements for payment by instalments constituted a binding contract. The Inland Revenue argued that no contract could have been formed because, among other things, Selectmove had provided no consideration. Selectmove, relying on **Williams** *v* **Roffey**, argued that the consideration provided was the 'practical benefit' to the Inland Revenue of Selectmove remaining in business so that it could continue to make payments, rather than going into liquidation, which would reduce the Inland Revenue's chances of recovery of the money owed. The Court of Appeal found in favour of the Inland Revenue, concluding that there was no binding contract and one of the reasons given was because no consideration had been given. Thus, while in relation to promises to supply goods or services, a renewed promise to perform an existing obligation can amount to good consideration if the other party receives a 'practical benefit', this is not sufficient for promises for the part-payment of a debt.

Exceptions to the rule in Pinnel's Case

Disputed claims The rule in **Pinnel's Case** does not apply if there is a genuine dispute about whether the debt is actually owed, or about the amount owed (**Cooper** *v* **Parker** (1885)). In such circumstances a part-payment by the debtor will be consideration for a promise not to enforce the rest of the alleged debt.

Unliquidated claims A liquidated claim is one for a fixed amount – a sum of money lent, for example, or the agreed price of goods or services supplied. Where the amount of a claim is uncertain, as in a claim for damages, or in connection with a contract specifying 'reasonable remuneration', it is said to be unliquidated. In such circumstances the rule in **Pinnel's Case** does not apply. Because the value of the claim is not known, a sum offered in part-payment could actually turn out to be more than the claim was worth, and in any case gives the creditor the practical advantage of avoiding legal action, which is not guaranteed to succeed; these benefits provide consideration for a promise to accept the part-payment in full settlement.

Composition agreements A debtor who owes money to several different people, and cannot pay, may offer to pay each one a percentage of their claim, which is often expressed as so much in the pound, and known as a dividend. As an example, if A owes £10 to B, £50 to C and £100 to D, and cannot pay, her creditors may agree to accept a 'dividend' of 10p in the pound in settlement of each debt, which will amount to £1 to B, £5 to C and £10 to D. Such an arrangement is called a composition agreement, and the courts have long held such an agreement to be binding, so that none of the creditors can later sue for the full amount – although it is hard to see what in the arrangement could amount to consideration.

Payment by a third party A creditor who accepts part-payment from a third party, in full settlement of the debtor's liability, cannot then sue for the outstanding amount. This was the situation in **Hirachand Punamchand** *v* **Temple** (1911). An army officer owed money to a moneylender, and the officer's father sent a draft (which works in a similar way to a cheque) for a smaller amount, saying it was 'in full settlement' of the debt. The moneylender cashed the draft, and then went on to try to sue the son for the rest of the money owed. The Court of Appeal rejected this claim, considering that by accepting the draft, the plaintiffs had agreed to the terms on which it was offered, and made an implied promise not to sue for the rest of the money. Although this implied promise was made to the father rather than the son, and the son had provided no consideration, the court stated that allowing the plaintiffs to succeed would be a fraud on the father and thus an abuse of the process of the court.

Promissory estoppel This is discussed on p. 80.

Existing contractual duty to a third party

In some cases two parties make a contract to provide a benefit to someone who is not a party to the contract, known as a third party. If one of them (X) makes a further promise to that third party, to provide the benefit they have already contracted to provide, that further promise can be good consideration for a promise made by the third party in return – even though nothing more than the contractual duty is being promised by X. In **Scotson** *v* **Pegg** (1861) Scotson contracted with A to supply a cargo of coal to A, or to anyone A nominated. Scotson was instructed by A to deliver the coal to Pegg who was a third party to the original contract between Scotson and A. Pegg promised to unload the coal at a stated rate of pay. He subsequently failed to do the agreed unloading. Scotson sued Pegg, claiming that their promise to deliver the coal to him was consideration for his promise to unload it. Pegg claimed this could not be consideration, since Scotson was already bound to supply the coal under the contract with A. The court upheld Scotson's claim: delivery of the coal was consideration because it was a benefit to Pegg, and a detriment to Scotson in that it prevented them from having the option of breaking their contract with A (in which case they would just pay damages to A) and having no liability to Pegg. However, there is some suggestion that Scotson had done more than he was bound to do under the earlier contract, and so provided additional consideration, and this means that the case is not entirely conclusive on the point we are discussing here.

Another case on the issue is **Shadwell** *v* **Shadwell** (1860). The plaintiff, a young barrister, was engaged to marry, and his uncle wrote offering to give him £150 a year, until such time as the plaintiff was earning 600 guineas a year from his practice at the Bar. The plaintiff duly got married. He never actually reached the point where he was earning 600 guineas a year, but the allowance promised by his uncle was not always paid. When the uncle died, the plaintiff brought an action to recover the arrears from his uncle's personal representatives. They argued that there was no consideration for the promise; all the plaintiff had done was marry his fiancée, which he was bound to do before the uncle wrote his letter (at this time a promise to marry was considered legally binding, and could be sued upon if broken). However, a majority of the court held that marrying his fiancée was consideration. It was a detriment to the plaintiff, because it involved incurring financial responsibilities which could have been problematic without the uncle's allowance (although the court did accept that marriage did also provide some benefit to the plaintiff!). There was also some benefit to the uncle, in that he would be pleased about the marriage of such a near relative. The judgment is not entirely satisfactory, in that it does not address the fact that the plaintiff was already bound to marry his fiancée, nor the fact that the marriage of a near relative is merely a sentimental benefit, which as we have seen would not usually be sufficient consideration, because it has no economic value.

Although neither of these judgments is entirely satisfactory on this point, the rule on promises to a third party being good consideration has been confirmed in the more recent cases of **New Zealand Shipping Co** *v* **A M Satterthwaite & Co** (*The Eurymedon*) (1975), and **Pao On** *v* **Lau Yiu Long** (1980).

Waiver and promissory estoppel

These doctrines are ways of making some kinds of promise binding even where there is no consideration. Waiver has traditionally applied where one party agrees not to enforce their strict rights under the contract by, for example, accepting delivery later than agreed. Subject to the usual principles of equity, that promise can be held binding, even without consideration.

An example of waiver in action is **Hickman** *v* **Haynes** (1875). A buyer asked the seller to deliver goods later than originally agreed, and then when the delivery was made, refused to accept it. The seller sued for breach of contract, and the buyer responded by arguing that in fact the seller was in breach, for delivering later than specified in the original contract. The court rejected this argument on the grounds that the late delivery was made at the buyer's request.

In **Charles Rickards Ltd** *v* **Oppenheimer** (1950) this principle was further developed. The defendant had asked the plaintiffs to do some work on his Rolls-Royce, to be completed within 'six or seven months'. In fact, the work was not finished by this time, but the defendant agreed to wait a further three months. Even after that, the work was still unfinished, at which point the defendant gave the plaintiffs notice that unless the work was done within another four weeks, the order would be cancelled. In the event, the work was not done for another three months, and the defendant then refused to accept the car. The plaintiffs sued him.

The Court of Appeal decided that although originally the completion date had been an important term of the contract, the first extension of it operated as a waiver. This meant that if the car had been delivered within that time, the defendant would have been bound to accept it; he could not insist on the original delivery date. Once the defendant gave the plaintiffs reasonable notice that delivery time was once again to be fixed, the plaintiffs' failure to complete the work put them in breach of contract, and their action against the defendant failed.

Promissory estoppel is a somewhat newer doctrine than waiver, and could be said to be a development of it. It is derived from equity and is therefore sometimes known as equitable estoppel. The case of **Hughes** *v*

Metropolitan Railway Co (1877), involving a landlord and his tenants, is usually seen as the starting point for the doctrine. Under the lease, the tenants were obliged to keep the premises in good repair, and in October 1874 the landlord gave them six months' notice to do some repairs, stating that if they were not done in that time, the lease would be forfeited. In November, the two parties began to negotiate the possibility of the tenants buying the lease, the tenants stating that in the meantime they would not carry out the repairs. By December, the negotiations had broken down, and at the end of the six-month notice period, the landlord claimed that the lease was forfeited because the tenants had not done the repairs. The House of Lords held, however, that the landlord's conduct was an implied promise to the tenants that he would not enforce the forfeiture at the end of the notice period, and in not doing the repairs, the tenants had been relying on this promise (the six-month notice period had started again from the date when the negotiations broke down). The promise was held to be binding.

Explaining the decision, Lord Cairns said:

> It is the first principle upon which all Courts of Equity proceed, that if parties who have entered into definite and distinct terms involving certain legal results – certain penalties or legal forfeiture – afterwards by their own act or with their own consent enter upon a course of negotiation which has the effect of leading one of the parties to suppose that the strict rights arising under the contract will not be enforced, or will be kept in suspense, or held in abeyance, the person who otherwise might have enforced those rights will not be allowed to enforce them where it would be inequitable having regard to the dealings which have thus taken place between the parties.

These principles were applied 70 years later by Denning J (later Lord Denning) in **Central London Property Trust Ltd** *v* **High Trees House Ltd** (1947). The case involved a block of flats owned by the plaintiffs. In September 1939, the plaintiffs had leased the block to the defendants, who planned to rent out the individual flats, use the income to cover their payments on the lease, and make a profit on top. Unfortunately, their plans were rather spoiled by the fact that the Second World War had just broken out, and many people left London, making it difficult to find tenants. As a result, many of the flats were left empty. The plaintiffs therefore agreed that the defendants could pay just half the ground rent stipulated in the lease. By 1945, the flats were full again, and the plaintiffs claimed the full ground rent for the last two quarters of 1945. The plaintiffs stated that the agreement was only ever intended to last until the war was over, or the flats fully let, whichever was the sooner. Both events had happened by the time payment for the last two quarters of 1945 were due, and so they believed that they were entitled to full payment for that period.

The court accepted this argument, holding that the full rent was payable for the two quarters in question, and from then on. Of more importance is the fact that Denning J went on to state that the plaintiffs would not have been entitled to recover the rent for the period 1940–45, even though there was no consideration for the promise to accept the reduced rent, because of the equitable principle laid down in **Hughes**. In fact though, this reasoning (which was *obiter*, because the plaintiffs were not actually seeking to recover all the past rent) went further than that put forward in **Hughes**. In the earlier case the landlord's rights had effectively only been temporarily suspended, but in **High Trees**, Denning J declared that the landlord's claim for their full contractual rights for the period 1940–45 had been destroyed – by accepting the reduced rent for the wartime period, they lost their right to claim for arrears of rent, rather than simply suspending it until the tenants could afford to pay.

The precise extent of the doctrine of promissory estoppel is still unclear. What is clear is that the following conditions must be fulfilled before the doctrine can be applied.

A pre-existing contractual relationship

The cases suggest that there must already be a contractual relationship between the parties before promissory estoppel can be raised.

A promise

There must be an obvious and unambiguous promise not to enforce a person's full legal rights. This promise may be implied from conduct, but silence, or failure to act, will not usually be sufficient. In **China Pacific SA v Food Corp of India** (1980), the parties had been involved in a complex commercial dispute, entailing a great deal of correspondence and discussion. The defendants claimed that the contents of one of the letters, and remarks made during a discussion between the two parties' barristers, provided grounds for promissory estoppel. On the facts of the case, the claim was rejected, as no unambiguous promise had been made.

Reliance

The promisee must have acted in reliance on the promise, in the sense that it must have influenced their conduct. In **High Trees**, for example, the lessees continued to rent out the flats, rather than, for example, trying to sell their leasehold interest to someone else.

It is not entirely clear whether or not an act of reliance has to be something which would put the promisee at a disadvantage if the promisor decided to reclaim their legal rights, or whether it can simply be some act which otherwise would not have happened. In **Hughes**, the tenants' failure to make repairs because they were relying on the landlord not to enforce the forfeiture clearly put them at a disadvantage, and in **Tool Metal Manufacturing** (see p. 84), Lord Tucker suggested that the act of reliance should involve such a disadvantage. On the other hand, there is no mention of such a requirement in **High Trees**, nor is it stated to be necessary in **Hughes**, even though there was in fact some disadvantage there. Where relying on the promise does not put the promisee at a disadvantage, it may be difficult to satisfy the next requirement described, that it must be inequitable for the promisor to go back on their word.

Inequitable to enforce strict legal rights

As an equitable doctrine, promissory estoppel will only be invoked where it would be inequitable for the promisor to go back on what was promised, and insist on their strict legal rights. Illustrations of such situations would be if the promisee cannot be restored to the position held before they acted in reliance on the promise, or if the party claiming promissory estoppel has acted in such a way that it would be inequitable to allow them to take advantage of it. The latter was the case in **D & C Builders** v **Rees** (1966). The plaintiffs were a small firm of builders who did some work costing £732 on the premises of Mr and Mrs Rees. The defendants had paid £250 before the work was finished, but then stated that they would pay no more than a further £300, alleging (apparently falsely) that the work was defective. The builders were in severe financial trouble, which the defendants knew about, and faced bankruptcy if they failed to secure the full amount owed. They pressed for payment over several months, but received nothing. Eventually, Mrs Rees again offered a cheque of £300, saying that it was in final settlement, and that if it was refused, the builders would be paid nothing. The plaintiffs, still being pressed by their own creditors, reluctantly agreed. They later sued for the balance of the original debt, and the court gave judgment in their favour. The majority of the court held that it was a straightforward application of the rule in **Pinnel's Case**, but Lord Denning's judgment also raised the possibility of promissory estoppel, explaining that although it might otherwise have applied, Mr and Mrs Rees could not rely on it because of their own behaviour – they had deliberately taken advantage of the builders' financial problems, effectively holding them to ransom, and there was also evidence that they had misled the builders about their own financial position, suggesting that they could not afford the whole price when in fact they were well able to pay. Given such behaviour, it would be inequitable to allow them to rely on promissory estoppel.

In **Re Selectmove Ltd** (1995) (discussed at p. 77 above), Selectmove tried to rely on equitable estoppel to prevent the Inland Revenue reneging on an alleged agreement for the payment of unpaid tax by instalments.

The Court of Appeal rejected this argument as, even if the agreement had existed, Selectmove had failed to make certain payments required by it. As a result of this failure, it would be perfectly equitable to allow the Inland Revenue to enforce its strict legal rights.

Future rights not destroyed

Promissory estoppel can usually only be used to prevent rights being exercised for a period of time; it cannot destroy them for ever. This was stressed in **Tool Metal Manufacturing Co Ltd** *v* **Tungsten Electric Co Ltd** (1955). A licence for the use of a patent provided that the licensees had to pay 'compensation' if they manufactured more than the agreed number of items using the patent. In 1942, owing to the war, the patent owners agreed to forego their right to 'compensation' in the national interest, with a view to a new agreement being made after the war. When the war was over, the patent owners had problems getting the licensees to make a new agreement, and eventually claimed the compensation that would have been due from the time the war ended.

The court held that the patent owners' promise was binding during the specified period, so they could not get back any money that would have been due if the agreement had not been made; but they could revive their legal entitlement to receive the compensation payments after that period, on giving reasonable notice to the other party. In other words, rights can be revived for the future but not claimed back for the past.

No new rights created

Promissory estoppel cannot be used to create entirely new rights or extend the scope of existing ones, only to prevent the enforcement of rights already held; it has been described as being 'a shield and not a sword'. This can be seen in **Combe** *v* **Combe** (1951) (see p. 72 above). Since there was no contract between them, Mrs Combe did not have a legal right to the payments her husband promised, even though she had relied on his promise in not applying for a maintenance order.

In **Baird Textile Holdings Ltd** *v* **Marks & Spencer plc** (2001), discussed on p. 42, Baird Textile Holdings (BTH) had been an important supplier of clothes for Marks & Spencer over a period of 30 years. In 1999 Marks and Spencer unexpectedly announced that they no longer intended to use BTH as their supplier. BTH took Marks & Spencer to court, and one of the arguments submitted to the Court of Appeal was that Marks & Spencer should be estopped from terminating their business relationship without reasonable notice. It alleged that Marks & Spencer had induced BTH to assume that the relationship was long-term, and terminable only on reasonable notice. BTH said that they had allowed Marks & Spencer to control and influence their business; they had invested money to be highly responsive to Marks & Spencer's needs; and had foregone the chance to establish relationships with other retailers. Reversing the finding of the High Court, the Court of Appeal rejected this argument, pointing out that promissory estoppel could not create a cause of action. The Court of Appeal acknowledged that, in the light of certain Commonwealth decisions, the House of Lords might well develop the law of estoppel in the direction favoured by BTH, but it had not yet done so.

The doctrine of waiver clearly has a lot in common with promissory estoppel, and in fact some academics have suggested that they are the same thing. Actually, there appears to be at least one main distinction between the two: in a case of waiver, the party waiving their rights is really only waiving the right to claim damages for breach of contract, or to terminate for breach where applicable. They can still claim for any payments which would have been due during the waiver. In promissory estoppel, such payments could not be claimed back, as established in **High Trees**.

Agreement by deed

There is one other way in which a promise can be made binding without consideration: it can be put into a document called a deed. An agreement by deed is often described as a 'formal' contract or a contract of 'speciality'; other types of contract are usually called 'simple' contracts. The procedure for making an agreement by deed is laid down in s. 1 of the Law of Property (Miscellaneous Provisions) Act 1989, and usually involves signing a formal document in the presence of a witness. Deeds are typically used to give binding legal effect to what might otherwise be a gratuitous gift, which would be unenforceable for lack of consideration.

Consideration and conditional gifts

We already know that a gratuitous promise is not usually enforceable by law – if Ann promises to give Ben her lawnmower for nothing, there is no consideration and no contract. If Ben promises to give Ann £5 in return, there is consideration and, assuming all the other requirements of a contract are met, the agreement will be binding. But what is the situation if Ann promises to give Ben the lawnmower, and Ben goes and fetches it from Ann's garden shed? At first sight it might appear that fetching the lawnmower is consideration for the promise, but in law it is nothing more than a condition of Ann's gift. The lawnmower is not being 'sold' to Ben for the price of fetching it, but given on condition that Ben fetches it.

This is clearly a tricky distinction to draw, but one approach is that in interpreting words describing a condition, it is useful (though not foolproof) to ask whether the condition is a benefit to the promisor – if so, it is more likely to amount to consideration. If, for example, our imaginary lawnmower was actually in the repair shop, and the repairers were threatening to impose a storage charge because it had been left there so long, Ben fetching it from there could well be consideration for Ann's promise to let Ben keep it, as Ann would receive the benefit of avoiding the storage charges.

Problems with consideration

The requirement for consideration can allow parties who make promises that ought, morally, to be binding, to escape liability. This has been one reason for the long history of judicial hostility to the doctrine. At the end of the eighteenth century, Lord Mansfield, a leading judge of the time, held that a moral obligation could amount to consideration. This view effectively destroyed the doctrine of consideration; by its very nature, making a promise implies a moral obligation to keep it, and so every promise would be supported by consideration. This approach was accepted for almost 60 years, but in **Eastwood v Kenyon** (1840) it was overruled and stated to be wrong.

Even today, the courts sometimes give a rather artificial interpretation to the principles of consideration, in order to prevent unjust avoidance of an agreement. This can be seen in cases such as **Ward v Byham** and **Shadwell v Shadwell**, above, where there were sound reasons of policy and justice for enforcing the promises, but the doctrine of consideration had to be considerably stretched in order to do so.

Rigid adherence to the requirement for consideration can mean that the parties' clear intentions are defeated – if there is an obvious agreement between two parties that they intended to be bound by their agreement, it seems unnecessary to impose a further requirement of consideration. In practice, the courts are reluctant to hold that mere lack of consideration prevents a business agreement, which has been satisfactory to the companies who made it, from being legally binding, and will stretch the doctrine as far as possible to accommodate such a situation – **New Zealand Shipping v Satterthwaite** (1974) is widely seen as an example of this (see p. 80 below).

The rules of consideration have also been criticized as highly artificial, and almost meaningless in many real-life situations. A gratuitous promise to give someone something is not binding, no matter how seriously it is made and how much the other party relies on it. Yet that same promise will be binding if the promisee hands over a peppercorn in return for it. To the parties concerned, the peppercorn adds nothing to the transaction, yet in legal terms it makes all the difference. The 'peppercorn' principle, and the fact that a promise can be made binding by putting it in a deed, also gives an enormous, and possibly unfair, advantage to a contracting party who can afford legal advice.

The rule that without consideration a promise to accept part-payment of a debt is not binding was criticized by Jessel MR in **Couldery** *v* **Bartrum** (1881):

> According to English Common Law a creditor may accept anything in satisfaction of his debt except a lesser amount of money. He might take a horse, or a canary or a tom-tit if he chose, and that was accord and satisfaction; but by a most extraordinary peculiarity of the English Common Law, he could not take [part-payment].

The reason for the requirement of consideration in part-payment situations has been to protect those creditors who are 'held over a barrel' by debtors – where, for example, firms with cash flow problems are forced to agree to accept part-payment because they cannot hold out any longer for the full amount (as in **D & C Builders** *v* **Rees**). It has been argued that such protection is now better performed by the expanding concept of economic duress (which we will discuss later), so that the rule in **Pinnel's Case** no longer serves any useful purpose.

In **Foakes** *v* **Beer** Lord Blackburn criticized the rule in **Pinnel's Case**, on the ground that part-payment often offered more practical benefit to the creditors than strict insistence on their full legal rights. A small business with cash flow problems might stand to gain more from accepting part of what others owe to them, than from being able to sue for the full amount, given that suing costs money, and they may well go bust in the meantime.

A possible reform would be to extend the decision in **Williams** *v* **Roffey** to part-payment cases, so that an agreement to accept part-payment would be binding where it offered a practical benefit. This would make the law more consistent and more satisfactory in its practical operation, and take account of the real needs of businesses. So far, such a development seems unlikely. It was considered in **Re Selectmove Ltd** (1995), where we have seen that Selectmove argued that the Inland Revenue had promised to accept its tax payments in instalments, and that this promise should be binding because there was no practical benefit for the Inland Revenue in the fact that it was likely to receive more by accepting the instalments than by winding up the company, which was the only alternative. The Court of Appeal felt unable to accept Selectmove's argument, because to do so would leave the principle in **Foakes** *v* **Beer** without any application: it would always be the case that the creditor who agrees to payment by instalments will see a practical benefit in doing so. Although the court could see merit in making such a contract enforceable, it considered that this effective overruling of **Foakes** *v* **Beer** was a matter for the House of Lords, or Parliament, rather than the Court of Appeal.

The future of consideration

Both promissory estoppel and the decision in **Williams** v **Roffey** have been seen as potentially major developments in the doctrine of consideration, and a great deal of speculation has been made as to their possible implications.

When the doctrine of promissory estoppel first appeared, it was widely thought to have eliminated the need for consideration. However, it is now clear that that is not the case. The doctrine can only be used where a contract has already been created, for which consideration will have been required. Further, as **Combe** v **Combe** shows, the doctrine cannot create new rights; so it cannot be used where, for example, one party promises to do more or pay more than a contract requires. Consideration is still required for that kind of promise. In addition, as an equitable doctrine, its protection cannot be claimed as of right.

The implications of **Williams** v **Roffey** are much less clear, as in legal terms, it is still a very recent case, and the boundaries of the rule are yet to be established. It clearly redefines consideration, giving it a wider definition and in many ways reducing the barriers to making modifications binding. It has been suggested that consideration in the shape of a **Williams** v **Roffey** practical benefit is likely to be present in the majority of agreed modifications made to commercial contracts, since in such situations the parties are unlikely to agree to any change unless it has some benefit for them. The **Williams** v **Roffey** view of consideration also allows the courts more discretion than previous, tighter definitions, since they will clearly be able to find a practical benefit in situations where traditional consideration was not present.

Hugh Collins (*The Law of Contract*, 1993) has suggested that the **Williams** v **Roffey** decision marks a new, and more realistic, approach to contracts, especially commercial ones. He argues that the traditional concept of consideration sees the parties' interests as diametrically opposed, whereas in reality there may be very good reasons why one party would accept what looks like less than was promised – the importance of maintaining good business relationships, and the possibility of losing a little on one contract, but gaining more business in the future, for example.

How far the doctrine will extend is still a matter for debate. Could a practical benefit be acceptable as consideration in the formation of a contract, for example? In theory there seems no reason why not, but no case on this point has yet arisen.

Williams v **Roffey** could also affect the rules on waiver and promissory estoppel. In waiver, the party waiving their rights can decide to withdraw the waiver later, but if it was found that there was a practical benefit to them in waiving those rights, would the modification then be final? Similarly, if in a case like **High Trees** there was a practical benefit to the landlord in reducing the rent (such as avoiding ending up with a bankrupt tenant and no rent at all), would that bar him from later returning to his strict rights by giving reasonable notice? So far, we do not know the answers to any of these questions, and it remains for relevant cases to reach the higher courts and establish the boundaries.

▶ Reform

The following proposals for reform were made in 1937 by the Law Revision Committee:

- A written promise should be binding, with or without consideration.
- Past consideration should be valid.
- Consideration should no longer need to move from the promisee.
- Performance of an existing duty should always be good consideration for a promise.
- A creditor should be bound by a promise to accept part-payment of a debt as full settlement. The reason for this proposal is that the development of the doctrine of economic duress is thought to offer sufficient protection for creditors who are forced to accept part-payment 'over a barrel'.
- A promise to keep an offer open should be binding. The Law Commission thought that such an offer should be binding if it is made in the course of a business, and the offeror promises to keep it open for a definite period of not more than six years.
- In a unilateral contract, the promisor should not be allowed to revoke an offer after the promisee has started to perform (as we have seen in **Errington** *v* **Errington** (1952), this may already be the law).
- That where a promisor knows, or could reasonably be expected to know, that a promise will be relied upon by the promisee, and the promisee acts upon that promise to their own detriment, the promise should be binding. As was noted above, such promises already have a limited effect under the doctrine of promissory estoppel, but this proposal would make them fully binding as contracts.

The latter proposal has also been suggested by Professor Atiyah. It would cover situations such as where A promises to pay B £300 the following day, and relying on this promise, B goes shopping and spends £150, which without A's gift she cannot afford to spend. A's promise is clearly gratuitous, because nothing was given in return for it, but B clearly relied on it, and in certain circumstances it would obviously be reasonable for her to do so – if A seemed very serious about making the gift, for example, or frequently made such presents to B or anyone else, B would have every reason to believe that she was going to get the money. Atiyah has argued that reasonable reliance on a promise, resulting in the promisee's detriment, should give the promisee the right to enforce the promise (which in our example would allow B damages of £300), or at least to recover the amount she has lost by relying on the promise (damages to B of £150).

▶ ANSWERING QUESTIONS

1 To what extent will the doctrine of promissory estoppel prevent a party to a contract from enforcing his or her legal rights? *Oxford*

You should start your answer by describing what promissory estoppel is, citing the case of **High Trees**. Point out, with reference to **Tool Metal**, that promissory estoppel does not cancel rights for ever – they can be resumed by reasonable notice. Then, mentioning relevant cases, go through the situations in which promissory estoppel will not apply: where there is no pre-existing contract; where the promisee has not relied on the promise (discussing whether such reliance has to be detrimental); where it would be inequitable to allow promissory estoppel. Your conclusion could sum up the situation by pointing out that promissory estoppel has an important effect where it applies, but that the restrictions in its use limit the number of cases where it can apply.

2 How far is it true that performance of an existing contractual duty can never amount to consideration?

Start by discussing the reason why performance of an existing contractual duty should theoretically not amount to consideration – the idea that consideration must be something given in return for something else. Then point out the two different categories of existing contractual duty (to the promisor and to a third party), and discuss them in turn (note that existing public duty is not relevant here – you are asked to discuss **contractual** duty).

You may want to start with existing duties to a third party, as there is rather less to say on this – highlight the fact that there are clear cases where performance of an existing duty to a third party is held to be consideration.

The bulk of your essay is likely to be devoted to the effect of **Williams v Roffey**. Explain the rule before **Williams v Roffey**, and the new rule on practical benefit created by it. You should look at the possible future implications of the case, including the possibility it might eventually lead to a change to the rule in **Pinnel's Case** and **Foakes v Beer**, despite **Re Selectmove**. Your conclusion might say that not only is it already incorrect to say that performance of an existing duty will never amount to consideration, but that the implications of **Williams v Roffey** suggest we may see even more exceptions to this rule in the future.

3 In August 1994 Idyllic Hotels employ Budget Builders to build a 50-bedroom luxury hotel for £20 million. The contract states that the hotel must be completed by 1 May 1996. After twelve months, work on the building has fallen behind and Budget Builders approach Idyllic Hotels to explain that they are in financial difficulties and will not be able to complete the hotel in time. The hotel is fully booked for the 1996 holiday season and Idyllic Hotels offer to pay an additional £125,000 to ensure that the hotel is built on time. Budget Builders agree to this arrangement and continue with the building work. In March 1996,

just before the hotel is completed, Idyllic Hotels Limited inform Budget Builders that they do not intend to pay the additional £125,000.
  Advise Budget Builders. *Oxford*

Clearly Budget Builders (BB) want to establish that the promise made by Idyllic Hotels (IH) to pay extra was binding; this will only be the case if there is consideration for it. BB have not given consideration in the traditional sense, because they have not done anything they were not already obliged to do. However, since **Williams** v **Roffey**, there will be consideration if the promise to pay more created a practical benefit for IH, or protected them from a disbenefit, and the promise was not secured by duress. Duress is discussed in a later chapter, but essentially what the courts look for is some element of taking advantage of the other party's position; if BB's financial difficulties are genuine, there seems no sign of that here, so there is probably no duress.

Is there a practical benefit? At first sight, it seems obvious that there is – IH need the work finished on time, so that they can accept guests who have already booked. But the evidence is not as strong as that in **Williams** v **Roffey**. The original contract price in that case had been too low; the alternative to promising more money (finding new contractors and then suing the original ones for breach) was impractical for reasons of time, and there was an additional benefit in that changes to the arrangements for working made it easier for other contractors to operate. None of these is present here – in fact, given that there is at least eight months between the date on which BB approach IH and the date by which the building must be finished, it might have been possible for IH to take on new contractors to finish the work, and sue BB for breach. The fact that BB's breach was anticipatory means they could have taken this action immediately; they did not have to wait until full performance was due (see p. 250 below). These factors do not mean that the courts will not find a practical benefit – for example, finding new contractors might have been possible but much less convenient – but they could be used by IH as arguments against the application of **Williams** v **Roffey**, and so you need to discuss them. You then need to say whether, on balance, you think **Williams** v **Roffey** would apply; if it does, IH are bound to pay the money. BB can sue them for it without finishing the building, because IH's statement that they do not intend to pay the money is an anticipatory breach.

4 Margaret has bought herself a new car. Greg had been her gardener for many years. She told him that as he had done such a good job in the garden that summer he could have her old car. Greg was delighted and sold his old car. Using the money from the sale of his old car he orally agreed to take out a four-year lease on a flat. The next week Margaret changed her mind and refused to give Greg the car.
  Discuss.

Greg does not appear to have provided consideration for Margaret's promise to give him her old car. The work he has done in her garden cannot amount to consideration because it is past: **Roscorla** v **Thomas**. Nor can Greg use the doctrine of promissory estoppel, because while he has acted in reliance on Margaret's promise, promissory estoppel can only act as a shield and not a sword: **Combe** v **Combe**. Thus he cannot bring an action against Margaret for delivery of the old car because that would be using promissory estoppel as a sword. However, Greg will be able to get out of the lease for the flat because this was a lease for more than three years and therefore should have been made by deed under the Law of Property Act 1925 (see p. 63).

Part 2

The contents of a contract

Although there are some contract cases where the central issue is whether or not there was a valid contract, more often both parties agree that they have made a binding agreement, but disagree as to the content of the agreement. This is obviously more likely to occur when an agreement is purely oral, with nothing in writing; but as we shall see, even where there is a written contract, there may be arguments about what the written terms mean, and about whether the written document comprises the whole of the contract – if, for example, you are promised a company car during a job interview, but your written contract of employment does not mention the car, there may be a disagreement about whether you are contractually entitled to the car. In addition, the law tries to control the use of unfair contract terms, so that while a term might appear to be a part of the contract, the law may exclude it because it is unfair to one of the parties.

7 Terms of the contract

The terms of a contract describe the duties and obligations that each party assumes under their agreement. As well as the contractual terms laid down by the parties themselves, called express terms, the courts may find that a contract contains what are called implied terms – terms which are read into a contract because of the facts of the agreement and the apparent intention of the parties, or the law on specific types of contract.

▶ EXPRESS TERMS

▶ Oral statements

In all but the simplest of transactions, there will be some negotiations before a contract is made. Companies making a deal for one to supply the other may hold detailed discussions about price, quality control and delivery; when hiring a firm to put in your central heating you might ask how long the job will take, what the price includes and who will do the work; and if you buy a tin of paint, a computer or a set of shelves, for example, you will want to know whether they are suitable for your particular purpose. In all these cases, oral statements will be made. Problems can arise when, although both parties agree that a certain statement was made, they disagree on whether that statement was part of the contract and therefore intended to be binding.

In looking at such questions, statements made during negotiations are classified by the courts as either representations or terms. A representation is a statement which may have encouraged one party to make the contract but is not itself part of that contract, while a term is a promise or undertaking that is part of the contract. Disputes generally centre around statements which have proved to be untrue: if that statement is a representation, it can give rise to an action for misrepresentation, whereas if it is a term, it can give rise to an action for breach of contract.

In some cases, a statement that was initially a misrepresentation later becomes incorporated into the contract as a term. In this situation the injured party has two possible causes of action: one for misrepresentation and the other for breach. In fact, although at one time the distinction was of major practical importance, developments in the law of misrepresentation (**Hedley Byrne** and the Misrepresentation Act 1967; see p. 150 below) mean it has less practical significance now.

Whether a statement is a representation or a term is largely a question of the parties' intentions. If the parties have indicated that a particular statement is a term of their contract, the court will carry out that intention. In other cases, the following guidelines may be used.

Importance of the statement

A statement is likely to be seen as a term if the injured party has made the other party aware that had it not been for that statement, they would not have entered into the contract. In **Bannerman** v **White** (1861) White was considering buying hops from Bannerman, and asked whether they had been treated with sulphur, adding that if they had, he would not even bother to ask the price. Bannerman said there had been no such treatment (believing this to be the truth) and, after negotiations, a contract of sale was made. Later though, it was discovered that sulphur had been used on some of the hops – five acres out of 300 – and when Bannerman sued for the price, White claimed that Bannerman's statement had been a term of the contract, and Bannerman had breached that contract, so he was justified in refusing to pay. The court agreed that the statement about the sulphur was indeed a term of the contract.

Special knowledge and skill

Where a statement is made by someone who has expert knowledge or skill that is relevant to the subject in hand, the courts will be more willing to deem that statement a term than if the same words were used by an amateur with no special expertise on the matter. This principle is illustrated by two cases involving the sale of cars. In **Dick Bentley Productions Ltd** v **Harold Smith (Motors) Ltd** (1965) the plaintiffs had said they were looking for a 'well-vetted' Bentley car. The defendant, a car dealer, stated that the car he had for sale had had its engine and gearbox completely replaced, and had only done 20,000 miles since then. After the plaintiffs bought the car, problems emerged, and it transpired that the car had in fact done almost 100,000 miles since the replacements. The Court of Appeal held that the dealer's statement was a term of the contract.

In the contrasting case of **Oscar Chess** v **Williams** (1957) the defendant, a private individual, wanted to trade in his old car and buy a new one. The price allowed for the old car depended on its age, and the defendant stated that it was a 1948 model, which was the year given in the vehicle's registration book (the equivalent of the car registration document used today). On this basis the plaintiffs allowed £290 off the price of the new car. Later, they discovered that the registration book had been altered, presumably by a past owner: the car was in fact a 1939 model, which was only worth £175. The car dealers therefore sued the defendant for the difference in price between the two valuations, on the grounds that his assertion that the car was a 1948 model was a term of the contract, and he was therefore in breach. The Court of Appeal rejected their claim, pointing out that the seller was a private individual who had innocently trusted the registration book, but the buyers were experienced car dealers and therefore likely to be able, if anyone was, to spot the car's real age. Consequently, the defendant's statement was not a contractual term.

Timing of the statement

In general, the more time that elapses between the statement being made and the contract being concluded, the less likely the courts will be to regard the statement as a term, though the cases show that this can only be an approximate guideline. In **Routledge** *v* **McKay** (1954) the parties had been discussing the sale of a motorbike. Both were private individuals without specialist knowledge of motorcycles, and the defendant, drawing his information from the registration book, stated that the motorbike under discussion was made in 1942. When a written contract was drawn up a week later, it did not mention the age of the motorbike. The motorbike turned out to be a 1930 model, and the buyer claimed that the date of manufacture was a term of the contract. His claim failed, because the interval between the statement being made and the contract concluded suggested that the statement was not a term.

In **Schawel** *v* **Reade** (1913) the plaintiff began to examine a horse that he was thinking of buying. The seller told him: 'You need not look for anything: the horse is perfectly sound', so the plaintiff did not make any further checks, and the sale was concluded three weeks later. When the horse in fact proved unsatisfactory, the House of Lords held the strength and importance of the seller's statement meant that it was a contractual term, despite the length of time between the statement being made and the contract being concluded.

Agreements in writing

Where the parties put their eventual contract in writing, any statement that appears in the written contract will usually be regarded as a term. Any statement made before the written contract but not included in it is likely to be regarded as a representation, on the grounds that if the parties draw up a written contract which leaves out an earlier statement, it is likely that they did not regard that statement as an important one. The fact that the contract in **Routledge** (above) was made in writing, and did not include the date of the motorbike's manufacture, was seen as significant by the court.

A dispute between some Newcastle United football supporters and their club was the subject of **Duffy & Ors** *v* **Newcastle United Football Co Ltd** (2000). In 1994 the club offered its season ticket holders the opportunity to buy what was described as a 'bond' for £500. This bond guaranteed a 'designated seat' for ten years, and the bondholder was entitled to have their name on the seat. Under the written terms and conditions of the bond, condition 9(b) stated:

> NUFC may determine at any time at its discretion that the Designated Seat shall no longer be available to the Bondholder (either for the balance of the current Season or any future Season) whereupon NUFC shall provide the Bondholder with an alternative seat in the Stadium and the Bondholder's Benefits shall apply in relation to such alternative seat.

Relying on this condition, the club sought to change the allocated seats of some of the bondholders to make way for a £42 million scheme to increase the capacity of the football stadium by 15,000. Under this scheme, more expensive seats with easy access to new bar facilities were going to be put where the bondholders currently sat.

Many bondholders objected strongly to the Club's attempts to move them. They argued that statements had been made, in the promotional material and media statements that had accompanied the issue of the bonds, that they would be guaranteed their seat for ten years. But the written terms and conditions of the bonds commenced by stating:

> The following Conditions should be read carefully and fully understood before you offer to purchase a United Bond from Newcastle United Football Company Limited. In offering to purchase a United Bond your offer will be deemed to incorporate all the Conditions listed herein and you will be required to sign an application form which acknowledges this fact.

The Court of Appeal concluded that the accompanying promotional material and media comments did not constitute terms of the contract, they were merely representations. These representations had not been false as there was nothing in any of the Club's literature or media statements which amounted to a binding representation that the claimants would have an absolute right to the use of their seats for the lifetime of the bond. The contract was interpreted by the court as allowing a seat relocation where the Club had 'good and sufficient reason'. On the facts, the stadium development scheme constituted a good and sufficient reason and the supporters' action failed.

Strength of the inducement

The more emphatically a statement is made, the more likely the courts will be to regard it as a term. In **Ecay** *v* **Godfrey** (1947) the seller of a boat told the buyer that it was sound, but suggested that nevertheless, the prospective buyer should have it surveyed. The court held that this suggested that the statement was never intended to be taken as a term of the contract. This result can be contrasted with that in **Schawel** v **Reade** (above), where the obvious strength and importance of the statement meant it was a term.

Written terms

Written terms can be incorporated into a contract in three ways: by signature, by reasonable notice and by a previous course of dealing. This issue arises most often in connection with exclusion and limitation clauses, and so is discussed fully in Chapter 8, but it is important to remember that the rules apply to any written term.

The parol evidence rule

Under this rule, where there is a written contract, extrinsic (parol) evidence cannot change the express terms laid down in that document. Extrinsic evidence includes oral statements, and written material such as draft contracts or letters, whether relating to pre-contract negotiations or the parties' post-contractual behaviour. The rule only prevents use of extrinsic evidence concerning the terms of a contract; where one side is seeking to prove whether or not a contract is valid (for example, by claiming that there was no consideration, or that there was misrepresentation) extrinsic evidence may be used even though the actual contract has been put in writing.

An example of the parol evidence rule in practice is **Henderson** v **Arthur** (1907). The plaintiff and the defendant were parties to a lease, which contained a covenant (a promise under seal) for the payment of rent quarterly in advance, although before the lease was drawn up, the parties had agreed that the rent could in fact be paid in arrears. When the tenant was sued for not making the payments in advance, he pointed out this prior oral agreement, but the Court of Appeal held that the terms of a prior oral agreement could not be substituted for the terms of a later formal contract concerning the same transaction. The written document effectively destroyed the previous oral agreement about the rent.

There are a number of exceptions to the parol evidence rule, with the following being the main ones.

Rectification
Where a document is intended to record a previous oral agreement but fails to do that accurately, evidence of the oral agreement will be admitted.

Partially written agreements
Where there is a written document, but the parties clearly intended it to be qualified by other written or oral statements, the parol evidence rule is

again displaced. In **Couchman** *v* **Hill** (1947), the defendant's heifer was up for auction. The sale catalogue described her as 'unserved', and also stated that the sale was 'subject to the auctioneers' usual conditions' and that the auctioneers took no responsibility for mistakes in the catalogue. The 'usual conditions', on display at the auction, contained a clause that 'the lots were sold with all faults, imperfections and errors of description'.

Before making a bid, the plaintiff asked both the auctioneer and the defendant to confirm that the heifer was 'unserved', which they both did. On this understanding, the plaintiff successfully bid for the cow. The animal was later discovered to be in calf, and because it was too young to bear a calf, it eventually died. On these facts the Court of Appeal found that the plaintiff could recover damages for breach of contract. They held that the documents (the catalogue and the 'usual conditions') were only part of the contract, and the oral statements could be placed alongside them, so that together they formed one binding transaction.

Implied terms

The parol evidence rule only applies where a party seeks to use extrinsic evidence to alter the express terms of a contract. Where a contract is of a type that is usually subject to terms implied by law, parol evidence may be given to support, or to rebut, the usual implication (see p. 108).

Operation of the contract

The parol evidence rule does not apply to extrinsic evidence which shows that the written contract was intended to come into operation, or to cease to operate, in the event of a particular circumstance. In **Pym** *v* **Campbell** (1856) the parties drew up a written agreement concerning the sale of a share in an invention. Evidence was admitted that one party had stipulated orally that the agreement should not become operative until an independent expert had approved the invention.

Evidence about the parties

Extrinsic evidence can be used to show the capacities in which the parties were acting when they made their contract – for example, where a person has apparently contracted as a principal (see p. 218 below), parol evidence is admissible in order to prove that he or she really acted as agent for someone else.

Aids to construction

If an express term is ambiguous, extrinsic evidence is usually admissible to help work out what the term should mean.

Proving custom

Where it is suggested that a term should be read in the light of local or trade custom, evidence of that custom is admissible to add to or explain a written agreement, though not to contradict it. Thus in **Smith** v **Wilson** (1832) evidence was admitted to the effect that, under local custom, 1,000 rabbits meant 1,200 rabbits – a sort of 'bakers' dozen'.

Collateral contracts

There is a way in which an oral statement can be deemed binding, even though it conflicts with a written contract and does not fall within any of the exceptions to the parol rule. If one party says something to the effect that 'I will sign this document if you will assure me that it means . . . ', the courts may find that two contracts have been created: the written agreement, and a collateral contract based on the oral statement.

In **City and Westminster Properties (1934) Ltd** v **Mudd** (1959) the terms of a lease included a condition that the premises could only be used for business purposes. However, the tenant was assured orally that the landlords would not object to his continuing to live on the premises (as he had been doing until that point), and on that basis, he signed the lease. Ten years later, the landlords attempted to make the tenant forfeit the lease, claiming he had broken its terms by living on the premises. Even though the oral statement contradicted the written lease, oral evidence of the statement was held admissible to prove that there was a collateral contract, which gave the tenant a defence for the breach of the lease.

It has been suggested that the device of finding a collateral contract based on an oral statement largely eliminates the parol evidence rule, and the above case does tend to support this view. Use of the device is, however, limited by the fact that a statement can only operate as a collateral contract if supported by separate consideration. This will often be provided by the act of entering into the main contract, as was the case in **City and Westminster Properties**. But entering the main contract will not be consideration for the collateral promise if that promise is made after the main contract is concluded; in that case entering the main contract will be past consideration, and therefore not valid.

Entire agreement clauses

Some contracts contain entire agreement clauses which state that the written contract contains the entire agreement. The aim of such clauses is to prevent one party from arguing later that an earlier written or oral statement is also part of the contractual agreement. An example of such a clause is:

> This Agreement contains the entire and only agreement between the parties and supersedes all previous agreements between the parties respecting the subject-matter hereof; each party acknowledges that in entering into this

Agreement it has not relied on any representation or undertaking, whether oral or in writing, save such as are expressly incorporated herein. (*Chitty on Contracts*, 27th edn, para. 12–102.)

An entire agreement clause will be effective, though it cannot exclude liability for misrepresentation (discussed on p. 145).

Oral and written statements

We have now seen that where parties enter into a written contract after one party has made oral assurances, there are at least three possibilities as to the status of those oral statements: the contract may be contained exclusively in the written document, with the oral statements being merely representations; the contract may be partly written and partly oral; or there may be two contracts, the main written one and a collateral one based on oral statements. However, it is important to know that different approaches can yield the same practical result. For example, in **J Evans & Son (Portsmouth)** *v* **Andrea Merzario** (1976) (see p. 48 above) some members of the Court of Appeal held that there was a partly written, partly oral contract, and others that the oral statements made constituted a separate, collateral contract. They were agreed that the result of either analysis was that the plaintiffs could recover damages for breach of an oral promise, even though the written contract between the parties did not mention the subject matter of the promise.

Construction of express terms

The courts sometimes have to determine the meaning of a contractual term. In doing this the judges try to discover what the parties appeared to intend the contract to mean. The task of ascertaining the intention of the parties has to be approached objectively. Thus, the court must seek 'the meaning which the document would convey to a reasonable person having all the background knowledge which would reasonably have been available to the parties in the situation in which they were at the time of the contract' (**Investors Compensation Scheme Ltd** *v* **West Bromwich Building Society** (1998)). The court starts by presuming that the parties intended what they said, so that their words must be construed as they stand. The meaning of a document must be sought in the document itself. At the same time, the courts will look at all the circumstances surrounding the making of the contract which would assist in determining how the language of the document would have been understood by a reasonable man.

Certain rules of construction have been formulated by the courts. Previously, these rules were applied rather rigidly. But Lord Hoffmann has advanced a more flexible approach where these rules are treated simply as guidance to assist the judges to reach a reasonable interpretation of the parties' intentions. In **Investors Compensation Scheme Ltd** *v* **West Bromwich Building Society** (1998) Lord Hoffmann stated that the modern approach to construction is 'to assimilate the way in which [contractual] documents are interpreted by judges to the common-sense principles by which any serious utterance would be interpreted in ordinary life'.

Where possible, words will be given their natural and ordinary meaning. But Lord Hoffmann has warned against taking this rule too far. In **Mannai Investment Co Ltd** *v* **Eagle Star Life Assurance Co** (1997) he observed:

> It is of course true that the law is not concerned with the speaker's subjective intentions. But the notion that the law's concern is therefore with the 'meaning of his words' conceals an important ambiguity. The ambiguity lies in a failure to distinguish between the meaning of words and the question of what would be understood as the meaning of a person who uses words. The meaning of words, as they would appear in a dictionary, and the effect of their syntactical arrangement, as it would appear in a grammar, is part of the material which we use to understand a speaker's utterance. But it is only a part; another part is our knowledge of the background against which the utterance was made.

Occasionally, the precise words used may appear to have an absurd meaning. In **Investors Compensation Scheme Ltd** *v* **West Bromwich Building Society** Lord Hoffmann said:

> The 'rule' that words should be given their 'natural and ordinary meaning' reflects the common sense proposition that we do not easily accept that people have made linguistic mistakes, particularly in formal documents. On the other hand, if one would nevertheless conclude from the background that something must have gone wrong with the language, the law does not require judges to attribute to the parties an intention which they plainly could not have had.

So the rule that words must be given their ordinary and natural meaning is liable to be departed from where that meaning would involve an absurdity or would create some inconsistency with the rest of the contract.

This approach was followed by the Court of Appeal in **Sinochem International Oil (London) Co Ltd** *v* **Mobil Sales and Supply** (2000). The case was concerned with the meaning of a clause in a contract between two international oil companies. In interpreting the clause, the Court of Appeal stated that the terms of the contract were inconsistent. The court's task was to construe the clause in a way which corresponded with its business purpose. To do so it was necessary to consider what meaning the clause conveyed to a reasonable businessman, rather than the meaning of the actual words used.

In **Bank of Credit and Commerce International SA** *v* **Ali** (2001) the House of Lords applied Lord Hoffmann's approach to the construction of a contract. The case was concerned with the interpretation of a redundancy agreement. Mr Naeem had been made redundant by the Bank of Credit and Commerce in 1990. The redundancy agreement contained a term that the money he received for his redundancy was 'in full and final settlement of all or any claims whether under statute, common law, or in equity of whatsoever nature that exist or may exist'. A year later the bank went into insolvent liquidation and it was discovered that a significant part of its business had been carried out in a corrupt and dishonest manner. Some former employees of the bank sought damages for the stigma of having been employed by the bank and the resulting difficulties in finding alternative employment. In the case of **Malik** *v* **Bank of Credit and Commerce International SA** (1997) (discussed on p. 109) the House of Lords ruled that such claims were sustainable in principle. Mr Naeem wanted to make such a claim in the present case, but the liquidators of the bank argued that his claim was barred because he had accepted that his redundancy package was in full and final settlement.

The House of Lords ruled that on a proper construction of the redundancy agreement Mr Naeem's claim was not barred. The majority cited with approval Lord Hoffmann's approach to the construction of contracts discussed above. Lord Bingham stated:

> A party may, at any rate in a compromise agreement supported by valuable consideration, agree to release claims or rights of which he is unaware and of which he could not be aware, even claims which could not on the facts known to the parties have been imagined, if appropriate language is used to make plain that that is his intention . . .
> . . . On a fair construction of this document I cannot conclude that the parties intended to provide for the release of rights and the surrender of claims which they could never have had in contemplation at all. If the parties had sought to achieve so extravagant a result they should in my opinion have used language which left no room for doubt and which might at least have alerted Mr Naeem to the true effect of what (on that hypothesis) he was agreeing.

Lord Hoffmann actually dissented in this case, while he agreed with the general rules of construction applied, he disagreed with the actual interpretation of the contractual terms.

An interesting example of a dispute over the meaning of a contract is **Martinez** *v* **Ellesse International Spa** (1999). Conchita Martinez is a top international tennis player. She had entered into a five-year sponsorship contract with Ellesse, a sportswear manufacturer, in 1995. The contract stated that if Martinez was ranked within the top ten professional singles players in each contract year, she was to be paid an annual retainer worth US$1,945,000 over the contract period. In addition, the contract stated that she would receive an annual bonus of US$550,000 if she reached number two in any month. It was the interpretation of the bonus clause that was the subject of the dispute, Martinez arguing that she was entitled to payment of the bonus for 1996 and Ellesse arguing that she was not. The contract stipulated that the ranking was to be based on 'the average of her best week's ranking in each month'. It was common ground that Martinez's best ranking added together and divided by 12 resulted in a figure of 2.5, and Martinez contended that she was therefore ranked second and entitled to a bonus. Ellesse argued that if the other players' rankings were averaged in the same way there were three other players ahead of her and Martinez was in fact fourth. It was this second interpretation that was accepted by the court of first instance and the Court of Appeal. Martinez was therefore not entitled to the bonus.

IMPLIED TERMS

As well as the express terms laid down by the parties, further terms may in some circumstances be read into contracts by the courts. These implied terms may be divided into four groups: terms implied in fact; terms implied in law; terms implied by custom; and terms implied by trade usage.

Terms implied in fact

These are terms which are not laid down in the contract, but which it is assumed both parties would have intended to include if they had thought about it – they may be left out by mistake, or because one or both parties thought them so obvious that they did not need to be spelt out. In order to decide what the intention of the parties was, the courts have developed two overlapping tests: the officious bystander test and the business efficacy test.

The officious bystander test

This test was laid down by MacKinnon LJ in **Shirlaw** *v* **Southern Foundries** (1926). He said:

> . . . that which in any contract is left to be implied and need not be expressed is something so obvious that it goes without saying; so that, if while the parties were making their bargain, an officious bystander were to suggest some express provision for it in the agreement, they would testily suppress him with a common 'Oh, of course!'

The business efficacy test

This test covers terms which one side alleges must be implied in order to make the contract work – to give it business efficacy. The leading case in this field is *The Moorcock* (1889). The defendants owned a wharf and jetty on the river Thames which people could pay to use to load and unload their boats. The defendants contracted with the plaintiffs for the unloading of the plaintiffs' boat, called *The Moorcock,* at their wharf. Both parties knew that the water level at the wharf was low and that the boat would have to rest on the riverbed when the tide was down. This would be alright if the river bed was soft mud, but would damage the boat if it was hard ground. In fact, the boat was damaged when it hit a ridge of hard ground at low tide. The contract did not expressly state that the boat would be moored safely. The plaintiffs brought an action for compensation for the damage to the boat on the basis that there had been a breach of contract. The Court of Appeal implied a term into the contract that the boat would be moored safely at the jetty. Such a term was necessary to give the contract business efficacy. Otherwise the boat owner 'would simply be buying an opportunity of danger'. The term had been breached and the action for damages for breach of contract was therefore successful.

The principle laid down in *The Moorcock* has since been clarified, and its limits defined. In **Reigate** *v* **Union Manufacturing Co** (1918) Scrutton LJ said:

> A term can only be implied if it is necessary in the business sense to give efficacy to the contract, i.e. if it is such a term that it can confidently be said that if at the time the contract was being negotiated someone had said to the parties: 'What will happen in such a case?' they would both have replied: 'Of course so and so will happen, we did not trouble to say that; it is too clear.'

Further definition was supplied by Lord Pearson in **Trollope and Colls Ltd** *v* **North West Regional Hospital Board** (1973):

> An unexpressed term can be implied if, and only if, the court finds that the parties must have intended that term to form part of their contract: it is not enough for the court to find that such a term would have been adopted by the parties as reasonable men if it had been suggested to them: it must have been a term that went without saying, a term necessary to give business efficacy to the contract, a term which although tacit, formed part of the contract which the parties made for themselves.

This statement makes it clear that a term will only be implied if the contract will not work without it; it will not be implied simply because it makes the contract more sensible, fairer, or better in any other way. It also seems that since business efficacy terms are implied on the grounds that the parties must have intended them, a suggested term which is inconsistent with some express term agreed by the parties will not be implied.

A case which illustrates the principle of business efficacy is **Alpha Trading Ltd** *v* **Dunnshaw Patten Ltd** (1981). In this case, one company was acting as agent for another (the principal) in promoting the sale of cement to a third party. The agent was to receive commission based on the tonnage sold. After contracting with the buyer, the principal then pulled out of the contract; since no sale took place, the agent stood to lose their commission. The cement company settled with the third party over their breach of the contract, but the Court of Appeal held that business efficacy required that there was an implied term that the principal would not withdraw from the contract so as to avoid the sale, and leave the agent without commission – without such a term, it would have been pointless for the agent to be a party to the contract. The cement company had breached this term and so their agent was entitled to recover damages.

Both tests are subjective

Both the officious bystander and the business efficacy tests are subjective: they ask what the parties in the case would have agreed, and not what a reasonable person in their position would have agreed. Consequently, attempts to imply terms in fact commonly fail for one of two reasons.

First, a term will not be implied in fact where one of the parties is unaware of the subject matter of the suggested term to be implied, or the facts on which the implication of the term is based. In **Spring** v **NASDS** (1956) a trade union claimed that it was an implied term of its contract with each one of its members that the union would comply with the 'Bridlington agreement', which laid down the rules under which members transferred from one union to another. The court rejected this argument, on the grounds that if anyone had asked the member concerned whether he had agreed to allow the union to comply with the Bridlington agreement, he would have been very unlikely to reply 'Of course'; 'What's that?' would have been a more likely answer.

Secondly, a term will not be implied in fact if it is not clear that both parties would in fact have agreed to its inclusion in the contract; there may be many cases where a term that one party sees as obviously implied is strenuously rejected by the other party, who regards it as against their interests. In **Luxor (Eastbourne) Ltd** v **Cooper** (1941) the defendant had instructed an estate agent to sell two cinemas, with commission to be paid 'on completion of sale'. The agent introduced a potential buyer, who offered the asking price, but the cinema owner did not proceed with the sale, leaving the estate agent without commission, despite having done the work asked of him. The estate agent argued that the contract between himself and the seller contained an implied term that unless there was a very good reason, the defendant should not refuse to sell to a person introduced by the agent. This claim was rejected by the House of Lords, on the grounds that although the estate agent may have thought it was obvious that the contract contained such a term, it was not clear that the seller would have thought the same.

The House of Lords recently emphasized that they would only imply such terms where it was strictly necessary. In **Equitable Life Assurance Society** *v* **Hyman** (2000) the House of Lords was concerned with a dispute relating to payments made by Equitable Life on some of their life insurance policies. The directors claimed to have a discretion to pay low bonuses on the termination of the policy. Article 65 of the articles of association, which governed the activities of the directors of Equitable Life, appeared to give the directors a very broad discretion. It stated that they could distribute bonuses 'on such principles, and by such methods, as they may from time to time determine'.

The House of Lords stated that a distinction had to be drawn between interpretation and implication. The purpose of interpretation is to assign to the language of the text the most appropriate meaning that the words can legitimately bear. The language of Article 65 contained no relevant express restriction on the powers of the directors. It could therefore not be interpreted as restricting the directors' discretion.

But it went on to say that the critical question was whether any such restriction could be implied into Article 65:

> It is certainly not a case in which a term can be implied by law . . . If a term is to be implied, it could only be a term implied from the language of article 65 read in its particular commercial setting. Such implied terms operate as *ad hoc* gap fillers . . . Such a term may be imputed to parties: it is not critically dependent on proof of an actual intention of the parties . . . This principle is sparingly and cautiously used and may never be employed to imply a term in conflict with the express terms of the text. The legal test for the implication of such a term is a standard of strict necessity . . . In my judgement an implication precluding the use of the directors' discretion in this way is strictly necessary. The supposition of the parties must be presumed to have been that the directors would not exercise their discretion in conflict with contractual rights. The implication is essential to give effect to the reasonable expectations of the parties.

Terms implied in law

These are terms which the law dictates must be present in certain types of contract – in some cases, regardless of whether or not the parties want them. In **Liverpool City Council** *v* **Irwin** (1977) the defendants lived in a council maisonette, which was part of a high-rise block in Liverpool. The whole building was in an extremely unpleasant condition, with unlit stairs, lifts that seldom worked and rubbish chutes that were frequently blocked, all due largely to persistent vandalism. The defendants (and others in the block) protested against the conditions by withholding their rent and, when the case went to court, claimed that the Council were in breach of an implied term in the contract of tenancy that communal areas should be kept in repair and properly lit. The Council argued that there was no such implied term. When they took up their tenancy, the Irwin family had been given a copy of the Council rules for tenants, which contained a list of tenants' obligations; but there was no written document containing the Council's obligations as landlord. The House of Lords held that a landlord who let property containing several homes in one building must be under some implied obligation in law to provide proper access to the individual dwellings. They stated that the appropriate implied term in this case was that the landlord should take reasonable care to keep the common parts of the block in a reasonable state of repair, and their Lordships held that the Council had in fact taken reasonable care to do so, and could not be expected constantly to repair damage done by vandals and by the tenants themselves. Consequently, the claim failed.

Following **Spring** *v* **Guardian Assurance plc** (1994), most contracts of employment include an implied term that an employer will furnish an employee who leaves his employment with a reference based on facts compiled with due care. Contracts of employment also include an implied term that employer and employee will not engage in conduct 'likely to undermine the trust and confidence required if the employment relationship is to continue'. This was accepted by the House of Lords' judgment in **Malik** *v* **Bank of Credit and Commerce International SA** (1997), one of a string of cases following the collapse of Bank of Credit and Commerce International SA (BCCI). The plaintiffs were employees of the bank who had been made redundant after it went into liquidation. They sought to be awarded, among other things, a payment that was described as 'stigma compensation'. They argued that their career prospects had been blighted by having worked over a long period for the bank. The House of Lords ruled that BCCI had breached the above-mentioned implied term in their employment contract by engaging in dishonest activities. Certain employees were therefore eligible for compensation; which employees would be a question of fact – for example, it was unlikely that a cleaner previously employed by BCCI would have any difficulties finding employment elsewhere, but this was not true of a banker.

Certain statutes imply terms into particular types of contract, and in some cases – notably consumer contracts – these terms must be read into the contract, regardless of either party's intentions. For example, under the combined provisions of the Sale of Goods Act 1979 and the Unfair Contract Terms Act 1977, goods sold to a consumer by someone acting in the course of a business must be of 'satisfactory quality', and it is not possible to exclude liability for breach of this term (for full details of the implied terms in consumer contracts, see Chapter 16). The Late Payment of Commercial Debts (Interest) Act 1998 provides that it is an implied term in commercial contracts that interest must be paid on certain debts.

▶ Terms implied by custom

Terms can be implied into a contract if there is evidence that under local custom they would normally be there (see **Smith** *v* **Wilson**, p. 101 above).

▶ Terms implied by trade usage

Where a term would routinely be part of a contract made by parties involved in a particular trade or business, such a term may be implied by the courts. In **British Crane Hire Corp Ltd** *v* **Ipswich Plant Hire Ltd** (1975) the owner of a crane hired it to a contractor, who was engaged in the same sort of business. It held that the hirer was bound by the owner's usual terms, even though these were not actually stated at the time the contract was made. The owner's terms were based on a model supplied by a trade association, and were common in the trade, and could therefore be implied into the contract in much the same way as terms implied by custom.

▶ THE RELATIVE IMPORTANCE OF CONTRACTUAL TERMS

Different terms in a contract (both express and implied) will clearly vary in their level of importance. For example, if I offer to sell you my car with the engine in good condition, the paintwork unscratched and the ashtrays empty, clearly the first two terms are of rather more importance to you than the last, and my breaching that term will cause you less of a problem than violation of either of the others. Consequently, the law seeks to classify terms according to their importance, with the implications of a breach for the innocent party varying according to the type of term breached.

For these purposes, there are three types of contractual term: conditions, warranties, and innominate terms.

▶ Conditions

A term which is clearly an important one, in the sense that a breach of it would have very significant consequences for the innocent party, will usually be regarded by the courts as a condition. Where a condition is breached, the innocent party is entitled to regard the contract as repudiated, and so need not render any further performance, and can also sue for damages.

An example of a term deemed by the courts to be a condition can be found in **Bunge Corp** *v* **Tradax Export SA** (1981). A seller had contracted to ship 5,000 tons of US soya bean meal by the end of June 1975, with the buyer taking responsibility for arranging for the ship to transport the goods. The buyer was supposed to give 'at least 15 consecutive days' notice of probable readiness of vessel' but in fact only gave notice on 17 June. The seller might have been able to load in 13 days rather than 15. However, the House of Lords held that it was clear that the seller's obligation to ship the produce before the end of the month was a condition, so that the buyer could terminate if loading was not finished until 1 July. It therefore followed that the buyer's obligation to give notice was a condition, because in a contract of this kind it would be unfair to deprive sellers of their full period of notice.

In some cases, the parties themselves may have described particular terms as conditions in a written contract. As an examination of the cases on innominate terms will show, the courts will not always regard such terminology as decisive. In general, they look for evidence that the parties actually intended the term to have its precise legal meaning (see **Schuler AG** *v* **Wickman Machine Tool Sales Ltd**, p. 112 below).

Certain types of term are held by law to be conditions. For example, the Sale of Goods Act 1979 states that certain terms relating to title to goods and their quality are not only implied into consumer contracts for sale, but are usually regarded as conditions as opposed to warranties. Case law also lays down that certain terms are to be regarded as conditions whenever they appear. In *The Mihalis Angelos* (1970) the owners of a ship hired it out by a charterparty (the name for the contract document in such a case). The document contained the clause 'expected ready to load under this charter about 1 July 1965'. In fact the ship could not have been ready by this time, and in the event was not ready until 23 July. The owners were obviously in breach of the term, but whether the charterers could terminate the contract depended on what sort of term it was. The House of Lords decided that an 'expected readiness' clause in charterparties was a condition. The judges based their decision on the fact that in previous sale of goods cases, similar undertakings had been construed as conditions, and that in commercial agreements, made by companies who bargain as equals, predictability and certainty are vital ingredients, and parties need to know the likely outcome of breaching any term before they can confidently agree to it.

▶ Warranties

The word warranty usually describes a contractual term which can be broken without highly important consequences – such as our example of the car ashtray, above. The Sale of Goods Act 1979, s. 61 defines a warranty as a term 'collateral to the main purpose of [a contract of sale]'. If a warranty is breached the innocent party can sue for damages, but is not entitled to terminate the contract.

▶ Innominate terms

Also known as 'intermediate terms', these are terms which can be broken with either important or trivial consequences, depending on the nature of the breach. If the effects of the breach are serious, the term will act as a condition; if they are minor, it acts as a warranty.

Innominate terms were first described in **Hong Kong Fir Shipping Co Ltd** *v* **Kawasaki Ltd** (1962), in which the defendants had chartered a ship from the plaintiffs for two years. Elderly engines and an inadequate and incompetent staff resulted in a total of 20 weeks of the charter being lost to breakdowns and repairs. The agreement contained a clause stating that the ship was 'in every way fitted for ordinary cargo service', so there was no doubt that the defendants were entitled to bring an action for damages for breach of contract, but instead of doing so, they decided to terminate the contract.

The plaintiffs then brought an action for wrongful repudiation, claiming that their breach did not entitle the defendants to terminate, only to claim damages. The Court of Appeal agreed, stating that the question to be asked was whether the result of the breach had been to deprive the defendants of the whole of the benefit to which they were entitled under the contract. As this was not the case, the breach did not justify termination.

The real importance of the case is in the Court of Appeal's statement that some terms, and this was one of them, did not lend themselves to the traditional form of legal analysis: they could not be clearly defined before breach as conditions or warranties. Lord Diplock stated:

> The problem in this case is, in my view, neither solved nor soluble by debating whether the shipowner's express or implied undertaking to tender a seaworthy ship is a 'condition' or 'warranty'. The correct approach was to look at what had happened as a result of the breach and then decide if the charterers had been deprived of substantially the whole benefit which it was the intention of the parties they should obtain.

In other words, there were terms where the effect of a breach should depend on the importance of that breach. The term as to seaworthiness was such a term, because it could be broken in many different ways, with different levels of seriousness.

As a result of the decision in **Hong Kong Fir**, the courts have shown themselves ready to find that a term is innominate, even if the parties themselves describe it as a condition. In **Schuler AG** *v* **Wickman Machine Tool Sales Ltd** (1973) the parties made a contract in which one party agreed to visit certain manufacturers at least once every week. The written contract described this promise as a condition of the agreement. The term was clearly one which could be breached with serious consequences if, for example, the weekly visits were rarely undertaken, but could also be breached in a much less important way if just one visit was missed.

The House of Lords held that use of the word 'condition' was an indication that the parties intended that the innocent party should be allowed to terminate if that term was breached, but it was only an indication. It was still important to discover their intention by looking at the contract as a whole, and one relevant consideration would be whether imposing the strict legal meaning of condition created a very unreasonable result: 'The more unreasonable the result, the less likely it is that the party intended it.' In this case, their Lordships felt the result would be unreasonable, since the term could be breached in very minor ways; the term was held not to be a condition and Schuler were not entitled to terminate the contract.

In creating the innominate term, the **Hong Kong Fir** decision approaches the effect of breach from the opposite direction to that traditionally adopted by the courts. Conventionally, as we have seen, the courts sought to determine what the status of a particular term was at the time the parties made their contract; the importance of a term at that stage dictated the consequences. The **Hong Kong Fir** approach deduces the relative importance of a term only after it is breached, from the consequences of that breach.

This strategy is clearly very logical where terms can be broken in a wide number of ways, ranging from the trivial to the really serious, as it would seem unfair to allow termination for a very minor breach. In **Reardon Smith Line** *v* **Hansen Tangen** (1976) the respondents agreed to charter a tanker, which was in the process of being built. The contract identified the tanker as 'Osaka No. 354', and that name identified the shipyard which was to build the vessel. In the event, the Osaka yard was unable to do the work, and the ship was instead completed – quite satisfactorily – by another shipyard, who acted as sub-contractors, with the effect that the vessel was then known as 'Oshima 004'. By the time the ship was finished, the tanker market had hit problems, and the prospective charterers were apparently looking for a way out of the contract. In order to do this without penalty, they claimed that the vessel did not correspond with the contract description of it; they pointed out that the Sale of Goods Act, s. 13 requires goods to match up to any description of them. However, the House of Lords decided the words used were merely labels, and not a description in the sense meant by the Act. The term breached was therefore not a condition, and the appellants were not entitled to terminate the contract.

One problem with innominate terms is their potential for uncertainty; until a breach has occurred, it may not be clear what kind of term is involved. This is clearly a potential source of inconvenience, especially in business, where, in order to plan their affairs, parties need to know exactly what obligations they are assuming, and what will be the result if they do not fulfil those obligations. Consequently, in subsequent cases the courts appear to have decided not to give the doctrine too broad a scope, as we can see in *The Mihalis Angelos* (above). The term regarding readiness for loading could have been broken with trivial consequences – if the ship was ready a day later than planned, for example – as well as with serious results, yet in the interests of certainty the court decided the term should be a condition.

However, there is no doubt that the innominate term has its place. In **Cehave NV** *v* **Bremer Handelsgesellschaft mbH** (*The Hansa Nord*) (1975) a dispute arose over a contract to ship 12,000 tons of citrus pellets 'in good condition'. Some of the cargo became damaged, though apparently not seriously. It was argued that a contract for the sale of goods was governed by the Sale of Goods Act, and since it was from this Act that the modern distinction between conditions and warranties was derived, such contracts could not contain 'intermediate' or 'innominate' terms; terms must either be conditions or warranties. The Court of Appeal rejected this argument, holding that the clause was indeed an 'innominate' term, and because the breach was not serious, the buyers were not entitled to repudiate the contract.

▶ ANSWERING QUESTIONS

1 'The essential flexibility, or fatal uncertainty, of innominate terms stems from the fact that it is not possible to predict before the time of the breach what the legal effects of the breach of such a term will be.' (Downes)
   Do you consider that innominate terms create an unacceptable level of uncertainty for contract law?

You need to define innominate terms and distinguish them from conditions and warranties, giving examples of each from case law. You then need to discuss the issues of flexibility and certainty, pointing out that both can have their place. Using the cases of **Schuler** v **Wickman** and **Reardon** v **Hansen**, you can highlight the potential unfairness of the traditional approach, and the way in which the innominate term deals with this. Then point out that the courts have also recognized that in some cases certainty will be more important, discussing *The Mihalis Angelos*, and explaining why contracting parties need to know the effect of a breach in advance. Your conclusion should state whether you think the use of innominate terms achieves the correct balance between the two, based on the points you have made.

2 Lisa saw a newspaper advertisement placed by M.J. Electrical in which VX48 video cassette recorders were available for £280 by mail order. Lisa sent a cheque for £280 but when she received the recorder, she discovered that it was a VX47. The next day, she received a letter from M.J. Electrical explaining

that VX48 machines had become very difficult to obtain. The letter enclosed a cheque for £50, representing the difference in value between the two machines, and went on to say that, unless Lisa returned the VX47 within two weeks, it would be assumed that she was satisfied with the deal.

As she was going away for a two-week holiday on the day that she received the letter, Lisa did not have time to consider the matter further, but when she came back she decided to try the machine. She found that it was perfectly adequate in playing pre-recorded cassettes, but produced inferior quality recordings, no matter what brand of cassette tape she used.

Accordingly, she sent the machine back to M.J. Electrical, explaining in a note that it was not the machine she ordered. M.J. Electrical refused to accept the machine or to make any refund of the purchase price. They argued that she had failed to return the machine within the two weeks specified and further pointed to two clauses contained in the documents sent with the machine. The first said that, in any dispute as to the quality of the goods, M.J. Electrical reserved the right to repair or replace the goods at its discretion. The second said that no liability for the quality of the goods would be accepted if any unauthorized repair or inspection of the goods had been made.

Before Lisa sent the machine back, she had allowed her friend to open it up to examine the recording heads. However, though there was clear evidence that this had been done, her friend had not removed, replaced or repaired anything.

(a) Explaining the relevant rules on formation of contracts, consider whether a contract for the purchase of the VX47 was made between Lisa and M.J. Electrical. *(10 marks)*

(b) On the assumption that a contract did come into existence, explain what terms it would contain and consider whether any have been broken. *(10 marks)*

(c) Consider what remedies may be available to Lisa and discuss M.J. Electrical's claim not to be liable in any way. *(10 marks)*

(d) Ignoring any question of appeals, consider in which court(s) the dispute between Lisa and M.J. Electrical would eventually be resolved and comment on the procedure likely to be used. *(10 marks)*

(e) How satisfactory is the protection currently afforded by the law to persons such as Lisa in their dealings with those such as M.J. Electrical? *(10 marks) AQA*

(a) The relevant rules here concern offer and acceptance (the requirements of intention to create legal relations and consideration pose no problems on these facts). You need to point out that what is needed for a contract to arise between Lisa and M.J. is an offer and an acceptance and then discuss whether these are present.

The first possible offer is the newspaper advertisement – as you know, in some cases these can be an offer (**Carlill** v **Carbolic Smoke Ball Co**), while in others they are deemed to be an invitation to treat (**Partridge** v **Crittenden**). You need to assess, by looking at the circumstances of the problem and comparing them with those in the cases, which side of the line you think this advertisement would fall.

Where, as here, the answer is not obvious, you should follow the two possible lines of argument through in turn. First, if the advertisement is an offer, it would seem to be accepted by Lisa sending her cheque – but the contract thus made was for a VX48, not a VX47. If the advertisement is not an offer, the offer might be Lisa's order, which could be accepted by sending the recorder (acceptance by performance). However, as acceptance must match the terms of the offer, sending a different machine becomes not acceptance, but a counter offer. For there to be a contract, Lisa would have to accept this offer. M.J. seem to be claiming that her failure to return the machine within two weeks amounts to acceptance, but in contract law, mere silence never amounts to acceptance (**Felthouse** v **Bindley**), so it would appear that no contract for the sale of the VX47 was made.

(b) Where you are asked to define the terms of a contract, remember that terms may be implied as well as express, and deal with each in turn. In this case, it is probably simplest to deal with the implied terms first, since these will be the usual Sale of Goods Act terms, described in Chapter 16. It seems that several of these have been broken: the machine appears to be neither of satisfactory quality nor fit for its purpose. In each case, you should briefly state what the implied term requires, showing how they have been broken.

Then discuss the express terms. The first possibilities here are the statements in the advertisement: the price and the model number. If the advertisement is deemed to be an offer, these will clearly be part of the contract, and we know that the second has been broken. Then there are the two clauses contained in the documents sent with the machine; here you need to consider whether they have been incorporated. Clearly there has been neither signature nor, as far as we know, previous course of dealing (see Chapter 8), so the only possibility is reasonable notice.

(c) Lisa clearly wants to get her money back, and she has two ways to do this. First, she can claim that there was no contract, following the explanation of offer and acceptance detailed above. Secondly, she can claim for breach of contract, and this is where M.J.'s claim not to be liable comes in. They are clearly relying on the two clauses in the documents delivered with the video recorder. Lisa can try to defeat this either by arguing that the statements were not part of the contract (the issue you discussed in part (b)), or by establishing that they are inoperative as a result of either the Unfair Contract Terms Act, or the Unfair Terms in Consumer Contracts Regulations 1999 (see Chapter 8). You need to examine each term in the light of these two.

(d) This part of the question raises issues that are outside the scope of this book, and which you will study as part of an English legal system course. A textbook by the same authors on the English legal system is available for this.

(e) This part requires an analysis of the law, rather than just description. You should aim to highlight any problems with the protection given by the law to consumers, and suggest any possible reforms; material on these issues is contained in Chapter 16.

8 Unfair contract terms

Sometimes contract terms are considered to be so unfair to one of the contracting parties that the legislature or the courts have been prepared to intervene to prevent an injustice.

This has tended to arise in the context of exemption clauses and these are controlled both by the common law and by the Unfair Contract Terms Act 1977. The European Union has also intervened by making a Directive to prevent the use of unfair terms in contracts; such a term might be an exemption clause, but it might be another type of contractual clause. We will look first at the controls that are specific to exemption clauses, and then the more general controls provided as a result of the intervention by the European Union.

▶ EXEMPTION CLAUSES

In some cases, one party to a contract may seek to avoid incurring liability for certain breaches of the contract, or may specify that their liability for such a breach will be limited, usually to a certain amount in damages. For example, photographic processing companies often include a clause in their conditions of trading stating that if a film is lost or damaged, the compensation payable will be limited to the value of a replacement film. This is called a limitation clause.

A clause which seeks to exclude all liability for certain breaches is called an exclusion clause: an example might be the terms often imposed by holiday companies, which exclude liability for holiday problems caused by events beyond the company's control, such as war or natural disasters. The term 'exemption clause' is commonly used to cover both limitation and exclusion clauses, and we have used it in that sense here. Such clauses are usually, though not always, contained in standard form contracts (see p. 20). Over the past 40 years, the law has sought to control the use of these clauses, first by the efforts of the judges, and later by statutory intervention in the form of the Unfair Contract Terms Act 1977 (UCTA) and the Unfair Terms in Consumer Contracts Regulations 1999.

▶ Common law controls

Modern judges – notably Lord Denning – have expressed considerable disapproval of exemption clauses, which were frequently used by larger and more powerful contracting parties to impose harsh terms on smaller and weaker ones. In general, the courts have found two ways to regulate exclusion clauses: first, they may question whether a clause has actually been incorporated into the contract, in which case it is for the party seeking to rely on the clause to prove incorporation; and, secondly, they may question whether the words used in the clause can be construed as covering the alleged breach.

Incorporation

There are three ways in which written exemption clauses (or in fact any other type of clause) may be incorporated into a contract: by signature; by reasonable notice; and by a previous course of dealing.

Incorporation by signature
If a document is signed at the time of making the contract, its contents become terms of that contract, regardless of whether they have been read or understood. This principle is known as the rule in **L'Estrange** *v* **Graucob** (1934), after a case in which a woman signed a hire-purchase agreement for a cigarette vending machine, without reading it. The agreement contained, in very small print, a broad exemption from liablity for the product. When the machine proved defective, it was held that signing the contract meant that the woman was bound by the exclusion clause, and therefore had no remedy.

The rule does not apply where there is any misrepresentation as to the nature of the document signed. In **Curtis** *v* **Chemical Cleaning and Dyeing Co** (1951) Ms Curtis took a wedding dress for cleaning, and was asked to sign a document exempting the cleaners from liability 'for any damage howsoever arising'. She queried the document, but was told it simply meant the cleaners would not accept liability for any sequins or beads on the dress. She then signed. When she collected the dress, it had a stain which was not there before, but the cleaners denied liability, relying on the exclusion clause. The Court of Appeal held that the statement made about sequins and beads misrepresented the effect of the clause, and therefore the cleaners could not rely on it, even though Ms Curtis had signed the document.

Incorporation by reasonable notice
If separate written terms are presented at the time a contract is made – by handing over a ticket, or listing them on a sign, for example – those terms only become part of the contract if it can be said that the recipient

had reasonable notice of them. Many of the rules on reasonable notice arise out of what are called the 'ticket cases', which occurred during the nineteenth century with the rise of companies providing public transport by rail.

The guiding principle was laid down in **Parker** *v* **South Eastern Railway** (1877). The plaintiff left his bag in a station cloakroom, paid the fee of 2d and received a cloakroom ticket in return. On the front of the ticket was printed details such as opening hours of the office, and also the words: 'See back'. On the back there was a clause limiting to £10 the company's liability for the loss of property left with them. When the plaintiff returned to collect his bag, it had been lost. The bag was worth £24 10s, so Mr Parker claimed that amount from the railway company; the company maintained that their liability was limited to £10. The Court of Appeal said that a party could be deemed to have had reasonable notice if they knew of the clause, or if reasonable steps were taken to bring the clause to their notice.

In deciding whether reasonable steps have been taken, the courts will look at when the notice was given, what form it took, and how serious and unusual the effect of the exemption clause is:

Time of notice   As a rule, an exemption clause is only incorporated into the contract if notice is given before or at the time of contracting. In **Olley** *v* **Marlborough Court Ltd** (1949) a married couple booked into a hotel for a week, and then went to their allotted room. On the wall of the room they found a notice stating that the hotel accepted no liability for loss of guests' property. While the couple were out, Mrs Olley's fur coats were stolen. The hotel disclaimed liability, relying on the words of the notice, but the Court of Appeal held that those words had not been incorporated into the contract, because they came to the Olleys' notice too late. The contract was made at the reception desk, and a new term could not then be imposed on them when they reached their room.

A similar issue arose in **Thornton** *v* **Shoe Lane Parking** (1971). The defendants ran a car park which motorists entered by taking a ticket from a machine, which triggered the raising of an automatic barrier. Mr Thornton did this, and parked his car, but when he returned to the car park later, there was an accident in which he was injured. The ticket stated that parking was subject to the conditions displayed on the premises, and various notices in the car park stated that the company did not accept responsibility for damage or personal injury (the latter claim would be inoperative now under UCTA).

When the plaintiff sued for damages, the defendants argued that they were exempt from liability, due to the clause. In deciding whether the clause was in fact part of the contract, Lord Denning analysed the transaction in terms of offer and acceptance, in order to decide when the contract was complete. He reasoned that the offer was made by the car park proprietors placing the machine ready to receive money. Acceptance took place when the customer drove up to the machine, and the contract was then complete. The terms printed on the ticket which was delivered a moment later by the machine therefore came too late.

Form of notice   The form in which notice is given is also important. In general, notice of an exemption clause will only be considered reasonable if it is given in a document which a reasonable person would expect to contain contractual terms. In **Chapelton** *v* **Barry UDC** (1940) the plaintiff wanted to hire two deckchairs on the beach. These were provided by the local council, which had posted a notice requesting those wanting chairs to obtain a ticket from the attendant and retain it for inspection.

The plaintiff bought two tickets, and put them into his pocket, without reading them. He then sat down on one of the chairs, which promptly collapsed, causing him some injury. He sued the Council, who relied on a term printed on the back of the ticket, which stated that they were not liable in the event of 'any accident or damage arising from the hire of the chair'. The Court of Appeal held that the clause was not part of the contract between Mr Chapelton and the Council, because such a ticket acted like a receipt – it merely acknowledged payment for the hire, and in most cases it would not be received until after the hirer had sat in the chair. A reasonable person would not have expected it to contain contractual terms.

A document will be considered to be contractual if the party to whom it is given knows it is intended to have this effect, or if the circumstances in which it was delivered provide reasonable notice of the fact that it contains conditions – so the mere fact that the document is called a receipt will not prevent it from having contractual effect if it is delivered in such a way as to allow reasonable notice of the terms within it.

Where an exemption clause is contained in a contractual document, it will usually be incorporated by reasonable notice if it is clearly set out or referred to on the front of the document. Notice is unlikely to be considered reasonable where an exemption clause is not on the front, and there are no words on the front referring to it. Equally, if a notice or ticket contains terms which are illegible or obscured in some way, the courts are likely to find that there was not reasonable notice. In **Sugar** *v* **LMS Railway Co** (1941) the ticket handed to a passenger carried the words 'For conditions see back' on the front, but these were hidden by the date stamp put on the ticket by the booking clerk. The court held that there had not been sufficient notice to incorporate the conditions into the contract.

Effect of the clause   Modern cases have stressed that the more unusual or onerous a particular term is, the greater the degree of notice required to incorporate it. Highly unusual or onerous clauses cannot be incorporated simply by handing over or displaying a document containing the clause; the party seeking to impose the clause must take special steps to draw attention to it. This principle formed part of the reasoning in **Thornton**: although it was fairly common for car park conditions to exclude liability for damage to cars, exclusion of liability for personal injury was not a term that motorists would usually expect in such a transaction. Consequently, even though the steps taken by the proprietor might have been sufficient to incorporate the more usual clauses excluding or limiting liability for property damage, they could not be deemed to have given reasonable notice of the more unusual term concerning personal injury.

This issue was central to the case of **Interfoto Picture Library** *v* **Stiletto Visual Programmes Ltd** (1988). The defendants were an advertising agency which borrowed some photographs from the plaintiffs, a picture library. These libraries work by supplying photographic material to companies who have requested particular types of picture. The photographs are left with the client for a specified period for approval, with a reproduction fee to be paid if any of the pictures are published, and then returned to the library.

The Stiletto agency had not dealt with Interfoto before but, on request, the picture library delivered 47 photographs, along with a delivery note. This stated that the pictures should be returned within 14 days, and included a list of conditions, one of which was that companies who kept the pictures longer than 14 days would be charged a holding fee of £5 per picture per day until they were returned. The advertising agency, apparently without reading the conditions, decided that the pictures were unsuitable for their project, put them aside, and did not return them until almost a month later. When they did so, Interfoto submitted an invoice for £3,783.50, the holding fee.

The Court of Appeal held that Stiletto were not contractually bound to pay the charge, stating that as the term concerned was 'very onerous', the other party's attention had to be drawn to it very explicitly for it to be incorporated by reasonable notice. The court echoed a previous statement by Lord Denning that: 'Some clauses which I have seen would need to be printed in red ink on the face of the document with a red hand pointing to it before the notice could be considered sufficient.' In this case, although the clause was not hidden in any way – it was plainly printed on the delivery note – it was sufficiently onerous to require that the picture library should take action to ensure that the agency knew about it, rather than just assuming they would read it. Picture libraries frequently do impose charges for late return, but £5 per transparency per day would be considered expensive even today, let alone at the time when the case took place, and it seems that the high price made the court consider the term particularly onerous (in fact the plaintiff was allowed to recover £3.50 per week for each transparency returned late, as being a reasonable sum due on a *quantum meruit* – see p. 286 below).

This case was applied in **O'Brien** v **MGN Ltd** (2001). The *Daily Mirror* had launched a scratchcard game in 1995. The claimant had bought a newspaper that came with a game card. On the card was printed 'Full rules and how to claim see *Daily Mirror*'. Rule 5 provided: 'Should more prizes be claimed than are available in any prize category for any reason, a simple draw will take place for the prize.' The claimant bought another copy of the *Daily Mirror* a few weeks later which contained a scratch card indicating two sums of £50,000. As was required, he telephoned a hotline and was informed by a message that he had won £50,000. Unfortunately 1,472 people were also informed that they had won £50,000. The game had been designed to produce only one or two £50,000 prizes each week, but a person responsible for determining winning combinations had made a mistake. The newspaper announced that it would hold a special draw for one £50,000 prize and a further £50,000 would be shared by the other cardholders. As a result, the claimant only received £34, as his share of the second £50,000 prize. In the claimant's action to recover the full prize, the issue was whether the contract between the parties incorporated the newspaper's rules of the game. The Court of Appeal agreed with the trial judge that the rules were incorporated into the contract. The case of **Interfoto Picture Library Ltd** v **Stiletto Visual Programmes Ltd** (1989) was applied. The test was whether the newspaper could be said fairly and reasonably to have brought the rules to the notice of the claimant and whether those rules were particularly onerous or unusual. Rule 5, although it turned an apparent winner into a loser, was neither onerous or outlandish. It merely deprived the claimant of a windfall for which he had done very little in return. In the particular context of the game, the court was satisfied that the newspaper had done just enough to bring the rules to the claimant's attention. There was a clear reference to the rules on the face of his card and they could be discovered from the newspaper office or from back issues of the paper.

Incorporation by a previous course of dealing

If two parties have previously made a series of contracts between them, and those contracts contained an exemption clause, that clause may also apply to a subsequent transaction, even if the usual steps to incorporate the clause have not been taken. In **Spurling** v **Bradshaw** (1956) the parties had been doing business together for many years. The defendant delivered eight barrels of orange juice to the plaintiffs, who were warehousemen, for storage. A few days later, he received a document from them, acknowledging receipt of the barrels. Words on the front of the document referred to clauses printed on the back, one of which exempted the plaintiffs 'from any loss or damage occasioned by the negligence, wrongful act or default' of themselves or their employees.

When the defendant went to collect the barrels, they were empty. He consequently refused to pay the storage charges, so the plaintiffs sued him. He counter-claimed for negligence and, in response, the plaintiffs pleaded the exemption clause. The defendant argued that the clause could not affect his rights because it was only sent to him after the conclusion of the contract. However, he admitted that he had received similar documents during previous transactions, though he had never bothered to read them. The court held that the clause was incorporated into the contract by the course of the previous dealings.

A contrasting case is **Hollier v Rambler Motors (AMC) Ltd** (1972). The plaintiff left his car with a repairer, on whose premises it was destroyed by fire, owing to the defendant's negligence. The plaintiff had used the same garage three or four times in the previous five years, and each time had signed an invoice containing the words: 'The company is not responsible for damage caused by fire to customers' cars on the premises.' Although no invoice had been signed on the occasion in question, the defendants argued that this term was imported into the contract by the previous course of dealing. This was rejected by the Court of Appeal, which held that the previous course of dealing was not sufficient to justify the inclusion of such a clause.

Interpreting exemption clauses

If it is established that an exemption clause has been incorporated into a contract, the courts will then check to see whether the clause actually covers the breach that has occurred. In doing so, they apply what is called the *contra proferentem* rule, which essentially means that where the words of an exemption clause are ambiguous, they will be interpreted in the way least favourable to the party relying on them. Since parties seeking to exempt themselves from liability will frequently use unclear and ambiguous language in order to conceal their purpose, the *contra proferentem* rule can be a useful tool.

Application of the rule can be seen in **Houghton v Trafalgar Insurance Co** (1954). The case centred on a car accident, involving a five-seater car which was carrying six people at the time. The policy under which the car was insured excluded the insurer's liability where an excessive 'load' was being carried, but it was held by the Court of Appeal that the word 'load' should be given a narrow interpretation, referring to goods and not people; consequently the clause did not exclude the insurer's liability where the car was carrying too many people, rather than too much weight.

An exemption clause in an insurance policy was also given a narrow interpretation in **Middleton v Wiggins** (1995). The plaintiffs owned a landfill site where waste was disposed of. The rotting of the waste produced gases which caused an explosion and destroyed a house nearby. They had to pay damages to the home owner and claimed this expense from their insurers. The insurance company refused to pay, relying on an exemption clause in the insurance policy which excluded liability for loss arising from the disposal of waste material. The Court of Appeal rejected this argument as the accident had not occurred from the disposal of the waste, but from the unforeseen escape of gas resulting from the process of decomposition.

Technically, the *contra proferentem* rule applies to all exemption clauses, but the courts tend to apply it less rigorously to those which merely limit liability, rather than exclude it completely. In **Ailsa Craig Fishing Co Ltd *v* Malvern Fishing Co Ltd and Securicor (Scotland) Ltd** (1983) Securicor had contracted to provide security services for certain ships moored in Aberdeen harbour. As a result of their incompetence, two ships sank. A clause in the contract limited Securicor's liability to £1,000, but the shipowners claimed that the clause was ambiguous and should therefore be interpreted in their favour. The House of Lords, however, upheld Securicor's reliance on the clause, stating that limitation clauses did not need to be construed as strictly as exclusion clauses, because limitation clauses were usually made with reference to the risks to which the deal exposed the party putting forward the clause, the price that party receives, and the possibility of the other party taking out insurance against the breach. In other words, the courts feel that limitation clauses are more likely to express the genuine intentions of the parties, and to be considered as part of the bargain than exclusion clauses.

Special applications of contra proferentem

The *contra proferentem* rule is applied particularly strictly where a party relies on an exemption clause to protect them from liability for negligence. Many clauses purporting to exempt a party from liability for negligence are inoperative under the Unfair Contract Terms Act 1977 (UCTA), and even where it remains possible to exclude liability for negligence, extremely clear words must be used for this purpose. Where a clause expressly refers to negligence, or uses a term that means the same, it will be effective. Clauses written in general terms, without express reference to negligence, will only allow the party concerned to avoid liability for negligence if the clause could not be interpreted as referring to any other kind of liability.

In **White *v* John Warrick & Co Ltd** (1953) the plaintiff hired a bicycle from the defendants. The contract between them stated that 'nothing in this agreement shall render the owners liable for any personal injury'. While Mr White was riding the bike, its saddle tilted forward, and he was injured. By supplying the defective cycle, the defendants could have been held liable both for breach of contract and for the tort of negligence. The Court of Appeal held that the clause was ambiguous; therefore the *contra proferentem* rule was applied. Construing the clause in the sense least favourable to the defendants meant that it referred to contractual liability only; therefore the defendants were not protected if they were found to be negligent in tort.

A contrasting case is **Alderslade** *v* **Hendon Laundry Ltd** (1945). Articles sent by the plaintiff for laundering were lost, and the laundry company sought to rely on a clause exempting them from liability for 'lost or damaged' articles. The court held that such a clause did exempt them from responsibility for negligence, since there was no other way in which the wording could be interpreted.

Fundamental breach

During the 1950s and 1960s, the courts developed the principle that as a matter of law no exclusion clause could protect a party from liability for a very serious breach of contract – even if the wording of the clause clearly covered the breach which had been committed. However, this 'doctrine of fundamental breach' was rejected by the House of Lords in **Suisse Atlantique Société d'Armement Maritime SA** *v* **NV Rotterdamsche Kolen Centrale** (1967). Their Lordships stated *obiter* that there was no rule of substantive law that an exclusion clause could never excuse liability for such a breach. Whether the clause covered the breach in question would always be a question of fact involving the interpretation of the contract.

This approach was confirmed in **Photo Production Ltd** *v* **Securicor Transport Ltd** (1980). Photo Production employed Securicor to protect their factory by means of a visiting patrol. A clause in their contract provided that 'under no circumstances shall the [defendant] company be responsible for any injurious act or default by any employee of the company'. One night, one of the Securicor guards lit a small fire inside the factory (for no rational reason so far as anyone could tell). The fire got completely out of control and destroyed the plaintiffs' premises, at a cost of £615,000. The House of Lords held that there was no rule of law that a fundamental breach could not be covered by an exclusion clause, and pointed out that since the **Suisse Atlantique** case, the Unfair Contract Terms Act 1977 had been passed, ensuring that exemption clauses could not be freely applied in consumer contracts. In commercial agreements, their Lordships pointed out, the parties were likely to be of roughly equal bargaining power, and to be able to cover their own risks by insurance (as in this case, where the case was actually being fought to decide which of the parties' insurance companies should pay for the damage). Therefore there was no need for a doctrine of fundamental breach. On the facts of the case, their Lordships decided that the exclusion clause clearly covered negligence, and so the defendants were allowed to rely on it.

Other common law controls

There are a number of other common law limitations on the effectiveness of exemption clauses. Although their importance is much reduced by the statutory provisions to be discussed later, they still have some practical importance in cases to which the statutory limitations do not apply.

Misrepresentation

Where the party putting forward an exemption clause misrepresents its effect, the clause will not be binding on the other party (see **Curtis** *v* **Chemical Cleaning & Dyeing Co Ltd**, p. 118 above).

Inconsistent oral promise

An exclusion clause can be made wholly or partly ineffective by an oral promise, given at or before the time of the contract, that conflicts with it. In **Mendelssohn** *v* **Normand Ltd** (1970) a customer was told by a garage attendant to leave his car unlocked. This instruction was held to override an exclusion clause disclaiming liability for goods stolen, so that the garage were not protected by the clause when valuables were stolen from the plaintiff's car.

Third parties

As a result of the doctrine of privity, which states that only the parties to a contract can sue on it (see Chapter 13), the courts have held that a person who is not party to a contract (called a third party) cannot be protected by an exemption clause in that contract, even if the clause is stated to apply to them.

The leading case in this area is the House of Lords' decision in **Scruttons Ltd** *v* **Midland Silicones Ltd** (1962). The case involved a contract to carry a drum of chemicals from the US to England, which contained a clause limiting the liability of the carriers to $500. The carriers employed Scruttons as stevedores (dock workers) to unload the ships, and the drum was damaged through Scruttons's negligence. It was held that the stevedores could not rely on the limitation clause in the contract between the carriers and the owners of the drum, because they were not a party to that contract. Nor could they rely on a similar limitation clause in the contract between the carriers and themselves, because the loss caused was to the chemical owners, who were not a party to that contract.

In practice, the case has been found commercially inconvenient and, to get round the problem, the courts seem ready to find that any reference in the contract to the third party can make them a party, and thereby give them the benefit of any active exemption clause. In **New Zealand Shipping Co Ltd** *v* **Satterthwaite & Co Ltd** (*The Eurymedon*) (1975), where the facts were similar to those in **Scruttons**, the courts found a collateral contract between the owners of goods for shipping and the stevedores who unloaded the goods, and thus allowed the stevedores the benefit of the exclusion clause.

Following the enactment of the Contracts (Rights of Third Parties) Act 1999 (discussed at pp. 215–17), it is now possible under this legislation for the benefit of an exemption clause to be given to a third party. So third parties will be able to avoid the difficulties in the common law.

Statutory controls

The most important limitations on exemption clauses are statutory, and most are contained in the Unfair Contract Terms Act 1977 (UCTA).

Unfair Contract Terms Act 1977

In some ways, the title of the Act is misleading, since it does not aim to provide a general standard of fair or unfair contract terms. Its basic purpose is to control the use of clauses excluding or limiting liability for breach of contract, particularly where one of the parties is a consumer.

Dealing as a consumer
Many of the provisions of the Act only apply where one of the contracting parties was dealing as a consumer. Section 12 explains that a party is 'dealing as a consumer' where they are not making the contract in the course of a business, and do not suggest that they are doing so, and the other party does act in the course of a business. Thus, in a contract where both parties are consumers, neither would be regarded as dealing as a consumer for the purposes of UCTA. In addition, where goods are supplied they must be of a type commonly supplied for private use (s. 12 also specifically states that anyone buying at auction or by competitive tender cannot be treated as a consumer).

The Court of Appeal has made it clear that the fact that a party is itself a business does not necessarily prevent it from 'dealing as a consumer' for the purposes of UCTA. In **R & B Customs Brokers Co Ltd** *v* **United Dominions Trust Ltd** (1988) the plaintiffs were a shipping company, owned and controlled by a Mr and Mrs Bell. The company bought a second-hand car from the defendants, for both business and personal use by the Bells; they had made two or three similar purchases in the past. The UCTA provision on which they sought to rely would only apply if they were dealing as consumers.

Despite the fact that the purchase was made by the company, and the car would be used partly for business purposes, the Court of Appeal held that the Bells were dealing as consumers. They stated that the question to ask was whether the transaction concerned was actually an integral part of the business, or merely incidental to it. If a contract related to the main purpose of a company (shipping goods in this case), the company concerned was acting 'in the course of a business' and could not be dealing as a consumer. However, if the contract was incidental to the company's main purpose, it would not be made 'in the course of a business', unless it was clearly something which the company did regularly.

The Bells' company was not in the business of buying cars, since it only bought one car at a time and had only previously bought one or two cars, so the court held that, regarding the contract in question, they were acting as consumers. If, for example, the Bells had been car dealers, or if the contract had been concerned with buying packing cases, or some other equipment required for their main purpose, that of shipping goods, the result would have been different.

Some doubt has been thrown on this narrow interpretation of the phrase 'in the course of a business' by the case of **Stevenson** *v* **Rogers** (1999) which is discussed at p. 308.

Other limitations on UCTA

UCTA does not apply to contracts concerning land, contracts which create or transfer most forms of intellectual property (such as patents or copyright), contracts relating to the formation or dissolution of a company, or any contract of insurance. The latter exclusion means that the Act has no application to a very important consumer area, where the imbalance of negotiating power is significant – insurance contracts are generally standard forms, and are notorious for exemption and limitation clauses which can be difficult to understand.

Impact of UCTA

UCTA uses two methods of controlling exemption clauses: declaring them ineffective, and making them subject to reasonableness. Clauses which are ineffective under UCTA simply do not apply, even if they are written into a contract; the courts decide their verdict as if the clause was not there. As far as reasonableness is concerned, the Act gives some guidelines on what is reasonable, and others have been provided by case law which will be discussed later.

Main provisions of UCTA

The following are the more important provisions of UCTA:

Liability for negligence (s. 2)

Liability for death or personal injury resulting from negligence cannot be excluded or limited – clauses purporting to do so will simply be ineffective (s. 2(1)). This includes liability for negligence in tort as well as contract.

Responsibility for negligence which causes some harm short of death or personal injury can only be limited or excluded where it is reasonable to do so (s. 2(2)). Both these provisions apply, regardless of whether one party is dealing as a consumer.

Negligence is defined under s. 1 as the breach of any express or implied contractual obligation 'to take reasonable care or to exercise reasonable skill in the performance of the contract' or 'of the common duty of care imposed by the Occupiers' Liability Act 1957'.

Non-performance (s. 3)
In a consumer contract, or when dealing on one party's standard business terms, a contract term cannot exclude or restrict liability for non-performance or for performance which is substantially different from what was agreed, unless it is reasonable to do so (s. 3). For example, a term in a contract for a package holiday which seeks to allow the tour operator to alter the date of the holiday or the accommodation would fall within this provision.

This issue arose in **Timeload Ltd** *v* **British Telecommunications plc** (1995). Timeload was setting up a free telephone inquiry service and had obtained the number 0800 192 192 from BT. After Timeload had begun to market its service, BT sought to withdraw the use of that number because 192 was the number for directory inquiries. BT relied on a clause of the contract on its standard terms which allowed for termination of the service. The Court of Appeal accepted that this clause fell within s. 3 of UCTA, as it would permit termination without good cause when Timeload would reasonably expect termination only with good cause. That is to say, it allowed a performance which was different from that reasonably expected and was therefore subject to the test of reasonableness. On the facts of the case, BT's interpretation of the clause would make the clause unreasonable.

Indemnity clauses (s. 4)
An indemnity clause is one which provides that one party will reimburse (indemnify) the other in the event of any loss arising from the contract. The effect of an indemnity clause is often to transfer liability away from the party who would normally be liable. Under s. 4 of UCTA such clauses are only valid if they are reasonable. For example, contracts for the hire of a lorry and driver sometimes contain a clause by which the hirer promises to indemnify the owner for any injury, loss or damage caused by the negligence of the driver; if there is an accident and the lorry owner has to pay for repairs to their own or any other vehicle, they can claim the money spent from the hirer. This indemnity clause would only be valid if it was found to be reasonable.

'Guarantees' of consumer goods (s. 5)
Sometimes manufacturers issue what they call a 'guarantee' of their goods. While this guarantee might offer a quick remedy for minor problems, occasionally it seeks to exclude liability for more serious matters, such as personal injury caused by the product. Under s. 5 of UCTA such exemptions in consumer guarantees are ineffective.

Implied terms in sale and hire-purchase contracts (s. 6)
Legislation, such as the Sale of Goods Act 1979 discussed on p. 308, implies certain terms into contracts for the sale of goods and hire-purchase

contracts. Exclusion of these terms is controlled by s. 6 of UCTA. The implied condition that the seller has the right to sell the goods in s. 12 of the Sale of Goods Act 1979 can never be excluded. Other terms implied by ss. 13–15 of the Sale of Goods Act cannot be excluded if one party deals as a consumer. Where neither of the parties is dealing as a consumer the exclusion clause will be subject to a requirement of reasonableness.

Implied terms in miscellaneous contracts (s. 7)

For certain contracts which are not contracts for the sale of goods or hire purchase contracts, such as building contracts, s. 7 of UCTA contains similar controls as those contained in s. 6.

Misrepresentation (s. 8)

Contractual terms in any type of contract, which seek to exempt a contracting party from liability for misrepresentation are subject to a test of reasonableness.

The meaning of 'reasonableness'

Clauses which are subject to reasonableness by UCTA obviously only apply if the courts decide it is reasonable for them to do so. The Act gives some guidelines as to the meaning of reasonableness for these purposes, and the concept has been interpreted by the courts. The onus of proving that a term is reasonable is always on the party seeking to benefit from the term (s. 11(5)). Under s. 11(1) the court should ask itself whether the term in question is 'a fair and reasonable one to be included having regard to the circumstances which were, or ought reasonably to have been, known to or in the contemplation of the parties when the contract was made'. Therefore, if the term was a fair and reasonable one in view of the parties' knowledge at the time the contract was made, it will not become unreasonable as a result of subsequent events.

Section 11(2) refers to Schedule 2 to UCTA, which lays down a number of issues that the court may consider when deciding whether a term is reasonable for the purposes of ss. 6 and 7. These are:

- the relative strengths of the parties' bargaining positions and other means by which the customer's requirements could have been met;
- whether the customer received an inducement to agree to the term (for example, if goods were offered more cheaply if the exclusion clause was accepted), or could have entered into a similar contract with another party without agreeing to that term;
- whether the customer knew, or ought reasonably to have known, about the term, bearing in mind any trade custom or previous course of dealing;
- where an exemption clause only comes into operation if a particular condition is not fulfilled, whether it was reasonable at the time of

contracting to expect that it would be feasible to comply with that condition; and

- whether the goods concerned were made or adapted to a special order.

Although the Act specifies that these issues are to be considered in relation to ss. 6 and 7, the courts have in practice used the same guidelines when considering reasonableness in relation to other parts of the Act.

UCTA also specifies in s. 11(4) that where the reasonableness of limitation clauses is being considered, the courts should bear in mind the resources which the party putting forward the term could expect to be available for meeting the liability if it should arise, and also how far it was practicable to take out insurance against the liability.

The first case on the issue of reasonableness under UCTA to reach the House of Lords was **George Mitchell (Chesterhall) Ltd** v **Finney Lock Seeds Ltd** (1983). The defendants were seed merchants, who sold the plaintiffs 30 lb of Dutch winter cabbage seed for £192. After planting, it became obvious that the seed was both a different kind from that stated (a spring rather than winter variety) and defective. The 63-acre crop was a complete failure, and the plaintiffs claimed compensation of £60,000, the value of the crop which they had lost. The defendants relied on a clause in their invoice, which purported to limit liability to replacing the seed or refunding the price. The House of Lords held that the clause was not reasonable, largely on the grounds that the defendants themselves admitted that in similar situations they had commonly made *ex gratia* payments to compensate farmers who had suffered losses, and their Lordships felt this suggested that the defendants recognized that the clause could operate unreasonably. Other factors thought relevant were that the breach was serious, the defendants had been very careless and that it was easier for the sellers to insure against the risk than for the buyers.

The courts have subsequently continued to explore the meaning of reasonableness under UCTA. In **Phillips Products** v **Hyland** (1987) the plaintiff hired from the defendant a digging machine with driver. The driver's negligence caused damage to the plaintiff's property, but the hire company claimed they were protected by an exclusion clause in their standard contract, under which the plaintiff was responsible for any damage caused by the digger. Under UCTA, s. 2 the clause was subject to the test of reasonableness, and the court held that it was not reasonable, on the grounds that the plaintiff did not regularly hire digging machinery, so was not likely to be familiar with the terms; the hiring was at short notice, with no time to negotiate the terms; and the plaintiff had no control over the risk for which he was expected to assume liability, since he did not choose the driver and knew nothing about operating the machine.

A further factor was introduced in **Smith** v **Eric Bush** (1990) which concerned a surveyor who was trying to limit his liability for an inaccurate report on the plaintiff's house. As well as echoing some of the factors considered in previous cases, such as the availability of insurance to each party, the court suggested that the difficulty of the task could be taken into account. In this case, surveying an ordinary house was not especially difficult, and this, combined with other factors, made it unreasonable for the surveyor to limit his liability as he was trying to do; but the court said that such limitation might be reasonable where the task was unusually difficult or complex.

In **Woodman** v **Photo Trade Processing** (1981) a photo processing contract provided that if the film sent for processing was lost, the processor's liability was limited to providing a replacement film. The court stated that on the facts of the case, the clause was unreasonable, but said that a similar clause might be reasonable if the processor also offered a premium service, which cost more but offered better protection.

▶ UNFAIR TERMS

Following the Maastricht Treaty, the European Union made the Directive on Unfair Terms in Consumer Contracts (1993). This instructed Member States to pass domestic legislation to provide consumer protection. As a result, the UK Government made the Unfair Terms in Consumer Contracts Regulations 1994, which have now been replaced by the Unfair Terms in Consumer Contracts Regulations 1999.

▶ Unfair Terms in Consumer Contracts Regulations 1999

These Regulations revoke and replace the Unfair Terms in Consumer Contracts Regulations 1994. The main aim of the 1999 Regulations is for UK law to be drafted more closely to the wording of the European legislation, to prevent potential discrepancies between the two. In most respects the 1999 Regulations are the same as those passed in 1994, the principal change being that more institutions are now able to enforce the legislation, beyond the Director-General of Fair Trading.

Application of the 1999 Regulations

The Regulations render ineffective certain unfair terms in contracts between consumers and sellers or suppliers (reg. 4(1)). Like UCTA, the Regulations can control the use of exemption clauses, but they can also control other clauses in the contract where they are considered unfair.

Regulation 3 has revised the definitions of 'consumer' and 'business' that were found in the 1994 Regulations, to make the definitions closer to those found in the Directive. 'Consumer' is defined as 'any natural person . . . acting for purposes outside his trade, business or profession'. 'Seller or supplier' is defined as 'any natural or legal person . . . acting for purposes relating to his trade, business or profession, whether publicly owned or privately owned'.

The Regulations apply to contract terms that have not been individually negotiated, or, under reg. 5(3):

> Notwithstanding that a specific term or certain aspects of it in a contract has been individually negotiated, these Regulations shall apply to the rest of a contract if an overall assessment of it indicates that it is a pre-formulated standard contract.

There are two important exceptions in this context that are laid down in reg. 6(2). Where terms are in plain, intelligible language the assessment of fairness shall not relate to:

- core contractual terms; or
- the adequacy of the price or remuneration for goods or services provided.

The purpose of the Regulations is to protect consumers from hidden injustice. When a person shops, they generally make sure that they are happy with the quality of the goods and the price of the goods, so these two things did not need to be controlled by the Regulations. For example, if I was a great admirer of the pop star Madonna and decided to pay £300 to buy a ticket for her concert, I would not be able to rely on the Regulations to argue later that I had paid an unfair price.

The regulation fails to lay down a clear definition of a core term. An illustration of the concept is provided by the Directive which cites a contract for insurance: the 'core' of an insurance contract consists of those terms which 'define or circumscribe the insured risk . . . since these restrictions are taken into account in calculating the premium paid by the customer'. A term such as that in **Thornton** *v* **Shoe Lane Parking** (1971) seeking to exclude liability for personal injury might not be considered as dealing with the main subject matter of the contract, which was the provision of parking facilities for a fee. By contrast, on the facts of **Houghton** *v* **Trafalgar Insurance Co** (1954) the exclusion clause in the car insurance policy limited liability where an excessive load was being carried and could be considered as a core term to which the test of fairness would not apply.

In addition, the Office of Fair Trading has stated that:

> In our view, it would be difficult to claim that any term was a core term unless it was central to how consumers perceived the bargain. A supplier would surely find it hard to sustain the argument that a contract's main subject matter was defined by a term which a consumer had been given no real chance to see and read before signing . . .

The case of **Director-General of Fair Trading** *v* **First National Bank** (2001) concerned a contractual term in the bank's standard loan agreement.

The term attempted to allow the bank to claim interest on judgments made in the bank's favour. The Bank argued in the House of Lords that the clause was excluded from the Regulations on the basis that it 'defined the subject matter of the contract or concerned the adequacy of the price or remuneration, as against the services supplied'. This argument was rejected by the House, which noted that the clause only came into operation after the borrower was already in default. The House of Lords explained that the 'core terms' provisions must be restrictively interpreted otherwise virtually anything could be construed as dealing either with the main subject matter of the contract or the price paid by the consumer, leaving 'a gaping hole in the system' of consumer protection under the Regulations.

Unlike the 1994 Regulations, the 1999 Regulations can apply to contracts relating to succession, family law and the incorporation and organization of companies. While there is no longer an express exclusion of employment contracts, these are excluded by the Directive and the Regulation will be interpreted in the light of the Directive.

Unfair terms

The definition of an unfair term is provided by reg. 5(1). This states:

> A contractual term which has not been individually negotiated shall be regarded as unfair if, contrary to the requirement of good faith, it causes a significant imbalance in the parties' rights and obligations arising under the contract, to the detriment of the consumer.

In addition, reg. 6 states that:

> . . . the unfairness of a contractual term shall be assessed, taking into account the nature of the goods or services for which the contract was concluded and by referring, at the time of conclusion of the contract, to all the circumstances attending the conclusion of the contract and to all the other terms of the contract or of another contract on which it is dependent.

Schedule 2 contains an indicative list of terms which may be regarded as unfair. This is identical to the list that was contained in the 1994 Regulations except in one respect. In the earlier Schedule, the list referred to clauses which enabled a business to alter unilaterally the contract terms without a valid reason being specified in the contract. This was then qualified to exclude changes in interest rates in contracts with a supplier of financial services. This exception has now been removed, so consumers have a better chance of challenging the fairness of a clause in a contract for the provision of financial services.

Unlike the 1994 Regulations, there is no list of factors to be taken into account when assessing the issue of good faith or unfairness. The 1999 Regulations simply provide that the assessment of unfairness will take into account all the circumstances attending the conclusion of the contract.

As the fairness of a term is decided in the light of the circumstances at the time of making the contract, the issue is not whether any actual detriment to the consumer has occurred as a result, but rather its potential to do so.

For a term to be unfair, the 'significant imbalance' it generates must be 'contrary to good faith'. The concept of good faith is not one which is familiar to lawyers in England and Wales, but in the light of the law in other European countries it is likely to require that contracting parties deal with each other in an open, honest way, taking into account their relative bargaining strengths. Bingham LJ observed in **Interfoto Picture Library Ltd** *v* **Stiletto Visual Programmes Ltd** (1989):

> In many civil law systems . . . [good faith] does not simply mean that they should not deceive each other, a principle which any legal system must recognise; its effect is perhaps most aptly conveyed by such metaphysical colloquialisms as 'playing fair', 'coming clean' or 'putting one's cards face up on the table'. It is in essence a principle of fair and open dealing.

In **Director-General of Fair Trading** *v* **First National Bank** (2001) Lord Bingham again discussed the issue of good faith and repeated that it was essentially a requirement of 'fair and open dealing'. He concluded that:

> Good faith in this context is not an artificial or technical concept; nor . . . is it a concept wholly unfamiliar to British lawyers. It looks to good standards of commercial morality and practice.

Effect of the 1999 Regulations

Under the 1999 Regulations, unfair contract terms are not binding on the consumer. The rest of the contract remains perfectly valid provided that it is capable of continuing in existence without the unfair term.

Enforcement

The Director-General of Fair Trading is required to consider any complaint made to him or her about the fairness of any contract term drawn up for general use. He or she can require traders to produce copies of their standard contracts and give information about their use, in order to facilitate the investigation of complaints and ensure compliance with undertakings or court orders. Where appropriate, the Director-General can seek an injunction to prevent the continued use of that term. Following a change made by the 1999 Regulations, this power to seek an injunction can now also be exercised by other regulatory bodies, including the local Trading Standards departments and the Consumers' Association. The right to issue court proceedings was used for the first time in **Director-General of Fair Trading** *v* **First National Bank** (2001). The case concerned a clause in the bank's standard loan agreement which stated:

Interest on the amount which becomes payable shall be charged in accordance with Condition 4, at the rate stated in Paragraph D overleaf (subject to variation) until payment after as well as before any judgement (such obligation to be independent of and not to merge with the judgement).

The Office of Fair Trading took exception to the provision that the bank should be entitled to interest after judgment. Normally, the law does not require the payment of interest on such sums. At first instance the trial judge decided that the term was not unfair. The judge took the view that the borrower would have been surprised to find that his financial obligations were lessened where the bank obtains a judgment against the borrower, which would be the effect of the law if the term did not apply. The Court of Appeal disagreed in the light of the inequality of bargaining power between the contracting parties and took a broad approach to the issue of fairness. It considered that while logically there was no reason why a person should be better off because a judgment had been obtained against them, in this case fairness and logic did not coincide. The statutory provisions might not be logical, but they served the socially desirable purpose of preventing those already in debt from finding their problems made even worse. It was therefore unfair for the bank to attempt to exclude it. The court commented:

> The Bank, with its strong bargaining position as against the relatively weak position of the consumer, has not adequately considered the consumer's interests in this respect. In our view the relevant term in that respect does create unfair surprise and so does not satisfy the test of good faith, it does cause a significant imbalance in the rights and obligations of the parties . . . and it operates to the detriment of the consumer.

The case went up to the House of Lords and the House allowed the appeal, accepting the original trial judge's approach to the case. The relevant term was not, when properly considered, unfair within the meaning of the Regulations, as it did not cause a significant imbalance in the parties' rights and obligations under the contract to the detriment of the consumer in a manner or to an extent that is contrary to the requirement of good faith.

The Office of Fair Trading has now established an Unfair Contract Terms Unit. Rather than invoking the power to go to court and get an injunction, the Director-General of Fair Trading has generally adopted an educative and negotiating strategy. The Unit publishes regular bulletins reporting on and explaining its work. In its fifth report, it observed that 3,000 complaints had been investigated and 1,200 contracts had been successfully challenged for unfairness since the 1994 Regulations came into force in July 1995. In its report in September 1996 it observed that unfair terms were widely in use by the majority of businesses. Such terms appear frequently in home improvement and furnishing businesses, and

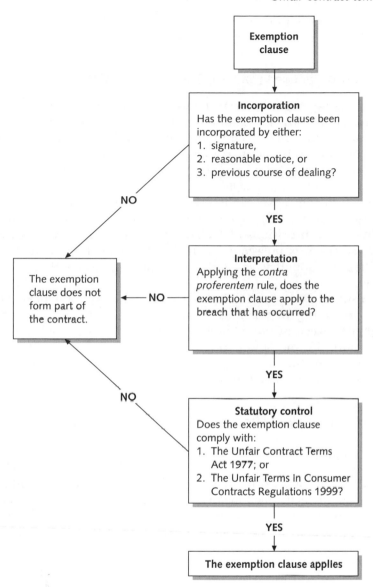

Figure 8.1 Contractual status of exemption clauses

where goods are sold in the home, such as double-glazing. They were also frequently found in contracts for holidays, mobile phones, funerals and cars.

Through the work of the Office of Fair Trading, the 1994 Regulations had a considerable impact in securing changes to unfair contract terms. The 1994 Regulations appear to have been effective and, with the new powers of additional bodies to enforce the 1999 Regulations, it is to be hoped that this progress will continue.

▶ Comparison between the 1999 Regulations and UCTA

There is a large area of overlap between the scope of the 1999 Regulations and UCTA. We have already noted that UCTA is primarily concerned with controlling exemption clauses, while the Regulations have a much broader application (though they do not cover the core terms referred to in reg. 3(2)). The Regulations are restricted to contracts between 'consumers' and 'sellers or suppliers', and a consumer can only be a human being, not a company. UCTA takes a broader approach to who 'deals as consumer', recognizing that a consumer can be a company. In addition, the provisions of UCTA extend to some contracts between businesses. There is no requirement in the Regulations that the terms be 'written', although it will only be in rare situations that this is not the case.

UCTA subjects exemption clauses to a test of reasonableness. The test applied under the Regulations is that of unfairness. The Regulations, through the Director-General of Fair Trading and other qualifying bodies, provide more flexible powers of enforcement.

In conclusion, the law would be a lot clearer if these two systems of control were amalgamated into one coherent piece of legislation.

▶ Other legislative controls

Product liability

Under Part I of the Consumer Protection Act 1987, where products are found to have defects which make them unsafe, manufacturers and certain other persons engaged in the distribution of products are liable in tort if the defect causes death, personal injury, or specified types of damage to property (this is called product liability). Section 7 of the Act provides that product liability cannot be limited or excluded by any contract term, notice or other provision.

Dangerous goods

Under Part II of the Consumer Protection Act 1987, it is an offence to supply goods which do not comply with the safety standard laid down by the Act and secondary legislation arising from it. Committing such an offence gives rise to a civil remedy for any person affected by the dangerous goods, and liability to that person cannot be excluded by any contract term, notice or other provision.

◗ ANSWERING QUESTIONS

When answering a problem question in this field, there are three basic questions which you need to consider:

1 Incorporation: is the clause part of the contract?
2 Construction: does the clause cover the factual situation that has occurred?
3 Legislation: is the clause affected by UCTA, the 1999 Regulations or both?

1 **Amanda is a successful businesswoman, who breeds pedigree cats as a hobby. She regularly buys three months' supply of cat food at a time from Happycat Ltd. The contract of sale provides that (a) the buyer must inform Happycat of any defects in the product within a week of purchase, and (b) any liability for defective products is limited to the contract price. Amanda's latest batch of cat food turns out to be defective, and most of her cats become ill and die within a month of eating it. Advise Amanda.**

This question raises issues concerning implied terms in contracts of sale, and the use of exclusion clauses; this is a common combination, so if you choose to revise one of these, it would be wise to do the other one as well. The facts of this case raise no difficulties in relation to incorporation under common law.

The next stage is to determine whether Amanda would have a claim if the exclusion clauses were not there – in other words, have Happycat breached the contract? Here you look to the terms implied into contracts by the Sale of Goods Act 1979; it seems clear that Happycat are in breach of the implied terms on fitness for purpose and satisfactory quality (see Chapter 16).

The question then is whether terms (a) and (b) of the contract have any effect on Happycat's liability for these breaches. Taking (b) first, this is a clear attempt by Happycat to limit their liability for breach of the implied terms on fitness for purpose and satisfactory quality. Section 6 of UCTA provides that where the buyer is dealing as a consumer, such liability cannot be restricted at all; where the buyer is not dealing as a consumer, such restrictions are subject to reasonableness. Do not be deceived by the description of Amanda as a businesswoman; we are told that breeding cats is her hobby, and therefore in this transaction she appears to be dealing as a consumer and the limitation clause would be invalid.

Term (a) does not exclude liability, nor reduce the amount which can be claimed, so does not fall within the protection of s. 6. However, s. 13 provides that where UCTA prevents the limitation of a liability, it also prevents making enforcement of that liability subject to restrictive or onerous conditions; assuming the cats did not begin dying within a week of purchase, expecting complaints to be notified within that time would seem to be an onerous condition.

It seems therefore that both terms are made ineffective by UCTA, and Amanda can claim damages for the death of her cats. Incidentally, do not be tempted to try to apply s. 2 of UCTA, concerning the restriction of liability for death or personal injury, to a problem concerning the death of animals; that provision only applies to people. Amanda's loss would be seen by the law as loss of or damage to property.

Although UCTA seems to cover this problem adequately, you can earn yourself extra marks by looking at the exclusion clauses in the light of the 1999 Regulations as well, and discussing whether the terms would be unenforceable against Amanda under their provisions.

2 Mary regularly parks her car in the customers' 'pay and display' car park at Jones Ltd department store. Inside the car park at all exit points are large notices stating in bold lettering, 'Cars parked at owner's risk'. Underneath is displayed in smaller letters a series of terms and conditions. One of the terms states:

> The company, its employees and agents accept no responsibility for any damage to customers' vehicles whatsoever and howsoever caused. Any term, condition or warranty whether express, implied or statutory covering damage to customer vehicles is hereby specifically excluded.

The next occasion Mary uses the car park she fails to see a notice placed at the entrance and before the automatic ticket barrier which states:

> Jones Ltd regrets the inconvenience caused to customers during the refurbishment and modernisation work. Customers are strongly advised to seek alternative parking during this period but may still use areas of the car park facility not undergoing refurbishing on the clear and express understanding that they do so entirely at their own risk and that the company, its employees and agents accept no responsibility whatsoever for any losses or damage howsoever caused.

Mary takes her ticket from the automatic machine and enters the car park. She suffers facial injuries and damage to the car when a brick is dropped through the car windscreen.

Advise Mary whether she can recover damages for her own injuries and for the damage to the car. *AQA*

An answer could be structured by looking firstly at the question of incorporation of the two notices into the contract, secondly their construction, thirdly their validity under the Unfair Contract Terms Act 1977 and finally the implications of the Unfair Terms in Consumer Contracts Regulations 1999. On all of these issues, each notice would need to be considered in turn.

Looking first at the question of incorporation of the notice placed at the exit points, this would not have been incorporated through the ordinary principles of reasonable notice, as the information would need to have been given before or at the time of contracting: **Thornton** v **Shoe Lane Parking**. However, it may have been incorporated as a result of the course of dealings between Mary and Jones Ltd, since we are told that Mary regularly parks her car in the car park. In **Hollier** v **Rambler Motors (AMC) Ltd** there was found to have been no course of dealing, but there the plaintiff had only visited the garage three or four times in the previous five years. This could therefore be distinguished, and **Spurling** v **Bradshaw** relied upon. The fact that the details of the exemption clause are in smaller print would not prevent it from being incorporated as the exemption is not particularly onerous or unusual – **Thornton** observed that it was fairly common for car park conditions to exclude damage to cars (see p. 119). The notice placed at the entrance point would be incorporated as it was visible before the time of contracting.

On the issue of interpretation, the terms of the first notice placed at the exit points seem clear and straightforward so there seems little scope for the *contra proferentem* rule. The terms of the second notice are, however, ambiguous, as they refer to parking being 'entirely at their own risk' and excluding liability for 'any losses or damage'. This does not clarify whether this is referring purely to losses or damage to property or whether it includes personal injury. This might be interpreted by a court under the *contra proferentem* rule to cover merely damage to property.

The Unfair Contract Terms Act 1977 would apply to this contract. Under s. 2(1) of this Act, any attempt under the notice placed at the exit point to exclude liability for personal injury will be ineffective if the facial injuries were caused by negligence. The exclusion of liability for damage to property resulting from negligence will only be applicable if it is reasonable (s. 2(2)). It would be up to Jones Ltd to prove that they were reasonable. A court will interpret this concept in the light of Article 11 and relevant cases, such as **George Mitchell (Chesterhall) Ltd** v **Finney Lock Seeds Ltd**.

Finally, consideration could be given to the Unfair Terms in Consumer Contracts Regulations. These would apply here as this is a contract between a consumer and a supplier, the terms of the contract have not been individually negotiated, and we are not concerned with core contractual terms within the meaning of reg. 6(2). The concept of fairness would be interpreted in accordance with reg. 5 and Sch. 2. It is unlikely that a court would find it unfair to exclude liability for damage to property, but they are likely to consider it unfair to exclude liability for personal injury.

Part 3

Vitiating factors

Even where a contract meets the requirements of offer and acceptance, consideration and intent to create legal relations, it may still not be binding if, at the time the contract was made, certain factors were present which mean there was no genuine consent. These are known as vitiating factors (because they vitiate, or invalidate, consent). The vitiating factors which the law recognizes as undermining a contract are misrepresentation, mistake, duress, undue influence and illegality. They will be dealt with in turn in the following chapters.

As we have seen, contracts are enforced by the law because they are expressions of the parties' own free will; the parties have consented to their contractual obligations. The reason why the vitiating factors undermine a contract is that they all in some way render invalid the parties' consent to their agreement – for example, if one party agrees to a contract because the other has threatened her, she cannot be said to have exercised free will.

The presence of a vitiating factor usually makes a contract either void or voidable, depending on which vitiating factor is present. Where a contract is declared void, the effect is that there was never a contract in the first place, so neither party can enforce the agreement. If a contract is voidable, the innocent party can choose whether or not to let the contract stand.

9 Misrepresentation

What is a misrepresentation?

A misrepresentation is an untrue statement of fact by one party which has induced the other to enter into the contract. A misrepresentation renders the contract voidable and it may also give rise to a right to damages depending on the type of misrepresentation that has occurred. For a misrepresentation to be actionable, it has to fulfil three requirements: it must be untrue; it must be a statement of fact, not mere opinion; and it must have induced the innocent party to enter the contract.

An untrue statement

The statement may be in any form – spoken, written or by conduct – but mere silence will not usually amount to a false statement, even though it means concealing some fact which is highly significant. Under the traditional rule of *caveat emptor* (Latin for 'let the buyer beware'), a purchaser is required to ask questions about important matters if necessary – the seller is not usually expected to volunteer information which may put the buyer off.

Even if one contracting party knows that the other has misunderstood some aspect of the situation, there is no duty to point this out. In **Fletcher v Krell** (1873) a woman applied for a post as a governess, without revealing the fact that she had previously been married. At that time, this may well have been a factor that would have affected the employer's decision to employ her. Despite this, the court held that her silence did not amount to a misrepresentation.

There are, however, four types of situation where the law does impose a duty to disclose information. To remain silent about a material fact in any of these circumstances can therefore amount to a misrepresentation.

Contracts requiring utmost good faith

These are often known as contracts requiring *uberrimae fidei*, which is Latin for utmost good faith. Examples are contracts for insurance, offers of shares in a company, sales of land (where utmost good faith is required on matters affecting title to the land, though not physical defects) and certain family arrangements. Failure to disclose a matter regarding which utmost good faith is required allows the innocent party to rescind the contract, though damages are not available.

The way the rule on utmost good faith works can be seen most clearly in insurance contracts, where the party taking out the insurance policy must tell the insurance company of **any** fact he or she knows about which might affect the company's decision on whether or not to accept the insurance risk, and what premium to charge. If the insured party fails to disclose any fact that affects those decisions, the contract is voidable, and the company is not required to pay out against a claim, even if that claim has no connection with the fact that was not disclosed. For example, if a client takes out a life insurance policy without revealing that they have a heart condition, and is then killed in a car accident which has no connection with the illness, any dependants will not be able to claim against the policy.

The basis for the rule is that the relevant facts are likely to be difficult or impossible for the other party to find out for themselves, so the law should ensure that one party does not have an unfair bargaining position over the other. It was applied in **Seaman** v **Fonereau** (1743) which concerned insurance of a ship while England was at war with Spain. The insured party had failed to reveal the fact that the particular ship was in a risky position when last sighted. In fact the vessel escaped that danger, but was subsequently captured by the Spaniards. It was held that the failure to disclose the ship's previous danger was sufficient to render the contract voidable.

The rule on utmost good faith is subject to the provisions of the Rehabilitation of Offenders Act 1974, which states that under certain circumstances a person cannot be required to disclose past convictions and sentences.

Subsequent falsity

A misrepresentation may occur where a statement was true when it was made, but due to a change of circumstances has become incorrect by the time it is acted upon. Keeping silent about the change can amount to misrepresentation. In **With** v **O'Flanagan** (1936) a doctor was selling his medical practice. He told a prospective purchaser that it was worth £200 per annum, which was true at the time. The seller then fell ill, and was unable to keep up with his work. Patients left the practice, and by the time the contract of sale was signed, four months later, there was almost no income. It was held that the failure of the seller to tell the buyer what had happened amounted to a misrepresentation.

Partial revelation

If one party makes a statement which is itself true, but which misrepresents the whole situation because of what is left unsaid, the statement may amount to a misrepresentation. In **Dimmock** *v* **Hallett** (1866) a seller of land told a prospective buyer that the farms on the land were let, but did not mention that the tenants were about to leave. Omitting this fact presented such a distorted picture of the true situation that the court held there had been a misrepresentation.

Fiduciary relationship

Sometimes it is the existing relationship between the parties, rather than the type of contract concerned, which gives rise to a duty to disclose important facts about a contract. The main types of relationship accepted by the courts as imposing such a duty (called fiduciary relationships) are those between parent and child, solicitor and client, trustee and beneficiary, and principal and agent. The courts have stressed that this list is not exhaustive, and it is always open to a party to show that the relationship between him or her and the other contracting party is such that one party necessarily places some trust in the other, and that other therefore has influence over them.

A statement of fact

The statement must be one of fact; merely delivering an opinion will not create an actionable misrepresentation. In **Bisset** *v* **Wilkinson** (1927) Bisset was selling land in New Zealand to Wilkinson, who planned to use it for sheep farming. The land had not previously been used as a sheep farm, but during the negotiations Bisset expressed the view that if the land were worked properly, it could support 2,000 sheep. This was not actually the case.

On the face of it, the statement looked likely to constitute a misrepresentation; a farmer's description of the quality of his land sounds exactly like a statement of fact. However, in this case it was regarded as no more than a matter of opinion, on the grounds that both parties were aware that the land had never been used for sheep farming, and therefore neither could expect the other to know, as a matter of fact, how many sheep it could support.

There are some cases in which what looks like a statement of opinion will be considered by the courts to be a statement of fact. An example is where one party falsely states their opinion. For example, A wants to sell a clock to B, and says she thinks the clock is 200 years old, when in fact she knows it was made the week before. Her state of mind is a fact, and she is lying about it; therefore she is making a misrepresentation of fact. This rule was laid down in **Edgington** *v* **Fitzmaurice** (1885) where a prospectus inviting loans from the public stated that the money would be used to improve the buildings and extend the business. The Court of Appeal held that this statement was a fraudulent misrepresentation of fact, since the person issuing the prospectus did not intend to use the money as suggested, and had therefore misrepresented the state of his mind. Bowen LJ commented that: 'The state of a man's mind is as much a fact as the state of his digestion.'

In addition, where circumstances are such that the party giving an opinion appears to be in possession of facts upon which the opinion can reasonably be based, that party is effectively stating that he or she **is** in possession of such facts, and if this is not the case, the statement will be a misrepresentation. In **Smith** *v* **Land and House Property Corporation** (1884) the plaintiffs were trying to sell a hotel and claimed that it was 'let to Mr Frederick Fleck (a most desirable tenant)'. In fact, Mr Fleck had been seriously in arrears with his rent, and only paid 'by driblets under pressure'.

The Court of Appeal held that the description of Mr Fleck as 'a most desirable tenant' was not a mere expression of opinion. Since the plaintiffs were clearly in a position to know Mr Fleck's record as a tenant, their statement suggested that they were unaware of any facts which could be regarded as making him an undesirable tenant, which was clearly untrue. The statement was therefore an actionable misrepresentation. Bowen LJ stated that:

> In a case where the facts are equally well known to both parties, what one of them says to the other is frequently nothing but an expression of opinion . . . But if the facts are not equally well known to both sides, then a statement of opinion by the one who knows the facts best involves very often a statement of material fact, for he impliedly states that he knows facts which justify his opinion.

To be an actionable misrepresentation, a statement must refer to an existing fact, not something in the future. The exception is a statement of intention, since this comes under the rule that a statement about the state of one's mind is a statement of fact: saying you intend to do something in the future implies that the intention already exists (**Edgington** *v* **Fitzmaurice**).

Mere 'sales talk' used to recommend a product to a potential customer will not amount to a statement of existing fact. In **Dimmock** *v* **Hallett** (1866) land for sale was described as 'fertile and improvable': this was held to be simply sales talk, and not a representation of fact. Clearly, this distinction will be difficult at times, but, in general, vague praise will be seen as mere sales talk, while more precise claims are likely to be viewed as misrepresentations of fact.

Statements of the law are not sufficient to amount to an actionable misrepresentation. In practice, it is not always clear when a statement is one as to law or as to fact. We will see in the next chapter that the distinction between mistakes of law and mistakes of fact has recently been removed by the House of Lords (p. 163). There is now a strong case for reconsidering this distinction in the context of misrepresentations.

Inducement

The misrepresentation must have been made by the other contracting party or by their agent acting within the scope of their authority, or the other contracting party must have known of the misrepresentation. The misrepresentation will only be actionable under contract law if it is at least one of the reasons for which the claimant entered into the contract. So if the claimant was not aware that the statement had been made, or knew it was untrue, or it did not affect the decision to enter into the contract, the misrepresentation will not be actionable.

Knowledge that another party's statement was untrue will only prevent that statement from being an actionable misrepresentation if it is genuine knowledge: mere suspicion, or possession of information which could reveal the lie if checked, are not enough. In **Redgrave v Hurd** (1881) a solicitor wanted to sell his law practice. He told the buyer that it was worth £300 a year and invited him to check this by inspecting the papers in his office. Had the buyer done this, he could have learnt that the practice was actually worth no more than £200 a year. However, the Court of Appeal held that the buyer had relied on the seller's word, and was entitled to do so, even if he had the means to discover that it was untrue.

Where the innocent party does not rely on the other's statement, and instead conducts their own investigations, or simply relies on their own judgement, the party making the misrepresentation will not be liable. In **Attwood v Small** (1838) the owners of a mine made rather exaggerated statements as to its earning capacity to the prospective buyers. The purchasers had these statements checked by their own surveyors, who wrongly reported that they were correct. The House of Lords held that the plaintiffs had been induced to enter the contract by their surveyors' report and not by the vendor's statements; if they had believed those statements they would not have had them checked.

Although a misrepresentation must be relied upon by the innocent party in order to be actionable, it does not need to be the only reason why the innocent party entered the contract. In **Edgington v Fitzmaurice** (see p. 147 above) the plaintiff was induced to loan money to the company, partly by a misstatement in the prospectus and partly by his own (mistaken) belief that the contract would give him some rights over the company's property. The plaintiff admitted that he would not have lent the money if he had not believed he would gain rights in the property, but the court nevertheless held that the statement made in the prospectus was still an actionable misrepresentation.

Constructive knowledge

In some situations a party to a contract may not have actual knowledge of a misrepresentation but for public policy reasons they will be treated as if they did have that knowledge, known as constructive knowledge. The issue of people being placed on inquiry and avoiding constructive knowledge is discussed in detail in the context of undue influence at pp. 204–7.

▶ Types of misrepresentation

There are four types of misrepresentation: fraudulent misrepresentation; negligent misrepresentation at common law; negligent misrepresentation under statute; and innocent misrepresentation. Which category a misrepresentation falls into depends on the state of mind of the person making the statement. The reason why the category matters is that the remedies for each type differ.

Fraudulent misrepresentation

This is also known as the tort of deceit. It was defined by Lord Herschell in **Derry** *v* **Peek** (1889). In this case, a company had procured the passing of an Act of Parliament which allowed it to run horse-drawn tramcars in Plymouth and, subject to the consent of the Board of Trade, to run tramcars powered by steam. The company's directors thought that obtaining the consent of the Board of Trade was a mere formality, and their share prospectus falsely stated that they had authority to run steam-driven tramcars. Relying on this assertion, the plaintiff, among others, bought shares in the company.

In fact the Board of Trade refused consent to steam-powered trams, and the company was wound up, with many investors losing money. The directors were sued in the tort of deceit. The House of Lords held that as the directors believed that the consent of the Board of Trade was more or less inevitable, given the passing of the Act, they were inaccurate, but not dishonest, and there was therefore no fraudulent misrepresentation. Their Lordships defined fraudulent misrepresentation as a false statement that is made '(i) knowingly, or (ii) without belief in its truth, or (iii) recklessly as to whether it be true or false'. In other words, a party makes a fraudulent misrepresentation if they make a false statement, and at the time of making it, do not believe it to be true.

Negligent misrepresentation at common law

In **Hedley Byrne & Co** *v* **Heller & Partners Ltd** (1964) the House of Lords stated, *obiter*, that in certain circumstances damages may be recoverable in tort for a negligent misstatement which causes financial loss. The plaintiff company had entered into some advertising contracts, on behalf of another company, called Easipower. Under the agreement, the plaintiffs were liable if Easipower failed to pay, so the plaintiffs wanted to check Easipower's creditworthiness. They contacted Easipower's bankers, who provided a credit reference. Unfortunately, Easipower did in fact default in their payment, so the plaintiffs sued the bankers.

The plaintiffs lost, because the reference was given with a disclaimer that it was 'without responsibility' (such a disclaimer would probably be inoperable under the Unfair Contract Terms Act 1977). However, the House of Lords stated *obiter* that there could be liability for negligent misrepresentation on the normal principles of tort, where there was a 'special relationship' between the parties.

It is still not completely clear what precisely is a 'special relationship' but, broadly speaking, it appears that such a relationship will only arise where the maker of a false statement has some knowledge or skill relevant to the subject matter of the contract, and can reasonably foresee that the other party will rely on the statement. This was held to be the case in **Esso Petroleum Co Ltd** *v* **Mardon** (1976). Esso's sales representative, who had 40 years' experience in the industry, had assured the defendant that a new garage development would be able to sell around 200,000 gallons of petrol a year. After this statement was made, the local authority insisted on changes to the plans of the site, and these meant the sales potential of the site was less than that detailed by the representative. Lack of care on Esso's behalf meant that this change was not communicated to the defendant, and in reliance on the representative's estimate, he signed a three-year tenancy agreement.

In fact petrol sales were less than half the estimate, and the defendants lost a lot of money. When Mardon fell into arrears with his rent, Esso sued him, so Mardon counter-claimed for damages for negligent misrepresentation. The court applied the **Hedley Byrne** principle and Mardon recovered on his counter-claim.

Misrepresentation under statute

Section 2(1) of the Misrepresentation Act 1967 states:

> Where a person has entered into a contract after a misrepresentation has been made to him by another party thereto and as a result thereof he has suffered loss, then, if the person making the misrepresentation would be liable to [pay] damages in respect thereof had the misrepresentation been made fraudulently, that person shall be so liable notwithstanding that the misrepresentation was not made fraudulently, unless he proves that he had reasonable ground to believe and did believe up to the time the contract was made that the facts represented were true.

Put more concisely, the section provides that where one party enters into a contract as a result of a misrepresentation by the other, the innocent party can claim damages, unless the other party can prove that at the time the contract was made, they believed the statement to be true, and had reasonable grounds for that belief. This effectively creates a type of negligent misrepresentation, but with the burden of proof reversed so that the person making the statement has to prove they were not negligent.

The fact that the party making the misrepresentation bears a heavy burden of proof under s. 2(1) is illustrated by **Howard Marine and Dredging Co Ltd** *v* **A Ogden and Sons (Excavations) Ltd** (1978). The plaintiffs were involved in major excavation work and needed to dispose of the clay that they had dug up. Having decided to dump it in the sea, they negotiated to hire two sea-going barges. The carrying capacity of these barges was crucial, since it would dictate how quickly the work could be done. The barge owner's representative misrepresented their carrying capacity, saying it was higher than it actually was; he had got his information from an official register of ships, which was usually accepted as an accurate source of such information, but on this occasion was wrong. The correct information was on file at the barge owners' head office. The Court of Appeal held that there was liability under s. 2(1); the defendants had failed to prove they had not been negligent. According to Bridge LJ, 'the statute imposes an absolute obligation not to state facts which the representor cannot prove he had reasonable ground to believe'.

A widely publicized case involving a s. 2(1) misrepresentation is that of **Spice Girls Ltd** *v* **Aprilia World Service** (2002). Spice Girls Ltd was a company formed to promote a pop group called the Spice Girls. At the start of 1998 there were five members of the group but one, Geri Halliwell, left on 29 May of that year. Aprilia is an Italian company which manufactures motorcycles and scooters for sale in Europe and the US. At the time of Ms Halliwell's departure the Spice Girls were in the final stages of a tour which, under a written agreement signed on 6 May 1998, was sponsored by Aprilia in return for the rights to use the Spice Girls' images and logos. The agreement referred to the group 'currently comprising' the five members and required the members to participate in filming a commercial for scooters which could be shown until March 1999. The commercial shoot took place on 4 May 1998.

Aprilia subsequently failed to pay for the advertising campaign and Spice Girls Ltd sued for payment. A counter-claim was brought by Aprilia that the contract had been induced by a misrepresentation. It argued that Ms Halliwell had declared her intention to leave the group before the agreement was signed and that Aprilia had not been told about this. As a result it had incurred expenditure and suffered loss by making the commercial shoot, and having to abandon plans for a limited edition of 'Spice Sonic' motor scooters featuring images of all five members. Aprilia asserted that, had it known of Ms Halliwell's intention to leave, it would not have signed the agreement.

The Court of Appeal ruled that by allowing a member of a singing group to participate in filming a television commercial, the group represented that she would remain a member for the period in which the commercial was to be used. As the group knew she intended to leave

during that period it was a misrepresentation. Spice Girls Ltd were ordered
to pay Aprilia damages.

Innocent misrepresentation

Before **Hedley Byrne** *v* **Heller**, the phrase 'innocent misrepresentation'
was used to describe all misrepresentations which were not fraudulent.
The appearance of two classes of negligent misrepresentation, one in
Hedley Byrne and the other in the Misrepresentation Act 1967, means
that innocent misrepresentation now applies only to misrepresentations
that are made entirely without fault. Where one party has entered into a
contract because of the other's false statement, the other party can avoid
liability for damages by proving that at the time the contract was made,
they believed the statement to be true, and had reasonable grounds
for that belief – this is the statutory defence laid down in s. 2(1) of the
Misrepresentation Act 1967.

Remedies for misrepresentation

The effect of a misrepresentation is generally to make a contract voidable,
rather than void, so the contract continues to exist unless and until the
innocent party chooses to have it set aside by means of rescission. Where
a contract is entirely executory, the innocent party may simply choose not
to perform their side of the bargain; the misrepresentation prevents the
other party from forcing the innocent party to perform. In some cases,
damages may be available, either instead of, or (in certain cases) as well
as, rescission.

Rescission

Rescission is an equitable remedy, which sets the contract aside and puts
the parties back in the position they were in before the contract was made.
It is available for all four types of misrepresentation.

An injured party who decides to rescind the contract can do so by
notifying the other party or, if this is not possible owing to the conduct of
the defaulting party, by taking some other reasonable action to indicate
the intention to rescind. In **Car and Universal Finance Co Ltd** *v* **Caldwell**
(1965) the defendant sold and delivered a car, and was paid by cheque.
The cheque bounced, by which time both the car and the buyer, whom
we will call A, had disappeared. The defendant immediately notified the
police and the Automobile Association, and asked the police to find the
car. While the police were investigating, A sold the car to a car dealer,
who knew that the car was not A's to sell. Finally, the car dealer sold the
car to the plaintiffs, who bought it in good faith. The Court of Appeal
held that by contacting the police and the Automobile Association, the

defendant had made his intention to rescind the contract sufficiently clear. As soon as he did this, the ownership of the car reverted to him. This meant that at the time the car was 'sold' to the plaintiffs, the car dealer had no legal right to sell it, and so it did not belong to the plaintiffs.

An injured party can also apply to the courts for a formal order of rescission, which provides that any property exchanged under the contract reverts to its former owner.

Indemnity payment

The courts can order a payment of money known as an indemnity. It is important to note that this payment is not damages; it is designed to put the parties back into their former positions, and is only available for obligations necessarily and inevitably created by the contract.

The distinction between an indemnity and damages can be seen in **Whittington** v **Seale-Hayne** (1900). The plaintiff was a poultry breeder, who carried out his business on a farm leased from the defendants. The defendants had told the plaintiff that the premises were in a hygienic condition, although this statement was not contained in the lease and therefore not a term of the contract. In fact, the water supply was poisoned. As a result, the poultry died, the manager of the farm became seriously ill and the local council ordered the plaintiff to repair the drains. The plaintiff claimed for his lost livestock, loss of profits, the cost of setting up the poultry farm and medical expenses, which amounted to £1,525. The defendants offered £20 to pay for the rent, rates and repairs to the drains (which under the terms of the lease the plaintiff was bound to pay). The court held that this was sufficient: the remainder of the plaintiff's claim did not inevitably arise under the terms of the lease, as the contract imposed no obligation to appoint a manager or stock the premises with poultry. Only expenses which inevitably arise from a contract will be compensated by indemnity (on the facts of this case, a different decision might be reached today if, for example, the defendants' statement was a negligent misrepresentation allowing an award of damages, but the case still provides valid authority on the distinction between damages and indemnity).

Where a misrepresentation is found to be fraudulent, an innocent party who rescinds the contract does not have to hand back whatever was received under the contract. So if someone defrauds an insurance company when taking out a policy, the insurance company is not only entitled to refuse payment of a claim against the policy, but also to keep any premiums paid.

Bars to rescission
There are some circumstances in which it is clearly unreasonable to put contracting parties back into their pre-contractual position, and in these

cases the injured party may lose the right to rescission. The three circumstances in which this may occur are where there is some practical reason why the parties cannot be restored to their original position, where a third party has gained rights under the contract, and where the innocent party affirms the contract.

Impossibility of restitution   The most common practical reason why parties cannot be restored to their original position is that the subject matter of the contract has been used up or destroyed. In **Vigers** *v* **Pike** (1842) the contract concerned a mine, and by the time rescission became an issue, it had been 'worked out' – there was nothing left in it to mine. Therefore rescission was impossible.

If, however, most of the subject matter of the contract can be restored to the other party, or if it can be restored, but not in its original condition, a court may order return of the property, along with financial compensation for the partial loss of value. This happened in **Erlanger** *v* **New Sombrero Phosphate Co** (1878) where the subject matter was again a mine, but where it had been only partially worked.

Third party rights   Rescission cannot be ordered where a third party has acquired rights under the contract. An example might be where A buys a car from B, who misrepresents its age, but A then sells the car on to C, without having rescinded the original contract with B. The car then rightfully belongs to C, so A cannot rescind the contract with B, since this would mean giving the car back. It is important to note that the rights acquired must be legal ones – if A had simply given the car to C, rather than selling it for consideration and so creating a new contract, A would have been able to rescind the original contract with B.

Affirmation   If an innocent party, once aware of the misrepresentation, states that they intend to continue with the contract, or does something which suggests an intention to continue with it, that party is considered to have affirmed the contract, and so will not be allowed to rescind.

Strictly speaking, simply doing nothing about a contract does not amount to affirmation, but the courts do appear to take into consideration the amount of time that elapses between a contract being made and a party asking for rescission. In **Leaf** *v* **International Galleries** (1950) the plaintiff bought a painting of Salisbury Cathedral, which the seller said was by Constable. When, five years later, he tried to sell it, he discovered that it was not a Constable at all, and so he immediately applied for the contract to be rescinded. The original seller's assertion that it was by Constable was not a term of the contract, and there was no suggestion that it had been made fraudulently.

The Court of Appeal refused to grant rescission, stating that: 'it behoves the purchaser either to verify or, as the case may be, to disprove the representation within a reasonable time, or else stand or fall by it.' It is important to remember that rescission is an equitable remedy, and the courts therefore have a discretion to refuse it where it is equitable to do so – in this case, for example, it might seem unfair to the original seller, who had not been trying to deceive the buyer, and, five years on, had every reason to believe that the picture had been accepted. The position may well have been different if the misrepresentation had been fraudulent – in that case, the courts would probably have taken account of the time that elapsed between discovery of the misrepresentation, and application for rescission, rather than the time since the contract was made.

In **Zanzibar** *v* **British Aerospace (Lancaster House) Ltd** (2000) the Zanzibar Government had purchased a jet from British Aerospace in 1992. They later failed to pay the full price of the plane and it was repossessed and sold. Several years after the original purchase of the plane, the Zanzibar Government initiated proceedings against British Aerospace, claiming that it had been induced to purchase the jet by virtue of representations made by British Aerospace as to the type of jet and its airworthiness, which were untrue. It sought to rescind the contract. The action was unsuccessful because the Zanzibar Government had delayed bringing the proceedings for several years after receiving the plane, so that their right to rescission had been lost.

Damages

Clearly there will be some cases in which the innocent party suffers a loss that cannot be put right by rescission, even if an indemnity payment is ordered. Suppose a food manufacturer buys a packaging machine, having been assured that it will keep products fresh for six months. In fact, the packaging only gives a shelf-life of two months, and everything goes off before it can be sold. Being told that the buyers can give back the machine and get their money back is not going to provide a satisfactory solution – their loss can only be compensated for by damages.

Where a party is induced to enter a contract by misrepresentation, they have a right to damages for any loss, unless the misrepresentation is innocent, where an award of damages is at the judge's discretion (see below).

Damages for misrepresentation are calculated using the tort measure, rather than the contract measure. Contract damages are designed to put claimants in the position they would have held if the contract had been performed as agreed, so they aim to provide any (foreseeable) financial benefit that successful performance of the contract would have provided. Tort damages aim to put the claimant back in the position held before the tort was committed (which, in the case of damages for misrepresentation, means the position at the time of the false statement before the contract was made), by making good any losses caused by the misrepresentation.

It is often said that as a result, tort protects a bad bargain and contract a good one. To illustrate the difference, imagine that Ann makes the following bad bargain. She wants to buy a particular type of vase to complete her collection of Wedgwood. Ben claims to be selling such a vase, which would normally be worth £500; realizing how much Ann wants it, Ben asks for £1,000 and Ann pays that sum. In fact, the vase is not a Wedgwood at all, and is only worth £100. On these facts, the damages for misrepresentation, calculated on the tort measure, would be £900 – Ann already has a vase worth £100, and receiving the £900 takes her as nearly as possible back to the position she started in. If contract damages were payable, she would receive £400 – if the contract had been performed as agreed (meaning if the misrepresentation had been true), she would have ended up with a vase worth £500, so the £400 tops up the value of the vase she has, to put her as near as possible to the position she would have been in. If, on the other hand, Ann had made a good bargain, contract damages would be more helpful. Suppose the vase would have been worth £1,500 if the representation was true, and Ann paid £1,000 for it, and then discovered that representation was false, and the vase was only worth £900. In tort, all she can recover is £100, whereas in contract she could recover £600.

Remoteness of damages

The courts will make a more generous award of damages where there has been fraudulent misrepresentation and misrepresentation under s. 2(1) of the Misrepresentation Act 1967, than for common law negligent and innocent misrepresentations. This is because in the former they apply a generous remoteness test, whereas in the latter the remoteness test is narrower. In the case of **Doyle v Olby (Ironmongers) Ltd** (1969) it was stated that for fraudulent misrepresentation a person can be compensated for 'all the actual damage directly flowing from the fraudulent inducement'. It does not matter that the loss was not foreseeable, essentially all that is required is that the misrepresentation caused the loss. So a person claiming for fraudulent misrepresentation will frequently be able to claim for lost profits.

The House of Lords was concerned with the calculation of damages for fraudulent misrepresentation in **Smith New Court Securities Ltd v Scrimgeour Vickers (Asset Management) Ltd** (1996). The plaintiffs had bought over £23 million of shares in the Italian company Ferranti at a price of 82.25p per share. They were induced to buy the shares by fraudulent representations that there were other possible purchasers actively in the market, which was not actually the case. At the date of the transaction, the shares were trading on the Stock Exchange at about 78p per share. Unknown to either party, the shares in the company were worth far less than the market price, because Ferranti had itself been the subject of a highly sophisticated fraud by a gentleman who had managed to sell Ferranti a worthless company for a large amount of money. Once this became known, the market in Ferranti shares took a steep downward turn and the plaintiffs were forced to sell their shares at a loss in excess of £11 million.

The question before the House of Lords was whether the plaintiffs' damages should be restricted to 4.25p per share which it had paid above the market price, or whether it could recover the whole of the loss it had suffered, including the much bigger loss caused by the hidden defect in the shares. The House held that the plaintiffs could recover the larger sum, stating that the damages had to be assessed to include all the losses flowing naturally from the original fraud.

There has been much debate as to the appropriate remoteness test for damages awarded under s. 2(1) of the Misrepresentation Act 1967. In **Royscot Trust Ltd** *v* **Rogerson** (1991) the Court of Appeal held that the same remoteness test should apply as for fraudulent misrepresentation. The result is that the measure of damages under s. 2(1) is now as good as where there is a fraud, without the difficulties of having to prove a fraud. In **Smith New Court Securities Ltd** *v* **Citibank** the House of Lords appeared to have reservations about the correctness of this approach.

The remoteness test for damages for common law negligent misrepresentation is that the loss must have been a reasonably foreseeable consequence of the misrepresentation (**The Wagon Mound (No 1)**). Unlike the position with regard to fraudulent misrepresentation, it is clear that liability is limited to the position assessed at the date of the wrong. The same remoteness test applies to awards of damages for innocent misrepresentation.

Damages or rescission?

Rescission is available to the innocent party regardless of which category the misrepresentation falls into. In the past, damages were only available for fraudulent misrepresentation. The case of **Hedley Byrne** made it clear that damages were available for negligent misrepresentation at common law, and the Misrepresentation Act 1967 further extended the availability of damages. First, under s. 2(1), a misrepresentor will be liable in damages unless they can prove reasonable grounds for believing the statement to be true. Secondly, under s. 2(2), the court has a discretion to award damages instead of rescission where the misrepresentation was not fraudulent 'if of the opinion that it would be equitable to do so'.

The practical result seems to be that there is a right to damages (assuming loss can be proved) for fraudulent and both types of negligent misrepresentation. Where a misrepresentation is innocent, the award of damages is at the court's discretion.

	Fraudulent misrepresentation: *Derry v Peek*	Negligent misrepresentation at common law: *Hedley Byrne v Heller*	Misrepresentation under s. 2(1) Misrepresentation Act 1967	Innocent misrepresentation
Rescission	Yes	Yes	Yes	Yes
Indemnity payment	Yes	Yes	Yes	Yes
Damages	Yes. Liable for all the actual damage directly flowing from the misrepresentation.	Yes. Liable for any loss that was a reasonably foreseeable consequence of the misrepresentation.	Yes. Liable for all the actual damage directly flowing from the misrepresentation.	Yes. Damages instead of rescission can be awarded under s. 2(2) of the Misrepresentation Act 1967.

Figure 9.1 Misrepresentation and remedies

Misrepresentation and terms

Section 1 of the Misrepresentation Act 1967 provides that where a misrepresentation becomes a term of the contract, the innocent party may bring an action for both misrepresentation and breach of contract.

Exemption clauses and misrepresentation

Under s. 3 of the 1967 Act, as amended by the Unfair Contract Terms Act 1977 (UCTA), exemption clauses which attempt to exclude or limit liability for misrepresentations are operative only if reasonable under the terms of UCTA (see p. 130 above).

This provision was applied in **Walker** *v* **Boyle** (1982). The seller of the house told the buyer that there were no disputes regarding the boundaries of the property. Unknown to the seller, this was not true. The innocent misrepresentation appeared to entitle the buyer to rescind the contract, but the contract contained a clause stating that 'no error, mis-statement or omission in any preliminary answer concerning the property . . . shall annul the sale'. The court granted rescission, stating that the clause was unreasonable.

ANSWERING QUESTIONS

1 Shirley wishes to set up an airplane service for business people flying between London and Rome. She answers an advertisement in a trade paper for the sale of a light aircraft. Two weeks before completing the contract Shirley

is advised by the seller, Dorianne, that the fuel capacity of the aircraft will enable her to fly between the two cities without the need to refuel. She purchases the airplane for £500,000 and sets up her business, Exec Jet Ltd. On a trial flight to Rome, she is forced to land and refuel before she reaches her destination. Further investigation reveals that the aircraft is only suitable for short flights and does not have the capacity to fly the distance she requires on a single tank of petrol. As a result Shirley is forced to abandon her business plans. The aircraft is worth £100,000 less than Shirley paid for it and, in addition, she has incurred considerable expense in setting up her business, which was expected to earn a substantial profit.

Advise Shirley whether she can recover any or all of her losses. *Oxford*

The main issue here is misrepresentation: Dorianne has made an untrue statement of fact which induced Shirley to enter the contract. Once you have established this, you need to look at the possible remedies. First, Shirley could rescind the contract, but this alone would not go far to solve her problems; she would get her £500,000 back, but would still have lost both the money spent on setting up the business and the potential profit. Nor would an indemnity be any help, as the case of **Whittington** shows, because none of her other losses arose inevitably from her contract with Dorianne.

As a result, Shirley will want to claim damages, and her ability to do this will depend to some extent on the type of misrepresentation. If Dorianne made the misrepresentation innocently, Shirley will not be able to claim damages as of right. However, the Misrepresentation Act 1967 and the case of **Howard Marine** make it clear that it will be difficult for Dorianne to prove negligent misrepresentation. If she cannot, the court has a discretion to award damages where it would be equitable to do so, so Shirley may succeed in this claim. If the misrepresentation was made fraudulently or negligently under the Misrepresentation Act 1967 (you should briefly define each type), Shirley definitely will be able to claim damages.

You now need to consider how much of her loss she will be able to claim in damages, bearing in mind that damages for misrepresentation are calculated using the tort measure, so the aim is to put Shirley in the position she held before the contract was made.

You should also consider the possibility that Dorianne's statement may be a term of the contract (applying the common law rules on incorporation), and point out that if this were the case, Dorianne's breach of that term would allow Shirley to reclaim all her foreseeable losses, because of the fact that contract damages are calculated to put her in the position she would have enjoyed had the contract been performed as agreed.

2 Critically assess the remedies available to a party who has made a contract on the basis of a misrepresentation.

The first thing to note here is that this question is very specific. However much you know about what misrepresentation is, if you know very little about the **remedies** for misrepresentation, then choose another question. You can pick up some marks at the beginning of your essay for a **brief** definition of misrepresentation, including an explanation of the different types, as defined in the Misrepresentation Act 1967 and common law, but you must devote the bulk of your essay to remedies.

Note too that your examination is required to be critical – merely listing the remedies is not going to get you a good mark. As well as pointing out any problems with remedies for rescission – such as the apparent unfairness in **Leaf** – you could, for example, contrast the availability of rescission and the availability and measure of damages for misrepresentation with those for breach of contract, pointing out the way in which tort protects a bad bargain and contract a good one.

10 Mistake

As we have seen, vitiating factors operate to prevent a contract being fully binding where one party has not given genuine consent, of their own free will. From this it might appear obvious that where one party (or both) is mistaken about some aspect of the contract being entered into, that party cannot be said to be consenting to it – they think the consent is to something different. However, the common law rules of contract take a rather restrictive view of the sort of mistake which negatives consent, and there are many types of mistake which, to the ordinary person, would suggest that one party was not truly agreeing to the contract, but which would not in law prevent the contract from being legally binding.

The common law rules on mistake can operate rather harshly, but they are mitigated to some extent by the fact that the courts have developed parallel rules in equity: where a mistake will not make a contract void under common law, it will sometimes make it voidable in equity.

General principles

There are two types of mistake, common mistake and cross-purposes mistake. We will discuss each in turn, but the following general rules apply to both.

Objective principle

As always in contract law, when deciding whether or not there has been a mistake sufficient to make the contract void, the courts will look at the facts objectively. They do not ask what the parties themselves believed they were agreeing to, but what an onlooker would have thought each was agreeing to.

In **Smith *v* Hughes** (1871) the defendant wanted to buy some old oats – for some reason new ones were of no use to him. The plaintiff apparently knew this, but still sold him new oats. There was no fraud, and the plaintiff had not done anything to suggest to the defendant that the oats were old but, nevertheless, that was what the defendant believed he was buying. The court held that the contract was binding, despite the defendant's mistake, because any reasonable onlooker would conclude that the parties were in agreement about what was being sold. Blackburn J said:

> If whatever a man's real intention may be, he so conducts himself that a reasonable man would believe that he was assenting to the terms proposed by the other party, and that other party upon that belief enters into the contract with him, the man thus conducting himself would be equally bound as if he had intended to agree to the other party's terms.

The mistake must precede the contract

In order to make a contract void, a mistake must be made before the contract is completed. In **Amalgamated Investment & Property Co Ltd** *v* **John Walker & Sons Ltd** (1977) a contract was made for the sale of a warehouse for £1,710,000. The sellers knew that the purchasers were buying the warehouse with the intention of redeveloping it. The day after the contract was signed, the Department of the Environment made the property a listed building (a device used to protect buildings of important historical interest from inappropriate alterations). This made it more difficult for the buyers to get permission to redevelop; without such permission, the warehouse would only have been worth £210,000. Neither party had been aware that the Department of the Environment was going to list the building.

The Court of Appeal held that the contract was valid; at the time of the agreement both parties were perfectly correct in their belief that the building was not listed, so there was no operative mistake (in fact it is quite likely that the mistake made in this case would not have made the contract void even if it had been made before the contract was completed).

Mistake must induce the contract

A mistake can only negate consent if it induced the mistaken party to enter into the contract. If a party thinks there is a possibility that they may be mistaken, but takes the risk, or is indifferent about that particular matter, the validity of the contract will not be affected.

Mistake of fact or law

In the past, only a mistake of fact could affect the validity of a contract, a mistake of law was not sufficient. Thus, if you made a mistake as to the cost of an item in a shop, you might expect the shop to refund the excess amount when you discovered the mistake. However, in law, the shop would only have been obliged to refund you if you had made a mistake of fact (you thought the price was £50 when in fact it was £5). It would not have been obliged to refund the money if you had made a mistake of law (you thought you had to pay VAT on top of the price of the item). The Law

Commission has pointed out in a recent report, *Restitution: Mistakes of Law and Ultra Vires Public Authority Receipts and Payments*, that this distinction was 'notoriously difficult to make' and led to a 'perceived unfairness'. The House of Lords abolished the distinction in 1998 in **Kleinwort Benson Ltd v Lincoln City Council**. It ruled that the remedy of restitution would now be available where there had been a mistake of law (for a discussion of restitution, see p. 283). A bank had paid money to local authorities under certain financial transactions which had been thought to be legal, but were later ruled by the courts to be illegal. The banks had made a mistake of law rather than fact in handing over this money, but the House of Lords accepted that the local authorities should pay the money back. They justified the overturning of the established principle that mistake of law was insufficient for these purposes, on the ground that the distinction between a mistake of law and a mistake of fact was not always clear cut, and that in order to do justice the money should be paid back. Other Commonwealth countries had already abolished the rule against mistakes of law and no such rule existed in many European systems. The experience of these countries showed that the fear of a flood of litigation resulting was unfounded so the House of Lords was prepared to adopt this reform.

One of the first cases to explore the implications of the House of Lords' ruling in **Kleinwort Benson Ltd v Lincoln City Council** was **Nurdin v Peacock** (1999). In that case the claimant had leased premises belonging to the defendant. The lease provided that an annual rental had to be paid of £207,000, which was payable in quarterly instalments. An additional £59,000 rent had to be paid for the fourth and fifth years of the lease. There was to be a rent review at the end of the fifth year, when the rent could be increased. No rent review took place, so the rent due reverted to the earlier £207,000. Nevertheless, the defendant continued to demand, and the claimant continued to pay, rent at the higher rate which had been payable in years four and five. Two years later, the claimant realized his mistake and informed the defendant that he would pay only at the lower rate and would set off the overpayments already made against future rent. Soon afterwards, the claimant received legal advice to continue paying at the higher rate and without set-off until the matter had been resolved through arbitration or through the courts, because otherwise the lease might be terminated. The legal advice was that, if successful in those proceedings, the claimant would be entitled to a full refund of any overpayment. The claimant thus paid, in May 1997, the quarterly rental at the higher rate. In fact the claimant had no legal right to recover that overpayment since it was aware that it might not have been due. In the proceedings, the claimant sought to recover all the overpayments. The court had no difficulty in ordering repayment of the excess payments made during the first two years before the claimant realized that he had made a mistake. These payments had been made under a mistake of fact and had to be paid back. The difficult issue was the payment made in May 1997.

At that time the claimant was no longer suffering from a mistake of fact, as he knew that the money was not due. The claimant sought to recover the overpayment made in May 1997 on the basis that he had been labouring under a mistake of law, namely that he would be entitled to recover that overpayment. The defendant counter-argued that money paid under a mistake of law could only be reclaimed if the mistake consisted of the claimant believing he was liable in law to make the payment. This argument of the defendant was rejected by the High Court. The money had been made under a mistake of law and, therefore, since **Kleinwort Benson Ltd** *v* **Lincoln City Council**, it was recoverable. It made no difference that the claimant's mistake was not about its liability to make the payment but about its right to recover the payment, since it was undesirable for the issue of recoverability to turn on an analysis as to the precise nature of the mistake. The key issue was that the payment would not have been made but for the mistake of law.

While this is a sensible approach, the decision does look peculiar if its logic is followed through. The legal advice to the claimant was that overpayment in May 1997 was recoverable. The advice was wrong. The claimant followed that advice. Therefore, the claimant paid under a mistake of law. Therefore, the money was recoverable as paid under a mistake of law. So in actual fact, the advice was right. So, no mistake was made. The court held that that unusual logical problem did not stand in the way of the conclusion it had reached.

Common mistake at common law

This is also known as identical mistake, shared mistake or mistake nullifying consent. In this situation, both parties make the same mistake – for example, if Ann buys a painting from Ben, which both parties believe is by Picasso, but which is in fact a fake, they have made a shared mistake. A shared mistake will only render a contract void if there is:

- a mistake as to the existence of the subject matter;
- a mistake as to the ownership of the subject matter; or
- a fundamental mistake.

Mistake as to the existence of the subject matter

This kind of mistake will usually concern goods to be sold – if, for example, A purports to sell her car to B, and it is then discovered that the car has been destroyed by fire, the contract will not be valid. However, it applies equally to other kinds of subject matter. In **Scott** *v* **Coulson** (1903) a life insurance policy was taken out, covering a Mr A.T. Death, who both parties believed was alive. In fact, Mr Death was, appropriately enough, dead. The agreement was held to be void at common law and the contract was set aside.

It is not always the case that non-existence of the subject matter will render a contract void, and there are several cases which make this area of the law difficult and rather unclear. A leading case is **Couturier** *v* **Hastie** (1856), which involved a contract to buy a cargo of corn which, at the time the contract was made, was supposed to be on a ship sailing to England from the Mediterranean port of Salonica. In fact, by that time, the corn had already been sold by the master of the ship, to a buyer in Tunis, because it had begun to go off – this was a common occurrence in the days before refrigerated transport, and the master's action was the usual solution. As far as the contract was concerned, the corn had therefore ceased to exist.

The sellers claimed that the buyer still had to pay; this may seem odd, but is explained by the fact that in such a transaction, which was always risky, the buyer would usually take out insurance against the goods not reaching their destination, and could simply reclaim the price paid. In this case the buyer did not have the appropriate insurance. The House of Lords held that the buyer did not have to pay for the corn: the contract was clearly assumed by both parties to refer to 'goods supposed to exist', and not to 'goods lost or not lost' (the terminology usually used in marine insurance policies). The court did not specifically mention mistake as to the existence of the subject matter, but that is widely thought to be the basis of the decision.

The decision in **Couturier** *v* **Hastie** was put into statutory form in s. 6 of the Sale of Goods Act 1893. This provision (now contained in s. 6 of the Sale of Goods Act 1979) states that: 'Where there is a contract for the sale of specific goods, and the goods without the knowledge of the seller have perished at the time when the contract is made, the contract is void.'

A contrasting case is **McRae** *v* **Commonwealth Disposals Commission** (1951), decided by the Australian courts. The defendants sold the plaintiff a wrecked oil tanker which was said to be 'on Jourmand Reef'. In fact the oil tanker did not exist, but the plaintiff did not discover this until he had spent a great deal of time and money searching for it. Consequently, he brought an action to recover the money he had spent on the search. Citing **Couturier** *v* **Hastie**, the defendants argued that since there was no tanker, the contract was void, and they owed him nothing. However, the High Court of Australia rejected this view. They stated that the important issue, in both **Couturier** and the case before them, was whether the contract contained an implied condition that the subject matter was in existence. They pointed out that in **Couturier**, the House of Lords had examined the terms of the contract, and concluded from them that the sale concerned a specific cargo, believed to exist, and this had been the basis of the decision.

On the facts of the case before them, the Australian court concluded that it had been an implied term of the contract that the tanker existed: 'if [the plaintiffs] had been asked, they would certainly not have said "Of course, if there is no tanker, there is no contract".' The defendants had breached that term, and so the plaintiff could claim damages. The court's decision may well have been influenced by the fact that the defendants appeared to have been grossly negligent on the facts – they were in possession of information which should have told them there was no tanker. As the court pointed out: 'In those circumstances it seems out of the question that they should be able to assert that no contract was concluded.'

Some guidelines on this issue were provided in **Associated Japanese Bank** *v* **Crédit du Nord** (1988). The case concerned a rather complex financial arrangement, the effect of which was that Associated Japanese Bank (AJB) bought some machines from a client, and leased them back to him, under a guarantee from Crédit du Nord (CDN). The client went bankrupt, and AJB attempted to sue CDN on the guarantee. It then turned out that in fact the machines had never existed and the whole scheme had been a fraud perpetrated by the client. The court held that the machines were security for the guarantee and were fundamental to the contract of guarantee; the fact that they did not exist made the contract void. They also laid down some basic rules as to when a mistake as to subject matter will render a contract void. The important factors were that the mistake must be substantially shared by both parties and it must render the subject matter 'essentially and radically different from the subject matter which the parties believed to exist'. The court pointed out that the rules on mistake as to subject matter were designed to deal with the impact of exceptional circumstances, rather as the doctrine of frustration does, the implication being that they are not to be used as an excuse to get out of undesirable or inconvenient obligations.

Mistake as to title

Very rarely, a situation will arise in which one party agrees to transfer property to the other, but unknown to both of them, the latter already owns that property. In such a case, the contract will be void for mistake. In **Cooper** *v* **Phibbs** (1867) the House of Lords set aside an agreement whereby one party had agreed to lease a fishery to the other, but unknown to either, the fishery already belonged to the party taking out the lease.

Fundamental mistake

Where the parties to the contract have made a fundamental mistake, this can render the contract void. The leading case is the House of Lords' judgment in **Bell** *v* **Lever Brothers** (1932). In that case, Bell and Snelling had been appointed chairman and vice-chairman of a company controlled by Lever Brothers. Their contracts were for five years but, before that time was up, a company merger occurred, which meant that there was no longer enough work for the two men. Consequently, at Lever Brothers' suggestion, Bell and Snelling agreed that their contracts should be terminated, and that they would be paid a total of £50,000 compensation.

Lever Brothers later discovered that both men had committed breaches of their contract, and so could have been dismissed without compensation. The company then sued the men to get the £50,000 back, arguing that their agreement was void for mistake, because they had made the compensation agreements in the belief that the service contracts were valid, when in fact they were voidable because of the breaches by Bell and Snelling. Both men had forgotten about the breaches, so they too were under the impression that their contracts were valid, and had not tried to defraud Lever in any way.

The House of Lords rejected Lever Brothers' argument, stating that the mistake made was not sufficiently fundamental to the parties' agreement to render the contract void. Nevertheless, the opinions given in the case clearly recognize that some mistakes as to quality may be sufficiently fundamental to render a contract void.

A rare recent example of a fundamental mistake rendering a contract void is the Court of Appeal's judgment in **Nutt** v **Read** (2000). The claimants had made two agreements with the defendants. First, they had agreed to sell a chalet to the defendants. Secondly, they had agreed to rent out to the defendants its pitch on a caravan site in Surrey for a monthly rent. Both parties to the contract had made a common mistake that the chalet was a chattel which could be sold independently of its pitch. The defendants failed to pay the rent and the claimants sought to eject them from the site. The defendants argued in their defence that the contracts were void for common mistake because the chalet could not in law be sold independently of its pitch. The Court of Appeal held that the first agreement for the sale of the chalet was void at common law due to the fundamental mistake of thinking that the chalet could be sold separately from the land – **Bell** v **Lever Brothers** was applied. The purchase price therefore had to be returned to the defendants. The second agreement to rent out its pitch was voidable for mistake in equity (discussed on p. 169).

In most cases a mistake as to the quality of the subject matter will not affect the validity of a contract. This is so even where the quality of the goods is a major factor in the decision to buy. In **Harrison & Jones** v **Bunten & Lancaster** (1953) the contract concerned the sale of some kapok (used to fill stuffed toys), which both parties believed to be of a certain standard of purity. In fact it fell below this standard and, as a result, was of no use to the buyer, but the contract was nevertheless held to be valid.

Occasionally a mistake as to the quality of the subject matter of the contract will be sufficiently fundamental to render the contract void. In **Bell** v **Lever Brothers Ltd** Lord Atkin said that a contract would be void if both parties were mistaken 'as to the existence of some quality which makes the thing without the quality essentially different from the thing as it was believed to be'.

In **Nicholson & Venn** v **Smith-Marriott** (1947) the defendants put up for auction some table napkins, described as 'with crest of Charles I and the authentic property of that monarch'. The napkins were bought, on the strength of this description, for £787 10s. They turned out to be Georgian, and consequently only worth £105. The buyer recovered damages for breach of contract, but Hallett J also suggested that the contract could have been treated by the buyer as void for mistake. If that approach had been taken, he said, the question would have been what the parties intended to achieve by the transaction. If their intentions were simply to buy and sell antique table linen, that was what they had done, and the fact that they had been mistaken as to its exact age, provenance or value would not be fundamental. If, by contrast, they intended to buy and sell an item associated with Charles I, their mistake **was** fundamental, and so made the contract void.

Common mistake in equity

There is some uncertainty as to the impact of equity where there is a common mistake. Under a traditional view of equity one might expect it to take a more lenient approach and allow a common mistake to render a contract voidable in circumstances where the common law was not prepared to render the contract void. However, in **Solle** _v_ **Butcher** (1950) Lord Denning laid down a test for common mistake in equity which required a fundamental mistake which appears to be the same test laid down in **Bell** _v_ **Lever Brothers** for the common law. Lord Denning stated:

> A contract is also liable in equity to be set aside if the parties were under a common misapprehension either as to facts or as to their relative and respective rights, provided that the misapprehension was fundamental and that the party seeking to set it aside was not himself at fault.

The problem with this approach is that it is difficult to see when the equitable doctrine should apply and when the common law should apply. On the facts of the case it seems that Lord Denning felt that as a matter of public policy the contract should not be void under common law, but equity could still apply. The defendant had agreed to let a flat to the plaintiff, at a rent of £250 a year. Both parties believed that the flat was not subject to the Rent Acts, but they were mistaken; under the Acts, the maximum rent to be charged was £140. Lord Denning felt that the contract should not be rendered void under common law because: 'it would mean that in the many cases where the parties mistakenly think the house is outside the Rent Acts when it is really within them, the tenancy would be a nullity, and the tenant would have to go, with the result that tenants would not dare to seek to have their rents reduced . . . lest they be turned out.' Consequently, equity stepped in to do justice because it could rescind the contract on terms. The Court of Appeal ruled that either the plaintiff should give up the flat or stay on at the maximum rent chargeable under the Rent Acts.

Thus, an advantage of a finding of common mistake in equity, as opposed to common law, is that the contract can be rescinded on terms, rather than the all-or-nothing approach of the common law. So, for example, in **Nutt** *v* **Read** (discussed on p. 168), the purchasers of the chalet had spent over £15,000 doing improvements to the chalet. When the contract for the rental of the pitch was rescinded in equity for common mistake, the court could have chosen to ask the sellers to compensate this money that had been spent on the chalet. In fact, the defendants had not asked for this compensation and the Court of Appeal therefore decided not to order it.

In a recent case, **Great Peace Shipping Ltd v Tsavliris Salvage (International) Ltd** (2001) Toulson J in the High Court expressed his confusion over the relationship of the common law and equity. He essentially seems to have concluded that there was no role for equity, because wherever the contract was valid under the common law it should also be valid under equity. With respect, the authors prefer the view that while Lord Denning spoke of a fundamental mistake being required for equity, this should be interpreted less strictly in equity than for the common law. Also, there should be occasions where, as a matter of public policy, equity, with its ability to rescind a contract on terms, could render a contract voidable, where the common law has not been prepared to intervene.

▶ Cross-purposes mistake at common law

This is also known as non-identical mistake and mistake negativing consent. It occurs where each party has a different view of the situation – where, for example, Ann thinks she is buying Ben's Rolls-Royce, when in fact it is his Daimler that is for sale. Two types of cross-purposes mistake are possible:

- *mutual mistakes*, where each party makes a mistake but they are different mistakes; and
- *unilateral mistakes*, where only one party is mistaken. The other either knows of the mistake or ought to know of it.

It is rare for a cross-purposes mistake to make a contract void at common law. The courts will simply decide whether a reasonable onlooker would have understood the contract to mean what one party thought it meant, or what the other party thought it meant. In **Wood** *v* **Scarth** (1855) the defendant was going to lease a pub to the plaintiff for £63 a year, and thought that his clerk had made it clear to the plaintiff that there would be an additional one-off charge of £500. In fact the clerk had failed to do this. The court held that the agreement was valid: as far as any reasonable onlooker was concerned, the defendant had made a precise and unambiguous offer, which the plaintiff had accepted, and the mistake did not negative that.

There are three situations where a cross-purposes mistake can make a contract void:

- the mistake was negligently induced by the other party;
- the parties are at such cross-purposes that a reasonable observer would not be able to say what they had agreed; and
- one party knew of the other's mistake (a unilateral mistake). A unilateral mistake will only make a contract void if it concerns the identity of one of the parties or the terms of the contract, and is fundamental to the contract. A unilateral mistake about the quality of the subject matter of the contract is not sufficient.

An example of parties at complete cross-purposes occurred in **Scriven Bros & Co** *v* **Hindley & Co** (1913). Bales of hemp and tow were put up for auction. Both hemp and tow are fibres used for making rope, but tow is of much lower quality than hemp. They were put into two lots, one of 176 bales of hemp, the other of the same amount of tow. Unusually, both lots bore the same markings. When the lot of tow came up for sale, the plaintiff thought it was hemp, and bid a price that was appropriate for hemp, which, not surprisingly, was immediately accepted. The contract was therefore concluded with one party thinking, correctly, that he was selling tow, and the other, wrongly, that he was buying hemp – neither was aware that they were at cross-purposes. It was obvious that there was no genuine consensus between the parties, but was there a contract when the transaction was viewed objectively? The court thought not as, in the circumstances, it was impossible to say that one or other commodity was being contracted for.

Unilateral mistake over the terms of the contract

Where one party is mistaken as to the terms of the contract and the other knows this, the contract will be void, regardless of whether the term is fundamental. In **Hartog** *v* **Colin and Shields** (1939) the defendants had some animal skins for sale, which they intended to sell at a certain price 'per piece', as was apparently the custom in the trade. By mistake, they offered them at the same price 'per pound' instead of 'per piece', which, at about three skins to the pound, obviously worked out much cheaper. The buyers accepted this offer. When they realized their mistake, the sellers refused to deliver the skins and were sued by the buyers for breach of contract. The court held that there was no contract, because the buyers were aware of the seller's mistake.

By contrast, in **Centrovincial Estates plc** *v* **Merchant Investors Insurance Co Ltd** (1983) a landlord offered, by mistake, to renew his tenant's lease at a rent of £65,000 a year; he had meant to offer it at £126,000. The tenant, unaware of the mistake, accepted the offer. The Court of Appeal held that the mistake had no effect upon the contract, because the tenant did not know of it, and the contract was therefore binding.

Unilateral mistake involving mistaken identity

Unilateral mistake is frequently relied upon where there is a mistake as to the identity of one of the contracting parties. A genuine mistake of this nature where the identity of the other party was of fundamental importance will render the contract void. The law draws a fine distinction between where a person intended to contract with someone else (the mistake renders the contract void), and a mistake which is merely as to a person's attributes rather than as to their identity. A mistake as to a person's attributes, such as thinking that they are creditworthy when they are not, will leave the contract intact.

Intention to contract with someone else

The main issue that the court will take into account in order to determine whether a person intended to contract with someone else, or whether they have merely made a mistake as to a person's attributes, is whether they made the contract at a distance or face to face. Where the parties made a contract at a distance (such as through the post or over the telephone) it will be easier to establish a mistake as to identity, because the identity of the person placing an order has to be known in order to deliver the goods and it is therefore easier to prove that it was of crucial importance to the making of the contract.

In **Cundy** _v_ **Lindsay** (1878) the plaintiffs received an order by post for a large number of handkerchiefs from a Mr Blenkarn of 37 Wood Street, Cheapside. Mr Blenkarn rented a room at that address, and further down the road, at number 123, were the offices of a highly respectable firm called Blenkiron & Co. On the order for the handkerchiefs, Blenkarn signed his name so that it looked like Blenkiron. The plaintiffs sent off the goods, addressed to Blenkiron & Co; Mr Blenkarn received them, and by the time the fraud was discovered, he had sold most of them to the defendant, Cundy, who bought them in good faith. The plaintiffs sued the defendant to get the goods back, and whether they could be successful in this depended on whether there was a contract between the plaintiffs and Blenkarn. If there was, Blenkarn would have become the owner of the goods and so would have been able to transfer ownership to the defendant; if not, the plaintiffs would be able to get their goods back. The House of Lords held that there was no contract between Blenkarn and the plaintiffs, because they had intended all along to deal with Blenkiron & Co, and not with a Mr Blenkarn, of whom they had after all never heard. The court concluded 'between him and them there was no consensus of mind which could lead to . . . any contract whatsoever'.

The fact that the parties contracted at a distance merely creates a presumption that the individual's identity was fundamental, and the facts of the case can rebut this presumption. In **King's Norton Metal Co** _v_ **Edridge, Merrett & Co Ltd** (1897) a Mr Wallis ordered by post some goods from the plaintiffs, using the name 'Hallam & Co', and placing the order on stationery showing a large factory, and claiming that 'Hallam & Co' had depots and agencies in Belfast, Lille and Ghent. The goods were delivered but never paid for. Again, the issue was whether there was a contract between them. The Court of Appeal held that there was: the plaintiffs intended to contract with the writer of the letter, and that they had done. The importance of their mistake did not concern the identity of the customer, but his attributes, in particular his credit-worthiness. **Cundy** was distinguishable because in that case the plaintiffs had a different customer in mind, not merely a different type of customer. The mistake in **King's Norton** was not sufficient to render the contract void, though in fact the agreement would be voidable for fraudulent misrepresentation.

Where the contract was made face to face the courts are likely to conclude that the parties intended to contract with the person in front of them and the only mistake was a mistake as to attributes. An illustration of this is **Lewis** *v* **Averay** (1972). The plaintiff had advertised his car for sale. A potential buyer introduced himself as Richard Greene, a film actor who was well-known at the time for playing the part of Robin Hood. Agreeing to buy the car, he signed the cheque 'R.A. Green', and when the plaintiff asked for evidence of identity, he produced a Pinewood Studios pass with his name and photograph on it. The plaintiff handed over the car, but a few days later was told by his bank that the cheque was worthless. In the meantime, the fake Richard Greene had sold the car to Mr Averay (who bought it in good faith and had no knowledge of the fraud) and disappeared. The question then became whether or not Mr Lewis's contract with the fake Richard Greene was valid; if it was, title to the car could pass to Mr Averay through the subsequent sale; if it was not, the car still belonged to Mr Lewis.

The Court of Appeal found that there was a contract, and Lord Denning based his judgment on the fact that Mr Lewis had reached an agreement with the person who turned up on his doorstep, and there was no evidence that he intended to contract with someone other than that person. He also seemed to be influenced by the idea that it was wrong to deprive the innocent purchaser, when he had 'acted with complete circumspection', and it was the seller who allowed the rogue to take the car. The result was that the contract between the seller and the fraudster was voidable for misrepresentation, but as he had failed to avoid it before a third party, Mr Averay, acquired rights in the property, title to the car had indeed passed to Mr Averay and the car was his to keep.

A second reason for the decision in **Lewis** *v* **Averay** was given by Megaw LJ, who based his judgment on the fact that the identity of the buyer was not of fundamental importance to Mr Lewis; the only importance was that he assumed a famous film actor would be credit-worthy. This was not enough to make the contract void for mistake.

Another case involving a contract made face to face is **Phillips *v* Brooks Ltd** (1919). A rogue went into a jewellery shop and examined some jewellery. He said his name was Sir George Bullough, and gave an address in St James' Square. He was allowed to take away the ring on credit without paying for it after the plaintiff had checked that a Sir George Bullough lived at the address given. The rogue then sold the ring to a third party and failed to pay for it. The plaintiff brought an action to recover the ring from the third party. The court rejected the claim, stating that the contract was valid as the plaintiff had intended to make the contract with the person in front of him in the shop. The mistake had been merely about the creditworthiness of the rogue, rather than as to his identity.

Again, the fact that the parties contracted face to face merely creates a presumption that any mistake about the other contracting party was merely a mistake as to attributes. This presumption can be rebutted by the specific facts of a case. Thus in **Ingram *v* Little** (1961) the Ingrams were two elderly sisters who advertised a car for sale. A man came to see it, and made an offer, stating that he would pay by cheque. The sisters refused this, and the man then gave the name of P. Hutchinson, and an address. The sisters checked the telephone directory, and finding that a P. Hutchinson was listed at that address, agreed to take the cheque. The cheque bounced, and the sisters discovered that the man was not who he claimed to be but, by this time, he had disappeared and the car had been sold to a dealer. The court held that the sisters' contract with the fraudster was void for mistake. They had made their offer to P. Hutchinson and, since the fraudster was someone else, there was no offer for him to accept. The judgment stated that the mere presence of an individual did not necessarily mean that the contract was being made with him or her: 'if he was disguised in appearance to represent someone else, and the other party, deceived by his appearance, dealt with him on the basis that he was that person and would not have contracted had he known the truth', there was no contract. Therefore, the court held, the same should apply where a person uses words to disguise their true identity.

Innocent purchasers of dishonestly obtained goods

A classic problem that has come to the courts is where a fraudster has approached a supplier of goods, and pretended to be another person who is credit-worthy. The supplier then hands over the goods on credit. The fraudster immediately sells the goods to an innocent purchaser and disappears without trace. The courts are left with a dispute between two innocent parties (the supplier of the goods and the innocent purchaser) who both claim to be entitled to the goods. Many of the cases discussed above raise this problem.

The fraudster has clearly made a misrepresentation as to his identity in order to induce the contract. However, misrepresentation merely renders the contract voidable, which means that the contract is valid and effective until it is rescinded by the supplier of the goods, so that the fraudster will have obtained good title in the goods until the contract is rendered void. If the fraudster has sold the goods on to an innocent third party prior to the fraud being discovered and the contract being rendered void then the innocent purchaser will have obtained good title and the supplier of the goods will be the party that loses out. It will be too late for the supplier of the goods to rescind the contract, because rescission will be barred.

The supplier of the goods therefore prefers to argue mistake rather than misrepresentation. Under the law on mistake the contract is immediately void and so the fraudster will never have obtained good title in the goods to pass on to the innocent purchaser. You can only pass title to goods if you have title in the first place. So I cannot sell you my neighbour's house, because I am not the owner who can sell it. Even if you pay me the full price for the house thinking that I am the owner, you will not become the owner of the house because I was not the owner to sell it to you.

Only a limited number of mistakes render a contract void. We have seen that a unilateral mistake as to a person's identity will render a contract void.

A recent case on the issue of mistake as to identity is **Shogun Finance v Hudson** (2001). On 10 June 1996 a fraudster visited the show-rooms of a car dealer in Leicester and agreed to buy a Mitsubishi Shogun for £22,250 on hire-purchase terms. The fraudster signed a draft finance agreement in the name of Durlabh Patel, producing a genuine, but stolen, driving licence as proof of his name and address. The dealer sent the signed document and a copy of the licence to Shogun Finance. Shogun confirmed the credit rating of Durlabh Patel and approved the sale. The fraudster paid a 10 per cent deposit and was allowed to drive away the car with its paperwork.

Because of the finance arrangements, the dealer sold the car to the finance company, who in turn hired it to the customer under the hire-purchase agreement. Thus, the finance company became the new owner, while the customer enjoyed merely possession of the car. The customer then has an option to purchase the car after paying all the hire charges.

The fraudster immediately sold the car to an innocent purchaser, Mr Hudson, for £17,000, and then disappeared. When Shogun discovered the fraud they traced the car to Mr Hudson and, as owners, sued him for the return of the car, or its value.

Mr Hudson's defence was that under the Hire-Purchase Act 1964, an innocent private purchaser of a motor vehicle subject to hire-purchase obtains good title. However, Shogun argued that the Hire-Purchase Act could not apply because the hire-purchase agreement in question was void. In particular, they argued that the hire-purchase agreement was void for mistake because they had intended to contract not with the rogue, but with Durlabh Patel. A majority of the Court of Appeal accepted this argument and ruled in favour of Shogun.

To defeat this argument of mistake, Hudson had to show that the hire-purchase agreement was merely voidable for fraud. The easiest way of achieving that was to establish that his case came within the face-to-face principle. But the fraudster's only contact was with the car dealer, and not the claimant finance company with whom he made the contract. Thus, the only way the face-to-face principle could be satisfied was if the car dealer was acting as Shogun's agent. The Court of Appeal found that the car dealer was not an agent with the authority to make a contract on behalf of the finance company, Shogun; he was merely a go-between whose role was to obtain and communicate information about the hirer to the claimant. Thus, the face-to-face principle could not apply. Even if he had been acting as Shogun's agent and had been the 'eyes and ears' of the claimant, the Court of Appeal said the face-to-face principle would not have applied because Shogun's evidence was that the identity of the customer was 'absolutely crucial'. At all material times it was to Mr Patel that Shogun intended to contract. Shogun had established that Durlabh Patel had resided at his address for nine years, held his job for five years and had no adverse credit references. Furthermore, under legislation, Shogun was obliged to send copies of the agreement and any default notices to the customer's home.

So the claimant, Shogun, could rely on unilateral mistake. The fraudster could pass no title to Hudson, as he had no title to pass, and Shogun's action was successful.

Equity and cross-purposes mistake

Like the common law, equity rarely allows a cross-purposes mistake to affect a contract, though it will occasionally refuse specific performance where the parties have made such a mistake.

As regards unilateral mistake, there are some rather rare situations in which equity has provided a remedy where the common law would not; it can offer relief to a party who has made a mistake which is not fundamental in the narrow common law sense, and has even intervened where a mistake has been made which merely affects the value of the thing sold.

Mistakes relating to documents

Where a mistake relates to a written document there are two special remedies: *non est factum* and rectification.

Non est factum

We have seen that, as a general rule, a person who signs a contractual document is bound by it, regardless of whether he or she has read or understood it (**L'Estrange** *v* **Graucob** (1934), see p. 118 above). However, where a person signs a document believing it to be something totally different from what it actually is, the common law remedy of *non est factum*

(Latin for 'this is not my deed') may make the contract void. In order to do this, the person seeking the remedy must prove three things: that the signature was induced by a trick or fraud; that they made a fundamental mistake as to the nature of the document; and that they were not careless in signing it.

The mistake made by the signer must concern the actual nature of the document, not just its legal effect. In **Saunders** *v* **Anglia Building Society** (1971) (also known as **Gallie** *v* **Lee**) an elderly widow had left her house to her nephew, a Mr Parkin, in her will. When he needed to raise some money, she handed over the deeds to the house for him to use as security. Parkin and an acquaintance called Lee came and asked her to sign a document, which they said transferred the title of the house to her nephew, so that he could raise the money he needed; she did not object to him doing this. In fact, the document was a deed of sale to Mr Lee, but the old lady did not read it because she had broken her glasses. Mr Lee later mortgaged the house to a building society and kept all the money, paying nothing to either the old lady or Parkin. Lee then defaulted on the mortgage repayments, and the building society sought possession of the house. By that time the widow had died, and Saunders, who was dealing with her affairs, sought a declaration of *non est factum* to make the agreement with Lee void. The House of Lords refused to issue this declaration. They agreed that the widow had been tricked into signing, but held that she was not mistaken as to the nature of the document, only as to its exact legal effect. In signing the document she intended to help her nephew raise money, and this was exactly what the document she did sign would have achieved if Lee had not been dishonest. A second reason for the decision was that the woman was careless in signing the document. Lord Reid said:

> The plea cannot be available to anyone who was content to sign without taking the trouble to find out at least the general effect of the document . . . the essence of the plea *non est factum* is that the person signing believed that the document he signed had one character or one effect, whereas in fact its character or effect was quite different. He could not have such a belief unless he had taken steps or had been given information which gave him some grounds for his belief. The amount of information he must have and the sufficiency of the particularity of his belief must depend on the circumstances of each case.

Rectification

Where some aspect of a written document is alleged not to reflect accurately the will of the parties, the equitable remedy of rectification may in certain circumstances allow the written document to be altered so that it coincides with the true agreement of the parties. In order for this remedy to be applied, three conditions must be satisfied: the parties must have agreed about the point in question; their agreement on that aspect of the contract must have continued unchanged up to the time it was put into writing; and the written document must fail to express the parties' agreement on that point.

If all three conditions are satisfied, equity will rectify the written document, and order specific performance of the rectified document. For example, in **Craddock Bros** *v* **Hunt** (1923) one party agreed to buy the other's house. While their oral agreement excluded an adjoining yard from the sale, the eventual written contract included it. Equity granted rectification of the document, so the buyer was not allowed to keep the yard.

Rectification is an exception to the parol evidence rule, as oral evidence can be admitted in order to show that the written document is in error.

Rectification will not be available where the written document accurately records the agreement, but the agreement is based upon a mistake. In **Rose** *v* **Pim** (1953) the plaintiffs were asked to supply a customer with 'feveroles'. Not knowing exactly what these were, they asked their suppliers, the defendants, who replied 'feveroles means just horsebeans'. This was genuinely the defendants' belief, but in fact 'feveroles' were a specific type of horsebean. The parties then made their written contract, using the term 'horsebean'. When the beans were supplied, they turned out to be another type of horsebean, and not feveroles at all. The plaintiffs were sued by their customer and, in order to cover their loss, the plaintiffs sought to rectify the written contract between them and the defendants. Their application was refused on the grounds that the written contract did accurately reflect the parties' agreement.

Criticism and reform

The case of **Shogun Finance** *v* **Hudson** highlights the unsatisfactory state of the law. Where there has been a fraud that has induced a supplier of goods to hand over their property to a fraudster, the logical argument of the supplier of the goods is that their property was obtained by a fraudulent misrepresentation. But this argument does not provide the remedy that the innocent supplier needs, and so the supplier's argument must centre instead on the artificial question of whether there was a unilateral mistake which rendered the contract void. This situation is unsatisfactory: the reality of the fraudster's wrongdoing is fraud, and it is perverse that the dispute between the supplier and a later innocent purchaser should focus instead on whether the fraudster's conduct induced a particular type of mistake.

The case of **Shogun Finance** also suggests that the law is not striking the right balance in protecting innocent purchasers of fraudulently obtained property. In that case the innocent purchaser, Mr Hudson, was forced to return the car that he had paid for to the finance company. But in fact it was the finance company who gave possession of the car to the fraudster without making sufficient checks about who he really was. Generally, the person who sells to a rogue is in a better position to check his honesty than the person who buys from a rogue, so that the rules of law should tend to protect the third-party purchaser. After all, no one with any sense parts with their car unless the buyer hands over cash or any equally secure means of payment, such as a bankers' draft. On these facts, the claimant was even more lax, allowing the rogue to take the car away on credit terms without any means of verifying that he was the person named in the driving licence.

Sedley LJ gave a powerful dissenting judgment in the case. He was scathing about Shogun's procedures. It gave £20,000 of credit on the strength of a driving licence and a credit check, which in no way confirmed that even the real Mr Patel could afford the instalments. The finance company had no good reason to be confident that it was Mr Patel it was dealing with. It could only afford this 'cavalier' approach because it could rely on repossessing the vehicle from an innocent purchaser. While Shogun successfully argued that the identity of the customer was 'absolutely crucial', Sedley LJ suggested that Shogun's actual practice suggested that this was not the case.

Over the years, there have been a number of suggestions to resolve the matter. The Law Reform Committee in its *Twelfth Report* in 1966 proposed abolishing the fine distinction between contracts void for mistake and those voidable for misrepresentation. Instead, it recommended that where

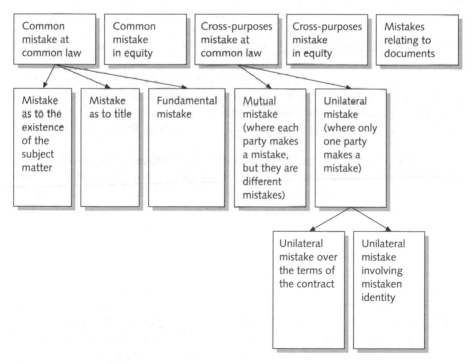

Figure 10.1 Mistake

goods are sold under a mistake as to the buyer's identity, the contract should be voidable, and not void. This solution would favour innocent purchasers because they would obtain good title, provided the fraud had not been discovered and the contract rescinded before they purchased the goods.

One option considered by the Law Reform Committee was of apportioning the loss according to the culpability of the parties. But this option was rejected by the Committee because of the practical difficulties of apportioning blame where the goods pass through several hands.

▶ ANSWERING QUESTIONS

1 In your opinion, does English contract law deal adequately with problems of common mistake?

Note that this question only requires you to deal with **common** mistake. Because of the large amount of law in this area, questions are often confined to certain types of mistake, and you will waste time if you discuss areas not specified.

Start your essay by defining what common mistake is. Then go through the three types – mistake as to existence of subject matter, title, and fundamental mistake – stating the law on each one. You are being asked about the success of the law so, as you explain it, you must highlight any problems. You could point, for example, to the very strict rules on mistake as to quality, which can seem unfair to buyers who end up with goods for which they have no use; or to the defendants in **Bell** who were held to a payment they had no legal obligation to make; and the lack of consistency between cases on existence of subject matter, with the explanations for these (such as the negligent behaviour of the defendants in **McRae**). You can then go on to point out the effects of equity on relieving some of the problems caused by the common law doctrine, using cases such as **Solle** v **Butcher**.

2 Faridah wishes to sell her valuable violin, so advertises it for sale. Germaine visits Faridah, explaining that she would like to buy the violin and they agree on a price. Germaine procures a cheque book, but Faridah hesitates, saying that she would prefer cash. Germaine then replies 'Look, you can see who I am', and produces various items of identity, bearing the same surname as a famous musician. Faridah is embarrassed and agrees to take the cheque, handing over the violin to Germaine.

A few days later Faridah is contacted by her bank, who informs her that the cheque from Germaine is worthless, and that Germaine cannot be traced. Faridah is upset at this, but to her surprise, a few days later she sees 'her' violin for sale in the window of a musical instrument supplier, Humbuskers. She tries to recover the violin from Humbuskers, but they claim that they paid a good price for it from someone going abroad, and would certainly not be prepared just to give it back to her.

(a) Advise Faridah as to whether she has any legal right to claim the return of the violin. (*40 marks*)
(b) If Faridah wishes to take legal action against Humbuskers, advise her as to how she may be able to get help with the cost of such an action. (*10 marks*)
(*Total 50 marks*) OCR

(a) This question raises the issue of a unilateral mistake as to the identity of the contracting party. The law draws a fine distinction between where a person intended to contract with someone else (where the mistake renders the contract void) and a mistake which is merely as to a person's attributes rather than as to their identity. A mistake as to a person's attributes, such as thinking that they are credit-worthy when they are not, will leave the contract intact. In determining this issue it is important to note that the contract between Faridah and the purchaser was made face to face. Where the contract is made face to face the courts are likely to conclude that the parties intended to contract with the person in front of them, and the only mistake was a mistake as to attributes. On the other hand, we are told that Faridah entered the contract because she was embarrassed, and this may have been because she thought she was in the presence of a famous musician. You would need to consider cases such as **Lewis** v **Averay**, **Phillips** v **Brooks Ltd** and **Ingram** v **Little**. If the court accepts that Faridah made a unilateral mistake as to identity, then the contract will be void and the third party, Humbuskers, will not have gained good title. Faridah will therefore be able to insist on the violin being returned. If the court decides that Faridah had merely made a mistake as to attributes, then there will be a valid contract with the purchaser, who will have passed on good title to Humbuskers, and who will therefore be able to keep the violin. Of particular interest on these facts is **Shogun Finance** v **Hudson**.

While the purchaser has made a misrepresentation, proving the existence of a fraudulent misrepresentation will not provide the remedy that Faridah needs. Fraudulent misrepresentation would only render the contract voidable, and Humbuskers would have already obtained a good title before the contract had been rescinded.

(b) This question is beyond the scope of a contract law book, and raises issues discussed in the authors' book on the English legal system, and, in particular, the availability of state funding and conditional fee agreements.

11 Illegality

Introduction

An agreement may possess all the requisite elements of a valid contract, such as offer and acceptance and consideration, but be unenforceable because it is illegal. The diversity of legal rules that can be breached and the wide scope of public policy make this branch of the law of contract rather complex. Contracts may be illegal at the time of their formation or because of the way they have been performed.

Illegal at time of formation

Contracts may be illegal when entered into because they cannot be performed in accordance with their terms without the commission of an illegal act. For example, the contract may involve a breach of the criminal law, or it may be a statutory requirement for the parties to the contract to have a licence which they do not possess. This type of illegality is illustrated by **Levy** *v* **Yates** (1838). There used to be a statutory rule that a royal licence was required to perform a play within 20 miles of London. In that case the contract was between a theatre owner and an impresario, for the performance of a theatrical production where no royal licence had been obtained. The contract was illegal at the time of its formation.

Illegal mode of performance

In some cases, a contract may be perfectly legal when it is made, but may be carried out in an illegal manner. This was the case in **Anderson Ltd** *v* **Daniel** (1924) where a statute provided that a seller of artificial fertilizer had to supply buyers with an invoice detailing certain chemicals used in its manufacture. The sellers failed to provide the necessary invoice. It was not against the law to sell artificial fertilizer, but it was against the law to sell it without following the statutory rules. As a result, the sellers were unable to claim the price when the defendants refused to pay.

▶ Violation of legal rules and public policy

A contract is clearly illegal where its formation, purpose or performance involves the commission of a legal wrong. But the law relating to illegal contracts extends beyond this. A contract is also regarded as being illegal where it involves conduct which the law disapproves of as contrary to the interests of the public, even though that conduct is not actually unlawful. In both cases the transaction is treated as an illegal contract and the courts will not enforce it. We will consider first where an agreement violates a legal rule and secondly where it is against public policy.

The contract violates a legal rule

The contract may constitute a crime or a tort. The violation may be of a statutory rule or of common law.

Breach of common law

There are a number of factors which may make a contract illegal at common law, the most important being where there is a contract to commit a crime or a tort. There are obvious reasons why the law would not want to uphold a contract between, for example, a contract killer and his or her client. Clearly, it is unlikely that many people employed to commit a criminal offence would sue for their fees, but this was effectively what happened in **Everet** *v* **Williams** (1725). Two highwaymen had agreed to share the spoils of their crime and when one tried to evade the agreement, the other sued for his share. Needless to say, he was unsuccessful. Of particular interest in practice are contracts in restraint of trade.

Contracts in restraint of trade. This issue is highly important in practice. Restraint of trade concerns contracts which limit an individual's right to use his or her skills for payment, or to trade freely. Such contracts fall into four groups:

- Contracts for the sale of a business where the vendor promises not to compete with the purchaser. This might arise where, for example, Ann buys a shop from Ben, and seeks to prevent Ben from opening up another similar shop just around the corner, which might attract the old shop's potential customers.
- Contracts between businesses by which prices or output are regulated. This category is now largely governed by legislation discussed on p. 185.
- Contracts in which an employee agrees that on leaving the company, they will not set up in business or be employed in such a way as to compete with that employer. This is common in businesses where personal skills and reputation attract custom, such as hairdressing or

advertising. Such contracts tend to provide that the employee should not set up a competing business, or take a job with a competitor, within a certain geographical area and/or within a certain period of time after leaving. The main reason for such contractual terms is the concern that the employee may take customers with them to the new employer or business.

• Contracts where a person agrees to restrict their mode of trade by, for example, only accepting orders from one particular company. This is sometimes called a *solus agreement*, and is frequently used for petrol stations; in return for the land or a lease, the trader promises to buy only the goods of the mortgagee or lessor.

Any of these types of contract may amount to what is called a general restraint, if the contract completely prohibits trading, or a partial restraint if it limits trading to a certain time or area. In **Nordenfelt v Maxim Nordenfelt Guns and Ammunitions Co** (1894) it was held that either type of restraint is contrary to public policy and therefore void, unless it can be shown that it is reasonable with regard to the parties, and is not unreasonable with regard to the public interest. If this can be done, the contract will be valid.

The court must be satisfied that the party making the restriction actually needs to protect their interests. The only legitimate interests employers may seek to protect are their relationship with customers and their trade secrets. Restrictions designed simply to prevent competition will not be upheld.

In considering reasonableness, the court must be satisfied that the agreement is no wider than is necessary to protect those interests and the scope of the restraint and the area and period of time it covers are all properly balanced against one another. Thus a restriction might be held void if applied over a large geographical area, or for a long time, but it might equally be valid if it only covered a small area or was to last for a short time.

In **Mason v Provident Clothing Co** (1913) the House of Lords held that a restriction on an employee which prevented him from working in the same trade within 25 miles of London was wider than was necessary to protect his former employer's business, and was therefore void. Similarly, in **Esso Petroleum Co Ltd v Harper's Garage (Stourport) Ltd** (1968) the owner of two garages entered into a contract in which he agreed, among other things, to sell only Esso petrol, in return for a discount on the price per gallon. This restriction was to run for nearly four-and-a-half years on one garage, but 21 years on the other. The House of Lords upheld the four-and-a-half-year agreement, but said the 21-year contract was unreasonable, because it was much longer than was necessary to protect Esso's interests, and therefore void. In reaching this decision the House of Lords took into account the recommendations of a report by the Monopolies

Commission, published in 1965, which recommended a five-year limit on all 'tied garage' agreements.

The purpose of invalidating agreements in restraint of trade is to promote competition, but there are cases in which it is recognized that it may be desirable to allow people to bind themselves not to compete. For instance, with the sale of certain types of business, it would simply be impossible to sell if you could not assure the buyer that you would not set up in competition and gain all their potential customers.

Breach of legislation

Some types of contract are expressly declared void by statute. An example of a contract that was illegal due to legislation is **Cope** *v* **Rowlands** (1836). The plaintiff, a stockbroker, did some work for the defendant, but the defendant failed to pay. Under statute, it was an offence for a stockbroker to work within the City of London without a licence, and the plaintiff did not have such a licence. As a result, his action was dismissed, on the grounds that the statute prohibited him acting as a broker, and therefore the courts could not enforce a contract that involved him doing so.

The two most important examples of contracts that are expressly declared void by statute are contracts in restraint of trade and wagering contracts.

Competition law

We have seen that the common law lays down some controls on contracts in restraint of trade. But these controls give only limited protection to third parties who may be adversely affected by these contracts. A more comprehensive approach to this problem has, since 1956, been made by legislation. One of the main goals of the European Union is to promote free trade between Member States, and clearly restrictive trade agreements can affect this policy. Where a restrictive trade agreement could affect trade between Member States, it will only be valid if allowed under both European Union and English law; if there is a conflict, European law should prevail, with the main provision contained in Article 85(1) of the European Community Treaty. Where an agreement is invalid under both, problems may arise as to which should determine the consequences of invalidity, but again, European law should, in theory, prevail.

The relevant UK legislation is now contained in the Competition Act 1998. This Act prohibits a number of anti-competitive practices; it does so in words which closely follow those of Article 85 of the European Community Treaty. The main difference between the two sets of provisions lies in their geographical scope. The Act applies to trade in the UK while Article 85 applies to trade in the whole of the European Union.

The 1998 Act applies to agreements between undertakings, decisions by associations of undertakings or concerted practices, which (a) may affect trade and (b) have as their object or effect the prevention, restriction or distortion of trade. Prohibited agreements are in general void unless an exemption is granted by the Director-General of Fair Trading (under the 1998 Act) or the European Union authorities (under the Treaty).

Prohibitions under the 1998 Act and Article 85 only apply where the agreement has an appreciable effect on competition, and not where that effect is insignificant. The crucial factor in determining whether the effect is appreciable is the percentage of the share of the market affected by it: a share of less than 5 per cent is probably not sufficient. Many of the agreements dealt with by the common law rules discussed earlier in this chapter would not have a sufficiently 'appreciable' effect to be prohibited by the legislation. This seems to reflect the different purpose of the two sets of rules. The legislation is concerned with the effect of agreements on the economy as a whole, while under the common law rules an agreement may be void by reason of its adverse effect on the party restrained by it.

Wagering contracts

Wagering agreements are bets, and are rendered void by the Gaming Act 1845. Section 18 of the Act provides:

> All contracts or agreements, whether by parole or in writing, by way of gaming or wagering, shall be null and void, and no suit shall be brought or maintained in any Court of Law or Equity for recovering any sum of money or valuable thing alleged to be won upon any wager . . .

The Act does not make wagering agreements illegal, it simply provides that neither party to such an agreement can legally enforce it. So if, for example, you bet a friend £10 that you will do better than her in your contract law exam, neither of you has done anything illegal, but, nevertheless, she cannot sue you for the £10 if she wins, and you cannot sue her for it if you win.

For the provisions of the legislation to apply, a wagering contract must be one in which there are two parties and the terms of the agreement are such that one party wins and the other loses. This means that football pools, for example, are not covered as its promoters take a percentage of the stake money and so gain by the transaction regardless of whether players win as well.

The Act also covers 'gaming', which is defined by the Betting, Gaming and Lotteries Act 1963 as 'the playing of a game of chance for winnings in money or money's worth'. Games of chance include games which depend partly on skill and partly on chance, but athletic games and sports are expressly excluded. Only the players of the game can make a gaming contract; if others bet on the outcome, they make a wagering contract and not a gaming contract. Under the Act, gaming is lawful if conducted in accordance with rules laid down by the Act, but gaming contracts are unenforceable.

In **Russell** *v* **Fulling** (1999) the claimant entered into an agreement with the defendant to establish a shopping 'goldcard scheme' whereby a retailer was furnished with scratchcards and, at his discretion, gave them away to customers or potential customers. Subsequently, the claimant made a claim for, first, the payment of a sum of money owing under the agreement and, secondly, the repayment of a loan made to the defendant in an attempt to rescue the failing scheme. The defendant contended that the scheme constituted an unlawful lottery, and that, therefore, the agreement and loan were unenforceable. The court accepted this view.

The contract is against public policy

Public policy is notoriously difficult to define, but essentially it assumes that there are some interests which are shared by most of society, which promote the smooth running of the type of society we have, and which should therefore be protected.

That does not mean that we all agree on exactly what those interests are, though most of us may agree on many of them. Although public policy is not the policy of any particular government or political party, it does involve political choices. For example, take the idea that it is public policy to promote free trade and competition, which is clearly accepted in English law. If you agree that free competition is the best way to ensure a balance of supply and demand, in which producers can only charge what the public are willing to pay, then you will agree that it is public policy to promote free trade and to limit the restrictions that can be placed on who makes what, and what they charge for it. On the other hand, you may feel that such a policy gives too much power to producers, especially where they are a small group of big organizations. If they all charge high prices, where does that leave the consumer? You might feel that rather than allowing them to trade freely, you want to restrict the prices they can charge. In that case, you would not consider it public policy to prevent such a restriction. Or you might consider it to be public policy to allow some restrictions and not others. This type of discussion has taken place recently in the context of car prices in the UK.

On almost any area of public policy there will be disagreements within society – even the idea that it is against public policy to uphold contracts with hitmen might be resisted by those who earn their living as contract killers! It is the job of Parliament and the judiciary to employ such public policy as will command the support of most people, though considering the élite background and conservative views of many judges, it is debatable whether this is always achieved.

Public policy changes over time as views and beliefs change. For example, in **Cowan** *v* **Milbourn** (1867) a contract for leasing a hall for a meeting of atheists was held to be illegal. Some 50 years later, in **Bowman** v **Secular Society** (1917) it was held that such a contract was not illegal at all, and today many people would regard even the suggestion that it might be as ridiculous.

It has been suggested that it is not open to the courts to find new ways in which a contract may be illegal on the grounds of being contrary to public policy. Given the rate at which social values have changed even in the last two or three decades – the position of women is an obvious example – this seems unlikely and undesirable. It may be, for example, that in the future a contract which involved discrimination on sexual or racial grounds could be deemed against public policy.

There are a range of contracts which are considered to be illegal because they are against the interests of public policy. The main categories of contract will be considered here.

Contracts promoting sexual immorality

In **Pearce** v **Brookes** (1866) the plaintiff had hired a carriage to a prostitute knowing that she would use it to see clients. He was unable to enforce the contract when she failed to pay the hire charge. But as our society has become more liberal, the courts seem to be less willing to treat a contract as illegal on this ground. **Armhouse Lee Ltd** v **Chappell** (1996) concerned a contract under which the defendants paid the plaintiffs to place adverts for telephone sex lines in magazines. When regulation of such publicity was increased the defendants terminated the contract as they no longer wished to advertise their services in this way. The plaintiffs brought an action for the money due under the contract, but the defendants argued that the contract was illegal and therefore unenforceable as it promoted sexual immorality. This defence was rejected by the Court of Appeal. The court stated that though the adverts were distasteful, the sex lines were generally accepted by society and were regulated by the telephone industry. There was no evidence that any 'generally accepted moral code condemned these telephone sex lines'. It considered that contracts should only be found illegal under this heading if an element of public harm clearly existed. Thus, in the light of today's society, the courts will probably only treat a contract as illegal for promoting sexual immorality where the behaviour concerned amounts to, or involves, a criminal offence such as prostitution.

Contracts prejudicial to the status of marriage

This category makes void any contract which seeks to restrict someone's right to marry or to choose their own partner, to charge for procuring a marriage partner, or to provide for the future separation of a married couple. For example, in **Hermann** v **Charlesworth** (1905) the plaintiff paid a special client's fee of £52 to the defendant under a so-called 'marriage brokerage' contract. Despite being introduced to several men by the defendant, the plaintiff did not become engaged or married to any of them. The Court of Appeal decided that this contract was invalid as it was contrary to public policy to enforce marriage brokerage contracts.

Contracts prejudicial to public safety

The main types of contract made illegal on this ground are transactions with those living in an enemy country during wartime, contracts to perform acts which are illegal in a friendly foreign country and contracts which are damaging to foreign relations. An example of the latter is **Foster** v **Driscoll** (1929) where a contract to smuggle whisky into the US, when the sale of alcohol was prohibited in that country, was illegal. The case of **Royal Boskalis Westminster NV** v **Mountain** (1997) arose from the Gulf War. The plaintiff was a company which had been working in Iraq when Kuwait was invaded in 1990. The United Nations imposed sanctions on Iraq and, in retaliation, the Iraqi Government seized the company's employees and assets based in their country. The company reached a deal with Iraq for the release of its employees and some of its assets, in return for making a lump sum payment to Iraq and waiving the money that was due for the work the company had carried out there. The lump sum payment was in breach of UN sanctions.

The plaintiff was insured by the defendant against the risks of war and sought reimbursement of the value of the waived claims, estimated at £84 million. The action was rejected and the Court of Appeal stated clearly that the agreement would not be given effect to by an English court as, by breaching the UN sanctions, it was contrary to public policy and illegal.

Contracts prejudicial to the administration of justice

An example would be an agreement not to report a criminal offence in return for payment.

Contracts to oust the jurisdiction of the courts

A contract which purports to deprive the courts of a jurisdiction which they would otherwise have is not enforceable. An example of this was **Bennett** v **Bennett** (1952) where a wife promised her husband that she would not apply to a divorce court for maintenance.

Contracts tending to encourage corruption in public life

A contract was held illegal on this ground in **Parkinson** v **College of Ambulance Ltd and Harrison** (1925). The plaintiff had given a charity

£3,000 after receiving assurances from its secretary that it could secure him a knighthood. It failed to do so, but he was not allowed to claim back his money due to the illegality of the transaction.

The effect of an illegal contract

The effect of an illegal contract will depend on whether it is illegal due to a statute or due to the common law. Where the contract is illegal because of a statute, in some cases the statute provides for the consequences of any illegality. For example, where an insurance company makes a contract to insure someone, and is not authorized to make that contract, the Financial Services Act 1986 nevertheless allows the insured person to enforce the contract. Where the statute does not expressly or impliedly state the effect of the illegal contract, the common law principles will apply.

Under common law an illegal contract is void and courts will not order it to be performed. A court will never 'enforce' an illegal contract, in the sense of ordering a party actually to do something that is unlawful or contrary to public policy. Illegal contracts are not devoid of legal effect, but no action on the contract can be maintained. Illegality, where operative, acts as a defence to the general right that a party would otherwise have to enforce a contract (that is, it acts as a defence to what would otherwise be a valid claim for damages for breach of contract, or to an action for the agreed price).

The precise effects of an illegal contract depend on whether the contract is illegal at the time of its formation or is illegal due to the way in which it is performed.

Contracts illegal at time of formation

In this case the contract is treated as if it was never made, so the illegal contract is unenforceable by either party. Where the making of the contract is unlawful, neither party can sue on it, not even one who is unaware of the facts which make it illegal and has been deceived by the other. An example of this basic principle is **Re Mahmoud and Ispahani** (1921). The sale of linseed oil was prohibited by legislation unless both the seller and the buyer had a licence. The plaintiff, who had a licence to sell, asked the defendant whether he had a licence to buy. The defendant replied untruthfully that he did. Relying on that representation, the plaintiff agreed to sell linseed oil to the defendant. The defendant refused to accept delivery and, when sued for damages for non-acceptance, successfully pleaded the illegality of the contract. The contract was expressly forbidden and the court would do nothing to enforce it. Another example is **Ashton** *v* **Turner** (1981) where two people had agreed (when drunk) to commit a burglary. One of them was injured when the other negligently drove the get-away car and sued for damages. The action failed as it would have been obviously contrary to public policy to allow such a claim.

Because the contract is unenforceable, property handed over under an illegal contract cannot be recovered, a point illustrated by the case of **Parkinson** v **College of Ambulance Ltd and Harrison** which concerned a donation made to a charity in order to get a knighthood (mentioned above).

There are two main exceptions to the general principle that the contract is unenforceable. The first is that a person will be able to recover their property if they can rely on some other cause of action which does not involve the illegal contract, for example, by relying on an independent tort. In **Bowmakers** v **Barnet Instruments Ltd** (1945) Bowmakers supplied certain machine tools to the defendants under three hire-purchase contracts. These contracts were illegal as they breached wartime regulations. The defendants, having failed to make all the hire-purchase payments, sold some of the tools and refused to return the others. They subsequently argued that Bowmakers had no remedy against them, because the hire-purchase contracts were illegal. The Court of Appeal allowed the plaintiff's claim, holding that they did not need to rely on the illegal contracts as, being the owners of the goods, they had a separate cause of action for conversion (a civil wrong which occurs when a party treats someone else's property as their own).

This approach was followed by the House of Lords in **Tinsley** v **Milligan** (1993). Two women lived in a house together. Both of them had provided money to buy it, but they had agreed for ownership to be in Tinsley's name only, so that Milligan could make false claims for social security payments (from which they both benefited). Despite this, there was an understanding that the house was jointly owned. They later quarrelled and Tinsley sought sole possession of the house, arguing that any earlier agreement between them was unenforceable because of its illegal nature. The House of Lords found that Milligan had rights to the house independent of any illegal contract. By contributing to the purchase price of the house and agreeing between themselves that the house was jointly owned, a right in equity (known as a trust) had been created in favour of Milligan.

The second exception to the general rule that a contract illegal at the time of its formation is unenforceable applies where one party is more at fault than the other (they are described as not being *in pari delicto*). In such a situation the courts may be prepared to view the less guilty party as the victim of the transaction and allow them to recover property transferred to the more guilty party.

Contracts illegal as performed

We have seen that a contract, perfectly lawful when made, may be carried out in an illegal manner. It will be possible to enforce the illegal contract if the illegal act was merely incidental to the performance of the contract. For example, a contract for the delivery of goods may not be tainted by illegality when the lorry driver who delivered the goods is caught speeding or parking his vehicle illegally during the delivery. In **St John Shipping Corp** *v* **Joseph Rank Ltd** (1957) the plaintiff had carried grain for the defendants from Alabama to England. In doing so, the plaintiff had overloaded its ship so that the loadline was submerged. That was a statutory offence, and the plaintiff was prosecuted and fined for it. The defendants then sought to withhold part of the payment due, on the basis that the plaintiff had carried out the contract in an unlawful manner. Devlin J held that the plaintiff was entitled to full payment as the illegal act was merely incidental to the performance of the contract.

Where the contract is merely illegal because of the way it has been performed, it is possible for either both or only one of the parties to intend illegal performance. It is customary to distinguish between the situation where the legally objectionable features were known to both parties and where they were known to only one of them.

Both parties aware of illegal performance
If both parties are aware that its performance is illegal, the consequences for this type of contract are the same as for a contract that is illegal at the time of its formation: neither party can enforce it. In **Ashmore, Benson, Pease & Co Ltd** *v* **AV Dawson Ltd** (1973) the defendants agreed to transport two boilers belonging to the plaintiffs, and did so by carrying the boilers on lorries which could not lawfully carry the loads in question. The goods were damaged in the course of transit, but the claim of the owner for damages was rejected; the owner of the goods not only knew that the goods were being transported in an illegal manner, but had actually 'participated' in the illegality in the sense of assisting the defendant carrier to perform the contract in an illegal manner. Another example is **Pearce** *v* **Brookes** (above) where the plaintiff knew that the prostitute was going to use the carriage for the purposes of her trade and therefore he was unable to enforce the contract.

Only one party aware of illegal performance
When one party did not know of the illegal performance of the contract by the other party, the innocent party can enforce it. An example might be where a person hires out their car, not knowing that it is going to be used to carry stolen goods. In such a case, all the usual contractual remedies are at the disposal of the innocent party, so long as they repudiate the contract or refuse to continue with it as soon as they know of the illegality.

Thus, in **Archbolds (Freightage) Ltd** *v* **S Spanglett Ltd** (1961) the A company agreed with the B company to carry goods in a van which, unknown to the B company, was not licensed for the purpose. The contract involved the commission of a criminal offence by the A company in using the van for this purpose. But since the B company was unaware of this fact, it was not prevented from suing the A company for failure to deliver the goods.

Where the innocent party has provided any performance of the contract, they may sue on a *quantum meruit* for its value (see p. 286 below). In **Clay v Yates** (1856) a printer had contracted to print a book for the defendant. During the printing, he discovered that part of the book was libellous and left out that part. The defendant refused to pay for the printing because of the omission, but the court held that the printer was entitled to be paid for the work he had carried out.

Where one party is completely innocent, the guilty party in these circumstances cannot sue on the contract for damages, or recover any property handed over, unless this can be done without relying on the illegal contract. In **Cowan v Milbourn** (1867) the defendant agreed to let rooms to the plaintiff, but later refused to carry out the contract when he learned that the rooms were to be used for giving blasphemous lectures. As this was an unlawful purpose, the plaintiff, who was the guilty party, had no remedy.

Severance

In some cases, it is possible to divide the illegal part of a contract from the rest, and enforce the provisions which are not affected by the illegality – this is called severance. It appears that the illegal parts of a contract can be severed if they are relatively unimportant to the contract and if the severance leaves the nature of the contract unaltered, because the words can be simply lifted out of the contract with no rewording required. If the unlawful part of a contract cannot be severed, the whole contract will be void. For example, in **Goldsoll v Goldman** (1915) the plaintiff bought the business of the defendant, who traded in imitation jewellery in the UK. It was a term of the contract that the defendant would not trade in either imitation or real jewellery in the UK, or in a number of specified foreign countries. The Court of Appeal decided that it was unreasonable for the defendant to restrict the plaintiff from trading in real jewellery, or from trading in either type of jewellery abroad, since the business interests he sought to protect were limited to selling imitation jewellery in the UK. Nevertheless, they said that this did not make the agreement void; the unreasonable parts could be severed from it and the remaining agreement could be enforced.

Criticism

The Law Commission has criticized this area of law for its complexity, its potential to give rise to unjust decisions and its lack of certainty (Law Commission, *Illegal transactions: the effect of illegality on contracts and trusts* (2000)).

Complexity

The Law Commission considers the law to be too complex because the courts have started with draconian principles, such as that illegal contracts are unenforceable and have then had to develop a large number of exceptions to these principles in order to do justice. According to the Law Commission, '[t]he law has thereby been rendered needlessly complex, technical and difficult to justify'.

Injustice

The Law Commission has argued:

> it has been widely recognised that the illegality rules may lead to injustice and, in particular, to the unjust enrichment of the defendant at the plaintiff's expense. Lord Mansfield made it clear in **Holman** v **Johnson** (1775) that an unmeritorious defendant could raise the illegality defence against the plaintiff's claim, despite the defendant's own involvement in the illegal act or purpose and even if the success of the defendant would leave the defendant with an unearned windfall.

Lord Goff commented in a dissenting speech in **Tinsley** v **Milligan**:

> It is important to observe that, . . . the principle is not a principle of justice; it is a principle of policy, whose application is indiscriminate and so can lead to unfair consequences as between the parties to litigation.

The courts frequently fail to take into account the gravity of the illegality and the culpability of the parties when determining the effects of the illegality. This was the case in **Mohammed** v **Alaga & Co** (1998) where the plaintiff entered into an oral agreement with the defendant solicitor. Under this agreement, the plaintiff would refer clients (Somali refugees) to the solicitor and assist the solicitor in preparing the clients' asylum applications in return for a share in the solicitor's fees from the Legal Aid Board. This agreement breached rules made under the Solicitors Act 1974, though the plaintiff did not know this. After making several referrals and carrying out the agreed work, the plaintiff claimed payment under the contract. Despite the trial judge's finding that it was highly blameworthy of the defendant to enter into such a contract, the plaintiff's claim was refused. The (guilty) defendant therefore benefited from the (innocent) plaintiff's work without being required to make any payment for it.

Uncertainty
There are several areas of the law on illegality where it is not possible to state with any certainty what the relevant rules are.

Reform

The Law Commission has provisionally proposed that the rules governing the effect of illegality should be reformed. It considers that the present technical and complex rules should be replaced by a judicial discretion. Under that discretion the court could decide whether or not to enforce an illegal transaction, to recognize that property rights have been transferred or created by it, or to allow benefits conferred under it to be recovered. Illegality would continue to be used only as a defence to claims under contract. It does not, however, recommend that the court should have an open-ended discretion to produce whatever it considers to be the just solution. Instead the proposed discretion would be structured in order to provide greater certainty and guidance. In exercising its discretion, a court would consider:

(i)   the seriousness of the illegality involved;
(ii)   the knowledge and intention of the party seeking to enforce the illegal transaction;
(iii)   whether refusing to allow standard rights and remedies would deter illegality;
(iv)   whether refusing to allow standard rights and remedies would further the purpose of the rule which renders the transaction illegal; and
(v)   whether refusing to allow standard rights and remedies would be proportionate to the illegality involved.

Where, however, a statute has expressly provided what should be the effect of the involvement of illegality on a transaction, the Law Commission recommended that the proposed discretion should not apply. In other words, it did not want the courts to be able to use the discretion to override the express provisions of a statute.

It hopes that its proposals would have two major advantages over the present law. First, a court would be able to reach its decision on the facts of a particular case using open and explicit reasoning, giving full effect to the relevance of the illegality on the transaction. Secondly, the proposals would result in illegality being used less frequently to deny claimants their usual rights or remedies. That is, under the discretion, illegality would only act as a defence where there is a clear and justifiable public interest that it should do so.

ANSWERING QUESTIONS

1 Jack agrees to sell his plumbing business in Wetherbridge to Nicola for £10,000. The written contract between them includes a term stating that Jack will not open a rival plumbing business within 25 miles of Wetherbridge for ten years, nor, during that period, will he approach any customers of the business

now owned by Nicola. Jack does not read the contract until after he has signed it. Five years later, Jack plans to set up a plumbing business in Maltham, five miles from Wetherbridge. Advise Nicola.

Nicola clearly wants to know whether she can enforce the contractual terms mentioned, and either prevent Jack setting up his new business by means of an injunction (discussed at p. 291), or claim damages for any effect it has on her own business. There seems little doubt that the clauses are part of the contract, even though Jack did not read them – see the rule in **L'Estrange** v **Graucob**.

Are they void for restraint of trade? Here you need to refer to the presumption set up in **Nordenfelt** v **Maxim Nordenfelt Guns and Ammunitions Co**, and the factors which dictate whether this presumption can be rebutted. Are the clauses reasonable with regard to the parties? Are they unreasonable with regard to the public interest – bearing in mind that the public interest includes competition in the marketplace? Is Nicola protecting a legitimate interest, or just trying to prevent competition? Are the clauses wider than is needed to protect her interests, and are the scope of the restraint and the area and period of time it covers properly balanced against one another? Whether Nicola can enforce the agreement will depend on the answers to these questions.

12 Duress and undue influence

Since a contract will only be binding if the parties voluntarily consent to it, it is obvious that where one party is forced to consent by threats or undue persuasion by the other, that consent should be invalid. The law has developed two doctrines to deal with this issue: the common law of duress, and the equitable one of undue influence. Both render a contract voidable.

Duress

Five conditions need to be satisfied in order for there to be a finding of duress:

1 Pressure was exerted on the contracting party.
2 This pressure was illegitimate.
3 The pressure induced the claimant to enter the contract.
4 The claimant had no real choice but to enter the contract.
5 The claimant protested at the time or shortly after the contract was made.

Each of these conditions will be considered in turn.

Pressure exerted on the contracting party

Traditionally, the common law doctrine of duress would only make a contract voidable where one party had obtained the other's consent by means of physical violence or threats of it, or unlawful constraint. Over the last 20 years, the courts have extended the scope of the doctrine to include what has come to be known as economic duress. Although still a relatively new doctrine, in modern times it appears to have more practical significance than the traditional concept of duress.

Economic duress occurs where one party was forced into the contract due to economic pressure. Of course, very few contracts are made without any economic pressure at all. How many of us would enter into employment contracts, for example, if we did not need to earn a living? Therefore, to constitute economic duress, economic pressure must go a great deal further than the ordinary pressure of the market, and most of the cases on the subject have been attempts to define just how much further.

Economic duress first arose in **North Ocean Shipping Co** v **Hyundai Construction Co (*The Atlantic Baron*)** (1979) which concerned a contract for the building of a ship. As is commonly the case where duress is raised, the dispute concerned not the formation of the contract, but a purported modification of its terms. Such a modification is only binding if both parties consent to it; if one party's consent is achieved by duress, the modification is not binding.

Although the price of the ship had been fixed at the outset, while it was being built the sellers decided to raise the price by 10 per cent, due to a drop in the exchange rate of the dollar. The buyers were not happy about this, but were unwilling to risk delaying completion of the ship, as they were already negotiating for it to be chartered (which means rented) by a major oil company. They therefore agreed to pay the increased price.

Eight months after the ship was delivered, the buyers tried to sue the sellers, claiming back the extra 10 per cent paid because, they said, it had been extracted from them under duress. The judge agreed that economic pressure such as that applied could constitute duress; the question was whether there had been any 'compulsion of the will', and this compulsion could stem from economic pressure as much as from physical force. In this particular case the buyers were not allowed to recover the extra 10 per cent. This was not because there was no duress – in fact the court held that there probably was – but because by waiting so long after delivery, they had effectively affirmed the modification.

The principle that economic pressure could amount to duress was confirmed in **Pao On** v **Lau Yiu Long** (1979), a rather complex case in which the plaintiffs threatened to break a contract to buy shares in a company unless the defendants, who were shareholders in that company, guaranteed them against losses which might arise when the value of the shares fluctuated. The defendants gave the guarantee, because they were concerned that if the contract did not go ahead, there might be a loss of confidence in their company. Applying the approach of *The Atlantic Baron*, the Privy Council held that there had been no 'compulsion of will', merely economic pressure that fell within the normal standards of business. Lord Scarman explained that a threat to break a contract was not in itself enough to constitute duress: 'It must be shown that the payment made or the contract entered into was not a voluntary act.'

Pressure exerted was illegitimate

Illegitimate pressure must have been exerted on the other contracting party. A threat to do an unlawful act (which includes breaking a contract) will always be illegitimate, but other lawful acts may also fit into the category, depending on the circumstances. This appears to have been the approach taken in **Atlas Express Ltd** *v* **Kafco (Importers and Distributors) Ltd** (1989). Here a small basketware company had secured a valuable contract to supply its products to Woolworths. They then contracted with a national firm of carriers to transport their products. After the contract with the carriers was made, the carriers insisted on raising their charges, threatening to stop deliveries unless the higher price was paid. This happened at a vulnerable time for Kafco, when the shops were beginning to require deliveries for the Christmas period, so they had no time to find an alternative carrier. They reluctantly agreed to the new terms, but later refused to pay the extra.

The court held that Kafco's agreement to pay extra had been obtained by duress, and was therefore not binding. The pressure applied was illegitimate, and Kafco had no realistic alternative but to agree. Had they had more time, they might have been expected to find an alternative carrier and then sue Atlas for breach, but in the circumstances this was completely impractical.

In **CTN Cash and Carry** *v* **Gallaher** (1994) the defendants were a cigarette supplier, who had a monopoly on the supply of the best-known brands. They supplied the plaintiff on credit terms. One of the plaintiff's orders was mistakenly delivered to the wrong warehouse, and when the plaintiff complained about this, the defendants admitted responsibility and agreed to re-deliver them to the correct address. Unfortunately, the consignment was then stolen before the defendants had a chance to re-deliver it. They supplied a new consignment to the correct address, and were paid for it, but then demanded payment for the stolen consignment as well. The plaintiff refused at first, but agreed when the defendants threatened that unless the payment was made, they would withdraw credit facilities. The plaintiff argued that their agreement to make that payment was obtained by duress, but the court held that this was not the case. The defendants had not threatened to break their contract, only to alter its terms, which was not unlawful. The court stated that a lawful act could constitute duress, but that it was unlikely to do so in a commercial situation.

Pressure induced the claimant to enter the contract

Duress must be one of the reasons for entering (or modifying) a contract, but it does not have to be the only or even the main reason. In the Australian case of **Barton** *v* **Armstrong** (1975) Armstrong, a former Chairman of a company, threatened to kill Barton, its Managing Director, if Barton did not agree to buy Armstrong's shares on terms which were decidedly favourable to Armstrong. Barton bought the shares, but there was some evidence that he in fact did so because it looked like a good business arrangement. Nevertheless, the Privy Council decided that the contract was voidable for duress. Armstrong's threats had contributed to Barton's decision to sign the deed, even if they were not the only reason.

Claimant had no real choice but to enter the contract

Universe Tankships *v* **International Transport Workers Federation** (*The Universe Sentinel*) (1983) concerned an industrial dispute. The ITWF insisted on a payment being made to its welfare fund before it would call off a strike, which was affecting a ship belonging to the plaintiffs. The payment was made, and once the strike was lifted, the shipowners sought to reclaim it, as having been paid under duress. In deciding that the payments had indeed been made under duress, Lord Diplock further defined the test. He suggested that compulsion of will alone could not form the basis of duress, since in all cases there is a choice, even though it may be between two unpleasant options – in other words, the shipowners had the choice of paying the money or losing revenue while the ship was stuck in port; they were not actually compelled to pay the money. He suggested that the issue should be whether they had any practical alternative to complying with the threat, and whether the pressure applied would be regarded by the law as illegitimate.

It now appears that economic duress will be present where there is compulsion of the will to the extent that the party under threat has no practical alternative but to comply.

Claimant protested at the time or shortly after the contract was made

In *The Atlantic Baron* (discussed on p. 198) it was because the claimant waited eight months after the ship was delivered that the claim for duress was unsuccessful.

▶ Undue influence

Undue influence is an equitable doctrine, which applies where one party uses their influence over the other to persuade them to make a contract. Where a court finds that a contract was made as a result of undue influence, it may set it aside, or modify, its terms so as to mitigate the disadvantage. The leading case on the subject is the House of Lords' judgment of **Royal Bank of Scotland** *v* **Etridge (No 2)** (2001). There are two types of undue influence: actual and presumed.

Actual undue influence

This arises where the claimant can prove that they entered the transaction as a result of undue influence from the other party. In these cases, the influence tends to be of a kind which is similar to, but falls short of, duress. An example might be where a person promises to pay money to someone as a result of a threat to report them for a criminal offence.

This falls short of duress, since we cannot say there is no practical alternative but to comply, nor that the pressure applied is illegitimate, but it might still be considered inequitable to uphold the promise. This form of undue influence is rare in practice.

Presumed undue influence

In certain circumstances an evidentiary presumption will be applied that shifts the burden of proof from the claimant to the wrongdoer, so that it is up to the wrongdoer to disprove the existence of undue influence. If the presumption of undue influence applies, this does not mean that undue influence exists, but rather that the burden of proof falls on the alleged wrongdoer to show that the transaction was not caused by undue influence. The alleged wrongdoer may satisfy this burden of proof and show that they did not exercise any undue influence over the other contracting party.

Undue influence may be presumed where there is a pre-existing relationship of confidence between the two parties to a contract, as a result of which one places trust in the other, and the contract between them is manifestly disadvantageous to the party who places trust in the other. Such a relationship of trust is called a fiduciary relationship, and it may arise in two ways. First, it may fall into one of several categories in which a relationship of trust is automatically presumed to exist. These categories are:

- parent and child;
- religious adviser and disciple;
- guardian and ward;
- solicitor and client;
- trustee and beneficiary; and
- doctor and patient.

Where the relationship does not come within one of these categories, a relationship of trust may nevertheless be established on the facts. In principle, any kind of relationship could be regarded as one of trust if this is justified by the circumstances of the case. Contracts between married couples or cohabitees can fall within this category or within actual undue influence depending on the facts of the case.

The defendant can rebut the presumption of undue influence by showing that the claimant entered into the contract freely, and this is usually done by establishing that independent advice was taken.

An example of a fiduciary relationship arising on the facts can be seen in **Lloyds Bank** *v* **Bundy** (1974). The plaintiff and his son both used the same bank. The son ran into business difficulties, and his father was asked to guarantee the son's overdraft, putting up his own farm as security. He did this, and when the son was unable to pay, the bank tried to possess the farm. The farmer claimed that the contract had been obtained by undue influence, on the basis that he had banked with Lloyds for a long time, and in that time had placed considerable trust in their advice, yet they had made no effort to warn him that it was not in his interest to give the guarantee. The Court of Appeal agreed that the presumption of undue influence had been raised; there was a relationship of trust on the facts, and the transaction was obviously disadvantageous. The bank were unable to rebut the presumption.

In **National Westminster Bank** v **Morgan** (1985) Mrs Morgan jointly owned the family home with her husband. As a result of his business problems, their mortgage payments fell into arrears, and the bank started to seek possession. Mr Morgan approached the bank to arrange a refinancing loan (this works as follows: if Mr Morgan's original mortgage was for £50,000, and he owed arrears of £5,000, he could replace the mortgage with a refinancing loan of £55,000, from a new lender, and start afresh). The bank agreed, but wanted the house put up as security, for which Mrs Morgan's signature was required. The bank manager went to see her, in the presence of Mr Morgan; she made it clear that she had little confidence in her husband's business, and wanted to talk to the manager alone, but this did not happen, and she eventually signed to prevent the house being repossessed.

The loan was not repaid, and Mr Morgan later died. When the bank tried to take possession of the house, Mrs Morgan pleaded undue influence, on the basis of **Lloyds Bank** v **Bundy**. The House of Lords held that there was no undue influence. The relationship between Mrs Morgan and the manager was no more than the ordinary one between banker and client; no relationship of trust had arisen, and so there was no duty to insist that she took independent advice. Nor was the transaction obviously to her disadvantage – as Lord Scarman pointed out, it could have been a means of saving her home.

Many of the recent cases have raised the issue of wives who allow the family home to be used to guarantee the husbands' debts or the debts of the husbands' business. This is important in practice as the family home is often the family's most valuable asset and frequently provided as surety to finance small businesses (with small businesses making up 95 per cent of all businesses in the UK). The law has to protect wives from being put under undue influence from their husband to provide the house as surety, as the danger for the wife is that she and her family may find themselves homeless if the husband falls into financial difficulty.

In **Royal Bank of Scotland** v **Etridge (No 2)** (2001) the House of Lords indicated that, in normal circumstances, a wife's agreement to charge the matrimonial home as security for her husband's business debts is not a transaction that calls for explanation. Undue influence connotes impropriety, and should only be found where the husband's influence has been 'misused'.

A manifestly disadvantageous transaction

Where a party seeks to rely on the existence of presumed undue influence, the transaction must be manifestly disadvantageous. It is not necessary in the case of actual undue influence to prove that the contract was manifestly disadvantageous to the party influenced (**CIBC Mortgages** v **Pitt** (1993)). This is because manifest disadvantage only helps to prove undue influence and so by definition is not needed where this has already been proved.

Manifest disadvantage will be found to be the case where it would have been 'obvious as such to any independent and reasonable persons who considered the transaction at the time with knowledge of all the relevant facts' (**Bank of Credit and Commerce International SA** v **Aboody** (1989)).

Determining whether there is a manifest disadvantage is a matter of weighing the advantages and disadvantages of the transaction in question. In **National Westminster Bank** v **Morgan** no such disadvantage was considered to be present. While the wife was taking a risk that executing the charge might result in the bank claiming the matrimonial home, at that point executing the charge was the only way to prevent the home being repossessed immediately.

By contrast, in **Cheese** v **Thomas** (1994) an 88-year-old plaintiff had agreed to buy a house with his great-nephew, the defendant. The house cost £83,000, of which the plaintiff contributed £43,000 from the sale of his flat. The defendant took out a mortgage to cover the remaining £40,000. The house was purchased solely in the name of the defendant but it was agreed that the plaintiff would reside there alone for the rest of his life. The defendant failed to keep up the mortgage payments and the plaintiff sought to withdraw from the transaction and recover his £43,000, on the grounds that he had been the victim of undue influence.

It was accepted that, on the facts, there was a presumption of undue influence, and the debate centred around whether the transaction was manifestly disadvantageous to the old man. In deciding this matter, the court had to weigh the advantages against the disadvantages to him. The advantages were that he was able to live in a house which was situated in an area where he had lived before and where his wife and daughter were buried; and he had been able to live in a property which he could not himself have afforded. The disadvantages were that he had used all his capital in the transaction, if he wished to move again he could not compel the defendant to sell the house or return any of his money and his position was insecure if the defendant failed to pay the mortgage. The court concluded that the disadvantages outweighed the advantages and amounted to a manifest disadvantage.

Undue influence and third parties

In **Lloyds Bank** v **Bundy** and **National Westminster Bank** v **Morgan** the undue influence was alleged to have been exercised by a bank employee and therefore it was clearly equitable that, if undue influence had been exercised, this could affect the bank's financial position. In **Barclays Bank v O'Brien** (1993) the undue influence was alleged to have been exerted by the husband and not the bank. Thus, the question was how far any undue influence by the husband should affect the financial position of the bank. The answer seems to be that the rights of a contracting party are affected by the impropriety of the third party if they knew of it or are deemed to have such knowledge (known as constructive knowledge). In these circumstances, the innocent contracting party is entitled to have the contract set aside. There have been a large number of cases which have come to the courts where wives have been asked to stand surety for the husband's debts or for the debts of the husband's business.

The facts of **Barclays Bank v O'Brien** were that Mr O'Brien wanted to put up the family home, jointly owned with Mrs O'Brien, as security for his business debts. He told her that it would guarantee an overdraft of £60,000, when in fact the true amount was £135,000. Mrs O'Brien was asked to go to a particular branch to sign the agreement; this was not her usual branch, but the manager of her usual branch had given strict instructions that the nature of the transaction should be explained to her and had left a letter for her to read. Owing to a mix-up, these instructions were not followed.

The husband's business later collapsed, and the issue of whether Mrs O'Brien was bound by the contract arose. As Lord Browne-Wilkinson pointed out, the problem was one which seemed to be arising frequently – there had been 11 Court of Appeal cases on similar facts in the previous eight years. Their Lordships decided that the bank had constructive notice of the undue influence. They then had to take steps to show that actually they did not have notice of the undue influence and were therefore still able to enforce the contract. The Court of Appeal found that the transaction had been so extravagantly improvident that it was difficult to explain in the absence of some impropriety, so that the bank was put on inquiry.

It is of course most unlikely that a bank will actually know of impropriety by one of the co-owners and still proceed with the mortgage. In practice, therefore, the courts are concerned with whether the bank had 'constructive knowledge'. It will have constructive knowledge if it had been placed 'on inquiry' that a third party may have committed some impropriety to induce the contract, and they have failed to take action to avoid having constructive knowledge of this impropriety.

Placed 'on inquiry'

Following **Royal Bank of Scotland v Etridge (No 2)** (2001) a bank will be put on inquiry in every case where the relationship between the surety and the debtor is non-commercial. This will always include where a wife stands surety for her husband's debts. The position is the same for unmarried couples, whether heterosexual or homosexual, where the bank is aware of the relationship. Cohabitation is not essential. A bank will also be put on inquiry where the wife became surety for the debts of her husband's company even where she was a shareholder, director or secretary of the company. This is because the wife's legal status does not always reflect the reality of the situation.

A lender will not be put on inquiry if the person standing surety for another person's debts is providing a commercial service. Banks and other financial institutions will provide this service for a fee. Those engaged in business can be regarded as capable of looking after themselves and understanding the risks involved in the giving of guarantees.

Also, if the loan is made to the parties jointly for their joint benefit, the lender is not put on inquiry unless it is aware that in reality the money is for the wrongdoer's purposes alone.

Avoiding constructive notice

Where a contracting party is placed on inquiry as to the existence of undue influence, they will only be able to enforce the contract if they can avoid being fixed with constructive notice of the undue influence. A contracting party will avoid having constructive notice by taking reasonable steps to satisfy itself that the other party's agreement had been freely given.

In **Barclays Bank** *v* **O'Brien** the Court of Appeal ruled that to avoid constructive notice in such cases, the creditor should arrange a private meeting with the wife (the husband must not be present), explain the full implications of the transaction, including the potential extent of her liability, and advise her to take independent advice. If this private meeting did not take place, and the husband did use undue influence (or misrepresentation), the bank's claim on the property would be subject to the wife's interests in it. Lord Browne-Wilkinson added that in exceptional cases where a creditor has knowledge of further facts which render the presence of undue influence not only possible but probable, the creditor to be safe will have to insist that the wife is separately advised.

The leading case on the subject is now **Royal Bank of Scotland** *v* **Etridge (No 2)** (2001). This case laid down guidelines for the banks on avoiding constructive knowledge of undue influence which apply to any transactions carried out after the date of that judgement. Transactions made prior to that judgment would still be governed by the earlier more flexible guidance laid down in **O'Brien**. **Etridge (No 2)** was a combined appeal of eight different cases which all raised similar issues. In seven of the cases the wife had allowed the matrimonial home in which she had part ownership to be used as surety for her husband's debts or the debts of the husband's company. The wife was thus a guarantor of the husband's debts (a surety) because the money lent by the bank was not given to both husband and wife, but only to the husband (or his company). The husband had got into financial difficulty and the bank had sought possession of the family home. The bank claimed an order for possession of the matrimonial home. The wife raised a defence that the bank was on notice that her agreement to the transaction had been obtained by her husband's undue influence. The eighth appeal concerned a claim by a wife for damages from a solicitor who acted for her when she provided her house as security for the husband's debts. Five of the appeals were allowed and three were dismissed.

In order to avoid constructive notice of undue influence, a bank had to take reasonable steps to satisfy itself that the wife had had brought home to her, in a meaningful way, the practical implications of the proposed transaction. Banks are not obliged to hold a personal meeting with the wife.

Ordinarily, it would be reasonable that a bank should be able to rely upon written confirmation from a solicitor, acting for the wife, that he or she had advised the wife appropriately.

Independent legal advice

In order to avoid having constructive notice of undue influence, the bank can rely on written confirmation from a solicitor that they have given the contracting party (usually the wife) appropriate advice. The bank should take steps to check directly with the wife the name of the solicitor she wished to act for her. The solicitor can also be acting for the bank or the husband of the contracting party. The advantages of a solicitor acting solely for the wife did not justify the additional expense that it would involve for the husband.

Solicitors should obtain from the bank any information needed to advise their client. If the bank failed for any reason to provide the requested information, then the solicitor should refuse to provide confirmation to the bank that the client had been advised. Exceptionally, there might be a case where the bank believed or suspected that the wife had been misled by her husband or was not entering into the transaction of her own free will. If such a case occurred, the bank had to inform the wife's solicitors of the facts giving rise to its belief or suspicion.

Solicitors should see their client in a face-to-face meeting, without the husband being present. They would need to explain to their client the purpose for which they had become involved. Typically, the solicitor would be expected to:

- explain the nature of the documents and their practical consequences for the wife;
- point out the seriousness of the risk involved;
- discuss the wife's financial means, including her understanding of the value of the property being charged;
- discuss the husband's financial position, including the amount of the husband's indebtedness and the amount of his overdraft facility;

- discuss whether the wife or her husband had any other assets out of which repayment could be made if the husband's business should fail; and
- state clearly that the wife had a choice whether or not to proceed with the transaction.

The solicitor should not give any confirmation to the bank without the wife's authority. The House rejected the Court of Appeal's suggestion that where a transaction is not one into which the wife could properly be advised to enter, a solicitor should in effect veto the transaction by declining to act further. The solicitor's duty is only to provide reasoned advice: it is up to the wife to decide whether to proceed. Only in 'exceptional circumstances' where it is 'glaringly obvious' that the wife has been 'grievously wronged' should the solicitor cease to act. If the solicitor considered the transaction was not in the wife's best interest, he would give reasoned advice to the wife to that effect. But, at the end of the day, the decision on whether to proceed was the decision of the client, not the solicitor.

The bank was entitled to proceed on the assumption that a solicitor advising the wife had done his or her job properly, unless it knew or ought to have known that this was not so.

It is not sufficient for a bank to instruct a solicitor to attend to the formalities in the signing of a legal charge, without expressly asking the solicitor to advise the wife. Without such an express request, the solicitor is merely acting for the bank and the wife will probably simply have attended the solicitor's office to sign documents, without receiving advice. This was the basis upon which some of the wives in the **Etridge (No 2)** appeal won their case.

Bars to relief

As undue influence is an equitable doctrine, relief will be barred on similar grounds to those discussed in relation to the limits on the right to rescission for misrepresentation (see p. 154).

▶ Inequality of bargaining power

In **Lloyds Bank** *v* **Bundy** Lord Denning suggested that economic duress was simply an example of a general principle of inequality of bargaining power. He argued that this general principle allows English law to give relief to anyone who, without taking independent advice, makes a contract on very unfair terms, or sells property for much less than it is worth, because their own bargaining power is seriously compromised by ignorance, infirmity or need. Clearly, this principle goes further than simple undue influence, since there is no suggestion that the other party had behaved improperly.

Lord Denning's reasoning has produced widely different reactions. Some overseas jurisdictions have regarded it as a bold, creative theory, but in England it has generally been disapproved by other judges. It is interesting to note, though, that in most of the cases where it has been criticized, the judges do nevertheless go to great lengths to analyse whether a transaction is substantively fair.

▶ ANSWERING QUESTIONS

1 Sheila consults her bank manager, Ms Suet, over her plans to sell her house. Sheila is a widow and she frequently consults Ms Suet on financial and personal matters. When told that Sheila intends to sell her house, Ms Suet offers to buy it at the current market price. Sheila accepts the offer and the sale is completed. Six months later house prices have risen by 25 per cent and Sheila is seeking to have the sale of the house set aside, on the grounds that Ms Suet has taken advantage of her position as Sheila's bank manager.

Advise Sheila. *Oxford*

The issue here is undue influence. As you know, this may be either actual or presumed; since actual undue influence requires illegitimate pressure, similar to, but short of, duress, there seems to be no sign of that here – Ms Suet simply makes an offer which Sheila accepts. Is there a presumption of undue influence? Two elements are required: a relationship of trust, and a manifest disadvantage for Sheila in the transaction. As far as the first requirement is concerned, as a matter of fact there does appear to be a relationship of trust and confidence between Sheila and Ms Suet: the case of **Lloyds Bank v Bundy** is relevant here.

If a relationship of trust is established – and it seems clear that it can be – the next question is whether the transaction was manifestly disadvantageous, as discussed in **Bundy**, **Morgan** and **O'Brien**. It is not absolutely clear whether there was a manifest disadvantage to Sheila in the transaction – on the face of it, being paid the going rate does not seem disadvantageous, but this might depend on whether it was obvious that house prices were going to rise drastically, or whether Sheila had a particular reason for selling at that point. It is perfectly reasonable to state that you would need more information in order to decide whether there was a manifest disadvantage, so long as you can state what difference the existence of such disadvantage would make – in this case, that if there was no manifest disadvantage, the contract would be valid, and that if there was manifest disadvantage, assuming the relationship of trust had been proved, the contract might be set aside, or its terms modified to counteract the disadvantage, unless Ms Suet could disprove the presumption by showing that Sheila had taken independent advice.

2 To what degree does the validity of a contract depend on the relative bargaining strengths of the parties?

Your introduction should set the question in its context, explaining that the basis of contract is voluntary agreement, and that since imbalances in bargaining strength can produce agreements that are not genuinely voluntary, contract law has developed rules aimed at helping the weaker party.

As far as the common law is concerned, the doctrines of duress and undue influence are the most important ways of doing this. Explain the effect of each, and, remembering that the question asks 'to what degree', highlight the limitations on each, using cases to illustrate your points. For example, in explaining that economic duress will only apply where the coercion involves more than mere commercial pressure, you could contrast the cases of **North Ocean Shipping** and **Pao On**, and **Atlas Express** v **Kafco** with **CTN** v **Gallaher**. Similarly, in relation to undue influence, you can highlight the fact that presumed undue influence will only apply where there is a manifest disadvantage, contrasting **Bundy** with **O'Brien** and **Morgan**.

You should also point out that statute has intervened to redress the balance between parties of unequal strength, particularly in the area of consumer sales, and describe the ways in which UCTA and the Unfair Terms in Consumer Contracts Regulations 1999 can be used to make contractual provisions invalid.

3 Janet, a partially sighted invalid, and John Smith, her husband, jointly own the family house which is mortgaged to the County Building Society. John Smith, an optimistic but unsuccessful businessman, is unable to meet the mortgage repayments, so the building society has started proceedings for repossession.

In order to avoid the loss of the house the Smiths approach their bank, the Mid West Bank plc, with a view to re-financing the mortgage. The loans manager of the Mid West Bank visits the Smiths at their home with the relevant documents. Janet Smith makes it absolutely clear that she has no confidence in her husband's business ventures, and will not sign any documents that cover her husband's business liability. The loans manager assures her that the document does not cover any business liability. He also states that if she does not sign, one of the consequences could be the loss of her home and she would therefore become homeless. The loans manager is extremely forceful and persistent in his insistence that she should sign the document. After hesitation and a request that the document be explained to her because she is unable to read it owing to disability and the size of the print, she eventually signs it.

She then discovers that the document secures a charge over the house covering not only the mortgage but also her husband's business debts.

Discuss the various grounds on which Janet Smith might avoid the contract. *AQA*

The first point to note here is that you are asked to discuss the **various** grounds on which Janet might avoid the contract. The facts of this problem at first glance appear very similar to those in the banking cases on undue influence, and it would be easy to assume that this is all the question is about, when in fact it raises several vitiating factors.

Since undue influence is the most obvious of these, it is probably a good starting point. In deciding whether Janet can rely on it, you need to look at both actual and presumed undue influence. Note that for presumed undue influence, the relationship between bank staff and their clients is not one of those where a fiduciary relationship is presumed to exist, so a fiduciary relationship would have to be established on the facts. We are not told whether Janet has banked with the Mid West Bank for a long time, or was in the habit of consulting them for advice, as was the case in **Bundy**; on the face of it, her relationship with the bank would appear to be more like that of Mrs Morgan in **Morgan**. For presumed undue influence, you also need to consider whether the transaction was manifestly disadvantageous to Janet; this is not necessary for actual undue influence.

Economic duress is another possibility you should discuss, given that Janet appears to be put under heavy pressure by the loans manager. In the light of **North Ocean Shipping** and **Atlas Express** v **Kafco**, you need to consider whether the loans manager was using pressure that would be regarded by the law as illegitimate, and whether Janet had any practical alternative but to comply.

Given Janet's partial sight, and her request to have the document explained to her, you will need to discuss the doctrine of *non est factum*. Note that this is a difficult doctrine to satisfy, as the case of **Saunders** v **Anglia Building Society** (see p. 177 above) shows. To avoid the contract on this ground, Janet would need to prove not only that she was tricked into signing the document, but that the trick had the result of her being misled as to the nature of the document, not just its legal effect. However, the fact that she asked for it to be explained will count in her favour, since the courts are less likely to allow a claim of *non est factum* where the person making the claim has been careless in some way.

Finally, you should consider misrepresentation. Did the loans manager make an untrue statement of fact, which induced Janet to enter the contract? Without a knowledge of land law, you will not be expected to know whether the remark about losing her home is true, but it is clear that the claim that the document did not cover John's business debts was untrue, and a statement of fact. It then only needs to be one of the reasons why Janet entered the contract.

Part 4

The rights and liabilities of third parties

The people who make a contract and provide consideration for it are the parties to the contract. Other people, who may receive a benefit or a burden from the performance of the contract, are described as third parties. For example, Ann may agree to buy Ben's car for £1,000. Ann may have told her daughter, Claire, that she will be able to drive the car once her mother has bought it. This transaction can be portrayed by the following diagram.

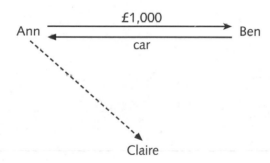

The traditional rule is that only the parties to a contract incur rights and obligations under the contract. This is known as the privity rule. But, increasingly, there are exceptions to this rule.

13 Third parties

The privity rule

A third party to a contract is a person who is not a party to the contract and has not provided consideration for the contract but has an interest in its performance. There has been a long-established rule that only the parties to a contract could incur rights and obligations under it. Described as the doctrine of privity, this principle meant that third parties could neither sue nor be sued under a contract.

Even where a contract was made for the benefit of a third party, that party still had no rights under it, as can be seen from the old case of **Tweddle** *v* **Atkinson** (1861). The plaintiff was engaged to be married and his father and future father-in-law made a contract providing that each of them would give a certain sum of money to the plaintiff. Even though the contract expressly provided that the plaintiff was to be entitled to enforce it, the court held that he could not do so.

The same approach was taken in the case of **Beswick** *v* **Beswick** (1968). The plaintiff's husband sold his business to his nephew in return for an annual allowance to be paid to himself and, after his death, to his widow. Once the husband died, the nephew refused to make payments to the widow. Despite the fact that the husband had clearly intended her to benefit from the contract, it was held that the widow could not sue the nephew on her own behalf, because she was not a party to the contract. However, in this case the court was able to get round the doctrine, because the widow was also the executor of her husband's estate and could, therefore, sue on behalf of the estate.

A large number of exceptions to the privity rule had been developed over the years, to avoid extreme cases of injustice, but these numerous exceptions rendered this area of law extremely complex.

Reform

There are two main aspects to the rule of privity. The first is that the third party cannot be made the subject of a burden imposed by the contract. The second is that a third party cannot enforce a benefit purported to be granted by the contract. The first principle has generally been regarded as just and sensible, as it would be odd if two contracting parties could oblige a third party to build a wall between their homes when the third party has nothing to do with the contract. But the second aspect of the rule has been heavily criticized in the past, and it is this aspect of the rule which has been the subject of a major reform.

There had been many calls for reform of the privity rules over the years. Back in 1937 the Law Revision Committee called for legislation to enable a third party who is expressly given rights under a contract to enforce those rights directly. Lord Scarman commented in 1980 in **Woodar Investment Development Ltd** *v* **Wimpey Construction UK Ltd** that: 'If the opportunity arises, I hope the House will reconsider **Tweddle** *v* **Atkinson** and the other cases which stand guard over this unjust rule.'

The Law Commission issued a report, in 1996, *Privity of Contract: Contracts for the Benefit of Third Parties*. This report proposed that, in certain circumstances, the privity of contract rule should no longer apply. This led to a major reform of the law with the passing of the Contracts (Rights of Third Parties) Act 1999, so that now the privity rule only has a very limited application. The Act has made a significant change to the way in which contracts can be enforced by third parties. Under the new Act, Mrs Beswick would probably be able to sue her nephew in her own capacity, rather than only as the executor of her husband's estate.

Contractual rights conferred on third parties

The privity rule now only has a very limited application following the passing of the Contracts (Rights of Third Parties) Act 1999. The impact of the Act can be understood by looking at the Law Commission's Report, where the Law Commission commented:

> it is important to emphasise that, while our proposed reform will give some third parties the right to enforce contracts, there will remain many contracts where a third party stands to benefit and yet will not have a right of enforceability. Our proposed statute carves out a general and wide-ranging exception to the third party rule, but it leaves that rule intact for cases not covered by the statute.

The rights conferred on third parties by the 1999 Act therefore have the character of a new statutory exception to the common law doctrine of privity. Prior to this Act, statute, common law and equity had all developed exceptions to the privity rule which will still be of interest where the 1999 Act does not apply, or as alternative grounds for founding a legal action. The 1999 Act does not affect any rights which third parties have apart from its provisions: thus it does not deprive third parties of rights which they have because their case falls within one of the other exceptions. Situations may arise in which it will be to the third party's advantage to rely on one of the old exceptions rather than on the new Act. The scope of the doctrine and these other exceptions therefore also need to be examined. The range of third party rights can arise under statute, common law or equity, and will now be considered.

▶ Statutory rights

Contracts (Rights of Third Parties) Act 1999

The Contracts (Rights of Third Parties) Act 1999 enables third parties to enforce contractual terms in certain situations. The Act received Royal Assent on 11 November 1999. It applies to contracts made on or after 11 May 2000, or to contracts made during the six-month period after Royal Assent if the contract expressly states that the Act applies.

Under the Act, people who are not parties to a contract can sue on it in two situations:

- the contract expressly provides that they may do so; or
- the contract purports to confer a benefit upon them, unless the parties did not intend it to be enforceable.

Express provision in the contract
The first situation is laid down in s. 1(1)(a) which gives third parties a right to enforce the contract if 'the contract expressly provides that he may'. This enables the contracting parties to provide expressly for a third party to be able to enforce a term of the contract. An illustration of when this might be useful is provided by the Law Commission report:

> A (a developer) and B (the client) might wish to designate C (a management company) as having the right to sue to enforce warranties in the construction contract for D–Z (the tenants).

The contract purports to confer a benefit
The second situation is laid down in s. 1(1)(b). This applies when the term of the contract 'purports to confer a benefit' on the third party. This is subject to an important proviso in s. 1(2), whereby it will not apply 'if on a proper construction of the contract it appears that the parties did not intend the term to be enforceable by the third party'. Thus, if the contracting parties do not want any other persons to have a right to enforce any part of the contract, they can expressly state this in the contract. It seems that a 'benefit' within s. 1(1)(b) can include any performance due under the contract, such as a payment of money, a transfer of property, the rendering of a service, or the benefit of an exclusion or limitation clause (s. 1(6)). The term must, moreover, purport to confer the benefit on the third party, so that it is not enough for third parties to show that they would happen to benefit from its performance. If, for example, Ann

agreed to pay Ben £20 for cutting the hedge which grew between her house and Tom's house, a court would probably consider that performance of the contract might benefit Tom, but it did not 'purport to confer a benefit' on Tom.

Identifying the third party

Under either limb it is not necessary for the third party to be specifically named: it is sufficient for him or her to be 'expressly identified in the contract by name, as a member of a class or as answering a particular description' (s. 1(3)). Hence phrases such as 'adjoining occupiers', 'successors in title', 'future owners and occupiers' and 'the owners of nos 1–5 Acacia Avenue' will be capable of conferring rights of enforcement upon these people in appropriate circumstances. Nor need the person be in existence at the time of the contract: rights could be conferred upon a company which is yet to be incorporated, an unborn child or a future spouse.

Consent to variations

The rights given under s. 1 would be of limited value if the contracting parties could at any time change their minds and remove the promised benefit. Section 2 deals with the issue of amending and cancelling the contract. This states that, unless the contract provides otherwise, the parties to the contract may not rescind the contract, or vary it so as to extinguish or alter the third party's rights, without his or her consent if the third party has either:

- communicated to the promisor their assent to the relevant term;
- relied on the term and the promisor knows of that reliance; or
- relied on the term and the promisor can reasonably be expected to have foreseen that reliance.

If one of these three situations applies, then any variations or cancellation can only take place with the consent of the third party. Take, for example, a situation where Tom has been promised £1,000 by Ann under a contract between Ann and Ben. The fact that he has, in reliance on that promise, spent some of the money he is expecting to receive will be enough to prevent Ann and Ben cancelling the promise, provided that Ann knew or could reasonably be expected to have known that Tom had relied on the promise.

The need for consent to variations can be dispensed with by the court if the third party cannot be traced or is incapable of giving consent (s. 2(4)), and if this occurs the court can order compensation to be paid to the third party (s. 2(6)).

The Act permits the contracting parties to vary the circumstances in which a third party's consent is required, or to exclude its requirement altogether (s. 2(3)).

Enforcement
Third parties have the same remedies as would be available to them if they were contracting parties, including the rights to damages and specific performance (s. 1(5)). Although the contract is enforceable by the promisee as well as the third party, there cannot be double liability for the promisor (s. 5), so any recovery by the promisee would have the effect of reducing any award subsequently made to the third party.

Defences
In an action by the third party, the promisor is able to rely on any defence arising out of the contract which would have been available to him or her had the claim been by the promisee (s. 3). Thus, if the promisee induced the promise by misrepresentation or duress, the promisor can use that as a defence to an action by the third party.

The promisor will also be able to rely on any set-off arising between the contracting parties from unrelated dealings. This could arise where Ann contracts with Ben that Ann will pay Tom £1,000 if Ben gives his car to Ann. If Ben owes £700 to Ann under a wholly unrelated contract, Ann could set off that sum against a claim by Tom for the £1,000 and only pay £300.

Excluding the Act
It must be remembered that the main contracting parties are still in control. They can decide that the provisions of the new Act should not apply and there will be nothing that the third party can do about it.

Insurance

The Married Women's Property Act 1882 provides that where a husband or wife takes out a life insurance policy for the benefit of their spouse or children, the contract can be enforced by the beneficiary.

The Road Traffic Acts make it obligatory for motorists to insure against liability for injury they may cause to other road users, and in certain circumstances those injured may claim directly against the insurance company, even though they are not a party to any contract with that company.

Similarly, under the Third Parties (Rights Against Insurers) Act 1930, where a person incurs liability to another, and is covered for that liability by an insurance policy, the other person can, in certain circumstances, claim on the policy.

Covenants relating to land

Under s. 56(1) of the Law of Property Act 1925, privity of contract does not apply to restrictive covenants (which are agreements not to do something) relating to land, providing they are registered in the land register. As an example of why this should be, suppose A sells the field beside her home to B, so that B can build a house there. Naturally, A will want to be sure that B will not build a nightclub instead, so she may make him promise, as part of the contract, that he will only build a house. This will be a restrictive covenant relating to land. In time, B may sell the field, and since A will have no contract with the new buyer, without the protection of s. 56(1) she would have been at risk of a nightclub next door all over again.

Bills of exchange

Under the Bills of Exchange Act 1882, a third party can sue on a bill of exchange, the most common form of which is a cheque. For example, B does some work for A, who pays by cheque. B happens to owe that amount to C, so endorses the cheque (by signing on the back, so that it becomes payable to whomever she gives it to) and pays C with it. If the cheque bounces, C may sue A on it, even though there is no contract between them. However, the Act does not allow either B or C rights against A's bank.

Section 6 of the Contracts (Rights of Third Parties) Act 1999 states that the Act does not apply to Bills of Exchange.

Common law exceptions

Agency

The term 'agent' has a specific meaning in this context, and applies to an individual who makes a contract on behalf of someone else, who is known as the principal. When the word 'agent' is used in everyday language it does not necessarily have this legal meaning; the fact that in ordinary language a car dealer might be described as a Fiat agent, for example, does not make that person an agent for the purposes of privity, since they will be buying and selling cars on their own behalf, even though all those cars may be made by Fiat.

An agent, in the sense we are using here, is viewed by the law as the intermediary of the principal, rather than a true party to the contract. In practice, one party to a contract made by agency is usually a corporation of some kind, such as a company or local authority, and the agent is their employee.

There are three circumstances in which a person will be treated as being the principal's agent: where there is express authority; where there is implied authority; and where there is apparent (also called ostensible) authority. Express authority is the most straightforward and means that the agent has been specifically asked to make the contract in question. Implied authority arises where the agent is asked to do something which by implication requires the contract to be made. An example might be where a driver is asked to take a car from London to Edinburgh, which would probably imply that the driver should buy petrol on the way on behalf of the principal, so that in the contract for the petrol the driver would merely be the agent.

Apparent authority can cause more problems. It arises where the principal's past behaviour gives the other party to the contract reason to believe that the agent has authority to contract on the principal's behalf. Take, for example, the common situation where a firm employs someone whose duties include buying stationery, and the agent simply orders the goods from the usual supplier, and has the bill sent to the firm. The employee later leaves the company, but the stationery supplier is not told. If the employee then apparently collects an order as usual, the firm may be liable for the price, even though the employee no longer has actual authority to buy for them.

Apparent authority cannot be created solely by the behaviour of the supposed agent. The fact that Ann claims to have authority to make a contract with Ben as the agent of Claire does not in itself make Claire liable on the contract as the principal; it will only do so if Claire has given Ben good reason to believe that Ann has such authority. If this is the case, Claire is liable, even though Ann is lying or mistaken.

Where an agent is covered by any of the three types of authority, the principal will be bound by any contract made that falls within that authority, as they are treated as having privity of contract. In **Waugh** *v* **Clifford** (1982) a firm of solicitors was employed to pursue certain litigation. In such circumstances, a solicitor generally has implied authority to negotiate a compromise with the other party, and so reach a settlement but, in this case, their client had specified that they were not to settle without reference to him. The other party to the litigation was unaware of this instruction, so assumed that the solicitors had the usual authority. The solicitors did in fact settle with the other side, but their client claimed he was not bound by this, because they were acting outside their authority. While the Court of Appeal recognized that the solicitors' implied authority had been terminated, it held that they still had apparent authority, and therefore their client was bound.

Where an agent makes a contract which lies outside the authority granted by the principal, or where the agent in fact has no authority at all, the principal may nevertheless choose to ratify the contract, so long as the agent was purporting to act on the principal's behalf at the time the contract was made, and the principal had the capacity to make the contract at that time. Once a contract is ratified by the principal, it becomes binding on the principal.

Undisclosed principals

In some cases, an agent may act for a principal without disclosing the principal's identity, or even the fact that there is a principal. English law nevertheless holds that it is the principal with whom the contract is made, so that it is effectively possible to make a contract with someone without even knowing that they exist. This is, of course, in complete contradiction with the usual principles of privity, but is nevertheless the law.

While the principal remains undisclosed, the agent is personally liable on the contract; once the principal is disclosed, if a claim arises, the other party to the contract can choose whether to sue the principal or the agent.

There is one important limitation on the creation of an agency situation where the principal is undisclosed. If the contract is such that it was reasonable to infer that the agent could only have been contracting on their own behalf, there will be no agency, and the purported agent will in fact be liable on the contract. The commonest example of this situation is where a service contracted for is one which relies on personal skill, such as painting a picture.

Warranty of authority

If an individual purports to make a contract on behalf of someone else, but in fact has no authority to do so, where does that leave the party contracted with? In **Collen** *v* **Wright** (1857) it was held that in such a situation it may be possible to hold that the purported agent has contracted that he or she does have authority. So the supposed principal would not be liable but the purported agent would be. Thus in **Penn** *v* **Bristol and West Building Society** (1997) a solicitor had put himself forward as acting as the agent of both the husband and wife who were joint owners of a house. When the house was sold he was found liable by the Court of Appeal for breach of warranty of authority to the building society who had lent money on the sale of the house, when it later transpired that the solicitor was only acting as agent to the husband, and the wife knew nothing about the sale.

Assignment

It is possible to assign (in effect, to sell) the benefit of a contract without the permission of the other party. A common example is where small businesses, having cash flow problems, sell the debts owed to them by others to what are called factoring houses. The factoring house buys the debt at less than its value, and so makes a profit when it collects from the creditor; the small business may lose a little of what it was owed, but gets its money quicker, and with less effort. Once a debt is assigned, the creditor owes the money to the party to which it was assigned, and not to the party originally contracted with.

It is not possible to assign the burden of a contract without the other parties' permission. There are obvious reasons for this rule; without it, for example, a debtor could simply assign the debt to someone who was bankrupt.

Negotiability

Certain types of contractual benefit can be assigned merely by being put into a written document and given to another party; the original owner of the benefit need not be notified. The written document is called a negotiable instrument, and the most common examples are banknotes and cheques.

A cheque, for example, represents money 'owed' by the bank to the chequebook holder (in the sense that the bank has in its possession money belonging to the chequebook holder, assuming they are not overdrawn). By writing a cheque to a shopkeeper, the chequebook holder effectively assigns the benefit of the bank's 'debt' to him or her, to the shopkeeper. In most cases, the shopkeeper then banks the cheque, but it is possible for them to endorse it (by signing on the back), and then use it to pay someone else, effectively assigning the benefit of the bank's debt to them. They could in turn do the same, without ever having to notify either the bank or the chequebook holder.

Section 6 of the Contracts (Rights of Third Parties) Act 1999 states that the Act does not apply to negotiable instruments.

Novation

As we have seen, assignment only transfers the benefits, and not the burdens of a contract. To transfer both burdens and benefits, a novation is required. The effect of novation is that the old contract is destroyed and a new one created. It requires the agreement of both the original parties to the contract, and the third party who is to take on the liability, and consideration must be given for the new contract.

Damages on behalf of another

One obvious problem with the doctrine of privity occurs when a contracting party buys something on behalf of others – not in the sense of an agent, where the buyer would be paid back, but as, for example, when a woman buys a holiday for herself and her husband, or a mother pays for a meal for the family. Where there is a breach of contract, the rules of privity mean that the party with whom the contract was made can claim for their own loss, but should not be able to claim for that of the other people for whom they have paid.

This problem was addressed in **Jackson** *v* **Horizon Holidays Ltd** (1975). The plaintiff bought a package holiday to Sri Lanka for himself and his family. The holiday was a complete disaster, and Horizon were clearly in breach of contract. There was no problem with Mr Jackson's claim for defects in his own holiday, as he was a party to the contract, but clearly his family had lost out as well. Could he claim for their loss? The rules of privity would suggest not, but the Court of Appeal unanimously decided that he could, Lord Denning explaining at some length that Mr Jackson had bought the holiday for the benefit of his family, and should therefore be compensated for their loss as well as his own.

Despite the obvious conflict with the doctrine of privity, it is easy to appreciate the logic of this decision. It was initially disapproved (though not overruled) by the House of Lords in **Woodar Investment Development Ltd** *v* **Wimpey Construction UK Ltd** (1980). The House accepted that the ultimate decision was correct, but suggested that it should be based on the fact that the loss of enjoyment by his family was itself a loss to Mr Jackson, and it was the loss to him of their enjoyment that should be compensated, rather than the loss to them. Alternatively, they said, it might be that contracts arranged by one person for the benefit of a group should be treated as a special case.

In more recent cases, the courts have been more willing to award damages to reflect the loss of someone other than the claimant. In **Linden Gardens Trust** *v* **Lenesta Sludge Disposals** (1994) the House of Lords considered the situation where a building contract was made between parties for the development of a site as shops, offices and flats. Ownership of the site was later transferred to a third party. The building work was not carried out to a satisfactory standard so that the third party was forced to incur expenses remedying the defects. In an action for breach of the building contract brought by the company which originally owned the site, the contractor argued that no loss had been suffered by the original site owner as the property no longer belonged to it when the alleged breaches occurred, and it was therefore entitled to no more than nominal damages. In other words, the defendant argued that while there was a technical breach of contract, the original site owner could not receive substantial damages as the loss had been suffered by the third party. This argument was rejected by the House of Lords. Their Lordships did not say that their earlier decision in **Woodar** *v* **Wimpey** was wrong, but instead distinguished it on its facts. Lord Browne-Wilkinson took an exception (to the general principle that plaintiffs can recover damages only in respect of their own loss) that had been developed in shipping law and applied it to contracts in general. He said:

> The contract was for a large development of property which, to the knowledge of both [parties], was going to be occupied and possibly purchased by third parties . . . Therefore, it could be foreseen that damage caused by a breach would cause loss to a later owner and not merely to the original contracting party . . . In such a case, it seems to me proper . . . to treat the parties as having entered into the contract on the footing that [the original owner] would be entitled to enforce the contractual rights for the benefit of those who suffered from defective performance.

Thus the majority's approach was that where many shops, offices and flats are being built it was foreseeable that the site owner does not intend to keep and occupy them all, but intends to sell or rent them at a profit to others on completion. Where it is foreseeable that property will be transferred, the person (usually a builder) contracting to carry out services (usually construction work) on that property would be treated in law as having contracted for the benefit of all persons who might, after the time of contracting, acquire interests in the property. Thus the original owner of that property will be able to sue for breach of contract for loss suffered by the future owner. The loss is treated as having been suffered by the third party rather than by the original site owner, but the original owner can nevertheless receive substantial damages for that loss.

This decision has subsequently been followed by the Court of Appeal in **Darlington BC** *v* **Wiltshier Northern Ltd** (1995). The plaintiff, a local authority, wished to develop land which it already owned as a recreational centre. It needed to borrow money to finance the project, but central government had imposed restrictions on local government borrowing. It could therefore not accept a direct loan from the bank. Instead two contracts were made. The first one was between the builders and the bank under which the builders undertook to carry out the building work. The second was between the bank and the local authority, under which the bank undertook to assign the completed building and the benefit of any contractual rights against the builders to the local authority. This second contract stated that the bank was not to be liable to the local authority 'for any incompleteness or defect in the building work'.

On completion of the building, the bank, in accordance with the second contract, duly assigned its rights against the defendant to the local authority. The local authority then claimed damages against the building contractor for defects in the work. It was accepted that the local authority could not be put in a better position under the assigned contract than the bank had been under that contract. Therefore the courts had to explore what rights the bank had enjoyed under the contract. The building contractor argued that the bank could not have recovered substantial damages since it had suffered no loss – it was always intended that the building would be transferred to the plaintiff and the plaintiff had agreed to pay the bank in full. They claimed, therefore, that the bank was in no way responsible to the plaintiff for the condition of the building. This argument was accepted by the court of first instance, which awarded only nominal damages, but the decision was overturned by the Court of Appeal. Applying **Linden Gardens**, it held that the bank could have recovered substantial damages from the defendant in respect of the local authority's loss, and therefore the local authority could also do so once that contract was assigned to it.

In **Panatown** *v* **Alfred McAlpine Construction Ltd** (2000) the House of Lords made it clear that, if the contractual arrangement between the parties in fact provided the third party with a direct remedy against the wrongdoer, the exceptional rule in **Linden Gardens** could not be relied upon.

Collateral contracts

Where one party makes contracts with two others, the courts will some-times use the device of 'finding' a collateral contract between the two others to evade the privity rule. An example of this is **Shanklin Pier Ltd** v **Detel Products Ltd** (1951). The plaintiffs owned Shanklin Pier, and needed to have it repainted. They contacted Detel to inquire about the qualities of its paint, and were told that it lasted for between seven and ten years. The plaintiffs then employed contractors to repaint their pier, and specified that Detel's paint should be used. The painting was done, but after three months the paint began to deteriorate. The pier owners could not sue the painters, since it was not they who had promised the paint would last, and the pier owners had no contract with Detel, since the paint was bought by the painters. However, the court held that there was in fact a collateral contract between the pier owners and Detel: Detel had promised that the paint would last, and the pier owners' request that the painters should use Detel paint was consideration for that promise.

This approach was also taken in **New Zealand Shipping** v **Satterthwaite** (*The Eurymedon*) (1974), though under rather more complex reasoning. In this case, an English company was selling a drilling machine to the plaintiff, a buyer in New Zealand. The seller entered into a shipping contract, known as a bill of lading, with the firm who were to carry the machine to New Zealand. A bill of lading allows the seller to transfer both ownership of the goods and their rights under the contract to the eventual buyer during the journey; therefore by the time the goods arrive, they belong to the buyer, and the carrier is liable to the buyer and not to the seller.

The carriers in the case employed a firm of stevedores to unload the drill, and unfortunately they dropped it, causing considerable damage. The buyer was unable to claim the cost of this damage from the carrier, because of an exclusion clause in the bill of lading, and therefore tried to sue the stevedores, the defendants. The stevedores argued in their defence that they were also covered by the exclusion clause, but the plaintiff sub-mitted that this could not be the case, since they were not a party to the bill of lading.

Unusually, the decision of the Privy Council was not unanimous, but by a majority they held that the stevedores were protected by the clause, because the terms of the bill of lading were expressed to cover third parties. There was therefore a contract between the buyers and the stevedores, on the terms of the bill of lading, with the carriers acting as agents, despite not knowing they were doing so. Consideration for the collateral contract could be found, it was said, in the stevedores' promise to unload; while this promise was already owed to the carriers, it was not owed to the buyers.

This case has subsequently been given a restrictive interpretation in *The Mahkutai* (1996). A cargo of plywood was damaged and an action was brought before the courts in Hong Kong by the owners of the plywood against the shipowners. The latter argued that the Hong Kong courts did not have jurisdiction to hear the case. In support of this argument, they sought to rely on a term of the contract for the carriage of the plywood entered into by the charterer of their ship, which gave exclusive jurisdiction to the Indonesian courts. They were not a party to this contract, but the contract stated that sub-contractors should have the benefit of 'exceptions, limitations, provisions, conditions and liberties' contained in it. This argument was rejected by the Privy Council. It interpreted this extension of the scope of the contract as being restricted to terms aimed at protecting the sub-contractors. It did not therefore extend to a mutual agreement, such as an exclusive jurisdiction clause. While the judges accepted that there were commercial advantages in the parties involved in the sale and shipping of goods being subject to the same allocation of risk, these policy considerations did not require such issues to always be tried in the same country. As a result, exclusive jurisdiction clauses would not be treated in the same way as clauses exempting or limiting liability for damages to the goods.

The Privy Council considered whether the time had come to take a further step and to recognize the situations currently dealt with by *The Eurymedon* principle as involving 'a fully fledged exception to the doctrine of privity of contract', thus escaping from the technicalities of needing to find a collateral contract. It concluded, however, that it was not appropriate in the present case to take such a step as they were faced with an exclusive jurisdiction clause rather than an exemption clause. Thus, it may be that in the future the courts might not seek to find a collateral contract when faced with a case like *The Eurymedon*, but might be ready to say that they were faced with an exception to the privity rule.

Exceptions in equity

Constructive trust

A contracting party can specify that the benefit of the contract is held by him or her in trust for a third party, in which case that third party will have enforceable rights to the benefit. At one time, the courts seemed willing to imply such a trust where there seemed to be an intention to create one, even though there was no specific reference to a trust in the contract. In **Les Affréteurs Réunis SA** *v* **Walford** (1919) Walford, a broker, negotiated a charterparty between the owners of a ship and a company wanting to hire it. The charterparty provided that the owners would pay Walford a 3 per cent commission on the estimated price of the hire. They failed to pay this, so Walford sued them for it, joining the charterers as parties to the action. The House of Lords upheld his claim, on the basis that even though Walford was not a party to the agreement, the charterers were trustees of the promise to pay him, and he could enforce his claim by joining them as parties to the action. If they had not been willing to help, he could have sued them as co-defendants, the court held.

However, more recent cases have shown the courts unwilling to assume such a trust unless there is a clear intention to that effect; in **Green** *v* **Russell** (1959) it was held that a mere intention to benefit a third party was not enough by itself.

Restrictive covenants

As well as avoiding the rules on privity of contract under statute, restrictive covenants concerning land avoid those rules in equity, following the case of **Tulk** *v* **Moxhay** (1848).

Arguments for the privity rule

Free will

This argument is based on the idea that only the parties to a contract should incur rights and responsibilities since only they have agreed to do so. This 'free will' theory underlies the whole of contract law.

Lack of reciprocal rights

It can be argued that it would be unjust to allow a party to sue on a contract, if that party could not be sued on it. Yet, as Treitel's *The Law of Contract* (1999) points out, unilateral contracts are a situation in which one party can sue but not be sued – for example, Mrs Carlill could sue the Carbolic Smoke Ball Company on the basis of their offer to pay anyone who used their smokeball and got flu, but the Smoke Ball Company could not have sued Mrs Carlill (or anyone else) for not using the smokeball (**Carlill** *v* **Carbolic Smoke Ball Co** (1893)). This appears to cause no great problems in unilateral contracts.

In addition, as Hugh Collins has observed in *The Law of Contract* (1993), the promisor has normally had full performance before the prospect of the third party suing arises – for example, in **Beswick** the nephew already owned the business. Similarly, in **Jackson** *v* **Horizon Holidays**, it was true that the holiday company would have no right to sue Mr Jackson's family for the price of the holiday, but in practice such a right was not necessary since Mr Jackson was liable for the whole price, and in any case it had already been paid before there was any reason for the family to want to sue.

Restriction of the contracting parties' rights

Allowing third parties enforceable rights limits the rights of the contracting parties to modify or terminate the contract. Again, this is refuted by

Hugh Collins, who argues that contracts could simply provide that third-party rights would be lost in the event of modification or termination, with third parties being allowed to claim for any reliance expenditure (see p. 274) if that should happen.

Making gratuitous promises enforceable

It is also argued that to allow third parties enforceable rights makes gratuitous promises enforceable. It is difficult to see how this could logically be the case. The promise would not be gratuitous, but part of a binding contract, for which consideration has been given; that does not change simply because the beneficiary, rather than the other contracting party, tries to enforce it. In **Tweddle** v **Atkinson**, for example, the promise which the bridegroom tried to enforce was not a gratuitous promise to him, but part of a binding contract with his father.

The 'floodgates' argument

There have been worries that the Contracts (Rights of Third Parties) Act 1999 exposes promisors to indefinite liability, making it impossible to foresee what they will owe, when and to whom. However, this is an exaggeration. While it is true that a contract must draw the line for the imposition of liability somewhere, there is no reason why that line has to be drawn where a person has the status of a contractual party. Liability can instead be restricted while including third parties identified in the contract.

The construction industry has been particularly worried about the implications of the 1999 Act and during the passage of the Act a spirited attempt was made to exclude construction contracts from its scope. The industry is concerned that the Act may lead to the unwitting creation of third-party rights. Prior to its enactment, construction projects involved the negotiation of a series of separate collateral warranties which stood alongside the main contract to allocate third-party rights. The Law Commission felt that there was a clear advantage in being able to deal with the issue of third-party rights in the main contract. Collateral warranties frequently limit liability to a specified share or a just and equitable share of the third party's loss, but the Law Commission points out that similar limitations can, in the future, be provided for in the main contract. As to the worries that unintended third parties may acquire rights of enforcement, this could be avoided by the parties defining the extent of third-party rights, or excluding them altogether.

Frequently, a construction contract will provide that the building works will not cause annoyance or nuisance to adjoining occupiers, and it has been questioned whether neighbours would now be able to sue for breach of contract. In many respects, this might seem an unlikely consequence of the Act, and in order to be actionable it would mean construing the phrase 'confer a benefit' widely. Nevertheless, the Law Commission clearly envisages that it will be possible for the adjoining owners to have enforceable rights in contract.

It seems that for the time being, parties to construction agreements will probably prefer to exclude the provisions of the Act, and continue to use the well-established route of collateral warranties to avoid the privity rule.

Variation of third-party rights

Where the privity rule is excluded, problems can arise over the issue of varying third parties' rights under a contract. This was one of the worries of the construction industry. Given the complex web of agreements and the number of persons involved in building projects, it will be inconvenient to have to obtain third-party consent to any contractual variation once the third-party rights have crystallized. The solution lies in the drafting of the contract. It is always open to the contracting parties to exclude the requirement for third-party consent, or to define in what circumstances third-party consent to a variation is required. Further, it is only variations to the contract itself that trigger the consent requirements. Although most construction contracts contain clauses permitting the employer to order variations to the work, these changes to the specifications are technically not variations to the contract, and so do not trigger the need for consent from any third party. This was the Law Commission's view, and it was confirmed during the Bill's passage through Parliament.

▶ Arguments against the privity rule

Extended litigation

The privity rule could lead to a chain of contract claims, because it prevented the party with the problem suing the party who actually caused it. A common example is where a consumer buys goods which have been badly manufactured. Because the consumer's contract is usually with the retailer, it is the retailer they must sue, even though the defect has been caused by the manufacturer. The retailer can then in turn sue the manufacturer under their contract, or if the retailer has bought from a distributor, the distributor is next in line to be sued, and the distributor then sues the manufacturer. In most cases this simply makes things a little more complicated and lawyers a little richer, but it can cause practical problems where one party in the chain goes out of business.

Irrational

While it seems reasonable that someone who is not a party to a contract should not incur obligations under it, it is less easy to understand why

English law was so firmly set against allowing third parties enforceable rights under a contract.

Intention of the parties

One of the arguments in favour of the privity rule was the concept of free will, but this can also work against the rule. Lord Steyn has observed in **Darlington Borough Council *v* Wiltshier Northern Ltd** (1995):

> The case for recognising a contract for the benefit of a third party is simple and straightforward. The autonomy of the will of the parties should be respected. The law of contract should give effect to the reasonable expectations of contracting parties. Principle certainly requires that a burden should not be imposed on a third party without his consent. But there is no doctrinal, logical, or policy reason why the law should deny effectiveness to a contract for the benefit of a third party where that is the expressed intention of the parties.

Hugh Collins further maintains in his book that, if we are talking about free will and agreement, why should the law not provide a mechanism for enforcing two parties' agreement that a third party should benefit from their contract? The fact that it does not do so may in fact go against what the parties have agreed and allow one party to revise the agreement without the consent of the other. In **Beswick**, for example, the nephew would have been able to go back on his promise to his uncle if his aunt had not been made executor.

Unjust enrichment

Cases like **Beswick** show that the doctrine of privity could allow parties to escape their contractual obligations, yet still themselves benefit from the contract. In that case, it was a lucky chance that the widow was made executor; that position could easily have been given to the nephew, in which case he would have been able to keep the business without paying most of the price.

Justifiable reliance

It can be argued that a contract should protect those who, while not a party to it, incur losses because they reasonably rely on its performance. This principle seems to have been behind the way in which the courts got round the privity rule by the use of collateral contracts, in cases such as **Shanklin Pier** and **New Zealand Shipping**. In the latter case, the owner of the machine had promised in the contract that their rights against the carrier and any sub-contractors would be limited, and it was reasonable for the sub-contractors to rely on this when considering their own insurance coverage.

International approach

Many modern legal systems have a much more flexible attitude to the issue of who can enforce a contract, including the US and most European countries. The Contracts (Rights of Third Parties) Act 1999 brings English law into line with these other legal systems.

Legal complexity

The sheer number of exceptions to the privity rule means that in practice it has caused fewer problems than might be expected, but this in turn has made the law very complex in this field. On the one hand, the 1999 Act adds to the complexity by adding another major exception to the privity rule. On the other hand, it will provide a means for contractors to avoid some of the more complex and legally questionable devices they had been forced to use in the past to avoid the privity rule. The legislation will be particularly important for businesses in the software, construction and oil and gas industries. Companies in these fields had, before the Act, been forced to rely on a web of collateral warranties, agency agreements and trust devices. The construction industry used separate collateral warranties in favour of investors, purchasers and tenants. Now, the relevant rights can be granted by a clause in the building contract. This means, for example, that landowners will be able to pursue sub-contractors for design errors.

▶ ANSWERING QUESTIONS

1 Was Parliament right to vote for the Contracts (Rights of Third Parties) Act 1999?

Reform of the privity rule is likely to be a very popular question with examiners for the next few years following the enactment of the Contracts (Rights of Third Parties) Act 1999. You need to take a critical view of the Act looking at both its strengths and weaknesses. You could start by explaining that the Act was passed to tackle the perceived problems with the privity rule and briefly explain the privity rule. The main material you will need to analyse whether the Act was required is contained in pp. 226–30. In particular, you could point out that some of the disadvantages of the privity rule were avoided in the past by relying on exceptions that existed prior to the passing of the 1999 Act. You could also discuss in detail the caution of the construction industry to the new legislation and the reasons for their concerns which are discussed at p. 227.

2 X received an advertisement through the post offering a special discount on cruise holidays if she booked within a month and paid by credit card. In February, she booked a two-week luxury Mediterranean cruise leaving in June. It cost £5,000 for herself, her husband and two children, and she paid a deposit of £500 using her credit card. In late May she received a letter informing her that the cost of the holiday would be £5,500 because of the unforeseeable repairs which had become necessary to the cruise ship. The total cost would now be more than the original would have been without the special discount offer. However, as it was so close to the time of the holiday, X and her family decided that they had no option but to go ahead with the cruise. The entire cruise proved to be very disappointing, as there were thunderstorms every day and the food was extremely poor. A waiter spilled red wine sauce over X's best evening dress worth £600, ruining it, and both children suffered food poisoning which confined them to their cabin for three days of the cruise.

Now that they have returned from the holiday, X, her husband and two children would like to claim compensation for the additional cost of the cruise, and the disappointing cruise. The children want compensation for the food poisoning which they have suffered. Advise each of them as to whether they can claim, and if so, how and from whom. *London*

The first issue to consider was the formation of the contract and whether the advertisement amounted to an offer or an invitation to treat. As the contract was made by post, the postal rule should be mentioned. It is clear that at the latest a contract was formed once the tendered payment of the £500 deposit had been accepted. The next stage in the question raises issues relating to the discharge of a contract, which are discussed in the next chapter. In summary, it is unlikely that this initial contract was frustrated (discussed at p. 240) by the need for unforeseeable repairs to the boat as these have merely rendered execution of the contract more onerous rather than impossible. Alternatively, by refusing to perform the contract as agreed (i.e. for £5,000) this may have constituted an anticipatory breach. X chose to affirm the contract despite the breach, but this can still leave a claim for damages.

This is a contract for both goods and services and would contain certain implied terms discussed in Chapter 16. Some of the terms of the contract have been broken, and the effect of these breaches will depend on whether they will be treated as conditions or warranties.

As regards the rights to compensation, a full discussion of the cases mentioned under the heading 'Damages on behalf of another' at p. 221 would be required. Particular emphasis should be placed on **Jackson v Horizon Holidays** due to the factual similarities. The children and the husband would have no right to bring an action themselves, but if X succeeded in receiving damages to reflect their loss, they may have a right to some of these damages.

This question also raises issues that stretch beyond the scope of this book to tort law and studies of the English legal system. These would consider questions of vicarious liability, the role of the county court and the growing use of methods of alternative dispute resolution such as arbitration by ABTA.

Part 5

Discharge and remedies

A contract is said to be discharged when the rights and obligations agreed in it come to an end. There are four ways in which this can happen: performance, agreement, breach and frustration. Where a contract is breached the innocent party will have a right to a remedy. This will in most cases be limited to financial compensation for loss suffered as a result of the breach, and it is only exceptionally that a court will order a party to fulfil their contractual obligations through an order of specific performance.

14 Discharge of contract

In this chapter we will look at the four ways in which a contract can come to an end: performance, agreement, breach and frustration.

PERFORMANCE

The most obvious way in which a contract is discharged is by both parties performing their obligations under it. In many cases this is quite straightforward, but there are circumstances in which one party may claim to have performed and therefore, for example, be entitled to payment, yet the other disagrees. As a result, the law has had to address the question of what will amount to performance.

The entire performance rule

The general rule is that performance must exactly match the requirements laid down in the contract, and this is known as entire performance. If the first party fails to perform, the other need pay nothing at all, even if the shortfall in performance actually causes no hardship.

Clearly, this rule has the potential to cause injustice, as can be seen in the case of **Cutter v Powell** (1795). A sailor had contracted to serve on a ship travelling from Jamaica to Liverpool. He was to be paid 30 guineas for the voyage, payable when the ship arrived in Liverpool, but he died during the journey. His widow sued for his wages up until his death, but her claim was unsuccessful. The court held that the contract required entire performance, and as he had not completed performance, she could claim nothing.

The rule can also allow parties who wish to escape from what has become an unprofitable contract to do so by taking advantage of the most minor departures from its terms. In **Re Moore & Co Ltd and Landauer & Co** (1921) the contract concerned the sale of canned fruits, which were to be packed in cases of 30 tins. On delivery, it was discovered that although the correct number of tins had been sent, about half the cases contained only 24 tins each. This actually made no difference at all to the market value of the goods, but the buyers pointed out that the sale was covered by the Sale of Goods Act 1979, which stated that goods sold by description must correspond with that description. The delivery sent clearly did not, and the buyers were therefore entitled to reject the whole consignment.

Mitigation of the entire performance rule

In practice, contracts requiring entire performance are the exception rather than the rule, although contracts for the sale of goods are usually entire. There are several ways in which the harshness of the rule is mitigated.

Substantial performance

Established in **Boone** v **Eyre** (1779) by Lord Mansfield, this doctrine allows a party who has performed with only minor defects to claim the price of the work done, less any money the other party will have to spend to put the defects right. The doctrine will only apply where the claimant has breached a warranty, or has breached an innominate term in a way that is not serious; it cannot be used where the claimant has breached a condition of the contract.

Substantial performance can be understood by contrasting two cases. In the first, **Hoenig** v **Isaacs** (1952), an interior decorator contracted to refurbish a flat for £750. The defendant had paid £400 in advance, but then refused to pay the remaining £350, arguing that the design and workmanship were defective. The court agreed that there were problems with the work done, but the cost of putting these right would only be £56. Consequently it was held that the decorator had substantially performed, and was entitled to the balance of the contract price, less the £56 needed to put right the defects.

In the second case, **Bolton** v **Mahadeva** (1972), a contractor had agreed to install a central heating system for £560. When the work was done, it was found that the system was unable to heat the house adequately, and emitted fumes. It would cost £174 to remedy these defects. The plaintiff claimed the contract price, less £174, on the basis that he had substantially performed, but the Court of Appeal rejected the claim. The proportion of the contract price required to put the work right was clearly greater than that in **Hoenig**, and the court considered that substantial performance had not taken place. Small domestic building contracts are usually treated as requiring entire performance. Builders carrying out such work have to complete all the work contracted for before they are entitled to be paid.

Severable contracts

A contract is said to be severable where payment becomes due at various stages of performance, rather than in one lump sum when performance is complete. Most contracts of employment are examples of this: employees are paid weekly or monthly, not all at once when they finally leave the company. Major building contracts usually operate in a similar way, with instalments falling due as various stages of construction are completed.

In a severable contract, the price for each stage can be claimed when that stage is completed, even though the party concerned may be in breach of the contract for not completing subsequent stages – so if you take on a childminder for the six-week school holidays and pay weekly, the child-minder can claim the first week's pay even if they then refuse to work the following five weeks.

Whether a contract is entire or severable is a question of construction.

Voluntary acceptance of partial performance

In some cases, while a contract may not originally have been intended to be severable, one party may later agree to accept and pay for part-performance from the other. Where such an agreement can be inferred from the circumstances, the claimant sues on a *quantum meruit*, to recover the cost of such performance as has been provided (see p. 286). The courts will only infer an agreement to accept and pay for part-performance where the party making the promise had a genuine choice – so, for example, this could not apply in **Cutter** *v* **Powell**, because the sailor was hardly in a position to offer the shipowners the choice of accepting part-performance or not.

The principle can be seen in **Sumpter** *v* **Hedges** (1898). A builder agreed to construct two houses and a stable on the defendant's land, for £565. However, he abandoned the project after completing £333 worth of work, so the defendant had to complete the building himself, and did so using materials left behind by the builder. The builder claimed on a *quantum meruit* for work done and materials supplied. The claim for the work failed; the defendant was not **choosing** to accept part-performance and finish the job himself; he had no real alternative but to complete the building, which would otherwise be just a useless mess on his land. However, he did not have to use the materials left behind, and so the builder was allowed to claim for these.

Prevention of performance by the other party

Where one party performs part of the agreed obligation, and is then prevented from completing the rest by some fault of the other party, a *quantum meruit* can be used to claim the cost of the work done.

In most of these cases, the innocent party can alternatively claim damages for breach of contract. This may be a higher amount, but there are circumstances in which a *quantum meruit* is more useful. An example is **Planché** *v* **Colburn** (1831) where the plaintiff was contracted to write a book on costume and ancient armour, for a fee of £100. After he had begun writing, the defendants decided to cease publishing the series of which the book was to form a part. The author was able to recover £50 on a *quantum meruit.*

Where one party cannot perform without the other's co-operation, rejection of an offer to perform (also called a tender of performance) will release the party tendering performance from any further obligation. In **Startup** *v* **Macdonald** (1843) the plaintiffs agreed to sell ten tons of oil to the defendants, to be delivered by the end of March. On the last day of March, the plaintiffs arrived with the oil at 8.30 pm, but the defendants refused to accept the delivery, saying it was too late in the day. The plaintiffs sued for damages, and were successful. The court held that they had done all they could to comply with the contract, and their tender of performance was sufficient basis for their claim (s. 29(5) of the Sale of Goods Act 1979 now provides that delivery must be made at a reasonable hour, so on the same facts a court might take a different approach today).

Slightly different rules apply to the tender of money, rather than goods. The party tendering the money is not obliged to repeat the offer, but the debt remains outstanding and the creditor can demand payment at a future date. Payment must also be of the exact amount due, and in the form of 'legal tender'. This means Bank of England notes for any amount, silver coins up to the value of five pounds, and copper up to the value of 20p – so if you decide to pay back your overdraft in 2p coins just to be annoying, the bank is perfectly free to reject it.

Breach of terms concerning time

What is the position when one party performs late, but in all other respects as agreed in the contract? The current law would appear to be that the effect of a delay in performance will depend on whether the time of performance is considered to be 'of the essence'. If this is the case, then late performance will give rise to a right to terminate the contract. Where time is not of the essence, late performance will not justify termination unless it amounts to a substantial failure in performance (though it is still a breach, which may give rise to damages if there is a resulting loss – **Raineri** *v* **Miles** (1981)). However, where the delay goes on so long that it becomes a frustrating event, it will, of course, be grounds for termination under the usual rules on frustration. When time is of the essence, any failure to perform on time justifies rescission, even if little or no hardship is caused.

There are three main ways in which a contract may be classified as one in which time is of the essence. First, the parties may explicitly state this in their agreement. Secondly, it may be inferred from the nature of the contract, or the circumstances surrounding it. Therefore in a contract to sell goods which quickly go off, or the price of which fluctuates very rapidly, time is obviously of the essence. For some types of contract, the rules on time stipulation are made by statute – for example, the Law of Property Act 1925, s. 41 states that time is not of the essence in contracts for the sale of land.

In the third category, a contract which is not originally one in which time is of the essence may become so if one party delays performance, and the other then gives notice of a time limit on performance. This was the case in **Charles Rickards Ltd** v **Oppenheimer** (see p. 80 above).

The current position was developed by the House of Lords in **United Scientific Holdings Ltd** v **Burnley Borough Council** (1978). The defendants in the case were landlords of premises leased by the tenants, under a 99-year lease running from 31 August 1962. For the first ten years, the rent was to be fixed, but there was provision for periodic rent reviews every ten years after that. If the landlords wished to take advantage of this provision, they were to take steps towards a rent review before the end of each ten-year period. In fact, the landlords did nothing about raising the rent until almost two months after the end of the first ten-year period. The tenant argued that time was of the essence, and that the landlords had therefore lost their chance to raise the rent, but this argument was rejected. Given the nature of the contract, the House of Lords held that there was a presumption that time was not of the essence, and so the landlords were still entitled to use the rent review procedure.

Where a contract does not specify a time for performance, performance must usually take place within a reasonable time.

Vicarious performance

Is a contract discharged if the contractual obligations of one of the parties are, at that party's request, performed by someone else? The answer depends on the type of contract. The general rule is that the other party cannot object to such vicarious performance unless it prejudices their interests. However, if the service contracted for is one which relies on the skill or judgement of one party, the other can insist on personal performance. Obvious examples are employment contracts, or a contract to paint a picture, or perform in a concert.

Clearly, a contract must also be performed personally if that is specified in the terms, or if, by implication, the terms prohibit vicarious performance. In **Davies** v **Collins** (1945) the defendant accepted a uniform for cleaning, under a contract stating that: 'Whilst every care is exercised in cleaning . . . garments, all orders are accepted at owners' risk.' The defendant sent the uniform to be cleaned by a sub-contractor, who lost it. It was held that this was a breach of contract, because the words 'every care is exercised in cleaning . . .' excluded the right to perform the cleaning operation vicariously.

Where vicarious performance is permitted, liability for performance nevertheless remains with the original contracting party. In **Stewart** *v* **Reavell's Garage** (1952) the plaintiff took a 1929 Bentley to the defendants' garage, to have the brakes re-lined. The defendants suggested that the work should be done by a sub-contractor and the plaintiff agreed. Unfortunately, the work was done badly, and the brakes failed, with the result that the plaintiff was injured. The defendants were clearly entitled to perform vicariously, as the plaintiff had agreed to their doing so, but they were still liable for the sub-contractor's defective workmanship.

FRUSTRATION

The basic principle here is that if, after a contract is made, something happens, through no fault of the parties, to make its performance impossible, the contract is said to be frustrated, and the obligations under it come to an end. Although there are many events which may make performance impossible, only certain limited types will allow a contract to be frustrated.

At one time, contractual responsibilities were generally regarded as absolute, and once a contract was made, subsequent events could not justify non-performance. This rule began to be relaxed with the case of **Taylor** *v* **Caldwell** (1863), from which the modern doctrine of frustration developed. The parties in the case had entered into an agreement concerning the use of the Surrey Gardens and Music Hall for a series of 'grand concerts, and day and night fetes'. Six days before the planned date for the first concert, the building was burnt down, making it impossible for the concerts to go ahead. The party planning to put on the concerts was sued for breach of contract, but the action failed because performance was impossible.

What will amount to frustration?

It is impossible to compile an exhaustive list of the situations in which a contract will become frustrated, but they fall into three broad categories: events which make performance or further performance impossible; those which make it illegal; and those which make it pointless.

Impossibility

A contract may become impossible to perform in any of the following ways.

- *Destruction or unavailability of something essential for contract's performance.* **Taylor** *v* **Caldwell** (1863) is an example of this.

- *Death of either party.* Contracts which require personal performance (as described above at p. 239) are discharged by frustration on the death of either party.
- *Unavailability of party.* Contracts requiring personal performance will be frustrated if either party falls ill or is imprisoned, providing that the non-availability of that party substantially affects the performance. In **Robinson v Davison** (1871) a piano player was booked to perform, but was ill on the day of the concert. He was sued for breach of contract, but it was held that the contract had been frustrated when his illness made it impossible to perform.
- *Method of performance impossible.* Where a contract lays down a particular method for performance, and this becomes impossible, the contract may be frustrated. In **Nickoll and Knight v Ashton Edridge & Co** (1901) a contract for the sale of cottonseed specified that it was 'to be shipped per steamship Orlando from Alexandria during . . . January'. The *Orlando* later ran aground in the Baltic, and could not therefore make the journey to Alexandria in January. A majority of the Court of Appeal interpreted the contract as requiring performance in the stipulated manner, and therefore held that the contract was frustrated since this could not be done. However, there may be cases where although a method of performance is stipulated, the contract can be interpreted as accepting an alternative method if necessary, and in this case, the contract will not be frustrated if the stipulated method of performance is impossible.

A contract is unlikely to be frustrated simply because performance has become more onerous or expensive than expected. This was established in a number of cases arising from the closure of the Suez canal during the 1956 'Suez crisis'. The canal was – and still is – an important 'short cut' for ships travelling between Europe and Asia, and when it was closed, journeys had to follow a much longer route, which was therefore much more expensive. Disputes arose where contracts were made before the closure of the canal, in the expectation that the shorter route would be used, but the courts held that if performance was still possible, the fact that it was now more expensive was irrelevant to the issue of frustration. An example of these cases is **Tsakiroglou Co Ltd v Noblee Thorl GmbH** (1962).

The leading modern case on frustration is **Davis Contractors v Fareham UDC** (1956). Davis, a building company, contracted to build 78 houses for a local authority. The job was to take eight months, at a price of £94,000. In fact, labour shortages delayed the work, which ended up taking 22 months and costing the builders £21,000 more than they had planned. The defendant was willing to pay the contract price, despite the delay, but as this did not cover the plaintiff's costs, Davis sought to have the contract discharged on the grounds of frustration, alleging that the labour shortages made performance fundamentally different from that envisaged in the contract (it intended to seek payment on a *quantum meruit* basis to recover its costs).

However, the House of Lords decided that the events which caused the delays were within the range of changes which could reasonably be expected to happen during the performance of a contract for building houses, and the changed circumstances did not make performance radically different from what was expected. It was a contract to build houses, and houses were in fact built. The problems incurred by the builder made his performance more burdensome to him, but they did not change the nature of what he was expected to do, and so the contract was not frustrated. Lord Radcliffe explained:

> It is not hardship or inconvenience or material loss itself which calls the principle of frustration into play. There must be as well such a change in the significance of the obligation that the thing undertaken would, if performed, be a different thing from that contracted for.

Supervening illegality

If, after a contract is formed, a change in the law makes its performance illegal, the contract will be frustrated. This happened to many contracts made just before the First and Second World Wars, as once war was declared, it became illegal to trade with enemy countries. In the leading **Fibrosa case** (see p. 245 below) a contract for the sale of machinery which was to be shipped to Poland was frustrated because the port was occupied by the enemy. Trade in various types of goods was also restricted, which again led to contracts concerning those goods being frustrated. Frustration by supervening illegality can of course happen outside wartime situations, but the two World Wars appear to have been a fruitful source of cases on this issue.

Performance made pointless

A contract can be frustrated where a supervening event makes performance of a contract completely pointless, though still technically possible. Another way of putting it is that there has been such a drastic change in circumstances that the contract becomes essentially different from that which was originally agreed. There are very tight limits on this aspect of the doctrine of frustration, and these are best illustrated by a pair of cases associated with the coronation of Edward VII in 1901. The coronation had been planned for a particular date, but in the event had to be postponed because the king fell ill. Since the postponement was made at the last moment, a great many preparations had been made and events organized, and it was from these that the two 'coronation cases' on frustration arose.

In the first case, **Krell** *v* **Henry** (1903), the defendant had agreed to rent from the plaintiff a suite of rooms in Pall Mall, for the day on which the coronation was to take place. The room offered a view of the coronation procession, and the defendant had intended to sell tickets to people wanting to watch from its windows. The contract did not mention the coronation, but the price to be paid reflected the significance of the day. Needless to say, when the coronation did not take place, the defendant no longer wanted the room, but the plaintiff nevertheless sued for the rent. The Court of Appeal held that although the contract was still capable of physical performance, it was frustrated, because the viewing of the procession was the 'foundation of the contract'. The court said that frustration could apply in cases where 'the event which renders the contract incapable of performance is the cessation or non-existence of an express condition or state of things, going to the root of the contract, and essential to its performance'.

The limits of this principle can be seen in the other well-known 'coronation case', **Herne Bay Steam Boat Co** *v* **Hutton** (1903). Here the defendant had hired a steamboat in order to take passengers to watch the naval review by the king, organized to mark the coronation. When the coronation was cancelled, so was the review, but the Court of Appeal held that the ability to watch the review was not fundamental to the contract; the defendant could still carry out pleasure trips on the boat. The contract was therefore not frustrated.

The contrast between these two cases is obviously an extremely fine one, and perhaps hard to justify. However, it is clear from more recent cases that despite the result in **Krell** *v* **Henry**, frustration cannot usually be invoked simply because one party has made what turns out to be a bad deal. This can be seen by **Amalgamated Investment & Property Co Ltd** *v* **John Walker & Sons Ltd** (1977) (see p. 163 above), where the fact that redevelopment of the buildings bought became difficult or impossible did not mean that there was no purpose at all to the contract, only that it was not as lucrative as expected.

Time of frustrating event

In order to frustrate a contract, the event in question must occur after the contract is made. If, for example, the hall in **Taylor** *v* **Caldwell** had burnt down, without the knowledge of the parties, before the contract was completed, the issue would be one of mistake, not frustration.

Limits to frustration

Though an event may occur which would usually frustrate a contract, the doctrine of frustration may be excluded if the contract makes provision for such an event; if the event was foreseen or foreseeable; or if it was due to the 'fault' of one of the parties.

Contractual provision

Some contracts make specific provision for the type of event which might otherwise frustrate a contract – for example, if you buy a house, the contract will often state that the responsibility for buildings insurance rests with the buyer once contracts have been exchanged. This means that if the house burns down between exchange and completion, you cannot say that the contract is frustrated by destruction of the subject matter, because you have already agreed to accept this risk. The contract goes ahead as planned and you claim against your insurance, assuming you have in fact organized it (the seller can claim the price anyway).

It is not possible to use contractual terms to exclude frustration by supervening illegality.

Foreseen and foreseeable events

Where the supervening event which interferes with performance is one which the parties foresaw, or could have foreseen, it is generally assumed that they made the contract with the knowledge of what could happen, and shaped their terms accordingly. If, for example, a shipbuilder contracts to build a ship at a time when it is generally thought that the price of raw materials is about to rise, it will usually take this into account when agreeing the price of the ship. In such cases, the fact that the event concerned does happen should not frustrate the contract, but there is no clear English case on this point. The exception is where the frustrating event is a wartime prohibition on trading with the enemy; the fact that the war was a foreseeable event does not prevent the prohibition from frustrating contracts.

Self-induced frustration

A contract will not be frustrated by any supervening event which is the fault of one of the parties. In the Canadian case of **Maritime National Fish Ltd** *v* **Ocean Trawlers Ltd** (1935) a ship, the *St Cuthbert*, was chartered for a year from the owners. Both parties were aware that the *St Cuthbert* was a type of ship that required a licence from the Canadian Government before it could be legally operated. The charterers were operating five ships, but were only granted three licences, which they used for three ships that they owned. They then claimed that the charter was frustrated by the Government's refusal to grant more licences. The Privy Council rejected this view, on the grounds that the charterers themselves had a choice, and decided not to use one of the available licences for the *St Cuthbert*.

Similarly, in **The Super Servant Two** (1990) the defendants contracted to carry the plaintiff's drilling rig in one of their two vessels designed for this purpose, the *Super Servants One* and *Two*. Before the contract was carried out, the *Super Servant Two* sank; the defendants said they could not use the *Super Servant One* because it was needed for another contract, and therefore claimed that the sinking frustrated the contract. The courts denied this claim: the defendants had chosen to use the *Super Servant One* on the other contract. The decision also seems to have been influenced by the fact that the other contract was finalized after the one made with the plaintiff, and the defendants continued to try to negotiate extra payments before deciding which contract to allocate to the *Super Servant One* – in other words, they seemed to be trying to use frustration to avoid an agreement which had become inconvenient.

Legal consequences of frustration

Once a court holds that a contract is frustrated, it is automatically terminated from the point at which the frustrating event occurred and the contract is described as being discharged. Obligations which would have arisen from that point on no longer exist, but the contract is not treated as though it never existed, so acts done before the frustrating event may have legal consequences. This can be contrasted with mistake where the contract is treated as void *ab initio* (meaning from the beginning).

The common law

The common law traditionally took the view that any loss resulting from the frustration should lie where it fell. Thus, if advance payments had been made under the contract prior to the frustrating event they would not be recoverable. This approach was softened slightly in the case of **Fibrosa Spalka Akeyjna** *v* **Fairbairn Lawson Combe Barbour Ltd** (1943) where the court stated that such advance payments would be recoverable if there had been a total failure of consideration. In that case Fairbairn was contracted to manufacture machinery for Fibrosa, a Polish company, in July 1939. The price was £4,800 and it was agreed that £1,600 should be paid in advance, though in fact only £1,000 was paid over. By September 1940 parts of Poland were under German occupation, including the area to which the machinery was to be delivered, so the contract was frustrated by the ban on trading with the enemy. Fibrosa claimed their £1,000 back. The Court of Appeal held that the money paid could be recovered because Fibrosa had received nothing at all in return for it. However, the court stated that if the party paying in advance had received some benefit under the transaction, even though it might not be complete performance, the money could not be recovered. This 'all-or-nothing' approach clearly had the potential to cause unfairness on both sides. First, where some consideration was given, parties making payment in advance could lose all their money, despite receiving very little benefit. Secondly, where there was a total failure of consideration, allowing the payer to claim back the whole payment could in some circumstances be unfair to the payee, who might have (and in the **Fibrosa** case had) already used the advance payment to finance the initial work on the contract. When the contract was frustrated, that work would be wasted. In other words, there were clearly circumstances in which the losses incurred by frustration were not being fairly allocated.

The Law Reform (Frustrated Contracts) Act 1943

The Act does not affect the law determining where a contract has been frustrated: that has been discussed on pp. 240–45; it simply alters the legal consequences once the contract is held to have been frustrated under the rules of the common law. It draws a distinction between obligations to pay money and other types of obligation that existed prior to the frustration.

Obligations to pay money
Section 1(2) of the Act provides that:

> All sums paid or payable to any party in pursuance of the contract before the time when the parties were so discharged (in this Act referred to as 'the time of discharge') shall, in the case of sums so paid, be recoverable from him as money received by him for the use of the party by whom the sums were paid and, in the case of sums so payable, cease to be payable:
>
> Provided that, if the party to whom the sums were so paid or payable incurred expenses before the time of discharge in, or for the purpose of, the performance of the contract, the court may, if it considers it just to do so having regard to all the circumstances of the case, allow him to retain or, as the case may be, recover the whole or any part of the sums so paid or payable, not being an amount in excess of the expenses so incurred.

The principal effect of the subsection is to entitle a person to recover money paid under a contract prior to the frustrating event, and it also removes any obligation to pay money that existed prior to the frustrating event. The court has no discretion over the question whether a sum already paid is recoverable: the only discretion concerns the allowance for expenses.

Section 1(2) goes beyond the common law rule laid down in **Fibrosa** in two respects. First, money paid is recoverable even upon a partial failure of consideration; the common law requirement that the failure be total has therefore been abolished in the case of frustration. Secondly, where the party to whom the money was paid or payable has incurred expenses as a result of the contract before the frustration occurred, the court can order that these expenses, or part of them, be kept back from the money recovered, or claimed from the other party, but only where the contract made provision for advance payment. Expenses may include overheads and the cost of work done.

Obligations other than to pay money
Section 1(3) states that:

> Where any party to the contract has, by reason of anything done by any other party thereto in, or for the purpose of, the performance of the contract obtained a valuable benefit (other than a payment of money to which the last foregoing subsection applies) before the time of discharge, there shall be recoverable from him by the said other party such sum (if any), not exceeding the value of the said benefit to the party obtaining it, as the court considers just, having regard to all the circumstances of the case and, in particular, –
>
> **(a)** the amount of any expenses incurred before the time of discharge by the benefited party in, or for the purpose of, the performance of the contract, including any sums paid or payable by him to any other party in pursuance of the contract and retained or recoverable by that party under the last foregoing subsection, and
> **(b)** the effect, in relation to the said benefit, of the circumstances giving rise to the frustration of the contract.

Thus, if before the frustrating event one party obtains a valuable benefit (other than money) because of something done by the other in performance of the contract, the party receiving the benefit can be ordered to pay a just sum in return for it. This provision has caused the most problems in practice for the courts. First, a court has to identify the valuable benefit; secondly, it has to award a just sum for that benefit.

As regards identifying the valuable benefit, the courts have had difficulties determining what exactly the benefit was: it could be the 'end product' of the services or the services themselves. In the leading case of **BP Exploration** *v* **Hunt** (1979) Robert Goff J pointed out that the provision of services would often not in itself be a valuable benefit, but the end result might be. He concluded that, in appropriate cases, it was the end product that was to be regarded as the 'benefit'. So, for instance, in a building contract the valuable benefit will not be the provision of so many hours of work, but the value, if any, which this adds to the owner's property. The effect of the frustrating event on the valuable benefit must be taken into account. Thus, if there was a building contract and the frustrating event was a fire, and this destroyed the work the builder had done, the building owner could not be said to have received a valuable benefit, and would not be obliged to pay for it.

In calculating the award of a just sum for the valuable benefit, the courts try to balance out the financial consequences of frustration, in order to prevent the unjust enrichment of one party at the expense of the other. In **Gamerco SA** *v* **ICM/Fair Warning (Agency) Ltd** (1995) the court concluded that there was: 'no indication in the Act, the authorities or the relevant literature that the court is obliged to incline towards total retention or equal division. Its task is to do justice in a situation which the parties had neither contemplated nor provided for, and to mitigate the possible harshness of allowing all loss to lie where it has fallen.' The emphasis is thus placed on the broad nature of the discretion which the court enjoys and the imperative to do justice on the facts of the case.

Regrettably, there is still a gap in coverage for those parties who incur expenses before the frustrating event, but whose contract does not specify advance payment: unless they have provided a valuable benefit, they will be stuck with these losses. The Law Revision Committee, on whose 1939 report the Act was based, argued that this was not a problem, since a contracting party who did not negotiate for advance payment would be voluntarily assuming the risk of such losses. However, since frustration concerns events which cannot be foreseen, it is hard to see how a contracting party could consciously assume the risk that these events might happen.

Scope of the Law Reform (Frustrated Contracts) Act 1943
Section 1(1) states that the 1943 Act does not apply to contracts concerning the sale of specific goods which are frustrated by the goods perishing, nor to most charterparties or contracts for the carriage of goods by sea or insurance policies. In addition, the parties may agree to place their contract outside the operation of the Act and specify this in the terms of their contract. In such cases the old common law applies.

The theory of frustration

It is not clear precisely what is the theoretical basis for the doctrine of frustration. Are the courts trying to give effect to the apparent intentions of the parties, as we would expect from the basic principles of contract law, or are they in fact merely imposing the solution which seems to them to be just in the circumstances? Two main schools of thought have developed on this point, known loosely as the 'implied term' and 'imposed solution' theories.

The implied term theory suggests that the contract is discharged because, by implication, the parties have agreed that it will no longer be binding if the frustrating event occurs – in other words, if anyone had asked the parties, at the time of contracting, whether they would consider themselves still to be bound if such an event happened, they would both have said 'Of course not'.

This approach was adopted by Blackburn J in **Taylor** *v* **Caldwell**, but it has been criticized as being artificial. As Lord Radcliffe pointed out in

Davis *v* **Fareham UDC** (1956) there is 'a logical difficulty in seeing how the parties could even impliedly have provided for something which *ex hypothesi* they neither expected nor foresaw'.

Current commentators favour instead the 'just solution' theory, which sees the courts as intervening to impose a fair solution when circumstances make the whole situation completely different from that originally envisaged by the parties. Under this interpretation, the courts ignore the intention of the parties and interfere with the contractual arrangement in order to do justice in a situation which is no fault of either party.

BREACH

A contract is said to be breached when one party performs defectively, differently from the agreement, or not at all (actual breach), or indicates in advance that they will not be performing as agreed (anticipatory breach).

Actual breach

An illustration of an actual breach of contract is **Pilbrow** *v* **Pearless de Rougemont & Co** (1999). The appellant had telephoned a firm of solicitors and asked to make an appointment with a solicitor. The appointment was arranged with an employee who was not a qualified solicitor. He was not informed that the employee was not a solicitor. The appellant was dissatisfied with the quality of the legal services he had received and refused to pay the outstanding fees. The firm sued for their fees. The Court of Appeal accepted that as a matter of fact the standard of legal services provided had been that of a competent solicitor. But it ruled that there had been a contract not just to provide legal services, but to provide legal services by a solicitor. The firm did not perform that contract at all. No legal services were provided by any solicitor; they therefore had no right to any payment. To avoid this problem in future, professionals should always make clear to the client whether their services are being provided by a qualified professional or not.

A case where breach of contract was not proven was **Modahl** *v* **British Athletic Federation Ltd** (1999). The claimant was a well-known British international athlete who was suspended from competition by the British Athletic Federation (BAF) because of an allegation that she had taken prohibited drugs to improve her performance. She successfully appealed against the doping allegation and brought an action for breach of contract and damages against BAF. She alleged that her suspension and the initiation of disciplinary proceedings were in breach of her contract with the defendant. She claimed damages for the financial loss suffered because she was unable to compete in international athletics for nearly a year. BAF was a member of the International Amateur Athletic Federation (IAAF). The IAAF had adopted its system of instant suspension followed by disciplinary proceedings in the belief that, although it might sometimes cause injustice in an individual case, it was necessary in the wider interests of the sport. The contract between Modahl and BAF was therefore interpreted as allowing the same procedures and no damages were awarded.

Anticipatory breach

Where an anticipatory breach occurs, the other party can sue for breach straight away; it is not necessary to wait until performance falls due. This was what happened in **Frost** *v* **Knight** (1872). The defendant had promised to marry the plaintiff once his father had died. He later broke off the engagement while his father was still alive, and when his ex-fiancée sued him for breach of promise (which was a valid claim in those days, though not any longer), he argued that she had no claim as the time for performance had not yet arrived. This argument was rejected and the plaintiff's claim succeeded.

In **Hochster** *v* **De la Tour** (1853) the parties had made a contract in April under which the plaintiff would be a tour leader in Europe for the defendant beginning on 1 June. In May the defendant informed the plaintiff that his services were no longer required. The plaintiff started his action for breach of contract on 22 May. The defendants argued that he should be required to wait until the date performance was due, which was 1 June, as there was no breach of contract until that date. The court rejected this argument. The plaintiff could commence proceedings immediately for damages, even though the date of performance had not yet arrived.

In some cases, the innocent party elects to wait until performance falls due, but this can mean they end up worse off than if they had sued immediately the anticipatory breach was known. In **Avery** *v* **Bowden** (1856) Bowden chartered Avery's ship and agreed to load up his cargo at Odessa within 45 days. However, Bowden later told Avery that he had no cargo and advised him to take the ship away. This was an anticipatory breach, and Avery could have sued for breach of contract immediately. Instead, he kept the ship available at the port, in the hope that Bowden would eventually fulfil his promise. Before the 45 days were up, the Crimean War broke out between England and Russia, so that performance became illegal and the contract was frustrated. The frustration then prevented Avery from suing for breach.

Lawful excuse

In some cases, an extraneous event which is not sufficiently serious to frustrate a contract will nevertheless provide an excuse for non-performance. For example, an employee who does not go to work because he is ill is not in breach, even though the illness is not serious enough to frustrate the contract.

Effect of breach

Any breach of contract will entitle the innocent party to sue for damages, but not every breach allows the wronged party to choose to discharge the contract (in contrast with frustration where the discharge is automatic). If the contract is not discharged, it will still need to be performed. There are three main circumstances in which the innocent party may choose to discharge.

Repudiation

This is where one party makes it clear that they no longer intend to be bound by the contract, either during its performance, or before performance is due (in practice it is usually the latter, and therefore an anticipatory breach). The courts are slow to find a repudiatory breach. In **Woodar Investment Development Ltd** *v* **Wimpey Construction Ltd** (1980) Lord Wilberforce stated:

> Repudiation is a drastic conclusion which should only be held to arise in clear cases of a refusal, in a matter going to the root of the contract, to perform contractual obligations.

An old illustration of a repudiatory breach is provided by **Frost** *v* **Knight** (1872) (see p. 250 above). A more recent illustration is provided by **Vaswani** *v* **Italian Motors (Sales & Services) Ltd** (1995). The appellant had paid a deposit on a Ferrari car to the respondents, who were sole distributors of such cars in Hong Kong. The price of the car was £179,500, a quarter of which had to be paid in advance by way of deposit. The car had to be specially ordered and took about a month to be delivered to the dealer. The contract of sale allowed the contract price to be increased to take account of increased costs, but the respondents sought to raise the price by £40,300 for a reason not allowed by the contract. They notified the appellant that the car was ready and required payment of the balance quoted at the higher price. Their letter stated that if the car was not collected and paid for by the specified date, they would treat the contract as repudiated and the deposit forfeited. The appellant challenged the respondents' right to do this, arguing that the demand for more money amounted to a repudiation of the contract.

The Privy Council held that, though the sellers did not have the right to demand the higher price, this did not on the facts amount to a repudiation of the contract. This was because they had honestly believed they had the right to increase the price in this way under the contract. In addition, the respondents' conduct had been consistent with the continuation of the contract. They were therefore entitled to keep the buyer's deposit. To avoid losing his deposit the appellant should have tendered the original correct purchase price.

Following the break-up of the highly successful pop group 'Take That' in 1995, one of its former members, Robbie Williams, unsuccessfully alleged that his manager, Martin-Smith, had committed a repudiatory breach of his management contract: **Martin-Smith v Williams** (1999). It seems that after the break-up of the group, a legal dispute had arisen between BMG and Williams. The dispute had been settled when Williams agreed to waive his right to commission payments from BMG in return for being released from Take That's recording agreement. Martin-Smith had been the group's manager and he sued Williams for commission on sums that, but for the compromise, Williams would have received under the recording agreement. Williams counter-claimed that Martin-Smith had been in repudiatory breach of his fiduciary duty arising under the management contract. It seems that after Williams had had a number of disagreements with the other band members in July 1995, he announced his intention to leave the band in January 1996. Two band members had, on Martin-Smith's advice, presented Williams with the choice of reconsidering his decision or leaving the band immediately. The Court of Appeal ruled that the manager of a pop group was authorized to act in the best interests of the whole group in priority to those of any individual member of the group. His advice was not unreasonable, it being in the best interests of all the members that there should be an immediate resolution of disagreements within the group. He had not, therefore, committed a repudiatory breach of the management contract. On the other hand, a waiver in relation to future royalties in the compromise with BMG was in breach of an express term of the management agreement. Even if it had not been, the court would have been prepared to imply a term preventing Williams from doing acts that would have deprived Martin-Smith of the commission for services rendered during the management agreement.

Breach of a condition

As we saw in Chapter 7, the terms of a contract can be divided into conditions, warranties and innominate terms, according to their importance. Breach of a condition allows the innocent party to terminate the contract; breaches of warranty do not justify termination, though they may give rise to an award of damages. In **Pilbrow v Pearless de Rougemont & Co** (see p. 249) the firm of solicitors was treated as having breached a condition, and the contract was discharged so that the appellant did not have to pay the firm's fees.

Serious breach of an innominate term

Where the relevant term is classified by the courts as innominate, it will be one which can be breached in both serious and trivial ways, and whether the innocent party is entitled to terminate or not will depend on how serious the results of the breach are. If the results are so serious as to undermine the very foundation of the contract, the innocent party will have the right to terminate.

Choice to affirm or discharge

Even when one of these three types of breach occurs, the contract is not automatically discharged; the innocent party can usually choose whether or not to terminate. As Viscount Simon stated in **Heyman** *v* **Darwins Ltd** (1942):

> Repudiation by one party standing alone does not terminate the contract. It takes two to end it, by repudiation, on the one side, and acceptance of the repudiation, on the other.

If the innocent party opts to treat the contract as discharged, that decision must be made known to the other party in a clear and unequivocal manner. The parties in **Vitol SA** *v* **Norelf Ltd** (1996) had entered into a contract under which Norelf sold Vitol goods which were to be shipped from the US and delivered between 1 and 7 of March. By 8 March loading was still not completed and the buyers, Vitol, sent Norelf a telex rejecting the cargo on the ground that delivery was overdue. It was later found that this telex breached the contract and amounted to a repudiation. The vessel completed loading on 9 March, and Norelf informed Vitol of this two days later, but took no further steps to perform the contract. Some four days afterwards, Norelf sold the cargo for substantially less than Vitol had agreed to pay and, after six months, commenced an action claiming damages for this loss.

The courts had to decide whether the conduct of the innocent party, Norelf, amounted to a clear and unequivocal acceptance of the repudiatory breach (if it did not, Vitol could have withdrawn it before acceptance and so have escaped liability for damages). Norelf had simply remained silent and failed to perform the contract. The Court of Appeal thought that this was not clear and unequivocal: a failure to perform was equally consistent with a misunderstanding by the innocent party of its rights or with indecision or even inadvertence. The House of Lords reversed the decision of the Court of Appeal, finding that the conduct of Vitol did in fact clearly and unequivocally demonstrate that they intended to treat the contract as terminated. The House pointed out that an acceptance of a repudiation required no particular form, and that in some circumstances mere silence and a failure to carry out their contractual obligations under the repudiated contract was sufficient to amount to acceptance of the repudiation. While it was accepted that silence is usually equivocal, Lord Steyn commented that '[s]ometimes in the practical world of business-men, an omission to act may be as pregnant with meaning as a positive declaration'.

Once the innocent party has made known to the other party that the contract is at an end, the choice is final, taking effect on communication to the other party; the innocent party cannot later decide that the contract should go ahead after all. The innocent party, once fully aware of the facts, can choose to affirm the contract by indicating with words, acts or even silence, an intention that the contract should continue despite the breach. In this case, apart from any claim for damages, the contract is treated as though the breach had never occurred. The innocent party's decision to affirm the contract is final; they cannot later decide to terminate for that breach.

In many cases, the party in breach will prefer the contract to come to an end, but if this is not what the innocent party wants, it is technically possible to continue fulfilling their side of the bargain, and then sue for the price, providing this can be done without co-operation from the other party, and the innocent party has a genuine interest in doing so.

An example of this fairly rare situation occurred in **White and Carter v McGregor** (1962) in which McGregor was a garage owner who had entered into a three-year advertising contract under which the plaintiffs would place advertisements for his garage on local litter bins. Later on the very day he made the contract, McGregor decided he wanted to cancel it. He immediately wrote to the defendants informing them of his decision. Even though the plaintiffs were aware that the advertising was no longer required, they went ahead with it, for the full three years, and then successfully sued for the price. The House of Lords held that the plaintiffs had a choice. If they opted to continue with the contract that was their right no matter how unreasonable. Lord Reid stated:

> The general rule cannot be in doubt . . . If one party to a contract repudiates it in the sense of making it clear to the other party that he refused or will refuse to carry out his part of the contract, the other party, the innocent party has an option. He may accept that repudiation and sue for damages for breach of contract, whether or not the time for performance has come, or he may if he chooses disregard or refuse to accept it and then the contract remains in full effect.

In contract law there is a general duty to take reasonable steps to mitigate one's loss (see p. 272). But this duty only applies where the contract has been discharged. The plaintiffs had made no attempt to mitigate their loss by looking for alternative advertisers. But, on the facts they were under no duty to mitigate because at this stage the contract had not been discharged, but continued to exist. The case is unusual because the plaintiffs were able to perform their side of the contract without any need for co-operation from the other party. Lord Reid justified the decision in the following terms:

> It might be, but never has been, the law that a person is only entitled to enforce his contractual rights in a reasonable way. One reason why that is not the law is no doubt, because it was thought that it would create too much uncertainty to require the court to decide whether it was reasonable or equitable to allow a party to enforce its full rights under a contract.

The outcome of the case has been criticized as absurd. It allows unwanted performance which can be highly wasteful.

Lord Reid laid down certain restrictions on when unwanted performance would be compensated. First, it would only be possible where no co-operation for its performance was required from the other contracting party. In most cases, by refusing to co-operate, the other party can be forced to restrict any claim to damages. Secondly, if the party has no legitimate financial or other interest in performing the contract other than claiming damages, they ought not to be entitled to perform.

These two limitations have been applied in some subsequent cases, in order to avoid a strict application of the **White and Carter** principle. Thus, it was emphasized in **Clea Shipping Corp** *v* **Bulk Oil International Ltd** (*The Alaskan Trader*) (1984) that the innocent party must have a genuine reason for continuing with the contract against the wishes of the other party. The case involved the charter of a rather elderly ship. The charterparty was for a specified period, but before the time was up, the charterers announced that they no longer needed the ship. They were therefore guilty of an anticipatory breach, and the shipowners could have sued for damages. Instead, they chose to behave as though the contract was still in existence, spending £800,000 on having the vessel repaired, and keeping a full crew standing by for the remaining period of the charterparty, after which they sold the vessel for scrap. They then sued for the full price, but the court considered that they had had no legitimate interest in continuing to perform and had simply tried to inflate the damages.

▶ AGREEMENT

In some cases the parties will simply agree to terminate a contract, so that one or both parties are released from their obligations. A distinction is generally made between bilateral discharge, in which both parties receive a benefit from the discharge, and unilateral, where the change is made for the benefit of one party only.

In general, an agreed discharge will be binding if it contains the same 'ingredients' that make a contract binding when it is formed, and the two which tend to present most problems are formality and consideration.

Consideration

Consideration is not usually a problem where both parties agree to alter their obligations, since each is giving something in return for the change. For example, Jean, a decorator, contracts to decorate Jack's kitchen and bathroom for £400 and, after the kitchen is finished, Jack decides that in fact he does not want the bathroom done after all. If Jean, perhaps having plenty of other work, agrees, Jack's releasing Jean from the obligation to decorate the bathroom is consideration for her releasing him from the obligation to pay the other £200 and *vice versa*.

Problems are more likely to occur where only one party's obligations change. If the other party agrees to the change, their agreement will only be binding if it is either put in a deed or supported by consideration. Where consideration is provided in return for one party's agreement to change, the agreement is called 'accord', and the provision of consideration for it is called 'satisfaction'; thus the arrangement is often called 'accord and satisfaction'.

As we have seen in Chapter 6, some problems of consideration where contracting parties change their obligations to each other can be avoided by the doctrines of promissory estoppel and waiver.

Formalities

This issue arises in connection with certain types of contract (mainly those concerning the sale of land) which must be evidenced in writing in order to be binding under the Law of Property Act 1925. Does the same requirement apply to an agreement to discharge such a contract? In **Morris** *v* **Baron** (1918) the House of Lords decided that this depended on how far the parties intended to alter their existing contractual relations, and those intentions had to be inferred from the terms of the discharging contract. There are three possibilities:

- *Partial discharge.* Where the second agreement suggests that the parties only want to modify the terms of their previous contract, without making really substantial changes, the agreed modification must be evidenced in writing. If this is not done, the original contract remains enforceable.
- *Complete discharge.* If the parties intend to abandon completely the original contract, and end their contractual relations, it is not necessary that this agreement be evidenced in writing – an oral agreement is sufficient.
- *Fresh agreement.* If the parties intend to abandon their original contract, but replace it with a new one, an oral agreement will be sufficient to

rescind the original contract, but the new one must be evidenced in writing.

In all cases, the question of what the parties intended is determined by the interpretation of the contract.

Novation

Novation is the name given to a specific type of discharge by agreement. It arises where there are two contracts, and the same person is a debtor under one contract and a creditor under the other – for example, A owes B £100, and C owes A £100. Novation occurs if C agrees to pay B £100 if he will release A from his debt to B; the first two contracts are discharged and a new one is created.

Condition subsequent

Sometimes contracting parties will agree at the start that if a certain circumstance occurs, the contract will come to an end. A common example is a manufacturers' guarantee offering to give a refund if a fault in the goods appears within a specified time. A recent case involving a condition subsequent is **Bland** *v* **Sparkes** (1999). Bland had been an international swimmer and was engaged as a consultant by the Amateur Swimming Association (ASA) to promote the ASA awards scheme. The consultancy contract allowed the ASA to terminate his engagement if he was convicted of any serious criminal offence or was otherwise guilty of conduct bringing the Association or himself into disrepute (the condition subsequent). The ASA discovered that before the contract was made, the claimant had received bribes or secret commissions to make commercial recommendations to the ASA's clients. It decided to terminate the contract. The claimant sought damages for breach of contract. The Court of Appeal held that the claimant's conduct had brought the ASA into disrepute and the ASA was therefore entitled to terminate the contract.

▶ ANSWERING QUESTIONS

1 'The doctrine of frustration is merely an excuse for people to escape from a contract because things have not turned out as they expected.' Discuss.
Oxford

Start by explaining what the doctrine of frustration is, and its effects on a contract, and illustrate this with some examples of cases in which frustration was successfully argued. You should write why it might not be considered reasonable to escape from an unwanted contract, looking at the importance of binding promises in a market economy, which is discussed in the introduction to this book. You can then go on to debate the accusation made in the quotation, by giving examples of cases which show the strictness of the doctrine – the Suez cases (for example, **Tsakiroglou v Noblee Thorl**), *The Super Servant Two*, and **Davis Contractors v Fareham UDC**. In all these cases, one party can be seen as trying to escape from a contract because of unexpected events which are to their disadvantage, but the courts have not allowed the doctrine to be used in this way. As a final example, you might contrast the two coronation cases, which show that, if anything, the doctrine of frustration can be regarded as leaning too far in preventing escape from contracts, since there was hardly much more point in hiring the steamship without the coronation events than there was in hiring the room overlooking the procession.

2 A had a contract with B to deliver 30 gallons of petrol weekly to B's garage from A's store. The contract was for a year and was to end in February. In September B told A that he would not take any more petrol but A simply stored the petrol, intending to sue B for breach in February. B objected, pointing out that A could have obtained a good price for the petrol from others. In January there was a fuel crisis and the government, exercising its statutory powers, issued an order confiscating all petrol stores without compensation.

A wishes to claim money from B. What factors would you identify as relevant in considering A's claim? *London*

The first issue here is whether A would have had a claim against B if the government confiscation had not occurred. B is clearly in breach of his contract, and such a breach would entitle A to claim any losses resulting from it. As B's breach is anticipatory, he could have done this as soon as B said he would not be taking any more petrol, and would have been able then to claim, within the usual rules on remoteness of damage, any losses made at that point – so if the market price of petrol had gone down, and he had to sell his stocks at a lower price than that agreed with B, A could claim the difference. However, A chose not to do this, but to continue to perform. Whether he had the right to sue for all the losses thereby incurred will depend on whether the courts feel he has a genuine interest in continuing to perform; the relevant cases here are **White and Carter v McGregor** and **Clea Shipping Corp v Bulk Oil International Ltd (***The Alaskan Trader***)**. If B's point about others being willing to pay a good price is true, the courts may well lean in favour of the second case and rule that there was no legitimate reason for A to continue to perform the contract and that therefore he could not claim all the losses which result from him doing so.

If the courts decide there was a genuine reason for continued performance, and that damages could have been claimed as a result, these will be affected by the government confiscation, which appears to have had the effect of frustrating the contract, since it has made further performance impossible. This brings any further obligations under the contract to an end (and this time A definitely has no choice in the matter). As far as obligations incurred before the frustrating event are concerned, A will only be able to claim under the Law Reform (Frustrated Contracts) Act 1943 for expenses incurred in storing the petrol if the contract stipulated advance payment. Since the storage of the petrol provided no valuable benefit to B, A cannot claim any money in respect of this.

3 Linda was a fashion designer who taught some classes at a college attended by Mark, a wealthy 18-year-old student. Mark became infatuated with Linda and, after his college course finished, he agreed to lend her £10,000 to establish a design business. The terms were very unfavourable to Mark. There was no interest payable on the loan, which was not due for repayment for 10 years. Mark was to be entitled to 5% of any annual profits over £20,000. When he discovered that Linda was not really interested in him, Mark began to realise that he might have been foolish to lend her the money.

Linda secured a contract with Nightworks to design and produce clothes for a forthcoming film starring Olivia. She was paid £1,000 in advance, with a further £5,000 to be paid on completion. In preparation, she paid £2,000 for materials to Paul, who assured her that he would be able to deliver within one month. When he gave this assurance, Paul knew that he was having considerable difficulty in getting materials from his supplier. Two months later, whilst Linda was still waiting for the material from Paul, Olivia died and Nightworks abandoned the film and informed Linda that they would no longer require her services.

(a) Consider whether Mark can terminate his agreement with Linda and recover the £10,000. *(15 marks)*

(b) (i) In view of Paul's statement to Linda about delivery, consider whether Linda has any rights and remedies against Paul in connection with the delay in delivery of materials.

(ii) Discuss the rights and duties of Linda and Nightworks following the decision of Nightworks to abandon the film. *(20 marks)*

(c) Explain and comment on the approach of the law to mistake in contract. *(25 marks)* AQA

(a) We are told that Mark is 18 years old so he had the capacity to make a binding contract (see p. 53). The only basis on which he could terminate the agreement with Linda and recover his £10,000 is if a court found that he had entered the contract as a result of undue influence. This is an equitable doctrine, which applies where one party uses their influence over the other to persuade them to make a contract. Where a court finds that a contract was made as a result of undue influence, it may set it aside, or modify its terms so as to mitigate the disadvantage. The leading case on the subject is the House of Lords' judgment in **Royal Bank of Scotland** v **Etridge (No 2)**.

Mark would need to argue that Linda had exercised undue influence over him. There are two types of undue influence: actual and presumed. Actual undue influence would be found if Mark could prove that he entered the transaction as a result of undue influence from Linda. This form of undue influence is difficult to prove in practice.

As regards presumed undue influence, in certain circumstances an evidentiary presumption will be applied that shifts the burden of proof from the claimant (Mark) to the wrongdoer (Linda), so that it is up to the wrongdoer to disprove the existence of undue influence. Undue influence can be presumed where there is a pre-existing relationship of confidence between the two parties to a contract, as a result of which one party places trust in the other, and the contract between them is manifestly disadvantageous to the first party. Such a relationship of trust is called a fiduciary relationship, and it may arise in two ways. First, it may fall into one of several categories in which a relationship of trust is automatically presumed to exist. The relationship of student/teacher that existed between Mark and Linda does not fall within one of these categories. Secondly, the relationship of trust may nevertheless be established on the facts. We are told that Mark had been one of Linda's students and had become infatuated with her. This would support the existence of presumed undue influence.

The defendant can rebut the presumption of undue influence by showing that the claimant entered into the contract freely, and this is usually done by establishing that independent advice was taken. We are not told that Mark received any such advice.

Where a party seeks to rely on the existence of presumed undue influence, the transaction must be manifestly disadvantageous (see p. 203). The terms of the loan would appear to satisfy this requirement.

As undue influence is an equitable doctrine, Mark will be prevented from terminating the agreement in three circumstances: where there is some practical reason why the parties cannot be restored to their original position; where a third party has gained rights under the contract; and when the innocent party affirms the contract (see p. 154). There is nothing to suggest that any of these three circumstances apply here.

(b) (i) Paul's statement to Linda that he would be able to deliver within one month was a misrepresentation (see p. 145). A misrepresentation is an untrue statement of fact by one party which has induced the other to enter into the contract. Paul's statement was untrue because he was having considerable difficulty in getting materials form his supplier. After two months, Paul had still not delivered the material to Linda. It was a statement of fact and not opinion (see p. 147). It is likely that the statement induced Linda to enter into the contract (see p. 149) though we are not expressly told what her time-schedule was to deliver the clothes to Nightworks.

The remedies available to Linda would depend on the type of misrepresentation that was committed. All misrepresentations render the contract voidable. Thus the contract continues to exist unless and until the innocent party chooses to have it set aside by means of rescission. Along with the remedy of rescission, the courts can order a payment of money known as an indemnity. An indemnity payment is designed to put the parties back into their former position, and is only available for obligations necessarily and inevitably created by the contract.

A misrepresentation may also give rise to a right to damages, depending on the type of misrepresentation that has occurred. There are four types of misrepresentation: fraudulent misrepresentation; negligent misrepresentation at common law; negligent misrepresentation under statute; and innocent misrepresentation. Which category a misrepresentation falls into depends on the state of mind of the person making the statement. When Paul made the statement, he knew that he was having considerable difficulty in getting materials from his supplier.

Looking first at fraudulent misrepresentation, it is very difficult to prove fraud. The leading case is **Derry v Peek** where it was stated that fraudulent misrepresentation is a false statement that is made: '(i) knowingly, or (ii) without belief in its truth, or (iii) recklessly as to whether it be true or false.' It is possible that Paul made his statement recklessly and that the statement will therefore amount to fraudulent misrepresentation. Alternatively, it was undoubtedly made negligently and would amount to negligent misrepresentation both under statute and under common law. Fraudulent and negligent misrepresentation both give rise to a right to damages.

In addition, it is possible that Paul's statement may have become a term of the contract. Whether a statement is a term of a contract is largely a question of the parties' intentions (see p. 95). In determining the issue, the courts will take into account the importance of the statement, the special knowledge and skill of Paul when he made the statement, the timing of the statement and whether the eventual agreement was made in writing. If Paul's statement has become a term, then it is clear that it has been breached, and the impact of this will depend on whether it was a condition (see p. 110) because time was of the essence (see p. 238). If the statement was a condition, then its breach will give rise to a right to terminate the contract as well as a right to damages.

(ii) Nightworks decided to abandon the film following the death of the leading actress, Olivia, and informed Linda that they would no longer require her services. The death of Olivia may amount to a frustrating event (see p. 241). If, after a contract is made, something happens, through no fault of the parties, to make its performance impossible, the contract is said to be frustrated, and the obligations under it come to an end. In this scenario we do not have the death of one of the contracting parties, but a death which may render performance of the contract between Linda and Nightworks pointless. Performance will be pointless if it was important that Olivia star in the film (see, for example, **Krell v Henry**). The legal consequences of frustration are discussed at p. 245. Once a court holds that a contract is frustrated, it is automatically terminated from the point at which the frustrating event occurred. Nightworks would therefore have no obligation to pay Linda the remaining £5,000 that was due to be paid on her completing the clothes.

Linda had received an advance of £1,000. Under s. 1(2) of the Law Reform (Frustrated Contracts) Act 1943, Nightworks would be entitled to recover money paid under the contract prior to the frustrating event. But a court can allow Linda to deduct any expenses she has incurred as a result of the contract from this sum. Thus, if Linda is obliged to pay Paul the £2,000 for the materials, she will be able to deduct this as an expense from her advance and thus she would not have to return anything.

If the contract has not been frustrated by Olivia's death, because it was reasonable to have found another actress to star in the film, then Nightworks would be in breach of their contract and would have to pay Linda damages (see p. 263).

(c) The material required to answer this part of the question is contained in Chapter 10 on mistake.

15 Remedies

This chapter is concerned with the remedies that are available to the innocent party in the event of a breach of contract. These can be divided into three categories. During the period when the English courts were split into courts of common law and of equity, each branch developed different remedies. Even though the courts are no longer divided in this way, it is still convenient to distinguish between common law and equitable remedies, since their separate histories have led to different rules about when they will be applied. The third category covers remedies which arise from the parties' own agreement.

COMMON LAW REMEDIES

All common law remedies are available as of right if a contract is breached.

Damages

An award of damages is the usual remedy for a breach of contract. It is an award of money that aims to compensate the innocent party for the financial losses they have suffered as a result of the breach. Damages for breach of contract are available as of right where the contract has been breached. The general rule is that innocent parties are entitled to such damages as will put them in the position they would have been in if the contract had been performed. When a contract is breached, a party may suffer pecuniary loss (that is to say financial loss) or non-pecuniary loss.

Pecuniary loss

Damages aim to compensate the innocent party for their financial losses that result from not receiving the performance bargained for. In general, such losses include physical harm to the claimants or their property and any other injury to their economic position.

Non-pecuniary loss

As we have seen, contract damages usually aim to compensate for financial (pecuniary) loss. They have traditionally not been available to compensate non-pecuniary loss, such as mental distress. This has been a key distinction between the law of contract and tort for, while in contract law damages for mental distress have not been available, such damages are available in tort law. In reality, following a breach of contract, a claimant might suffer not only financial loss but also mental distress, such as disappointment, hurt feelings or humiliation, but damages for such non-pecuniary losses are generally not recoverable in contract. The main policy consideration for this seems to be a concern to keep contractual awards down, to provide fair compensation without encouraging unnecessary litigation by offering excessive compensation. In **Hayes** v **Dodd** (1990) Staughton LJ stated:

> ... the English courts should be wary of adopting ... the United States practice of huge awards. Damages awarded for negligence or want of skill, whether against professional men or anyone else, must provide fair compensation, but no more than that. And I would not view with enthusiasm the prospect that every shipowner in the Commercial Court, having successfully claimed for unpaid freight or demurrage, would be able to add a claim for mental distress suffered while he was waiting for his money.

Damages for mental distress are not awarded in commercial contracts. The leading authority for this is **Addis** v **Gramophone Co Ltd** (1909). The plaintiff had been employed as a manager of a company in India. He was wrongfully sacked for alleged dishonesty. He brought an action claiming that the manner of his dismissal had been harsh and humiliating. He had been ostracized by the British community in Calcutta. As a result he had suffered mental pain and anguish. The House of Lords held that he could recover the usual damages for loss of salary and commission, but not for the injury to his feelings caused by the way in which he was sacked.

However, recent cases have developed the principle that, in a limited number of situations, injury to feelings (generally called mental distress) and loss of amenity will be compensated. Initially, such compensation was limited to cases involving contracts whose whole purpose was the provision of pleasure, relaxation and peace of mind. More recently, the House of Lords has allowed damages for non-pecuniary loss where a major object (though not the whole purpose) of the contract was to provide pleasure, relaxation and peace of mind. In addition, mental suffering can be compensated if it is related to physical inconvenience and discomfort caused by the breach of the contract.

Contracts where the whole purpose is pleasure, relaxation and peace of mind

The leading case on the provision of damages for non-pecuniary loss where a contract for recreation has been breached is **Jarvis** v **Swans**

Tours Ltd (1973). The plaintiff was a solicitor who had booked a two-week winter sports holiday that was described in the brochure as a 'house party'. The brochure stated that there would be a welcoming party, afternoon tea and cakes and a yodelling evening. In the event, there was no welcoming party, the afternoon teas consisted largely of crisps and the yodeller turned out to be a local man who arrived in his working clothes, sang a couple of songs and then left. The 'house party' also left something to be desired, consisting of 13 holidaymakers in the house in the first week, but in the second week Mr Jarvis was the sole member of the 'house party'.

The holiday had cost £63. The holiday company was clearly in breach of contract and the judge at first instance awarded Mr Jarvis half the contract price, on the basis that Mr Jarvis had received some benefit, in the shape of transport and accommodation, and the sum awarded was the difference in value between what he expected and what he got. Not surprisingly, Mr Jarvis appealed. The Court of Appeal raised the damages to £125 on the basis that merely giving him back the cost of the holiday would not adequately compensate his loss, and instead the damages should take account of his disappointment and distress. Lord Denning explained:

> It is true he was conveyed to Switzerland and back and had meals and bed in the hotel. But that is not what he went for. He went to enjoy himself with all those facilities which the defendants said he would have. He is entitled to compensation for the loss of those facilities, and for his loss of enjoyment.

The case was compared with where a man plans to go to an evening opera performance in Glyndebourne. He arranges to hire a car for the night, but the car fails to turn up and he misses the performance. He would be entitled to claim from the car hire company, not just the cost of his ticket, but also for his disappointment at missing the concert.

This case was affirmed in **Jackson v Horizon Holidays Ltd** (1975) (discussed on p. 221). In the Scottish case of **Diesen v Samson** (1971) the defendant had been booked to take photographs at the claimant's wedding. He failed to attend and damages were awarded to the bride for the distress of having no wedding photographs. This was not a purely commercial contract that fell within the rule in **Addis v Gramophone Co**. Instead, it was a contract under which the bride would get pleasure looking at the photographs in the years ahead.

In **Heywood v Wellers** (1976) the plaintiff, Sheila Heywood, was a single parent living in Penge who met a married man with whom she had an affair. Later, they split up, but he began stalking her. The plaintiff went to the defendants, a firm of solicitors, to seek an injunction against her former companion. The defendants negligently failed to do so, with the result that the plaintiff had to suffer further harassment. The Court of Appeal held that she could recover for the mental distress caused by the breach of contract.

Where a contract is for the provision of a product for leisure activities and this contract is breached, damages for loss of pleasure and amenity may be awarded. In **Ruxley Electronics and Construction Ltd** *v* **Forsyth** (1995) a contract had been entered into for the construction of a swimming pool for £70,000. The plaintiff made it clear that one end of the pool had to be 7 ft 6 in deep as he needed this depth to feel safe when diving. In fact, on completion, it was only 6 ft 9 in deep. Mr Forsyth had contracted for a swimming pool for reasons of pleasure, and in this sense his expectation had not been fulfilled. The trial judge awarded the defendant £2,500 for loss of amenity and pleasure, an award that was approved by the House of Lords. This was to compensate the pleasure lost by the defendant by not feeling safe when he dived into the swimming pool.

Contracts where a major object is pleasure, relaxation and peace of mind
The House of Lords further considered the issue of the award of damages for loss of amenity in **Farley** *v* **Skinner** (2001). Mr Farley was thinking of buying a house in the Sussex countryside, where he would spend his retirement. He paid a chartered surveyor, Mr Skinner, to look at the property, and specifically instructed him to assess the impact of aircraft noise on the property. The house was 15 miles from Gatwick airport. The surveyor was negligent in carrying out this work and advised Mr Farley that it was 'unlikely that the property will suffer greatly from such noise'. After Mr Farley had spent a considerable amount of money renovating the house and had moved into the property, he discovered that the house was in fact badly affected by aircraft noise, particularly at weekends. It seems that the house was positioned near a navigation beacon and at busy times aircraft flew around this beacon while they waited for a slot to land. Mr Farley's enjoyment of the house was badly affected. He brought an action against the surveyor for the difference in the value of the house between what he paid and what it was worth with the aircraft noise. This part of his claim was unsuccessful because it was found that the price he paid was the market value for the house taking into account the aircraft noise. In addition, he included a claim for non-pecuniary damages for the loss of amenity caused by the aircraft noise. At first instance, the claimant was awarded £10,000 for distress and inconvenience. The House of Lords upheld this award. The House held that it did not matter that the object of the contract with the surveyor was not entirely to give pleasure, relaxation or peace of mind, since this was nonetheless a major and important object of the contract. The surveyor had been specifically asked to report on aircraft noise. It would be perverse to allow someone to recover damages if they had just asked a surveyor to report on aircraft noise, but not where the client (like Mr Farley) had specifically asked the surveyor about that issue as well as some other

matter. That would be a distinction of form and not substance. From now on, 'it is sufficient if a major or important object of the contract is to give pleasure, relaxation or peace of mind'. The House emphasized that awards of damages in this area should be modest. While they allowed the trial judge's award of £10,000 to stand, it noted that this was at the very highest end of the scale. They did not want the award to encourage a litigation culture.

Mental suffering caused by physical inconvenience

Mental suffering can be compensated if it is caused by physical inconvenience and discomfort resulting from the breach of contract. In **Perry** *v* **Sidney Phillips and Son** (1982) the plaintiff bought a house relying on a survey prepared by the defendants. Their report stated that the house was in good order, but it was found to have many faults, including a leaking roof and a septic tank that gave off an offensive odour. These problems with the property caused the plaintiff distress, worry and inconvenience. As well as awarding damages for the reduced value of the property, the Court of Appeal awarded damages for the physical inconvenience and discomfort caused by having to live in the house while the builders were doing repairs and for mental distress.

In **Bailey** *v* **Bullock** (1950) the plaintiff brought an action against his solicitor for failing to act to recover possession of a house which had been leased to a third party. As a result of the delay, the plaintiff was required to live in a small house with his parents-in-law. Damages for discomfort were awarded.

The House of Lords noted in **Farley** *v* **Skinner** that the concept of physical inconvenience should not be narrowly interpreted, and could include the harmful effects of aircraft noise. The House stated that 'aircraft noise was something which affects the plaintiff through his hearing and can be regarded as having a physical effect on him'.

Limitations on awards of damages

The general rule is that innocent parties are entitled to such damages as will put them in the position they would have been in if the contract had been performed, but there are three limitations, which will be considered under the headings of causation, remoteness and mitigation.

Causation

A person will only be liable for losses caused by their breach of contract. The defendant's breach need not be the sole cause of the claimant's losses, but it must be an effective cause of their loss. It is not enough if the breach merely provided the claimant with the opportunity to sustain loss. Intervening acts between the breach of contract and the loss incurred may break the chain of causation. Those events which were reasonably foreseeable will not break the chain of causation. Sometimes a loss can be caused partly by a breach of contract and partly by some other factor. The general rule is that where breach can be shown to be an actual cause of the loss, the fact that there is another contributing cause will not prevent the existence of causation.

In **County Ltd** *v* **Girozentrale Securities** (1996) the plaintiffs' bank agreed to underwrite the issue of 26 million shares in a publicly quoted company. The defendants were stockbrokers who were engaged by the plaintiffs to approach potential investors in the shares. The brokers breached the terms of their contract and, in due course, the plaintiffs found themselves with some 4.5 million shares on their hands which, the price of the shares having fallen, represented a loss of nearly £7 million. They sued the stockbrokers and the main issue in the case was whether the plaintiffs' loss was caused by the defendants' breach of contract. In effect, the plaintiffs would not have suffered their loss if there had not been a concurrence of a number of events, of which the defendants' breach of contract was but one. The Court of Appeal held that the brokers' breach of contract remained the effective cause of the plaintiffs' loss; the breach did not need to be the only cause. The defendants were therefore liable to pay damages.

In **Quinn** *v* **Burch Bros (Builders) Ltd** (1966) the plaintiff was an independent sub-contractor carrying out such building work as plastering on a building project. In breach of their contractual undertaking to supply equipment 'reasonably necessary' for the work, the defendant failed to supply a step-ladder. The plaintiff found a folded trestle, and stood on it to do the work. He slipped and broke his hand. The Court of Appeal held that the cause of the plaintiff's injury was his own choice to use unsuitable equipment. The defendant's breach of contract was only the occasion for the accident, not its legal cause.

Remoteness
There are some losses which clearly result from the defendant's breach of contract, but are considered too remote from the breach for it to be fair to expect the defendant to compensate the claimant for them. Take, for example, the situation where a taxi driver is booked to take a passenger to the airport in time for a certain flight to New York, where the passenger expects to complete a deal worth £1 million. If the taxi driver breaches the contract by arriving late and makes the passenger miss the flight, the taxi firm may be liable for expenses such as any extra cost for getting the next flight, but is unlikely to be expected to compensate the passenger for the lost £1 million.

The rules concerning remoteness were originally laid down in **Hadley** *v* **Baxendale** (1854). The case concerned a contract for delivery of an important piece of mill equipment, which had been sent away for repair. The equipment, an iron shaft, was not delivered until some days after the agreed date. This meant that the mill, which could not work without it, had stood idle for that period. The mill owners attempted to sue for loss of the profits they would have made in the time between the agreed delivery date and the actual delivery. The court laid down two situations where the defendant should be liable for loss caused by a breach of contract:

1 Loss which would arise naturally, 'according to the usual course of things', from their breach.
2 Loss 'as may reasonably be supposed to have been in the contemplation of the parties at the time when they made the contract, as the probable result of the breach of it'.

In practice, it is the second 'reasonable contemplation' test which has proved the most important in subsequent cases. In this case, they did not consider the lost profit to fall within either category. The fact that the mill could not work without the equipment was not considered to be a loss that arose in the usual course of things, because there could well have been a spare; nor could such a loss be said to be within the contemplation of the defendants, because the mill owners had failed to make it clear that the mill could not work without the shaft. It is therefore important to inform the other contracting party at the time of contracting of circumstances which affect performance, to prevent a subsequent loss being found to be too remote.

The approach in **Hadley** *v* **Baxendale** was reaffirmed in **Victoria Laundry (Windsor) Ltd** *v* **Newman Industries Ltd** (1949) and then discussed again by the House of Lords in *The Heron II* (1969). These two cases addressed particularly the problem of abnormal losses – those which could not be said to occur 'in the normal course of things', but which, on the other hand, the defendant might well have been able to contemplate when making the contract.

In **Victoria Laundry** the plaintiffs were launderers and dyers, who needed to buy a large boiler in order to expand their existing business and take on a very well-paid Government contract. They contracted to buy such a boiler, second-hand, from the defendants, making it clear that it was needed for immediate use. As the defendants dismantled the boiler in preparation for delivery, it was damaged, and so the delivery was considerably later than agreed. The launderers claimed loss of profits under two heads: £16 per week for the loss of 'normal' profits, which represented the additional ordinary work they could have taken on with the extra boiler; and £262 per week for the loss of a lucrative dyeing contract with the Government.

Evidence was given that although the defendants knew the plaintiffs wanted the boiler working as soon as possible, they did not know about the Government contract, or the fact that it was so much more lucrative than the laundry's other work. As a result, the Court of Appeal held that they were liable for the £16 per week, but not for the £262. The Court stated that a defendant should only be liable for such losses as were 'reasonably foreseeable' as arising from the breach.

In **The Heron II** (1969) the plaintiff chartered a ship, the *Heron II*, to carry sugar to Basrah, where the cargo was to be sold. The journey was to take 20 days, but the shipowner strayed from the normal route and took 29 days. During the period between the agreed delivery date and the actual delivery, the market price of sugar at Basrah fell significantly. The late delivery put the shipowner in breach of contract, and the plaintiff claimed the difference between the price he would have got for the sugar had the delivery been made on time and the going price when the delivery was actually made. The shipowner had not been told that the plaintiff intended to sell the sugar as soon as it arrived in Basrah, but he did know that there was a market for sugar at Basrah. From this the court held that 'if he had thought about the matter he must have realized that at least it was not unlikely that the sugar would be sold in the market at market price on arrival'. In view of this, the House of Lords held that the plaintiff's intention to sell the sugar at Basrah when the ship arrived was so probable that it should be regarded as arising in the normal course of events, and would therefore be within the contemplation of the parties at the time the contract was made.

In **The Heron II** the House of Lords discussed the level of probability required for an event to be considered to be within the contemplation of the parties. They disapproved of the phrase 'reasonably foreseeable', as used in **Victoria Laundry**, on the grounds that it suggested a very low degree of probability (similar to the remoteness test used in tort law). They stated that in order for a plaintiff to be held responsible for a loss, that loss must be such that both parties would, at the time the contract was made, have regarded as 'liable to result' from the breach; the fact that they knew there was a very remote chance that the loss might occur would not be enough.

The above two cases make it clear that where a loss only results from a breach because of special circumstances (such as the unusually lucrative contracts in **Victoria Laundry**), the defendant will only be liable for that loss if they knew about the special circumstances at the time the contract was made, and contracted on the basis that such circumstances existed.

One way of looking at the two tests laid down in **Hadley** *v* **Baxendale** is that the first applied to normal losses (where the loss arose in the usual course of things) and the second applied to abnormal losses (where they were within the reasonable contemplation of the parties). In practice, the courts have not favoured this distinction and have preferred to see **Hadley** *v* **Baxendale** as laying down a single principle. Under this single principle, as the likelihood of the loss occurring diminishes, the degree of knowledge on the part of the defendant must increase for the loss to be recoverable in damages.

In **Satef-Huttenes Albertus SpA** *v* **Paloma Tercera Shipping Co SA,** *The Pegase* (1981) Goff J discussed the two rules laid down in **Hadley** *v* **Baxendale**. He stated that in the light of the subsequent cases, the case should now be seen as laying down a single principle, whereby remoteness depended on 'the degree of relevant knowledge held by the defendant at the time of the contract in the particular case'. The test was now whether:

... the facts in question come to the defendant's knowledge in such circumstances that a reasonable person in the shoes of the defendant would, if he had considered the matter at the time of making the contract have contemplated that, in the event of a breach by him, such facts were to be taken into account when considering his responsibility for loss suffered by the plaintiff as a result of such breach.

A claimant does not have to contemplate the breach of contract in question; it is only the type of damage that must be contemplated. So long as the loss is of a type that could reasonably have been contemplated, the fact that the loss may turn out to be much greater than could be foreseen does not prevent the defendant from incurring liability for it. In **Vacwell Engineering Co Ltd** *v* **BDH Chemicals Ltd** (1971) a scientist dropped an ampoule of chemicals into a bin which caused an explosion, killing both the scientist and a colleague, and causing extensive damage to property. Rees J stated that: 'the explosion and the type of damage being foreseeable it matters not in the law that the magnitude of the former and the extent of the latter were not.'

In **Wroth** *v* **Tyler** (1974) the defendant had contracted to sell his house to the plaintiffs for £6,000, but wrongfully repudiated the contract before the sale could take place. By the time the case came to court, house prices had begun to rise very quickly, and the house had gone up in value to £11,500. The plaintiffs claimed the difference between the contract price and the market price, as is usual in such a case. The defendant claimed that he was not liable for the full amount, because although he could have foreseen some increase in value, he could not have contemplated that prices would rise so sharply. His argument was rejected: Megarry J said that the defendant could escape liability if he could not have contemplated that a particular type of loss could result from his breach, but not simply because he could not have contemplated its extent.

The same point was made in **Brown** *v* **KMR Services Ltd** (1995). The case arose from the losses made by the 'Lloyd's names' (who had provided financial security for certain insurance policies). They had incurred substantial losses when large claims were made under the insurance policies. The action was brought against those who had encouraged the Lloyd's names to take on excessive liabilities. The losses were financial and therefore of a type which it could readily be foreseen might be incurred as a result of the breach of contract, but their extent went well beyond that which might in any year arise 'in the usual course of things'. The Court of Appeal said that such losses were recoverable. Only the type of loss needs to be foreseeable. The test was whether, at the time of making the contract, damage of the kind for which the plaintiff claims compensation was a reasonably foreseeable consequence of the breach of contract. If the kind of damage was reasonably foreseeable, it does not matter that the extent of the damage is not. The difficulty with this reasoning is that in the case of financial loss, it will not be easy to differentiate kinds of loss.

A recent case on remoteness is **Balfour Beattie Construction (Scotland) v Scottish Power plc (1994)**. Balfour Beattie were building a section of motorway near Edinburgh. They needed a continuous supply of electricity to make concrete. The defendants agreed to set up a temporary electricity supply for the concrete plant. When this supply failed, a bridge under construction could not be completed and later had to be rebuilt. Balfour Beattie claimed the cost of rebuilding the bridge. The House of Lords held that the loss incurred was too remote. There was no evidence that Scottish Power knew that the concrete plant needed a continuous supply of electricity. The parties had to have reasonable knowledge of the other's business, but not every technical fact particularly of something as vast and complicated as major motorway construction.

Mitigation

Claimants cannot simply sit back and allow losses to pile up and expect the defendant to pay compensation for the whole amount if there is something they could reasonably do to reduce the loss. Claimants are under a duty to mitigate their loss, and cannot recover damages for losses which could have been avoided by taking reasonable steps. For example, if Jane has a contract with David to repair the machines in his factory, and fails to carry out her duties as agreed, David cannot simply keep the factory idle for years and submit a claim for lost profits; he will only be able to claim for such losses as he could not reasonably avoid by taking steps such as finding a replacement machine, or an alternative source of repairs.

The claimant does not have to prove that reasonable steps have been taken; it is up to the defendant to prove that the loss could have been mitigated, or better mitigated. Nor are claimants expected to make enormous efforts to mitigate the loss; they need only do what is reasonable.

In **Pilkington v Wood** (1953) the defendant, a solicitor, was in breach of contract for wrongly advising that the title to the plaintiff's house was good. The defendant argued that the plaintiff should have mitigated his loss by taking proceedings against the seller of the house for having conveyed a defective title. However, this would have involved complicated litigation, which would not necessarily have succeeded, and the court held that the purchaser was not required to take such onerous and uncertain steps in mitigation.

In the leading case of **Brace** *v* **Calder** (1895) the defendants, a partnership consisting of four members, had agreed to employ the plaintiff for two years as manager of a branch of their business. Five months later, two of the members retired and the partnership was dissolved, with the business being transferred to the remaining two. Legally, the dissolution of the partnership constituted wrongful dismissal of the plaintiff, but the two remaining partners offered to re-employ him, on the same terms as before. He rejected the offer and brought an action for breach of contract, seeking to recover the salary that he would have received had he served the whole period of two years. The claim was refused and only nominal damages awarded, on the grounds that it was unreasonable to have rejected the offer of continued employment.

Another illustration of the requirement of mitigation is **British Westinghouse Electric Co Ltd** *v* **Underground Electric Rys Co of London Ltd** (1912). The appellants had contracted to supply electricity turbines to the respondents' specification. The turbines delivered did not match these specifications, and the respondents replaced them with some other turbines made by a different manufacturer. These turbines were much more efficient, so that the replacement machines paid for themselves in a short time. The respondents claimed damages for the cost of replacing the original turbines, but the House of Lords rejected the claim. The respondents had rightly mitigated their loss, and had been so successful that most of the losses had been eliminated. They were therefore only entitled to compensation for the period of time when the original turbines were running inefficiently.

Calculating loss

Once it has been established that a loss is one for which the defendant is liable, the court must calculate the sum of damages – what amount will compensate the claimant for the loss? There are two main ways in which the losses of a claimant in a contract action can be calculated: the loss of expectation and the reliance loss.

Loss of expectation

Where loss of expectation is the basis for calculating damages, the courts aim to put claimants in the position they would have been in if the contract had been performed. Thus the parties would have expected a certain result from the performance of the contract and the damages will compensate for the loss of this expectation. This can be described as the difference in value measure, that is the difference in value between the promised performance and the actual performance. If, for example, a claimant was buying goods with the intention of selling them and the supplier failed to supply the goods, the claimant can claim the profit that would have been made on that sale. A claimant who is forced to sell goods at a lower price when the original buyer pulls out can claim the difference between the contract price and the price at which the goods were eventually sold. Expectation losses provide an incentive to perform a contract: if the party contemplating a breach of contract knows that by failing to perform they will be liable for the full loss of profits, they are discouraged from breaking the agreement.

Reliance loss

Where reliance loss is the basis for calculating damages, the damages seek to put claimants in the position they were in before the contract was made. The damages will therefore compensate for the actual wasted expenditure and other losses incurred because of the contract which has been breached. Reliance loss is the normal test in tort law.

The case of **Anglia Television Ltd** *v* **Reed** (1972) established that reliance loss compensation can include money spent before the contract was made. The television company had planned to make a film for television, and had signed up an actor called Robert Reed to star in it. Reed signed the contract to perform in the film and then later pulled out in breach of contract. As a result, the film was not made. Clearly, the potential profits on a project such as a film are extremely difficult to predict; it could be a huge success, or sink without trace. Consequently, Anglia sought instead to claim back the money they had spent on making the film.

The amount they had spent after contracting with Reed was clearly recoverable, since it had been spent in reliance on him performing as agreed, but the film company also wished to claim money spent in the preparatory stages, before Reed was signed. It could not be said that this was spent in reliance on Reed, but the court said that there was, nevertheless, no reason why such expenditure should not be recovered, so long as it satisfied the rules on remoteness; if Reed could have been expected to realize that such losses were likely to result from his breach, he was liable for them. As Lord Denning MR pointed out, Reed would have known that money had been spent on the film before he signed up, and that that money would be wasted if the film was not made. Therefore Anglia were allowed to recover all they had spent on the film before and after the contract was made with Reed.

Choosing between the expectation and reliance principles

As a rule, a claimant can choose whether to base a claim on loss of expectation or on reliance. In **Anglia Television** *v* **Reed** (1972) Lord Denning stated that a claimant could not claim for both expectation loss and reliance loss due to the risk of being compensated twice for the same loss. This is because wasted expenditure is normally included within a claim for lost performance, as the innocent party's expenditure would be taken into account when calculating how much profit they would have made from the performance of the contract. However, provided the claimant avoided such overlapping claims, there is no reason why they should not claim for both.

In practice, loss of expectation is the usual basis for calculating contract damages. Reliance loss is generally less generous than the loss of expectation measure. However, it may be seen as fairer in that it compensates for actual losses, rather than relying on guesses as to what the future gains from the performance of the contract would have been.

Limits on the claimant's choice
There are two main restrictions on the claimant's choice between the expectation and the reliance principles. These are the bad bargain rule and the speculative damages rule.

The bad bargain rule. If the claimant would have made a loss from the contract, then he or she will only be entitled to nominal damages, and will not be entitled to claim their expenses on the basis of reliance loss. To compensate on a reliance basis would mean that the injured party would be placed in a better position as a result of the breach than they would have been in if the contract had been performed. In **C and P Haulage** *v* **Middleton** (1983) the plaintiff had a licence to use premises in Watford for six months, with the possibility that the contract could be renewed. He spent money on fixtures and fittings knowing that the contract stated that these could not be removed when the licence expired. When the contract was breached, the Court held that the plaintiff could not recover for his expenditure and was entitled to nominal damages only. He could not claim for his wasted expenditure on the fixtures and fittings, because this would have been wasted even if the contract had been performed as agreed. If Robert Reed in the **Anglia Television** case could have shown that Anglia Television would not have made any money from the film anyway, the television company could not have claimed back the money they spent.

Expectation losses are 'too speculative'. The reliance basis for calculating damages must be used where it is virtually impossible to calculate what profit the claimant would have made if the contract had been performed correctly. In practice, the courts are reluctant to conclude that damages are too speculative and are prepared to base their awards on a certain amount of guesswork.

McRae *v* **Commonwealth Disposals Commission** (1951) was an Australian case heard by the Australian High Court. The plaintiff had successfully tendered for the salvage rights to an oil tanker, said to be wrecked on a reef approximately 100 miles north of Samarai. Despite being given an exact map reference for the location of the tanker, the plaintiff's salvage expedition failed to find the tanker, and it was eventually agreed that it was not in fact there at all. The plaintiff attempted to claim for loss of the profit he expected to make on salvaging the ship, but the court refused to allow this, on the grounds that it was impossible to calculate the value of a ship that did not exist. However, McRae was allowed to recover the wasted costs of the salvage trip – in other words, his reliance loss.

Damages were considered too speculative in **Sapwell** v **Bass** (1910). The plaintiff was a breeder of racehorses and the defendant the owner of a stallion who was paid £315 so that his stallion could 'serve' the plaintiff's mares. The defendant sold the stallion to a third party in South America, making it impossible to carry out the contract. The plaintiff claimed damages for the foals which he had lost, including the possibility he had lost a valuable prize-winning animal. The court held that these damages were too uncertain and instead made a nominal award.

Quantifying the expectation loss

Contract damages based on expectation loss aim to put the non-breaching party in the position they would have been in had the contract been performed as agreed. In calculating damages, the focus is on the claimant's loss. Claimants cannot recover more than their actual loss. If the claimant suffers no loss, they will only receive nominal damages. An award of damages can include compensation for a loss of profit which would have been made but for the breach of contract. The damages are essentially seeking to compensate the difference in value between the promised performance and the actual performance.

The market price rule
Where a contract has been breached, the law assumes that the wronged party will immediately mitigate their loss by buying similar goods which they had contracted for from another source or selling the goods which they had contracted to sell to another source. The wronged party will then suffer a loss only if they had to pay more for the substitute goods on the open market than they had originally contracted to pay, or had to sell the goods at a lower price. The buyer's damages will therefore be assessed by subtracting the contract price from the market price at the time of breach. A market price exists when goods can be bought and sold at a price fixed by supply and demand. This mode of calculating loss is expressly laid down for certain breaches of contracts for the sale of goods in ss. 50 and 51 of the Sale of Goods Act 1979, but the principle applies more generally.

As a result of the market price rule, the wronged party will often suffer no loss, as there is often no difference between the market price and the contract price. Take the example where Ann has two bags of flour and contracts to sell them to Ben at the market price of £10 per bag. If Ben later wrongfully refuses to accept the flour, Ann will almost certainly be able to sell them to Claire at the same price. Only nominal damages will be awarded. Ann may argue that she has lost profit because she would have been able to sell another two bags of flour to Claire. This argument may succeed if supply is greater than demand, that is to say that Ann had access to more sacks of flour which could have been sold to Claire, so that there is one lost sale.

An illustration of how the law applies in practice is **Thompson Ltd** *v* **Robinson (Gunmakers) Ltd** (1955). The buyers of a car were in breach of contract for refusing to accept delivery of the car from the sellers, who were car dealers. The dealers had to sell the car at the manufacturer's list price, which meant the market and contract prices were effectively the same. At the time, there was little demand for the type of car in question and supply was exceeding demand. Realizing that they were unlikely to find another buyer, the dealers persuaded their suppliers to take the car back. The buyers admitted that they were in breach, but argued that the plaintiffs had in fact suffered no loss, as there was no difference between market and contract price at the time when they refused to accept delivery. The court disagreed, pointing out that s. 50 of the Sale of Goods Act was merely a *prima facie* rule which did not apply in this situation. The sellers were awarded £61, the profit they would have made on the sale. On the facts the dealers had lost a sale, which could not be mitigated. A contrasting case is **Charter** *v* **Sullivan** (1957). Here the facts were similar, except that the car was of a type which was in such demand at the time that the sellers admitted that they were easily able to sell every example they could get their hands on. As a result, it was easy to find another buyer, and the sellers were only awarded nominal damages.

Exclusion of the market value rule. The market price rule will not be used as the measure of loss either where there is no available market or where, in the circumstances, the non-breaching party is not expected to avail itself of the market to mitigate its loss. Where there is no market, the loss has to be quantified by the court estimating the actual value of the goods. There is no market for unique goods because alternative substitute goods cannot be obtained. In **Lazenby Garages Ltd** *v* **Wright** (1976) the sale of a second-hand car was treated as a sale of a unique item, but it is unlikely that every second-hand car would be treated as unique. There will be no market for goods where they have been specially manufactured to the exact specifications of the buyer, so that it is very unlikely that a different buyer would have ordered precisely the same goods.

Cost of cure

Cost of cure is the other possible way of calculating expectation loss. In some cases, claimants may have wanted the performance of a contract for personal ('subjective') reasons. These subjective reasons are the value to the consumer of contractual performance which is over and above the market value of that performance. They can be described as the consumer surplus. Thus, an award of damages based on an objective difference in value between the contractual performance and the market value of the performance received will not compensate them for their loss.

The cost of cure may be significantly greater than the difference in value from that contracted for. The question, therefore, is whether the courts should take account of the consumer surplus and award higher cost of cure damages. Cost of cure damages will only be awarded where this would be reasonable. They will not be awarded where they would be out of all proportion to the consequences of the breach and there is a risk of unjust enrichment where the claimant is awarded cost of cure damages but then does not use the money to remedy the breach.

In a US case, **Jacob & Youngs** *v* **Kent** (1921), the plaintiffs had specified in the contract for the construction of a house that a particular brand of piping had to be used for the plumbing work. A different make of piping of identical quality was in fact used. The court refused to allow damages on the basis of cost of cure, and allowed only the difference in value between the two types of pipe, which was purely nominal.

A leading case on the issue is **Ruxley Electronics and Construction Ltd** *v* **Forsyth** (1995). This case was discussed on p. 266. The plaintiff had contracted for the construction of a swimming pool in his garden. He had specified that the pool needed to be 7 ft 6 in deep so that he would feel safe when diving. The completed pool was only 6 ft 9 in deep. The cost of rebuilding the pool (the cost of cure) was out of proportion to the loss suffered and so the House of Lords held that the cost of cure was not recoverable. The House of Lords gave an example of the construction of a house where the owner specifies that some of the lower bricks should be blue. Instead of using blue bricks, yellow bricks are used. To conform with the contractual requirements, the house would have to be knocked down and rebuilt, but this would be disproportionately expensive. It would therefore be unreasonable to award cost of cure damages. By contrast, if a house was built so defectively that it is not inhabitable, it would be reasonable to award cost of cure damages.

Loss of opportunity damages

The loss of an opportunity is recoverable in damages if the lost chance is quantifiable in monetary terms and there was a substantial chance that the opportunity might have come to fruition. Otherwise, the loss of opportunity will be treated as too speculative. The leading case is **Chaplin** *v* **Hicks** (1911) in which the defendant, Sir Edward Seymour Hicks, was a theatre producer. He advertised a competition in the *Daily Express* for young women to send photographs to the newspaper to be shortlisted by readers for a prize. The winner of the competition would be offered a part in one of the defendant's plays. Six thousand photographs were sent in, each woman paying one shilling to take part in the competition. For the purposes of the competition, the country was divided into four areas, and the winners from each area were to attend the final round. The plaintiff, Eva Chaplin, came top in her area but was only informed of this at a very late stage, and was then unable to attend the final round. She sued for the loss of the chance to win the competition. The Court of Appeal held that she was entitled to damages for breach of contract. The mere fact that such damages were difficult to assess did not in itself mean that the plaintiff could not succeed. The court stated that in calculating the damages the jury 'must of course give effect to the consideration that the plaintiff's chance is only one out of four and that they cannot tell whether she would have ultimately proved to be the winner. But having considered all this they may well think that it is of considerable pecuniary value to have got into so small a class, and they must assess the damages accordingly.'

Lord Reid in **Davies** v **Taylor** (1974) put forward the requirement that there must have been a substantial chance that the opportunity would have come to fruition.

> The issues and the sole issue is whether that chance or probability was substantial. If it was it must be evaluated. If it was a mere possibility it must be ignored. Many different words could be and have been used to indicate the dividing line. I can think of none better than substantial on the one hand, or 'speculative' on the other.

The distinction between loss of a chance and speculative loss was discussed in **Allied Maples Group Ltd** v **Simmons and Simmons** (1995) in which the plaintiff sued a firm of solicitors for negligence in failing to pursue a claim. The court stated that the plaintiff could only succeed if the chance was substantial rather than speculative.

Tax

As we have seen, the aim of contract damages is to put the claimant in the position that they would have been in had the contract been performed. This means that, as a rule, the claimant should not make a profit from the defendant's breach if the profit would not have been made had the contract been performed as agreed. Therefore where a claimant's claim includes money on which they would have had to pay income tax if it were earned by performing the contract, the amount of tax payable can be deducted from the damages.

This principle was established in **British Transport Commission** v **Gourley** (1956). This was actually a tort case, but the same principle applies to contract damages. The plaintiff had been seriously injured as a result of negligence by the defendants and was claiming for lost earnings of £37,000. The court awarded him the sum that he would have earned after paying tax, since that was what he would have received had the injury not occurred.

If the damages will themselves be subjected to tax, then the courts do not have to deduct tax themselves when calculating the damages, because this would lead to tax being deducted twice.

Profit made by the defendant

Contract damages are not intended to be a means of punishing the party in breach. For this reason, with minor exceptions, when calculating damages, the courts do not take into account any profit the party in breach has made by breaking the contract, only the loss caused to the innocent party. So if, for example, Bill, a greengrocer, fails to make a delivery to Jill because a top chef has just come in and bought all his stock at a vastly inflated price, Bill will be liable to compensate Jill for any extra cost she incurred in buying elsewhere, but does not have to hand over the extra profit he made on the sale to the chef. The party breaking the contract has calculated that it is more profitable to break the contract than to perform it. In **Occidental Worldwide Investment Corp** v **Skibs A/S Avanti, The Siboen and the Sibotre** (1976) shipowners had contracted to charter their vessels to the plaintiffs. In 1973 the market price for chartering vessels increased and the shipowners chose to break their contracts with the plaintiffs in order to charter the vessels at higher prices to other customers. As a result they made an additional profit of over 3 million dollars. The plaintiff claimed damages, including an award of this profit. The Commercial Court held that they could only claim for their own loss and not the profits made by the defendants.

A leading authority rejecting profit-based damages is **Surrey County Council** v **Bredero Homes Ltd** (1993). The Council sold land to the defendant property developer, who covenanted not to build more than 72 houses on it. Without seeking a variation of the covenant, the developer built an additional five houses. The developer deliberately breached the covenant in order to make more profit. The Council claimed damages based on its estimate of what the defendant would have had to pay as the 'price' for variation of the covenant. While the developer had been 'unjustly enriched', the Council had not suffered any loss. Normal contract damages were not recoverable, because the plaintiff was already in the position it would have been in had the contract not been breached. The question for the Court of Appeal was whether the deliberate breach of the contract should in some way be sanctioned by making the defendant hand over part of its profit. The court did not think it should.

Exceptionally, the courts will now order a party in breach of a contract to hand over any profits that they have gained from the breach of contract. This development in the law was laid down by the House of Lords in **HM Attorney-General** v **George Blake & Jonathan Cape Ltd** (2000). In that case Blake had been a member of the Secret Intelligence Service. In 1951 he became an agent for the Soviet Union. From that time until his arrest in 1960, he worked as a spy, disclosing valuable secret information.

In 1961 he was convicted of committing offences under the Official Secrets Act 1911 and was sentenced to 42 years' imprisonment. Five years later he escaped from Wormwood Scrubs and made his way to the Soviet Union, where he now lives as a fugitive from justice.

The publishers, Jonathan Cape Ltd, agreed to pay the defendant £50,000 on signing a contract to write a book of his experiences, £50,000 on delivery of the manuscript and a further £50,000 on publication of the autobiography. In 1990 the book was published. The information in the book was no longer confidential and nor was its disclosure damaging to the public interest.

By the time the Government knew about the book, Blake had already received £60,000, which could not in practice be recovered. Approximately £90,000 remained payable by the publisher and the present action was brought to prevent its payment to Blake.

In 1944 Blake had signed a declaration under the Official Secrets Act 1911 which included an undertaking not to divulge any official information gained as a result of his employment. The House of Lords held that this undertaking was contractually binding and had been breached by Blake.

The House accepted that following a breach of contract an account of profits could, in exceptional circumstances, be ordered. Under this order the defendant would have to hand over to the claimant any profits received from the breach of contract. This order could be made when the claimant's interest in performance made it just and equitable that the defendant should retain no benefit from the breach of contract. The House of Lords said that such an order would only be made in exceptional circumstances and that:

> A useful general guide, although not exhaustive, is whether the plaintiff had a legitimate interest in preventing the defendant's profit-making activity and hence, in depriving him of his profit.

Lord Steyn stated that four conditions would need to be satisfied before there could be an order for an account of profits for a breach of contract:

- There must be a breach of a negative stipulation (in this case not to disclose official secrets).
- The contract breaker has obtained a profit by doing the precise opposite of what he promised not to do.
- The claimant has a special interest greater than the financial one of having the contract performed.
- Specific performance or an injunction (both discussed below) would be an ineffective remedy.

The House considered that three facts would not in themselves be a sufficient ground for departing from the normal basis on which damages are awarded:

the fact that the breach was cynical and deliberate; the fact that the breach enabled the defendant to enter into a more profitable contract elsewhere; and the fact that by entering into a new and more profitable contract the defendant put it out of his power to perform his contract with the plaintiff.

In 1997 the Law Commission issued a report, *Aggravated, Exemplary and Restitutionary Damages*, in which it considered the question of damages when the contract breaker has profited from their breach. It came to the conclusion that the law in this area should be left to the courts rather than being developed by statute. They pointed out that it would be difficult to draw the distinction between 'innocent' and 'cynical' breaches of contract, which were based on the parties' own commercial reasons. Thus any legislative provisions based on this distinction would lead to greater uncertainty in the assessment of damages in commercial and consumer disputes. It would also be difficult to show which profits were a direct result of the breach of contract.

Action for an agreed sum

Where a contract specifies a price to be paid for performance, and payment has not been made, the party who has performed can claim the price owing by means of an action for the agreed sum. Although the claim is obviously for money, this is not the same as a claim for damages. This is a claim for a debt and not a claim for damages. The claimant is not seeking compensation, but simply enforcement of the defendant's promise to pay. However, where the claimant has suffered additional loss, beyond not receiving the agreed price, damages can be claimed alongside the agreed sum and the claim for damages follows the usual rules on remoteness and so on.

There are many advantages of an action for an agreed sum over an action for damages. The amount claimed is known from the beginning, so that questions of quantification, remoteness, causation and mitigation do not arise. In addition, because the issues at trial are frequently uncomplicated, there is a streamlined procedure for claims for unpaid debts (known as a summary judgment).

An action for the agreed sum can only be brought once the duty to pay has arisen, which will depend on the terms of the contract. Where the party failing to pay has wrongfully repudiated the contract, the injured party will have had the choice of terminating the contract or affirming it. If the injured party has chosen to terminate, he or she cannot sue for any sum which, under the contract, only became due after the date of termination. Damages can, however, be claimed for wrongful repudiation, and in calculating these the court may take into account any sums which should have been received under the contract.

▶ Restitution

Restitution is the remedy available when there has been unjust enrichment. Where money has been paid under a contract, or purported contract, and performance has not been received in return, or has not been adequate, the payer may want to claim the money back, rather than claiming damages (if, for example, no additional loss has resulted from the failure to perform). Restitution is not a remedy for a breach of contract. Rather, restitution seeks to restore money paid or the value of a benefit conferred in circumstances in which no contract exists, or in which there is no longer any obligation to perform under a contract.

Contract remedies and restitution do not overlap. In practice, restitution will therefore be available where there is no contract. There may be no contract for one of the following reasons:

- a contract has not been made (e.g. because of a lack of agreement, uncertainty or the absence of consideration);
- the contract has been discharged; or
- the contract was void (e.g. due to illegality).

Restitution will be available, for example, where one party has provided some performance to the benefit of another party in anticipation of a contract being made, but the contract is never made. The recipient of the performance has received a benefit which will have cost the other party to provide, and it would be unjust to allow the benefit to be retained without payment of some kind.

Restitution can apply in many legal contexts, but in the context of contract law, restitution will allow an injured party to recover money paid, or claim the value of benefits conferred for the services rendered at the other's request; this is called a *quantum meruit*.

Total failure of consideration

In general, restitution will only be possible if there has been a total failure of consideration so that restitution will prevent unjust enrichment. There is a total failure of consideration where one party has provided a benefit to another party, but has received nothing in return. There need not be any breach of contract. In this context, there may have been consideration at the time of the formation of the contract, but in practice the consideration has not actually been performed as promised by the contract. Performance may be impossible because the contract has been frustrated, or because unknown to the parties the subject matter of the contract had been destroyed before the contract was made. In each case, a person may recover money paid in advance even though the failure of performance does not amount to a breach of contract. Where there has been a breach of contract, the appropriate remedy is damages and not restitution.

An example of restitution where there is a total failure of consideration is **Fibrosa Akcyjna** v **Fairbairn Lawson** (see p. 245 above). The seller of goods was prevented from completing performance of a contract by delivering the goods due to the outbreak of war, because the purchaser was in enemy-occupied territory. The contract was frustrated. The purchaser had paid part of the price of the goods in advance, but had received none of the goods. They were able to claim back these advance payments due to the total failure of consideration under the principles of restitution.

In order for there to be a total failure of consideration, it is not sufficient that one party had received nothing under the contract; what has to be shown is that one party had not performed any of their contractual duties. Thus, in **Stocznia Gdanska SA** v **Latvian Shipping Company** (1998) the defendants had ordered some vessels from the claimants, which were not delivered. The House of Lords considered that the claimants' contractual obligations included designing and building the vessels. Since some of this work had been performed, there had not been a total failure of consideration.

Restitution may be available where a contract is void for illegality where the parties are not equally at fault. Following the House of Lords' judgment of **Kleinwort Benson Ltd** v **Lincoln CC** (1999), if money has been paid under a void contract as a result of a mistake of law, the money can be recovered even though there is no total (or partial) failure of consideration.

Partial failure of consideration

Where there is only a partial, rather than a total, failure of consideration (for example, if part of a job is done, or part of a consignment of goods supplied), the general rule is that there is no right to recover back money paid. There is an exception to this rule: under the Law Reform (Frustrated Contracts) Act 1943, money paid in advance under a contract which is later frustrated can be recovered, even if the failure of consideration is only partial. This is because in such a case the party making payment has no other remedy, since damages cannot be claimed when a contract is frustrated.

There is a second exception where restitution is possible when there is partial or defective performance. This is where a party chooses to give back any benefit received, bringing about a total failure of consideration, so that money paid can be recovered. This is not, however, possible where the nature of the benefit received is such that it cannot be returned to the other party. An example would be a bad haircut.

Where the subject matter can be returned, handing it back will only bring about a total failure of consideration if the injured party has not received a benefit from it, for example, by using the goods, or occupying a property. Simply testing goods does not count as benefiting from them, but any further use may prevent a total failure of consideration. In **Hunt v Silk** (1804) an agreement for a lease provided that the tenant would take possession immediately, the landlord would undertake specified repairs and the lease would be executed within ten days, with the tenant paying £10 when it was executed. The tenant duly took possession, and paid his £10, but the landlord failed to do the repairs, or to execute the lease within ten days. The tenant waited a few more days, then left, and claimed the £10 back. His claim was rejected, and the case has generally been taken as establishing a strict rule that, if a party has received any part of the benefit due under the contract, failure of consideration is not total. Although the decision in the case seems reasonable, since the tenant could presumably have claimed damages instead, the rule itself is open to criticism, because it has the potential to prevent a claim for the recovery of money even where the benefit received is negligible or of no practical use.

The courts are sometimes prepared to find a sufficient failure of consideration for the purposes of restitution, where that failure appears to be less than total by apportioning the consideration. Consideration is apportioned by finding independent promises, one of which fails totally and can be the subject of restitution. This approach can be seen in **DO Ferguson Associates v M. Sohl** (1992). The defendant employed the plaintiffs as building contractors to renovate shop premises in Kensal Green. The price agreed was £32,194. After disputes between the parties, the builders walked off the site and did not return. They had already been paid £26,738. The defendant employed another firm of builders who completed the work for less than it would have cost under the original contract. The builders brought an action for the rest of the contractual price, and the defendant counter-claimed for damages and repayment of an overpayment made by him. The Court of Appeal held that the plaintiff had repudiated the contract which was discharged by the defendant's acceptance of the breach. The value of the work done by the plaintiffs was only £22,065. The defendant had therefore overpaid by £4,673. The defendant received £1 nominal damages for the plaintiff's breach of contract. In addition, the court awarded the defendant restitution of the £4,673 overpayment for work which had not been done. In other words, there was a total failure of consideration of this part of the contract. Hirst LJ stated:

> It matters not that at some stage or other that sum of money formed part of a larger instalment.

The Law Commission in its Working Paper, *Pecuniary Restitution on Breach of Contract (No 65)*, had provisionally recommended that restitutionary recovery ought to be available in cases of partial failure of consideration. However, it changed its mind in a later Report (No 121).

Quantum meruit

Where work has been done or goods supplied but no payment has been received and cannot be obtained under a contract, an action is available called a *quantum meruit* (Latin for 'as much as is deserved'), under which claimants can claim a reasonable price for their performance. Payment cannot be obtained under a contract where there is no contract, or where the price has not been specified in the contract. A *quantum meruit* is based on restitutionary principles and is different from damages, since it merely aims to pay for performance, not to compensate for loss. So long as there is a contract between the parties, under which the claimant was intended to be paid, the court will order payment of a reasonable sum for the performance rendered – essentially the market price or 'going rate'. Where there is no contract because the contract is void, the court will still be able to order a *quantum meruit* for performance rendered.

In **Sir Lindsay Parkinson & Co Ltd** *v* **Commissioners of Works** (1949) contractors agreed to do some building work. The price was £5 million, but the contract allowed for extra work to be ordered, and also provided that the price paid should provide a profit of between £150,000 and £300,000. In the event, the Commissioner did order extra work, taking the cost to over £6 million. The contractors claimed for extra profit on a *quantum meruit*. The court allowed their claim, stating that the express provision concerning the maximum profit only applied to works worth about £5 million.

A *quantum meruit* based on extra work done or goods supplied will only be allowed if the defendant had the choice of accepting or rejecting the extra benefit. In **Forman & Co Proprietary Ltd** *v* **The Liddesdale** (1900) the contract concerned repairs to a ship, for which a price had been agreed. Materials had been specified in the contract, but the repairer chose to use alternative ones, which were more suitable for the job and more expensive. The shipowner then refused to pay for the work. The Privy Council held that the repairer could recover nothing for the work he had done. He could not claim for the agreed sum, because he had not performed as agreed and he could not use a *quantum meruit* because the shipowner had never been asked whether he wanted the extra benefit.

For an example of the operation of this principle, see **British Steel Corp** *v* **Clevleand Bridge & Engineering Co Ltd** (1984). Work had begun at the request of the defendants, on the provision of some steel before all the elements of the contract for the steel had been agreed. Both sides confidently expected to reach agreement without difficulty. In fact, final agreement was never reached. The plaintiffs successfully claimed a *quantum meruit* for the work they had done.

The **Cleveland Bridge** case was distinguished in **Regalian Properties plc** *v* **London Dockland Development Corp** (1995). In that case the plaintiffs had not carried out the work at the request of the defendants, but had done it in order to win the contract from the defendants. The negotiations had been conducted on a subject-to-contract basis, so that such expenditure was at their own risk. It was not recoverable when they failed to obtain the anticipated contract.

Where there is precise provision for remuneration, a *quantum meruit* cannot usually be used to alter the price, even if extra work is done. In **Gilbert and Partners** *v* **Knight** (1968) Knight employed a firm of surveyors to supervise building work for a fee of £30. The surveyors did more supervision than Knight had asked for and submitted an account for £30 plus £105 for the additional work. Knight refused to pay the extra £105 and the court upheld his case. The original contract had fixed the payment and it was still in existence.

The following are circumstances in which the courts will allow a *quantum meruit* claim even though a price has been fixed.

Incapacity Where necessaries are sold and delivered to a minor, they need only pay a reasonable price for them, even though there may have been an agreement to pay more (see Chapter 4).

Wrongful prevention of performance If one party begins performance but is prevented from finishing by the other party's breach, the innocent party can claim a *quantum meruit* at the agreed rate for the work done (see **Planché** *v* **Colburn**, p. 238 above).

Agreed partial performance Where a party performs only part of their contractual obligation, but this part-performance is voluntarily accepted by the other party, a *quantum meruit* can be used to secure a reasonable payment for the work done. In **Miles** *v* **Wakefield Metropolitan District Council** (1987) the House of Lords held that a worker on industrial action, in the form of a 'go slow' could not claim his wages under his contract of employment because he was deliberately working in a manner designed to harm the employer. He was, however, entitled to be paid on a *quantum meruit* basis for the value of the reduced work performed and accepted by the employers.

Contract void Remuneration on the basis of a *quantum meruit* may be recoverable where performance is rendered under a contract which, unknown to both parties, is void. In **Craven-Ellis** *v* **Canons Ltd** (1936) the plaintiff had been appointed and carried out work as a managing director of the defendant company, but it turned out that his contract of employment was void. The Court of Appeal held that he could recover the reasonable value of his work on a *quantum meruit*. This principle would also apply where a contract with a company is void because when the contract was made the company was not yet legally in existence or had been dissolved, and where goods have been supplied under a contract of sale which is void for a mistake as to the purchaser's identity.

Contract frustrated   Where work is done under a contract before it is frustrated, a *quantum meruit* is not available at common law, but the party can make a claim in respect of a valuable benefit conferred by the work under the Law Reform (Frustrated Contracts) Act 1943. Work done after the frustrating event can be claimed for on a *quantum meruit*, on the principle of **Craven-Ellis** *v* **Canons Ltd** (1936).

▶ EQUITABLE REMEDIES

Where common law remedies are inadequate to compensate the claimant, there are a range of equitable remedies. However, these are not available as of right, merely because the defendant is in breach. They are provided at the discretion of the court, taking into account the behaviour of both parties and the overall justice of the case.

▶ Specific performance

An order of specific performance is a court order compelling someone to perform their obligations under a contract. As we have seen, the common law will not force a party in breach to perform (except where the performance is simply paying money), even though this may seem a fairly obvious solution to many contract problems. The equitable remedy of specific performance does compel the party in breach to perform. In practice, specific performance only rarely applies, as the making of such an order is subject to the following restrictions.

Damages must be inadequate

Specific performance is only granted where damages alone would be an inadequate remedy (though damages may be ordered as well as specific performance). It is not, therefore, applied where the claimant could easily purchase replacement goods or performance. Where the goods that are the subject of the contract are in some way unique, then specific performance can be available. For this reason, specific performance is mainly applied in contracts to sell land (which includes land with buildings), since each piece of land is thought to be unique, and impossible to replace exactly.

Where the damages would only be nominal, specific performance may be ordered to avoid one party being unjustly enriched. The latter circumstance applied in **Beswick** *v* **Beswick** (1968) (discussed at p. 213 above) where the plaintiff's husband sold his business to his nephew in return for an annual allowance to be paid to himself and, after his death, to his widow. Once the husband died, the nephew refused to make payments to the widow. Despite the fact that the husband had clearly intended her to benefit from the contract, it was held that the widow could not sue the nephew on her own behalf, because she was not a party to the contract. However, the widow was allowed to sue as the executor of her husband's estate. The circumstances were such that the husband suffered no loss, because he had died before the nephew stopped paying the annuity, so damages would only have been nominal. It was clearly unjust for the defendant to keep the entire benefit of the contract without himself performing much at all. As a result, specific performance was ordered.

Hardship to the defendant

Because specific performance is a discretionary remedy, the court will not apply it to cases where it could cause the claimant great hardship or unfairness. In **Patel** v **Ali** (1984) the plaintiff had requested specific performance on a contract for the sale of a house. The claim was delayed by four years (through no fault of either party) and in this time, the seller's husband had gone bankrupt and she had become disabled. As a result, she needed to be near friends and relatives, and moving house would have caused her hardship. Consequently, the court refused specific performance and ordered damages instead.

Contracts made unfairly

Equity also allows the court to refuse specific performance of a contract which has been obtained by unfair means, even if they do not amount to the sort of vitiating factor which would invalidate the contract. In **Walters** v **Morgan** (1861) the defendant, who had just bought some land, agreed to grant the plaintiff a mining lease over it. When the party who had asked for the lease tried to enforce the agreement by specific performance, the court refused, on the grounds that the plaintiff had taken advantage of the fact that the defendant had not really known the value of the lease at the time the agreement was made.

Contracts unsuitable for specific performance

Some types of contract are, by their nature, unlikely to be the subject of an order for specific performance. The two main types are contracts involving personal services (such as employment contracts), where specific performance would infringe personal freedom, and contracts which involve continuous duties. In the latter case, it is impractical for the courts to supervise proper performance, but more importantly, failure to perform after an order for specific performance can lead to a charge of contempt of court, and the courts are not keen to envisage a series of contempt actions arising from a long-running contract. In **Ryan** *v* **Mutual Tontine Association** (1893) the lease of a flat promised tenants that a resident porter would be 'constantly in attendance'. The person appointed had other employment, and so was in fact often absent from the flats. The court refused specific performance of this term of the lease because it would require a level of constant supervision beyond that which the court was able to assess.

However, there is flexibility, and the courts are willing to weigh up the degree of supervision required, and the balance of hardships if the order is made against those if it is not. These were said to be the issues taken into account when the court decided to grant specific performance in **Posner** *v* **Scott-Lewis** (1986) where the tenants of a block of 'luxury' flats sought to enforce their landlords' obligation to provide a resident porter.

In **Co-op Insurance Society Ltd** *v* **Argyll Stores (Holdings) Ltd** (1997) the plaintiffs were developers of a shopping centre. They had granted the defendants a 35-year lease to operate a Safeway supermarket in the largest shop unit. This store was central to the success of the centre, as it would attract customers, generating business for the smaller shops. The lease therefore contained a promise to keep the store open as a supermarket during ordinary business hours and only allowed for closure for a maximum of four months during the lease. In 1995, the supermarket was losing money and the defendants informed the plaintiffs that they intended to close it down, despite the fact that 20 years remained on the lease. The plaintiffs in turn proposed that the defendants keep the supermarket open at a reduced rate until they found a suitable tenant to replace them. Without replying, the defendants closed the supermarket, which constituted a serious breach of contract. The plaintiffs sought an order for specific performance to compel the supermarket to come back and carry on the tenancy for the rest of the lease. This had been granted by the Court of Appeal, but was refused by the House of Lords.

The House considered that while it would be difficult to arrive at an accurate figure for the loss which was going to be caused to the plaintiffs over the next 20 years, taking into account the impact on the smaller shops in the centre, this was not sufficient to justify an order for specific performance. Lord Hoffmann, in delivering the principal judgment, was clear that 'the established practice may justify a refusal of specific performance even when damages are not an adequate remedy'. It was settled practice not to make such orders where this would compel someone to carry on a business, since this would require constant supervision by the court. Moreover, the only tool at the court's disposal to ensure compliance was the draconian criminal sanction for contempt of court, which he considered to be an unsuitable rod to hold over a commercial party being compelled to trade. The result of ordering someone to run a business which was uneconomic might well be to cause them loss which was completely out of proportion to that caused to the other party by the original breach of contract. While the Court of Appeal had clearly been influenced by what they considered to have been blatantly dishonest conduct by the defendants, the House of Lords followed the traditional common law path of refusing to treat the nature of the defendants' conduct as relevant. Finally, Lord Hoffmann distinguished between contracts requiring someone to carry on an activity over a period of time and contracts for results. In the latter case, supervision by the courts was less problematic, as the court could often simply view the end result. This distinction was used to explain the fact that specific enforcement had been ordered in the past in relation to building contracts.

Specific performance will not be applied to a contract which is vague as to the performance required, nor to a promise which is only supported by nominal consideration or contained in a deed. It is not used where a contract allows the party concerned to terminate it (since if specific performance were ordered, the party in breach could simply exercise the right to terminate).

An order for specific performance is also subject to the principle of mutuality, which means that it will not usually be ordered against a defendant if it could not have been ordered against the claimant, had they been the one in breach. So, for example, specific performance is never ordered when the claimant is a minor, because it cannot be ordered against a minor.

The courts tend to make the order where substitute performance cannot be bought.

Injunction

An injunction normally orders the defendant not to do a particular thing. For example, Ken, a horse owner, rents a field from Julie, and it is a term of their agreement that no buildings should be put up on the land. If Julie discovers that Ken is about to build a stable, she could apply to the court for an injunction to prevent him doing so. This is called a prohibitory injunction.

Where the action has already taken place (if Ken has already built the stable, for example) the court may make a mandatory injunction, which orders the defendant to take action to restore the situation to that which existed before the defendant's breach – so Ken would have to demolish the stable.

When considering an application for a mandatory injunction, the court applies a balance of convenience test, and may refuse the remedy if the defendant would lose a lot more by restoring the original position than the claimant would gain. However, in deciding this issue, they will also take into account the nature of the breach and the circumstances, and a mandatory injunction may be applied even where the defendant's loss in the event of restoration outweighs the claimant's gain – if, for example, the breach was committed knowingly and damages would not be an adequate remedy.

Injunction and specific performance

As we have seen, specific performance will not be granted for a contract concerning personal services, such as an employment contract. However, there are borderline cases where an injunction has the potential to be used, for all intents and purposes, to bring about the effect of specific performance. In **Warner Bros Pictures Inc** *v* **Nelson** (1937) the actress Bette Davis had signed a contract with Warner Brothers, under which she agreed not to work for any other film company for a year. During this period, she contracted with another company, in breach of the Warner Brothers contract, and Warner Brothers sought an injunction to stop her actually working for the rival company. Although the practical effect was to make Ms Davis work for Warner Brothers, because she could not work for anyone else, the order could be distinguished from specific performance on the grounds that it was an encouragement to work for the plaintiffs, and not a compulsion, because in theory she could have simply made her living in some other way, and not acted in anyone's films.

In practice, the courts place limits on the use of injunctions in such circumstances. In **Page One Records Ltd** *v* **Britton** (1968) the defendants were a pop group called The Troggs, who were at that time very well known. They had engaged one of the plaintiffs as their manager, and agreed not to employ anyone else to do that job. Later, they wanted to terminate the agreement and the plaintiffs responded by seeking an injunction to stop the group from taking on another manager. The injunction was refused, on the grounds that its practical effect would be to force the group to employ the plaintiff as manager, because without a manager they would not be able to work.

Recent cases seem to suggest that the courts are watching out for the use of injunctions as a means of achieving specific performance 'by the back door'. **Warren** *v* **Mendy** (1989) concerned a contract between a boxer and his manager, Warren. The contract gave Warren exclusive rights to manage the boxer for three years, but during that period the boxer apparently lost confidence in Warren and asked advice on his career of Mendy. Warren sought an injunction against Mendy, to prevent him from inducing a breach of Warren's contract with the boxer. The Court of Appeal declined to grant the injunction to enforce the agreement, on the grounds that doing so would indirectly compel performance of the contract. The general view seems to be that an injunction should not be granted unless it leaves the employee with some other reasonable means of earning a living.

▶ REMEDIES AGREED BY THE PARTIES

Many contracts, particularly commercial ones, specify the kinds of breach which will justify termination, and/or the damages to be paid by each party in the event of certain types of breach. For example, building contracts often contain provision for specified damages to be paid in the event that the building is not completed on time, and holiday contracts often state that the tour company is allowed to keep a percentage of the price paid if the customer cancels at a late stage. This sort of provision allows both sides to know in advance what their liability will amount to, and to plan accordingly.

There are two types of contract clauses concerning damages: liquidated damages clauses and penalty clauses.

▶ Liquidated damages

Liquidated damages is the term used where a contract specifies the amount of damages to be paid in the event of breach, and this amount represents a genuine attempt to work out what the loss would be in the event of such a breach. In such a case, the court will allow the claimant to recover this amount without proof of actual loss, even if the actual loss is larger or smaller than the sum laid down in the contract. The usual rules as to damages are excluded (damages which are not fixed by a contract, and must be calculated using the rules described in the first part of this chapter, are described as unliquidated damages).

▶ Penalty clauses

If a contract states that a particular sum is to be paid on breach of the contract, and that sum is not a genuine pre-estimate of the loss that would be suffered in the event of breach, but is designed instead to threaten to penalize a party in breach, this is a penalty clause. Where the damages laid down in a contract amount to a penalty clause, the clause will be found to be invalid and the award of damages will be determined by the ordinary principles of contract law instead, discussed in the first half of this chapter.

Guidelines for determining when specified damages should be considered penal were laid down in **Dunlop Pneumatic Tyre Co Ltd** *v* **New Garage and Motor Co Ltd** (1915). The plaintiffs supplied tyres to the defendants, under a contract providing that the defendants would not resell them at less than the list price. If they breached this provision, they were to pay £5 for every tyre sold at less than list price (an arrangement which would now be illegal).

The House of Lords held that the provision was not penal and was in the nature of liquidated damages. Undercutting the list price would have been very damaging to the plaintiff's business, and although it was impossible to calculate the loss precisely in advance, the sum specified was reasonable in the circumstances.

Lord Dunedin described the factors to be taken into account when deciding whether damages were penal or not. Damages would be regarded as penal if the sum laid down was 'extravagantly greater' than any loss which might conceivably result from the breach. This would include a situation where the breach consisted of not paying a certain sum of money and that sum was smaller than the damages stipulated for not paying it. There is a presumption (but no more) that damages are penal if 'a single lump sum is made payable . . . on the occurrence of one or more or all of several events, some of which may occasion serious and others but trifling damage'.

Lord Dunedin made it clear that even if the parties themselves describe the damages they set as either 'liquidated' or 'penalty' this will not be conclusive, though it may be relevant. The court should look at the substance of the agreement and decide what the terms really amount to; if there was a genuine attempt to pre-estimate the consequences of a breach, damages would not be considered penal, even if such consequences could not be precisely calculated in advance.

▶ EXTINCTION OF REMEDIES

As we saw in Chapter 14, where one party has a right of action for breach of contract, this right may be extinguished by agreement between the parties, either by a release under seal or by accord and satisfaction. Such a right can also be extinguished by the passage of time, under the Limitation Act 1980. The Act lays down various time limits for different kinds of action, and once these have expired, the claimant is said to be 'statute-barred' from claiming.

▶ The statutory time limits

Contract proceedings should normally be brought within six years of when the cause of action accrued. 'Cause of action' means the facts giving rise to the action and will usually be when the contract is breached.

An action based on a contract made by deed must be brought within 12 years of the date on which the cause of action accrued.

There are contract cases where the claimant does not know that there is a cause of action at the time when the situation occurs, and may not know for some time afterwards, possibly even not until the ordinary limitation period has passed. This issue is addressed in the Latent Damage

Act 1986, which provides that where the cause of action could not be discovered when it arose, the claimant can sue within three years of the time when it could be discovered. In addition, s. 32 of the Limitation Act 1980 provides that when a claimant is unaware of the cause of action at the time it accrues because of mistake or fraud by the defendant, the period of limitation does not begin until the claimant has discovered the fraud or mistake, or until such time as they could have discovered it by using reasonable diligence.

Section 32 was applied in **Applegate** v **Moss** (1971). The defendant, a builder, was contracted to build a house on a specific type of foundations. He did the work on the foundations very badly, with the result that several years later the house was found to be unsafe to live in. By this time the six-year limitation period was over, but the court held that there had been concealment of the defective foundations and allowed the action to proceed.

Where a claimant is under a disability, for example, they are a minor, or of unsound mind at the time when the cause of action accrues, the limitation period does not begin until the disability has ceased to operate. Therefore a minor can bring proceedings relating to contractual matters that arose while they were a minor, for six years after their eighteenth birthday.

Acknowledgement

The limitation period may be extended if, before it expires, the defendant acknowledges the claim or pays part of it (s. 30). If this happens, the limitation period starts again on the date of the acknowledgement or part-payment (s. 29). If, for example, under a contract between A and B, A was due to pay B £300 in December 1987 and failed to do so, B's right to sue would be barred after six years; he would have to sue by December 1993. But if in July 1992 A pays B £50 as part-payment of the debt, or simply acknowledges that she does owe the money, the time limit of six years starts again, so that B now has until July 1998 to sue for the rest of the money.

In order for an acknowledgement to have this effect, it must be in writing, signed by the person making it, and must clearly acknowledge the debt, not just the fact that a dispute exists. It must also apply to a debt or some other liquidated sum.

Equitable claims

Section 36(1) of the Limitation Act 1980 makes it clear that the statutory limitation periods do not apply to claims for specific performance, an injunction or other equitable remedies. Instead, the equitable doctrine of 'laches' (delay) is applied: if, taking account of all the circumstances of the case, the court considers that the claimant has been too slow in bringing the action, the equitable remedy sought will be refused.

It is not possible to lay down strict rules on when laches will prevent a claim; in each case, it will depend on the length of the delay, how diligent the court believes the claimant ought to have been and the nature of the contract. Thus, where a defendant is seeking specific performance, a lengthy delay will be less acceptable if the contract concerns goods whose value fluctuates rapidly than in a case where prices remain steady.

In **Pollard** *v* **Clayton** (1855) the defendants agreed to extract all the coal in a particular mine, and sell it to the plaintiffs at a fixed price per ton. They began to perform as agreed, but later refused to deliver any more coal to the plaintiffs, and began selling it elsewhere. Naturally, the plaintiffs objected, but the defendants simply referred them to their solicitors. The plaintiffs waited 11 months, and then made a claim for specific performance. It was refused, on the grounds that too long a delay had occurred between the plaintiffs becoming aware of the breach of contract and bringing their action.

Problems with remedies

A cursory look at this chapter might suggest that the range of remedies on offer provides a solution for every breach. In fact, there are two main problems with the law's provision for breach of contract.

The interests protected

The law focuses mainly on one type of loss: financial loss to the party concerned. It generally ignores the mental distress, anxiety and sheer inconvenience which a breach of contract may cause. For example, the directors of large businesses may not lose any sleep over a supplier's failure to deliver, but the situation is very different for a small business, where such a breach may involve the proprietor in extra work finding alternative stock or, if this cannot be done, customers may be disappointed and shop elsewhere. The injured party may be able to claim for the cost of buying goods at a higher price, or the loss of the profit from the goods that should have been supplied, but will not be able to claim for the stress caused by extra work, or for the incalculable long-term damage caused by disappointing customers.

There are kinds of interest which contract law is simply not equipped to consider. Take, for example, a situation where a rich environmentalist, Sue, makes a contract with a farmer, Giles, under which she pays him not to tear up the hedgerows around the farm. What if Giles pulls up the hedges anyway? Sue could probably get her money back, but she has made the contract in order to protect the environment; not only will no damages be payable, as she has suffered no financial loss, but no damages could restore the position that would have existed had the contract been performed.

The law of contract needs to recognize that consumers tend to contract for reasons other than financial profit, so that remedies which focus entirely on their loss of economic bargain are inadequate.

Practicalities

Even where the available remedies would provide an adequate solution, there are many situations in which it is completely impractical for the claimant to make a claim, because the costs and/or time and effort involved in litigation are out of proportion to the amount that could be claimed. Because of this, it will frequently be obvious to a party considering breaching a contract that no action will be taken against them if they do, especially where they are the stronger party.

An additional problem is that in many cases, the injured party does not know they have a right to claim. Even the considerable amount of consumer protection legislation enacted in recent years cannot protect a consumer who does not know what they are entitled to when buying goods or paying for a service.

Limitation periods

The Law Commission has produced a report, *Limitation of Actions* (2001), in which it has highlighted problems with the current law on statutory time limits. For example, it can be difficult to determine which time limit applies to certain cases. The report recommends a single regime of limitation periods to apply to all claims. There would be a primary limitation period of three years from the date on which claimants knew or ought reasonably to have known the facts relevant to their case. The maximum time possible to bring a claim would normally be ten years from the date on which the relevant events took place. An exception to the maximum ten-year rule would be personal injury, where the three-year rule could be disapplied at the discretion of the court.

Restitution

Restitution was discussed at p. 283. In its 1997 Report, *Aggravated, Exemplary and Restitutionary Damages*, the Law Commission considered whether the remedy of restitution should be laid down in legislation. It rejected this suggestion, on the basis that this would 'freeze' the position. Instead, it recommended that the availability of such damages should be left to be developed by the common law.

▶ ANSWERING QUESTIONS

1 Anne-Marie, a joiner, decides to set up her own business. She contracts with John, a builder, to convert her garage into a workshop. The price is £10,000, and the work is to be completed by 1 March. However, problems with labour and materials mean that John does not finish the work until 1 June. Anne-Marie now wants to know whether she can claim damages to cover:

(a) The loss of profit from cancelled joinery jobs for the period between March and June.

(b) The loss of a special contract she had with a local stately home, to make rather expensive shelving for its library.

(c) The mental distress which Anne-Marie's inability to get her business up and running has caused to Anne-Marie and her husband Trevor.

(a) The question here is whether the loss of profit was something that would arise naturally from the breach, or which 'may reasonably be supposed to have been within the contemplation of the parties at the time when they made the contract' (**Hadley v Baxendale**). If the loss falls within this principle, Anne-Marie can claim damages to put her in the position she would have been in had the contract been performed as agreed, which would cover her lost profit.

(b) The cases to consider here are **Victoria Laundry** and *The Heron II*. John will be liable if he knew about the contract with the stately home, or if Anne-Marie's losses through losing the contract were reasonably foreseeable as liable to result from his breach, but not if he is only aware that there is a remote possibility of such a loss.

(c) Here Anne-Marie has little chance of an award for the distress, for three reasons. First, the rule of privity prevents her from claiming for any loss to Trevor, and none of the exceptions to the rule seem to apply here. Secondly, damages for mental distress have so far been confined to cases where peace of mind or enjoyment are the object of the contract, such as **Jackson**. Thirdly, it was specifically stated in **Addis v Gramophone** that damages for mental distress are not available in commercial contracts; since both John and Anne-Marie are acting for the purposes of their businesses, this would seem to be a commercial contract.

2 Analyse the factors the courts will take into account when awarding damages for breach of a contract, where there is no provision for this in the contract. *Oxford*

The material you need to answer this question is primarily contained in this chapter at pp. 263–82 and you could follow the same structure for your answer.

You are asked to analyse the law and should therefore take a critical approach, evaluating the current law in the field. You might point out that the law attempts to strike a balance between adequately compensating the claimant and imposing an unfair burden on the defendant, and show how the cases on remoteness of damage and mitigation have achieved this balance. You should highlight any problems with the case law – you may feel, for example, that the rules on damages for mental distress are too harsh, and cite the case of **Addis** v **Gramophone Co Ltd**. You could also highlight the problems with contractual remedies discussed at p. 296.

3 Amy knew that her friend Claire was thinking of buying a new sofa and armchairs, so she said to her, 'Are you going to sell the ones you already have? If so, I could pay you £100 for them.' Claire said she would think about it. Two weeks later, not having seen or spoken to Amy, who was not on the telephone, Claire posted a short note to Amy which read, 'I am having new furniture delivered tomorrow and I want to take you up on your suggestion that you pay me £100 for my existing sofa and armchairs. Please give me a ring so that we can make the arrangements.'

Shortly after returning from posting the note, Claire received a letter in the post from Amy which informed her that she had gone away for a few days but that, before she did so, she had been able to buy a new sofa and armchairs at a bargain price from a local store.

In fact, when Amy returned home after a three-week holiday, she discovered that the furniture that she had bought in a sale from Princeway Stores was lumpy and uncomfortable, that the material was slightly frayed at the bottom of the back of the sofa, and that there were slight variations in colour between the two armchairs. When she complained to Princeway Stores, she was reminded of the prominent notices displayed on the walls of the store which read, 'No refunds on any sale items'.

(a) Explain the relevant rules on the formation of contracts and apply those rules to determine whether a contract for the sale to Amy of Claire's furniture ever came into existence. *(10 marks)*

(b) Amy made a contract with Princeway Stores for the purchase of the furniture in the sale. Explain what obligations are placed on Princeway Stores under that contract and consider whether any have been broken. *(10 marks)*

(c) Assuming that Amy and Claire had a contract which Amy would not fulfil and that Princeway Stores was in breach of its obligations to Amy, discuss what remedies might be available to Claire against Amy and to Amy against Princeway Stores. In your answer, discuss the effect of the notice displayed in the store. *(10 marks)*

(d) Compare the respective merits of legislation and case law as mechanisms for changing rules of law such as those in contract. *(10 marks)*

(e) How far would you agree that the law has now succeeded in overcoming the problems formerly created by inequalities in bargaining power between parties to contracts? *(10 marks) AQA*

This question covers material from across this book, including issues from the next chapter. Each sub-part of this question will be considered in turn.

(a) A discussion was required of the rules of offer, acceptance and an intention to create legal relations, which were discussed in Chapters 1 and 3. The important thing for a question like this is to have recognized the relevant issues, and to have applied the law logically to the facts. The actual conclusion that is reached as to the existence or absence of a contract is less important, as a court could have reached either conclusion.

On the issue of offer and acceptance, you needed to consider whether Amy's suggestion that she could pay £100 for Claire's furniture was an offer or merely some preliminary stage of negotiation, known as an invitation to treat. If a court did regard it as an offer, it would have to decide whether it remained in existence after two weeks so as to be capable of valid acceptance. No time was specified for how long the offer would remain open, so it would be treated as continuing for a reasonable length of time. As in this instance the offer was concerned with the purchase of non-perishable goods any offer is likely to be treated as still in existence after two weeks. If a court treated Amy's suggestion as an offer and found that it was still in existence after two weeks, the next issue is whether it was validly accepted before Claire received Amy's letter which made it clear that she was no longer interested in buying Claire's furniture. You would need to consider the postal rule, and the fact that under cases such as **Byrne** v **Van Tienhoven**, where an acceptance has been posted before a revocation has been received, the acceptance will be binding.

In relation to the requirement of an intention to create legal relations, on the one hand the friendship between Amy and Claire and the probable social occasion on which any offer was made would suggest an initial presumption against such intention. On the other hand, the subject matter of the deal and the apparent seriousness of both parties at various stages of the process offered powerful evidence in rebuttal.

You are asked to discuss only the 'relevant' rules on formation of a contract, and thus only a passing mention needs to be made of the rules of consideration, privity and capacity.

(b) The main issues raised in this part of the question are dealt with in the next chapter. The important obligations placed on Princeway Stores in relation to Amy's purchase of furniture are implied into the contract by the Sale of Goods Act 1979, as amended by the Sale and Supply of Goods Act 1994. So the contract would be subject to terms as to description (s. 13), satisfactory quality (s. 14(2)) and fitness for purpose (s. 14(3)). On whether any of these terms had been broken, it is unlikely that the term as to description had been infringed or that Amy's perception that the furniture was 'lumpy and uncomfortable' was sufficient to render it not fit for its purpose. On the other hand, it might have been argued that the furniture was not of satisfactory quality in view of the fraying of the material and the colour variations, though this would have to be considered in the context that these defects may have been the reason for the 'bargain' price.

(c) To answer this part of the question a distinction should be drawn between the remedies available to Claire and those available to Amy. Claire's remedy would lie in common law for damages, there being no apparent reason why a claim for specific performance should be entertained by a court. The measure of damages awarded would be the difference between what Amy had offered and the price at which Claire could now sell.

By contrast, Amy's remedies against Princeway Stores would have stemmed from the Sale of Goods Act 1979, discussed in the next chapter, and would thus have included rejection of the goods and recovery of the purchase price; or, should rejection no longer be available due to acceptance derived from use of the furniture or by lapse of time, damages for breach of a warranty. The measure of damages in this context would be the difference between the value of the goods contracted for and those actually supplied. Even if the notices displayed on the wall of the shop were found to contain a term incorporated into the contract in accordance with the common law requirements of notice, they would be ineffective due to the Unfair Contract Terms Act 1977.

(d) This question goes beyond the scope of this book, and is covered by the authors' book on the English legal system. Advantages of legislation include the fact that it is the product of a democratic process that takes place in public, with the possibility of a wide input of information, consultation and advice. The danger is of delays and the problems with interpreting the legislation when it needs to be applied to particular situations. Case law has the advantage of responding directly to problems occurring, and is flexible, providing scope to be adapted gradually to particular circumstances. On the other hand, case law is the product of an unelected judiciary, is dependent on relevant litigation to arise for its development and can produce uncertainty.

(e) Material to answer this question can be found in the introduction to this book. Your point could be illustrated by reference to the consumer protection legislation, such as the Sale of Goods Act 1979 (and amendments), the Supply of Goods and Services Act 1982, the Consumer Protection Act 1987, the Unfair Contract Terms Act 1977 and the 1999 Regulations. You could also have discussed the common law attempts to control the use of exemption clauses – the rules on incorporation, restrictive interpretation and the development of devices such as fundamental breach. You could have considered the law in relation to minors and the law on duress and undue influence.

Drawing from English legal system material, you could have discussed issues concerning access to justice (cost, delays, small claims arbitration, state funding, etc.) as rights and remedies are of no practical significance if parties are effectively denied access to them.

4 Harry had recently opened a fitness centre and was still trying to improve his stock of fitness machines. He knew that his friend, Jim, the manager of another fitness centre, had a spare step-machine and he asked him how much he would sell it for. Jim said, 'Probably £700'. The next day, Harry telephoned Jim's home and left a message on his answering machine saying, 'I will give you £650. No need to reply if that is all right. I will pick it up next week.' Jim kept the machine for Harry and so he was very annoyed when, two weeks later, Harry told him that he had changed his mind and did not want it after all.

Harry agreed with Kevin that Kevin would service all the machines for an annual fee of £5,000. The written contract stated that Kevin would service and repair any machine within 48 hours of being requested to do so, or would supply

a replacement. During the first three months, Kevin twice took 55 hours to return machines and did not supply a replacement on either occasion. Harry terminated the contract with Kevin and demanded the return of the £5,000 fee.
(a) Consider whether there is a contract between Harry and Jim for the purchase of the step-machine. Assuming there is a contract, discuss what remedy Jim may pursue. *(25 marks)*
(b) Consider the rights, duties and remedies of Harry and Kevin in connection with the terms of the agreement to service and repair the machines and Harry's decision to end the agreement. *(25 marks)*
(c) How satisfactory are the rules on formation of contracts? *AQA*

(a) Looking first at whether there is a binding contract between Harry and Jim, you need to break down the transaction into the legal concepts of invitation to treat, offer and acceptance. Harry starts the negotiations by asking how much Jim would sell his spare step-machine for. This is merely a request for information. Jim responds 'Probably £700'. This is too uncertain to amount to an offer. An offer can be defined as a communication which indicates the terms on which the offeror is prepared to make a contract and gives a clear indication that the offeror intends to be bound by those terms if they are accepted by the offeree. The use of the word 'probably' means that the terms on which Jim is prepared to be bound are not certain and he does not appear to intend to be bound by any acceptance. Instead of being an offer, this would be treated as an invitation to treat. You could refer to the cases of **Gibson v Manchester City Council** and **Harvey v Facey** to illustrate how the law has been applied in practice.

The next day Harry telephones Jim stating 'I will give you £650. No need to reply if that is all right. I will pick it up next week'. This is an offer.

Jim then kept the machine for Harry and to determine whether this had led to the formation of a contract, you needed to consider the case of **Felthouse v Bindley**. In that case an uncle wrote to his nephew offering to pay £30 and 15 shillings, saying 'If I hear no more about him, I consider the horse mine at that price'. The nephew was on the point of selling off some of his property in an auction. He did not reply to the uncle's letter, but did tell the auctioneer to keep the horse out of the sale. The auctioneer forgot to do this, and the horse was sold. It was held that there was no contract between the uncle and the nephew. The court felt that the nephew's conduct in trying to keep the horse out of the sale did not necessarily imply that he intended to accept his uncle's offer, and so it was not clear that his silence in response to the offer was intended to constitute acceptance.

In **Re Selectmove Ltd** the Court of Appeal stated that an acceptance by silence could be sufficient if it was the offeree who suggested that their silence would be enough to complete the contract.

On the facts before us, like **Felthouse v Bindley**, it is the offeror suggesting that silence will be sufficient and not the offeree. The question for the court will therefore be whether Jim has done enough to make it clear that he intended to accept the offer. He does not appear to have done any more than the nephew in **Felthouse v Bindley**, so a court is likely to find that he has not effectively accepted the offer and there is therefore no binding contract.

The question asks you to consider what remedies Jim would have if there had been a contract. The main remedy in contract law is damages. This is an award of money that aims to compensate the innocent party for the financial losses they have suffered as a result of the breach. The general rule is that innocent parties are entitled to such damages as will put them in the position they would have been in if the contract had been performed. Here Jim has suffered a pecuniary loss, which the courts are more willing to compensate than non-pecuniary losses.

When calculating the amount of damages to be awarded, three main restrictions apply: causation, remoteness and mitigation. On the issue of mitigation (p. 272), Jim will be required to mitigate his loss, so he cannot recover damages for losses which could have been avoided by taking reasonable steps. On these facts Jim will therefore be expected to have tried to secure an alternative sale of the step-machine. On the issue of remoteness (p. 268), he will only be able to claim for losses which are not too remote. The main question for the court will be whether any loss of profit will be compensateable. The test to be applied was laid down in the case of **The Pegase**, which is whether:

> . . . the facts in question come to the defendant's knowledge in such circumstances that a reasonable person in the shoes of the defendant would, if he had considered the matter at the time of making the contract have contemplated that, in the event of a breach by him, such facts were to be taken into account when considering his responsibility for loss suffered by the plaintiff as a result of such breach.

The likely basis for the calculation of Jim's loss is his expectation (p. 273). This means that if he manages to sell the step-machine to a third party he will be compensated for the difference in price he received for the machine (the market price) and the £650 that Harry had promised to pay.

(b) Under the contract between Harry and Kevin, there is an express term that Kevin will service and repair any machine within 48 hours of being requested to do so or he would supply a replacement. Kevin has breached this term because on two occasions he has taken 55 hours to return machines and did not supply a replacement on either occasion. The effect of the breach will depend on the type of term that has been breached. Terms can be divided into three types: conditions, warranties and innominate terms (see p. 110).

A term which is clearly an important one, in the sense that a breach of it would have very significant consequences for the innocent party, will usually be regarded by the courts as a condition. Where a condition is breached, the innocent party is entitled to regard the contract as repudiated, and so need not render any further performance, and can also sue for damages. An example of a term deemed by the courts to be a condition can be found in **Bunge Corp v Tradax Export SA**.

The word warranty usually describes a contractual term which can be broken without highly important consequences. If a warranty is breached the innocent party can sue for damages, but is not entitled to terminate the contract.

Innominate terms are terms which can be broken with either important or trivial consequences, depending on the nature of the breach. If the effects of the breach are serious, the term will act as a condition; if they are minor it acts as a warranty.

It will be up to the court to determine whether the contractual term broken in Harry and Kevin's contract was a condition, warranty or innominate term. The term has been broken in two ways: first, there has been delay and, secondly, no replacement machine has been provided. The effect of delay in performance will depend on whether the time of performance is considered to be 'of the essence' (see p. 238). If this is the case, then late performance will give rise to a right to terminate the contract. Where time is not of the essence, late performance will not justify termination unless it amounts to a substantial failure in performance. It is unlikely that time was of the essence for this type of contract.

(c) To answer this question you could have looked at the sections headed 'Problems with offer and acceptance' at p. 37, 'How important is intention to create legal relations' at p. 51 and 'Problems with consideration' at p. 86.

Part 6

Although the common law principles of the law of contract (covering issues such as offer and acceptance, consideration and vitiating factors) apply to all contracts, in recent years there has been increasing intervention by Parliament in certain types of contract, with the result that many are now covered by special rules governing both the way in which they are made and the terms they may include. The three most important types of contract in which Parliament has intervened in this way are employment, landlord and tenant and consumer contracts; the latter are the subject of this chapter. These are the kind of contracts we make when, as an ordinary individual, we buy or hire goods, or pay to have services, such as plumbing or hairdressing, done for us.

The reason for intervention in consumer contracts is a move away from the traditional idea that the parties should be left to negotiate the best possible bargain for themselves, and a recognition that in many modern situations, ordinary consumers will be contracting with large, powerful organizations and effectively have no power to negotiate a favourable deal, or sometimes even a fair one. An example of this is the standard form contract offered when you engage in many common transactions, from hiring a car to having clothes dry-cleaned. Often, roughly the same form will be used by all the businesses in a particular industry, and, if unregulated, they have the potential to remove choice from the purchaser, the only options being to contract on those terms or not at all.

16 Consumer contracts

History

Recognition that consumers could be at a disadvantage in contracting with businesses came as early as the nineteenth century. The courts began to imply terms into contracts, especially those for the sale of goods, which made sure the buyer got a fair deal, by, for example, requiring that the goods were fit for their purpose. Unfortunately, the fact that businesses were richer and more powerful than their consumers also meant that they had access to good lawyers, and as fast as the courts found terms to imply into contracts, businesses found ways to draw up contracts excluding themselves from those liabilities.

In 1893 the first Sale of Goods Act was passed, but it merely codified the existing case law, and by the twentieth century, it was clear that more drastic action was needed. The supply of goods and services was by then largely dominated by big companies, who were able to draw up contracts which were extremely favourable to themselves; the consumer had the choice of buying goods and services on those terms or not at all, since even competitor companies would be offering much the same terms. The courts attempted to curtail the power of companies by construing contracts strictly against them, and finding ways round the various exclusion clauses, but it was clear by this time that the common law simply could not provide adequate protection for consumers.

As a result, since the 1960s, Parliament has passed a series of Acts designed to protect the interest of consumers, including the Consumer Protection Act 1961, the Trade Descriptions Act 1968, the Fair Trading Act 1973, the Consumer Credit Act 1974, the Unfair Contract Terms Act 1977, the Consumer Safety Act 1978 and the Consumer Safety (Amendment) Act 1986, the Sale of Goods Act 1979, the Supply of Goods and Services Act 1982 and the Sale and Supply of Goods Act 1994. All of this legislation aims, in varying ways, to even out the balance of power in contracts by providing protection for the individual.

> ## Contracts for the sale of goods

These are largely covered by the Sale of Goods Act 1979, as amended by the Sale and Supply of Goods Act 1994. Section 2(1) of the 1979 Act defines a sale of goods contract as one 'by which the seller transfers or agrees to transfer the property in goods to the buyer for a money consideration, called the price'. Thus the Act applies only to goods sold for money and does not cover other kinds of transaction such as the swapping or exchanging of goods.

'Goods' has been interpreted broadly. It has been held to include packaging surrounding goods and instructions appearing on the packaging. It does not cover services, which are covered by the Supply of Goods and Services Act 1982 (see p. 315 below).

In the course of a business

Certain provisions of the 1979 Act apply only when goods are sold 'in the course of a business'. Difficulties have arisen in determining when a sale is in the course of a business. There is clearly a range of different types of sale transactions. At one end of the spectrum is a sale by a retail organization, like a supermarket selling eggs and cheese, or a clothes shop selling a pair of trousers. There has never been any doubt that such a sale is in the course of a business. At the other end of the spectrum is a purely private sale by a member of the public, like the sale of a private car through an advertisement in the local newspaper. There has never been any doubt that this sort of sale is not in the course of a business and the relevant protections in the Sale of Goods Act 1979 do not apply.

In the middle of the spectrum are sales of goods by a business, where the sale does not fall within the normal business activity of the company. Is this a sale in the course of a business or not? For example, if a solicitors' firm has some old computers that it no longer needs and decides to sell them, is this sale in the course of a business or not? Following the decision of the Court of Appeal in **Stevenson** *v* **Rogers** (1999), this type of case is now clearly caught by the wording 'in the course of a business'. Rogers, the defendant, was in business as a fisherman. In 1988 he sold his only fishing boat, *The Jelle*, to the claimant and replaced it with *The Marilyn Jane*. The claimant was dissatisfied with *The Jelle* and brought an action against the defendant, complaining that he was in breach of the implied term, incorporated into the sale contract by s. 14(2) of the Sale of Goods Act 1979, that the boat should be of 'merchantable quality' (the contract was made before the 1994 Act came into force, replacing the test of 'merchantable quality' with that of 'satisfactory quality' discussed at p. 310). The implied term only applied to a sale of goods made by the seller 'in the course of a business'. So, as a preliminary issue, the Court of

Appeal was required to decide whether the sale of *The Jelle* was made in the course of Rogers' business as a fisherman.

The court gave the phrase a very wide scope, in order to impose as few limitations as possible on the remedies available to a person buying goods as a consumer. It looked at the legislative history of the Sale of Goods Act 1979, including the relevant Law Commission Report and the parliamentary statements and debates recorded in Hansard at the time it was enacted. The court decided that the wording 'in the course of a business' was intended to have a wider meaning than the narrower wording found in earlier versions of the Act, and was thus intended to catch all sales of goods made by businesses, whether or not the sale of such goods was the regular trade of that business. The expression 'in the course of a business' in s. 14 of the Sale of Goods Act did not require any regularity of dealing, or indeed any previous dealing at all. It considered that it was the intention of the legislators that a broad construction should be applied to s. 14, so as to reflect the emphasis on consumer protection which underlies the more recent reforms. It concluded that the sale by the defendant was made in the course of a business and, accordingly, was subject to the implied term as to merchantable quality.

Implied terms in contracts for the sale of goods

Whatever the terms agreed by the parties under the Sale of Goods Act 1979 a set of terms concerning the goods is implied into all contracts covered by the Act.

Title

Under s. 12(1) of the 1979 Act, a condition is implied into any contract for the sale of goods that the seller has a right to sell the goods and is able to pass good title to the buyer. A breach of this condition amounts to a total failure of consideration and the buyer may claim back the price of the goods, even if they have been used for some time.

Sale by description

Section 13(1) of the 1979 Act states that 'where there is a contract for the sale of goods by description, there is an implied condition that the goods will correspond with the description'.

Sale by description in practice covers all but a minority of transactions, where the parties agree on a specific article without describing it in any way – such as, for example, offering to sell 'my car', without specifying its make, age or colour. Section 13(3) specifies that goods sold by self-selection, as in a supermarket, are included within the category of sales by description (on the basis that they are usually labelled in some way).

In **Beale** *v* **Taylor** (1967) the plaintiff responded to an advertisement for a 'Herald, convertible, white 1961'. On going to inspect the car, he noticed on the back a disc marked '1200'. In fact the car consisted of the rear of a 1961 Herald 1200 welded to the front part of an older model. The Court of Appeal held that the advertisement and disc together constituted a sale by description and, as the vehicle clearly did not conform to this description, there was a breach of s. 13.

The potential strictness of s. 13 can be seen in **Re Moore & Co and Landauer & Co** (1921) (see p. 235 above), where a seller was entitled to reject goods which did not comply with their description, even though that fact caused him no hardship at all and there was no defect in the goods.

In many cases, the implied term as to description will also be an express term of the contract. If you buy a sweater which you are told is cashmere, that is likely to become an express term of the contract, alongside the implied term that the goods correspond with that description.

As s. 13 is not limited to sales 'in the course of a business' it can apply to private sales.

Satisfactory quality

Section 14(2) of the Sale of Goods Act 1979 required that goods sold in the course of a business should be of merchantable quality, but this term caused problems because it was considered imprecise. The Sale and Supply of Goods Act 1994 now replaces it with a requirement that such goods should be of 'satisfactory quality', which means that they should 'meet the standard that a reasonable person would regard as satisfactory', taking into account their price, description and other relevant circumstances. In assessing the quality of goods, the courts may take into account their fitness for their usual purpose, their appearance and finish, freedom from minor defects, safety and durability. The old condition on merchantable quality was held not to be an absolute and consistent standard, but one based on value for money – so, for example, defects which might be acceptable in a very cheap coat might not be acceptable in a very expensive one. Similarly, goods clearly sold as second-hand were not to be required to meet the same standards as new ones. This balance seems to be preserved by the 1994 Act.

The requirement of satisfactory quality will not apply where any defect or other matter is specifically drawn to the buyer's attention before the contract is made, or which ought to have been revealed by the buyer's own examination of the goods. There is no obligation for a purchaser to examine the goods, and a cursory look at them – without opening the packaging for example – is not expected to reveal defects. On the other hand, where a purchaser does examine the goods before buying, any defects he or she should have spotted will not be covered by the implied condition on satisfactory quality.

The old provision on merchantable quality was held to cover the whole of what is supplied, including packaging or anything else which is part of the consignment, and it seems this will also apply to the new term on satisfactory quality. The importance of this can be seen in **Wilson** v **Rickett Cockerell & Co Ltd** (1954). The plaintiffs purchased a ton of a solid fuel called Coalite. Unfortunately, it ended up heating their home rather more comprehensively than expected, since part of the delivery contained an explosive substance, which detonated when the Coalite was burnt. The defendants argued that the fuel itself was not defective, and it was the presence of an additional substance that had caused the damage. The court rejected this argument and held that there was a breach of the implied condition on merchantable quality since the goods supplied, taken as a whole, were not fit for use on a domestic fire.

The implied term on satisfactory quality only applies to sales in the course of a business, and so not to private sales (see p. 308).

Fitness for purpose
Section 14(3) of the Sale of Goods Act 1979 states:

> where the seller sells goods in the course of a business and the buyer, expressly or by implication, makes known . . . to the seller . . . any particular purpose for which the goods are being bought, there is an implied condition that the goods supplied under the contract are reasonably fit for that purpose, whether or not that is a purpose for which such goods are commonly supplied, except where the circumstances show that the buyer does not rely, or that it is unreasonable for him to rely on the skill or judgment of the seller.

This subsection basically means that if a buyer tells the seller the goods are required for a particular purpose, and the seller goes ahead and sells them, they must be fit for that purpose, even if it is an unusual one. So if you buy a very large raincoat, telling the seller you want it for your pet elephant, it must be able to stand up to the strains of such a use, unless it is clear that in making your choice you were not relying on the seller's advice.

For the section to apply, the buyer must make known any special purpose for which the goods are to be used. In **Griffiths** v **Peter Conway Ltd** (1939) a woman with abnormally sensitive skin developed dermatitis as a result of wearing a tweed coat. She sued for breach of the implied condition of fitness for purpose, but failed, because she had not made known to the seller the fact that she was assuming the coat would not irritate her skin.

There is often an overlap between the conditions on fitness for the purpose and satisfactory quality. Where the purpose for which the buyer claims to want the goods is their ordinary purpose, the ability of those goods to fulfil that purpose may also be a measure of their satisfactory quality. For example, in **Preist** v **Last** (1903) the buyer asked for 'a hot water bottle', and this request was taken to mean that he wanted goods fit for the purpose of filling with water and heating his bed, without splitting. When the bottle did split, this was therefore a breach of both the implied condition on merchantable quality (and would now be a breach of the requirement for satisfactory quality) and that on fitness for its purpose.

The condition of fitness for purpose will be implied only where the goods are sold in the course of a business.

Correspondence with sample

Section 15 of the Sale of Goods Act 1979 provides that where goods are sold by sample, there is an implied condition that the bulk of the goods will correspond with the sample, that the buyer will have a reasonable opportunity of comparing the bulk with the sample, and that the goods will be free from any defect, rendering them unsatisfactory, which would not be apparent on reasonable examination of the sample.

Remedies for breach of the Sale of Goods Act 1979 implied terms

In the past, all the above terms were implied conditions, which, as we have seen, means that any breach entitles the buyer to terminate the contract, in practice by returning the goods and getting their money back. This situation created problems, as the buyer had the right to reject the goods for even the most trivial breach. The Law Commission therefore recommended reform in 1987, and its recommendations were incorporated into the Sale and Supply of Goods Act 1994. The 1994 Act amended the Sale of Goods Act 1979, inserting a new s. 15A, which deems a breach of the conditions implied by ss. 13–15 to be merely a breach of warranty under certain circumstances. These circumstances are that the buyer does not deal as a consumer and breach is so slight that it would be unreasonable to reject the goods. As a result, the buyer is not allowed to reject the goods, but has only a right to claim damages.

In addition, the Sale of Goods Act 1979 used to provide that once the buyer had 'accepted' goods, or part of them, any breach of the implied terms would only be treated as a breach of warranty, so that the buyer could not get back the money paid and could only sue for damages for any loss. Problems were caused by the way in which acceptance was deemed to have taken place. First, a buyer was deemed to have accepted the goods if they did something that was inconsistent with the seller's ownership of them. This meant that if, for example, you bought a pair of trousers and turned up the hems, you could be regarded as accepting them at that point, and if they fell apart shortly afterwards, you would have no right to reject them. Alternatively, acceptance could be signified by failure to return the goods within a reasonable length of time. Problems here were caused by the fact that it is perfectly possible to buy something, such as a sewing machine or a lawnmower, and use it only infrequently, so that any defects do not appear for some considerable time. This might have been for such a long period that, under the old provisions of the 1979 Act, a court would deem the goods to have been accepted, leaving the buyer with no right to claim back the purchase price.

The Sale and Supply of Goods Act 1994 attempts to address these problems. Although acceptance will still be deemed to have taken place unless the seller is told otherwise within a reasonable length of time, this length of time is now required to be long enough to give the buyer a reasonable opportunity to examine the goods, which may mean that goods used infrequently would be allowed a longer period for acceptance. In addition, the 1994 Act provides that doing something which is inconsistent with the seller's ownership of the goods will not mean that the buyer loses the right to reject them until they have had a reasonable opportunity of examining them to see if they conform to the contract. Asking for or accepting a repair to defective goods does not amount to acceptance, and therefore does not cancel the buyer's right to reject the goods.

An additional protection is provided by s. 11 of the 1979 Act, which states that the restrictions on terminating a contract for breach of an implied term do not apply where there is an express or implied term to the contrary in the contract of sale. So if, for example, a shop claimed that faulty goods could be returned for a refund at any time, it would not matter that, in terms of the legislation, the buyer might be deemed to have accepted them.

The remedies available are subject to the limitation period, which is discussed on p. 294.

Excluding the implied terms in contracts of sale

The Unfair Contract Terms Act 1977 (UCTA) lays down rules concerning the exclusion of terms implied by the Sale of Goods Act 1979, which are described in Chapter 8. The provisions of UCTA are strengthened by the Consumer Transactions (Restrictions on Statements) Order 1976, as amended. This order, made under the authority of the Fair Trading Act 1973, makes it a criminal offence to purport to introduce into a consumer transaction a term which is void by virtue of s. 6 of UCTA. The idea behind this provision is to prevent unscrupulous traders from misleading consumers about their rights, by, for example, stating that no refunds will be given. Further protections are provided by the Unfair Terms in Consumer Contracts Regulations 1999, which are also discussed in Chapter 8 (although they cover all types of unfair terms).

Passing of ownership

The basic rule is that the parties themselves agree on the point at which ownership passes from seller to buyer, but if they do not make such an agreement, the Sale of Goods Act 1979 lays down rules on when ownership

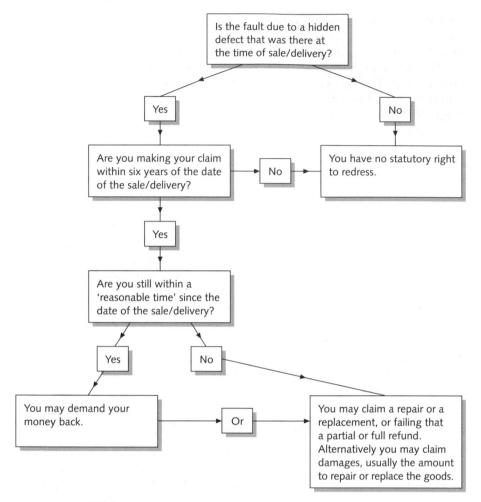

Figure 16.1 The limitation period

Source: The Sale of Consumer Goods Directive Consultation Paper, http://www.dti.gov.uk. At the time of writing the above was a likely description of the rights that will exist once Directive 1999/44/EC has been transposed in the UK, probably in the first quarter of 2003. However, these had still to be finally agreed and no date was available.

will pass. This will usually, but not always, be when the goods are physically delivered or handed over, and from that point the buyer is normally responsible for the goods.

The Sale of Goods (Amendment) Act 1995 amended the 1979 Act, laying down special rules on how ownership passes when there is a contract for a sale of a specified quantity of unascertained goods forming part of an identified bulk, for example, a contract for the sale of a gallon of petrol from a tankload. The buyer of such unascertained goods will now become an 'owner in common' of an identified bulk of goods.

▶ Contracts for the supply of services

These are largely governed by the Supply of Goods and Services Act 1982. As well as straightforward services, such as hairdressing, window cleaning or plumbing, it covers contracts in which a service is performed and goods supplied at the same time, often called work and materials contracts. An example would be the decoration of a house, in which the decorator supplied the wallpaper and paint as well as applying them, or the mending of a car where new parts are provided.

There are some cases where it is difficult to say whether a contract is one for goods or services: for example, in **Lockett** *v* **A and M Charles Ltd** (1938) the contract concerned a restaurant meal, which clearly involved the services of cooking and serving, but the court decided that on balance, the contract should be seen as one of sale, and would therefore be covered by the Sale of Goods Act 1979. In **Robinson** *v* **Graves** (1935), concerning a contract to paint a portrait, Greer LJ said the contract was one of service because the buyer was essentially purchasing the artist's labour and skill in producing the painting; the fact that some materials, in the form of paint and canvas, might also pass to the buyer was a secondary consideration.

Implied terms in contracts for services

Under the Supply of Goods and Services Act 1982, the following terms are automatically implied in contracts for the supply of a service.

Care and skill

Section 13 provides that 'where the supplier is acting in the course of a business, there is an implied term that the supplier will carry out the service with reasonable care and skill'. Note that this does not mean that a job must be carried out successfully. If, for example, you employ some-one to cure the damp in your house, and they fail to do so, that will only be a breach of the implied term if the damp could have been cured using reasonable care and skill. If reasonable care and skill would not have solved the problem, there is no breach of the implied term (though there may be breach of an express term, if the firm promised that they could eradicate the damp).

Time

Section 14(1) provides that in a business transaction, where the parties do not specify a time by which the job should be finished, 'there is an implied term that the supplier will carry out the service within a reasonable time'.

What is a reasonable time is a question of fact, and will obviously depend on the nature of the work done. The section only applies to contracts entered into in the course of a business.

Price

Section 15(1) states that where the parties have not fixed a price 'there is an implied term that the party contracting with the supplier will pay a reasonable price'. Again, the reasonable price is a question of fact, depending on the nature of the service, and the term only applies to business contracts.

Property

Where a service contract also involves the transfer of property to the customer (as in the decorating and car repair examples above), ss. 2–5 of the 1982 Act imply terms as to title, description, satisfactory quality, fitness for purpose and sample, which are basically the same as those implied into contracts for sale by ss. 12–15 of the Sale of Goods Act 1979.

Remedies for breach of the Supply of Goods and Services Act 1982 implied terms

The implied terms in the 1982 Act are referred to as terms. They are therefore treated by the courts as innominate terms and the consequences of breach depend on the seriousness of that breach.

Excluding the implied terms in service contracts

UCTA lays down rules concerning the exclusion of the implied terms under the 1982 Act, which are described in Chapter 8.

▶ Hire contracts

The Supply of Goods and Services Act 1982 also covers contracts where goods are hired, and s. 6 defines such a contract as one under which one party gives possession of goods to another, to be used for purposes agreed between them, in return for consideration. The section does not include hire-purchase agreements.

Under ss. 6–10, hire contracts are covered by implied conditions on satisfactory quality, fitness for the purpose and correspondence with description or sample, which are similar to those implied into other service contracts. Under s. 7, there is an implied condition in contracts of hire that the party hiring out the goods has a right to transfer possession of the goods by way of hire, or will have such a right at the time of the hiring.

▶ Manufacturers' liability

As far as contract law is concerned, consumer protection generally involves rights against retailers, since it is the retailer with whom the contract is usually made (except on the rare occasions when a consumer buys direct from the manufacturer). There are, however, three ways in which manufacturers may be liable directly to the consumer: under a manufacturer's guarantee; as a result of the manufacturer's negligence; and under the provisions of the Consumer Protection Act 1987.

Manufacturers' guarantees

Many manufacturers provide a guarantee with their products, but is the guarantee legally enforceable? It is difficult to see it as a contract, since the product has usually been bought before the guarantee is given, so there is no consideration. In most cases, of course, manufacturers will honour a guarantee voluntarily, in the interests of good customer relations, but it is debatable whether they are legally obliged to do so.

It may be possible for a consumer to argue that they have a collateral contract with the manufacturer, on the basis that the goods were bought in return for the promise made in the guarantee – **Carlill** v **Carbolic Smoke Ball Co** (1893) could be seen in this way. To make this claim, the buyer would need to have been aware of the guarantee before buying the goods.

In the past, manufacturers used guarantees as a way of depriving consumers of their common law or statutory rights. The consumer would sign away those rights in order to gain the protection of the guarantee, which may have given them fewer rights than they already possessed in law. Section 5 of UCTA makes any exclusion of such rights by a guarantee ineffective.

Under the Sale of Consumer Goods Directive 1999 (discussed on p. 325) guarantees offered by manufacturers or retailers will be legally binding. They will have to be written in plain language with clear information on how to claim.

Negligence

If goods actually harm the end consumer, the manufacturer may be liable for negligence. An important line of cases arising from **Donoghue** v **Stevenson** (1932) established the principle that a manufacturer of goods is under a duty of care not to put on the market goods which could harm the ultimate consumer, and this line of cases is now backed up by statute. It gives an additional layer of protection in that the consumer is not required to have a contractual relationship with the manufacturer in order to have rights against them.

Manufacturers can defend themselves against a claim for negligence by showing that the goods were manufactured using reasonable care and skill. The burden of proving that the manufacturer is negligent lies on the consumer, and can be extremely difficult to discharge, given the complexity of modern manufacturing processes. A tragic example from the

1960s concerned a drug, Thalidomide, which was used to treat morning sickness in pregnant women. It produced serious deformities in the children who were born to them. Only after three years was it discovered that the deformities were caused by the drug and, even then, negligence by the manufacturer was never actually proved.

The difficulty of proving negligence with regard to products can also be seen in **Daniels *v* R White & Sons Ltd** (1938). Mr Daniels bought a bottle of R White's lemonade and a jug of beer from his local pub, took them home and mixed lemonade shandies for himself and his wife. On drinking the shandy, both felt burning sensations in their mouths; the lemonade was later shown to be contaminated with carbolic acid. It was proved that carbolic acid was used in the defendant's bottle-cleaning plant, but the plaintiff could not show where in the manufacturing process the negligence had occurred and his claim failed. By contrast, Mr Daniels also claimed in contract against the pub licensee, Mrs Tabard, and this claim succeeded. Liability in contract is strict and Mrs Tabard was in breach of the implied condition of merchantable quality, then applied by the legislation governing the sale of goods.

The somewhat unsatisfactory result of the case was that although both Mr and Mrs Daniels were injured, only Mr Daniels could recover damages (because of privity of contract); and those were recovered from a party, Mrs Tabard, who was not responsible for the problem and could have done nothing to prevent it, as the lemonade was sold in sealed containers.

The courts nowadays tend to impose a less rigorous burden of proof in negligence cases than that borne by the Daniels, and have also imposed stricter responsibilities on manufacturers, such as a duty to carry out research to discover whether a product is dangerous (**Vacwell Engineering Co Ltd *v* BDH Chemicals Ltd** (1971)).

Liability for negligence with regard to products only covers damage to person or property, and not economic loss (loss of profits). This was established in **Muirhead *v* Industrial Tank Specialities Ltd** (1986) where a fish merchant installed a fish tank to keep lobsters alive out of season. When the motor which powered the tank failed, all the lobsters died, causing substantial loss of potential profit. The supplier of the motor had gone into liquidation, so the fish merchant sued the manufacturer. The court held the relationship was not sufficiently proximate to allow recovery of pure economic loss.

Consumer Protection Act 1987

This Act was passed as a result of the EC Directive of July 1985, which sought to harmonize the law of Member States on liability for defective products. In compliance with this goal, s. 1(1) provides that the Act is to be construed in accordance with the Product Liability Directive.

The Act establishes strict liability for damage caused by defective products. This means that a claimant does not have to establish that the manufacturer was negligent; unless the manufacturer is covered by one of the defences provided by the Act, it will be held responsible for the damage. This obviously makes things easier for the injured party than an action in tort.

Liability under the Act

Section 2(1) of the Act lays down the basic liability for damages caused by a defective product. 'Product' is widely defined to mean 'any goods or electricity', with only unprocessed agricultural products and game being outside the scope of the Act. Thus the Act applies to all the usual consumer goods.

Liability under the Act cannot be limited or excluded by any term or notice (s. 7). The statute obliges the supplier of a defective product (usually a distributor or retailer) to identify its producer when requested to do so by the victim of the defective product. Suppliers who do not give the name of a person who is primarily liable, or the name of the person who supplied the product to them, will face liability for the damage themselves.

Who may be liable?

The Act imposes liability on the producer of a product. In most cases this will be the manufacturer, but in the case of 'own brands' (products made by manufacturers but sold under the names of supermarkets and large chain stores) the retailer whose name appears on the pack will be regarded as the producer (s. 2(2)).

Defects

Section 3(1) states that there is a defect in a product 'if the safety of a product is not such as persons generally are entitled to expect'.

Damage

'Damage' is defined in s. 5(1) as death, personal injury or loss of or damage to property. It does not include damage to the product itself (s. 5(2)), nor damage worth less than £275 (s. 5(4)). In these cases, any claim must be made on the basis of pre-existing law.

Defences

The Act offers four defences.

- *Contributory negligence* The manufacturer will have a defence where the consumer has done something which contributes to the damage – an obvious example might be where the consumer has interfered with the workings of the product.

- *Compliance with legislation* There is a defence where the defect is a result of the manufacturer's compliance with any Act of Parliament or European Union obligation.
- *The 'development risks' defence* This is a controversial provision, allowing a defence on the basis that, when the product was being produced, the state of scientific and technical knowledge was insufficiently advanced for the producer to be expected to discover the defect. The implications for a case such as that of the Thalidomide victims are obvious: if the manufacturer can prove that at the time a drug was made, scientific knowledge was such that they could not be expected to discover that it had side-effects, victims could be left with no compensation at all. Opposition to the provision was strong, led by the Consumers' Association, but, not surprisingly, industry, and especially the drug industry, was in favour of it.

   The provision clearly weakens the Act's requirement of strict liability, but some protection for consumers is offered by the fact that the burden of proof to establish this defence is on the producer. The drafting of this defence was found to be in conformity with the Directive it was implementing in **Commission of the European Communities *v* United Kingdom** (1997). The argument of the European Commission that the defence was considerably broader than the equivalent provision in the Directive was rejected.
- *Time limits* A right of action under the Act is extinguished ten years after the date when the product was put into circulation.

Consumer protection by the criminal law

In many ways, the criminal law is the most important source of consumer protection. While protection in contract and tort is only useful to consumers who know, or can discover, their rights, and are prepared to spend time and money on pursuing them, the criminal law allows authorities such as trading standards officers to take action against unscrupulous traders. This approach also has the merit of seeking to prevent harm or loss before it occurs, rather than merely awarding compensation afterwards. The following are the principal Acts that offer consumer protection enforced by the criminal law, and their main provisions.

Consumer Protection Act 1987, Part II

This contains a general requirement that goods sold must be safe. Section 10 creates a new offence of supplying consumer goods (defined as goods for ordinary private use or consumption) which fail to comply with this general safety requirement, by not being reasonably safe in all the circumstances.

Against such a charge, there is a possible defence of due diligence, where the defendant can show that all reasonable steps were taken, and due diligence exercised, to avoid committing the offence.

The Act also empowers the Secretary of State to make safety regulations, concerning, for example, the composition, design and labelling of goods. A 'prohibition notice' can be used to prevent the supply of a particular type of goods, and where dangerous goods have already been sold, a 'notice to warn' can order the trader to warn consumers of the danger.

Fair Trading Act 1973

This set up a mechanism by which certain types of trading practice can be kept under constant review and created the Office of Fair Trading, headed by the Director-General of Fair Trading. The Director-General has powers to act against businesses whose practices persistently cause unfairness to consumers.

Trade Descriptions Act 1968

This Act made it an offence, when in the course of a business, to apply a false trade description to any goods, or supply or offer to supply goods with a false description. It has proved to be an extremely important piece of legislation, and there are over 30,000 prosecutions a year under it. An example of its application is the well-known practice of turning back the milometer on a car (known as 'clocking') in order to suggest that the car has driven fewer miles than it actually has. Under the Act, the mileage on the clock amounts to a description that the car has done that mileage; clearly, if the milometer has been turned back, this description is false, and the only way in which a dealer can avoid liability for this false description is to state very clearly that the mileage shown should not be relied on to be true.

Consumer Protection Act 1987, Part III

The Trade Descriptions Act 1968 was also designed to deal with the problem of misleading information on price – such as 'half price' labels when the product had never been sold at a higher price anyway. Although the Act went some way towards dealing with this malpractice, it was not as effective as was hoped. Part III of the Consumer Protection Act 1987 attempts to meet some of its shortcomings, and makes it an offence, when acting in the course of a business, to give consumers any misleading indication concerning the price of goods, services or accommodation.

A Code of Practice gives guidance to traders on how to avoid giving misleading price information; failing to follow this guidance is not an offence, but the Code's provisions may be used in evidence where legal action is taken under Part III of the 1987 Act.

The first prosecution under the above provision concerned an estate agent who had claimed in a newspaper advertisement that the price of a particular house had been reduced from £194,950 to £164,950. In fact, although another firm of estate agents had valued the house at the higher price, it had never been offered for sale at that price. The estate agents were fined £800.

Unsolicited goods

Some unscrupulous companies send goods to consumers who have not requested them, and then demand payment for the goods – usually stating that unless the goods are returned or rejected within a specified time, the company will assume the 'customer' wants them. As you will realize by now, under common law this in itself imposes no obligation whatsoever on the consumer – the case of **Felthouse** *v* **Bindley** (1862) (see p. 19 above) states that one party cannot make an offer to another and insist that silence will be taken as acceptance.

However, the average consumer has, unfortunately, not read this book, and as so often happens with consumer transactions, the practice has caused great confusion and anxiety. Some companies found it easy to give the impression that people were obliged either to pay for the goods or return them at their own expense. In other cases, customers assumed that since they had not ordered the goods, they were not bound to pay for them and duly used the goods, only to find that if the common law judged that this amounted to acceptance, they were liable to pay. Consequently, in 1971 Parliament decided to regulate this method of selling and the result was the Unsolicited Goods and Services Act 1971.

The Act defines unsolicited goods as goods sent without the recipient's request and with a view to the recipient acquiring them. Anyone receiving such goods is under no obligation to buy them, nor to send them back. They have two options. First, to keep the goods safe for six months and, if they are not reclaimed by then, to do what they like with them, with no obligation to pay. Secondly, to write to the sender, stating that the goods were unsolicited and giving an address from which they can be collected. If the sender does not collect the goods within 30 days of the notice, they will belong to the recipient.

In either case, if goods are accidentally lost or damaged before the statutory period expires, the recipient will not generally be liable, though they are not entitled to destroy them during this time.

Section 2 of the Act makes it a criminal offence for traders to demand payment for unsolicited goods, where they have no reasonable cause to believe that there is a right to payment, or to threaten legal proceedings to enforce such a payment.

▶ Consumer credit

During this century, and particularly the past 20 years, there has been an enormous increase in the number of people using credit to make purchases. Where once credit was only used for major purchases, such as cars or furniture, the advent of easily available credit cards now means that all kinds of everyday purchases are made in this way.

Given that the providers of credit are generally large and powerful organizations, and their customers often ordinary consumers, the inequality of bargaining power could easily lead to transactions which are clearly much more favourable to the credit suppliers. In addition, there is a danger that heavy promotion of credit services may lead consumers to take on more debt than they can realistically afford. For these two reasons, the Consumer Credit Act 1974 was passed to regulate credit transactions.

Hire-purchase

Widely used for cars and other major purchases, hire-purchase is generally arranged by the seller of the goods. The buyer chooses a purchase, and fills in a form, which the seller then passes to a finance company (usually the same one for all their transactions). The finance company checks the buyer's credit-worthiness and, if satisfied, accepts the deal. The goods are then sold not to the buyer, but to the finance company. The buyer takes possession of the goods, and pays regular instalments to the finance company. The goods remain the property of the finance company until some agreed point (usually when the final payment is made). In effect, what happens is that the finance company hires the goods to the buyer, with an option to buy them. The contract of sale is therefore between the buyer and the finance company, not the buyer and the original seller.

The 1974 Act covers hire-purchase agreements where the credit given is no more than £15,000 – note that does not mean the purchase price must be less than £15,000, as in many cases the buyer will have put down a cash deposit. Interest is also excluded from the £15,000 total.

Where a hire-purchase agreement falls inside this total, there are a number of provisions to protect the consumer. These include strict rules on the formalities of the agreement: it must be in writing, with even the print and paper regulated by the Act, and the consumer must be given at least one copy.

As with any other contract, the consumer can cancel at any time before the offer is accepted by the finance company, but the Act provides an additional means of escape. Where the finance company's negotiator (often the seller of the goods) has made oral representations to the buyer, and the agreement was signed somewhere other than the business premises of the buyer, the seller, the finance company or anyone involved in a linked transaction, the consumer is allowed a 'cooling off' period of five days from receiving a copy of the agreement that was signed. During this time, the consumer may cancel, in writing (which takes effect on posting), return the goods and get back any money paid; the transaction is then treated as though it had never been made.

Contract law and consumer protection

As this chapter shows, the majority of consumer protection provisions have been developed not, like most contract law, by the common law, but by legislation. Part of the reason for this is the fundamental clash between the idea of protecting one party against the other and the roots of contract law in the idea that parties should be left alone to make their own agreements and protect their own interests.

There are, however, other reasons why statutory intervention has been needed. First, the fact that criminal sanctions have been seen as the only way to deal with certain trading practices clearly required legislation; there is general agreement that criminal offences should only be created by Parliament.

Secondly, only the highest courts are really involved in developing the common law, and consumer problems rarely reach those courts. The vast majority do not get to court at all, and those that do tend to be dealt with in the lower courts, so there is little opportunity to set new precedents.

Thirdly, much of the pressure for reform has come from consumer groups, notably the Consumers' Association. Such pressure groups cannot directly influence the decisions of the courts, and can only bring about change in the law through publicizing problematic issues and then pressing for legislation. Many changes in the law on consumer contracts have been influenced by such campaigns.

Reform

Government White Paper

The Government has issued a White Paper, *Modern Markets: Confident Consumers* (1999). This sets out a range of initiatives that it is considering to improve consumer protection. These include the approval by the Office of Fair Trading of codes of practice laying down business standards. These would require the use of truthful advertisements, clear and adequate pre-contract information for clients, clear and fair contracts, effective complaints procedures and effective redress for problems without resort to the courts. A hallmark to identify companies that applied the codes of practice would be introduced. Trading Standards Offices and the Office of Fair Trading would be given new powers to tackle companies defrauding customers. Companies that repeatedly cheated consumers would be barred from trading. There would be a speedy procedure for the introduction of secondary legislation to outlaw fraudulent practices as they arise. A new consumer advice network would be established, with an internet consumer service and a local consumer helpline. There would be an ongoing review of consumer protection legislation to ensure that it was still achieving its objectives, was necessary and was cost-effective. The National Consumer Council would be relaunched.

The Sale and Supply of Goods to Consumers Regulations 2002

The European Union issued a Directive, the Sale of Consumer Goods Directive 1999 to try to harmonize the basic provision of consumer protection across Europe. This Directive was supposed to be brought into force in the Member States by January 2002. The UK Government missed this deadline, as it was still in the process of deciding what changes were required to be made to the UK legislation in order to make it conform to the European Directive. The UK Government has now produced the Sale and Supply of Goods to Consumers Regulations 2002, which are intended to implement the changes made by the Directive and are due to be brought into force in late 2002.

The Department of Trade and Industry is responsible for implementing the changes to the UK legislation, and has stated that only a few changes will be required. The changes will be incorporated into the existing legislation to try to keep the law as accessible as possible to the consumer seeking to know their rights. The Government has indicated its intention not to reduce current provisions for consumer protection where the Directive falls below current levels of protection.

The main changes that are likely to be made to the UK legislation by the proposed regulations include the following:

Implied terms
Sections 13 and 14 of the Sale of Goods Act 1979, discussed at p. 309, imply certain terms into contracts for the sale of goods. The provisions of these sections will be extended by requiring that the seller delivers goods to the consumer which conform to the contract of sale. In particular, the seller will be liable for public statements made by the producer or its representative, particularly in advertising or on labels. There is a presumption that consumer goods are in conformity with the contract if they: comply with the description given by the seller; are fit for any particular purpose made known by the consumer; are fit for the purposes for which goods of the same type are commonly supplied or normally used; are of satisfactory quality and performance given the type of the goods, the price and taking into account any public statements made by the seller, the producer or its representatives, especially in advertising or on labelling.

Incorrect installation of a product by the seller, their representative or the consumer (where this has been caused by deficiencies in the installation instructions) is deemed to be equivalent to a lack of conformity of the goods.

Parallel amendments are also proposed to the very similar provisions on quality and fitness in the Supply of Goods (Implied Terms) Act 1973 and the Supply of Goods and Services Act 1982.

A change in the burden of proof

For the first six months after purchase or delivery of goods, the burden of proof will be reversed in relation to faulty goods, in that there will be a presumption that the fault existed at the time of delivery. It will therefore be up to the seller to show that the goods were not faulty when delivered.

Guarantees

Guarantees offered by manufacturers or retailers will be legally binding. They will have to be written in plain language, with clear information on how to claim.

Remedies

The current remedies are a right to return the goods within a reasonable time, or damages. Additional remedies will be added to conform with the Directive where defects appear within two years of delivery. There will be a right to have goods repaired or replaced. If a repair or replacement is not possible or practical, or has not been provided within a reasonable time, the consumer will have a right to a price reduction or to rescind the contract. The consumer will not have a right to rescind the contract if the lack of conformity is only minor. These remedies are already widely offered by retailers and manufacturers in the UK, but the consumer has not had a legal right to them.

The two existing remedies will be preserved. But where a consumer asks for one of the new remedies of repair or replacement, they must give the seller a reasonable opportunity to comply before using the existing right to return the goods.

Definition of consumer

Currently, the 1999 Directive, the Unfair Terms in Consumer Contracts Regulations 1999 and the Unfair Contract Terms Act 1977 use different definitions for the term 'consumer'. It is proposed that the legislation will be harmonized so that they all have the same meaning for consumer which will become:

any natural person who, in the contracts covered by the Regulations, is acting for purposes which are outside his business.

▶ ANSWERING QUESTIONS

1 While in a shoe shop owned by E, D tried on a pair of shoes. These were to D's satisfaction and she offered to purchase them for £30. The sales assistant informed D that the shoes were only a sample and not for sale, but that there was an identical pair in the stockroom. D was in a hurry and agreed to take the pair from the stockroom, which were packaged in a box, and she paid the £30. When D opened the box at home, she discovered that, although the shoes were very similar to the pair she had tried on, the soles were of man-made material and not real leather, as the sample pair had been. She also noticed that one of the heels was loose and would soon be torn away after some use. D is concerned that a notice she had read in the shop declared that goods would not be replaced or money refunded to customers under any circumstances.

What are D's rights regarding her purchases? What is the legal effect, if any, of the notice in E's shop? *London*

This question clearly covers the terms in sales contracts implied by the Sale of Goods Act 1979. E appears to be in breach of two of these. First, the requirement that goods sold by sample should correspond with that sample seems clearly to be breached, because there are major differences in quality between the two. You also need to consider whether D was given a reasonable opportunity to examine the shoes she actually bought, as required under s. 15.

Secondly, the requirement for satisfactory quality – look at the problems with the shoes by reference to the kinds of factors which the Act allows the courts to take into account, and remember that price is important.

Assuming one or both of these terms have been breached, what rights does D have? Here you need to talk about remedies – does she have the right to demand a refund, under the amended rules on acceptance discussed at p. 312 above?

Finally, analyse the notice in the shop. This is covered by the Unfair Contract Terms Act 1977, and you will find more detailed information in the chapter on exclusion clauses, but essentially the notice has no legal effect as far as D is concerned, because the Sale of Goods Act 1979 implied terms cannot be excluded in consumer sales. You should also discuss the fact that such a notice may make E liable for a criminal offence, under the Consumer Transactions (Restrictions on Statements) Order 1976, which is discussed at p. 313.

2 'There is no room for a doctrine of freedom of contract in modern consumer protection legislation.'

Critically evaluate this statement in relation to twentieth-century consumer protection legislation. *WJEC*

You should begin by defining what freedom of contract is, with a little of the historical and political background to it – this material can be found in the introductory chapter. Then explain why freedom of contract caused problems for consumers – due to their inequality of bargaining power. Mention the growth of standard contracts and the use of lawyers by big companies to ensure contracts were agreed in their favour. Go on to explain some of the ways in which legislation has protected the consumer by interfering with freedom of contract – discuss the Sale of Goods Act 1979, Supply of Goods and Services Act 1982, Sale and Supply of Goods Act 1994, Unfair Contract Terms Act 1977 and other consumer legislation concerning contract terms referred to in this chapter. You should also mention the Unfair Terms in Consumer Contracts Regulations 1999, covered in Chapter 8. You might then point out briefly that this approach alone has not been entirely successful, because giving consumers greater rights under contracts only protects those consumers who are aware of their rights, and that, as a result, stronger policing of freedom of contract has been thought necessary, in the form of criminal sanctions, and the new power to ban unfair contract terms without litigation by affected individuals contained in the 1999 Regulations.

Your conclusion should say whether you agree that there is now no place for freedom of contract within consumer contracts and, on the basis of the points you have made, whether this should be considered a good or bad development in the law.

3 Henry drove into town to do some shopping and parked his car in a car park which he had used a few times before and which was operated by Safeparks. At the entrance to the car park was a notice which stated: 'For the sole use of customers of the shops in this precinct. Exit by token available from shops with any purchase.' As he walked towards one of the shops, Henry met an old friend who had acquired a token which he did not need and who now gave it to Henry. Henry decided that he no longer needed to buy anything from the precinct shops and, leaving his car in the car park, went off and ordered a dining room carpet from Comfyfloors. When he later tried to leave the car park, he was stopped by security staff doing a spot check on customers and it was discovered that he had not bought anything in the shops, despite having a token. The security staff pointed to a notice displayed at the exit barrier and to a notice at the entrance to the shops (some distance from the entrance to the car park) which stated that exit without a token would cost £25. Henry was told that he could not now go and make a purchase and he had to pay the £25 before the security staff would open the barrier.

Henry engaged Ken, a carpet-fitter, to lay the carpet for him and, after a brief inspection of the completed work, signed a document to say that he was completely satisfied. When he was able to examine the carpet and the fitting more carefully, he discovered that there were variations in the colour and pattern and that Ken had cut it short in three or four places, so that it did not reach the wall. When he complained to Comfyfloors, he was reminded that the delivery note which he had signed informed him that no liability for any defects would be accepted once the carpet had been cut by anyone other than Comfyfloors' employees or authorized agents. Additionally, Henry complained to Ken about the fitting, but Ken rejected the complaint by reminding Henry of the document that he had signed on completion of the work.

(a) Discuss the rights, duties and remedies between Safeparks and Henry arising out of the above incidents. *(15 marks)*
(b) Discuss the rights, duties and remedies arising out of the incidents involving Henry and Comfyfloors and Henry and Ken. *(15 marks)*
(c) Explain the mechanisms, both formal and less formal, which exist for the resolution of the disputes between the various parties. *(10 marks)*
(d) Assess the contribution made by the judges to the development of the rules which you have explained and applied in answering parts (a) and (b) above. *(10 marks)* AQA

(a) This part of the question concerned the formation of contracts and remedies for breach. A court would be likely to find that Safeparks had made a unilateral offer to all those who wished to park, the terms of which were contained in the notice at the entrance to the car park. Henry accepted this offer by parking his car. The case of **Thornton v Shoe Lane Parking**, discussed at p. 119 above, is very important on these facts and should be considered in depth. The consideration for this contract would normally be the provision of the car-parking facility and the purchase of merchandise from one of the shops in the precinct. In fact, Henry makes no such purchase and instead obtains a token provided by an old friend, which might be viewed as past consideration (see p. 68 above). The case of **Chappell & Co Ltd v Nestlé Co Ltd** (at p. 71 above) could also be considered.

In the light of **Thornton v Shoe Lane Parking** and **Olley v Marlborough Court Ltd**, the notice at the entrance of the car park stating 'Exit by token available from shops with any purchase' is likely to be viewed as a term of the contract. A court would probably interpret this clause to require a purchase to be made by the car user, despite the fact that this is not expressly stated, as this would reflect the purpose of the contract – **Investors Compensation Scheme Ltd v West Bromwich Building Society** (p. 102 above).

The requirement to pay £25 on failing to satisfy the conditions of entrance was not mentioned in the notice at the entrance to the car park. Therefore, in the light of **Thornton v Shoe Lane Parking** and **Olley v Marlborough Court Ltd**, this has not been incorporated into the contract by giving Henry reasonable notice of the penalty. Consideration could be given as to whether it has been incorporated through a course of dealings (see p. 122), that is to say, by Henry having used the car park in the past. If this was found not to be a term of the contract, then Safeparks would have to rely on the remedies of damages or an injunction.

(b) Your answer should be divided into two parts. First, consider the contract between Henry and Comfyfloors, this would be affected by the Sale of Goods Act 1979. This Act imposes an obligation that the carpet should be of 'satisfactory quality' (see p. 310). Given the importance of the aesthetic qualities of carpets to customers, a court might well find that the deficiencies described do not satisfy this implied term. Under s. 6 of the Unfair Contract Terms Act 1977, liability for breach of this implied term cannot be excluded as Henry was acting as a consumer (see p. 129). You should also consider whether the delivery note was incorporated into the contract under common law and whether its terms would be considered unfair under the Unfair Terms in Consumer Contracts Regulations 1999. If the carpets are not of a satisfactory quality, Henry will have a right to damages. He is unlikely to have a right to reject the goods because, while he has contacted Comfyfloors promptly about the defects, Ken has already cut the piece of carpet delivered (pp. 312).

Secondly, the contract between Henry and Ken would be affected by the Supply of Goods and Services Act 1982. This contains an implied term that reasonable care and skill will be used in the provision of services. Again, this term could not be excluded by an exclusion clause (UCTA, s. 6). In addition, the clause would not have been incorporated into the contract as Henry did not sign the document at the time of making the contract (p. 118).

(c) This question requires information that is outside the scope of this book and which is covered in the authors' book on the English legal system. As regards formal mechanisms or resolution, you would need to include a discussion on the courts, including the relevance of the size of the claim to determine which court has jurisdiction, and a discussion of the small claims procedure. As regards less formal procedures, you could explore the trade schemes available for arbitration and the growing importance of alternative methods of dispute resolution.

(d) In answering this part of the question you could draw on material contained in the introductory chapter under the headings 'The origins of contract law', 'Freedom of contract' and 'Contract and fairness'. You could point out that most of the general principles of contract, including those concerning the formation of a contract, were created and developed by the judges as part of the common law. On the other hand, the judges' role in developing consumer protection has been more limited due to their adherence to the principle of freedom of contract. They tended to restrict their scrutiny of contracts to formalities and avoided assessment of their substance, as can be seen in their approach to exemption clauses. But it should be noted that judicial contribution continues even where there is legislation through their role in statutory interpretation.

Appendix

A t the end of each chapter in this book, you will find detailed guide-lines for answering exam questions on the topics covered. Many of the questions are taken from actual A-Level past papers, but they are equally relevant for candidates of all law examinations, as these questions are typical of the type of questions that examiners ask in this field.

In this section, we aim to give some general guidelines for answering questions on contract law.

Citation of authorities

One of the most important requirements for answering questions on the law is that you must be able to back up the points you make with author-ity, usually either a case or a statute. It is not good enough to state that the law is such and such, without stating the case or statute which says that that is the law.

Some examiners are starting to suggest that the case name is not essen-tial, as long as you can remember and understand the general principle that the case laid down. However, such examiners remain in the minority and the reality is that even they are likely to give higher marks where the candidate has cited authorities by name; quite simply, it helps give the impression that you know your material thoroughly, rather than half-remembering something you heard once in class.

This means that you must be prepared to learn fairly long lists of cases by heart, which can be a daunting prospect. What you need to memorize is the name of the case, a brief description of the facts, and the legal principle which the case established. Once you have revised a topic well, you should find that a surprisingly high number of cases on that topic begin to stick in your mind anyway, but there will probably be some that you have trouble recalling. A good way to memorize these is to try to create a picture in your mind which links the facts, the name and the legal principle. For example, in the case of **Routledge** *v* **Grant** (1828) the defendants made a provisional offer to buy the plaintiff's house at a specified price, 'a definite answer to be given within six weeks from date'. The principle established in the case was that the offeror had the right to withdraw the offer at any moment before acceptance, even though the time limit had not expired. You could remember this case by imagining the actress Patricia Routledge trying to buy a house from the *EastEnders* character Grant Mitchell, with Grant telling Patricia that he has the right to withdraw his offer at any time before acceptance. Or turn the names into objects – you can remember **Fisher** *v* **Bell**, for instance, by imagining a fisherman trying to sell flick knives to a bell, and the bell replying, 'Putting those knives in your window is not an offer, but an invitation to treat.' The more bizarre the image, the more likely you are to remember it.

Knowing the names of cases makes you look more knowledgeable, and also saves writing time in the exam, but if you do forget a name, referring briefly to the facts will identify it. It is not necessary to learn the dates of cases, though it is useful if you know whether it is a recent or an old case. Dates are usually required for statutes.

You need to know the facts of a case in order to judge whether it applies to the situation in a problem question. However, unless you are making a detailed comparison of the facts of a case and the facts of a problem question in order to argue that the case should or could be distinguished, you should generally make only brief reference to facts, if at all – long descriptions of facts waste time and earn few marks.

When reading the 'Answering questions' sections at the end of each chapter in this book bear in mind that for reasons of space, we have not highlighted every case and statute which you should cite. The skeleton arguments outlined in those sections **must** be backed up with authority from cases and statute law.

There is no right answer

In law exams, there is not usually a right or a wrong answer. What matters is that you show you know what type of issues you are being asked about. Essay questions are likely to ask you to 'discuss', 'criticize', or 'evaluate', and you simply need to produce a good range of factual and critical material in order to do this. The answer you produce might look completely different from your friend's but both answers could be worth the same marks.

Breadth and depth of content

Where a question seems to raise a number of different issues – as most do – your will achieve better marks by addressing all or most of those issues than by writing at great length on just one or two. By all means spend more time on issues which you know well, but be sure to at least mention other points which you can see are relevant, even if you can only produce a paragraph or so about them.

The structure of the question

If a question is specifically divided into parts, for example (a), (b) and (c), then stick to those divisions and do not merge your answer into one long piece of writing.

Law examinations tend to contain a mixture of essay questions and what are known as 'problem questions'. Tackling each of these questions involves slightly different skills so we consider each in turn.

▶ Essay questions

Answer the question asked

Over and over again, examiners complain that candidates do not answer the question they are asked – so if you can develop this skill, you will stand out from the crowd. You will get very few marks for simply writing all you know about a topic, with no attempt to address the issues raised in the question, but if you can adapt the material that you have learnt on the subject to take into account the particular emphasis given to it by the question, you will do well.

Even if you have memorized an essay which does raise the issues in the question (perhaps because those issues tend to be raised year after year), you must fit your material to the words of the question you are actually being asked. For example, suppose during your course you wrote an essay on the advantages and disadvantages of the privity rule, and then in the exam you find yourself faced with the question 'Should the privity rule be abolished?' The material in your coursework essay is ideally suited for the exam question, but if you begin the main part of your answer with the words 'The advantages of the privity rule include . . .', or something similar, this is a dead giveaway to the examiner that you are merely writing down an essay you have memorized. It takes very little effort to change the words to 'Abolition of the privity rule would ignore certain advantages that the current law has . . .', but it will create a much better impression, especially if you finish with a conclusion which, based on points you have made, states that abolition is a good or bad idea, the choice depending on the arguments you have made during your answer.

During your essay, you should keep referring to the words used in the question – if this seems to become repetitive, use synonyms for those words. This makes it clear to the examiner that you are keeping the question in mind as you work.

Plan your answer

Under pressure of time, it is tempting to start writing immediately, but five minutes spent planning each essay question is well worth spending –

it may mean that you write less overall, but the quality of your answer will almost certainly be better. The plan need not be elaborate: just jot down everything you feel is relevant to the answer, including case names, and then organize the material into a logical order appropriate to the question asked. To put it in order, rather than wasting time copying it all out again, simply put a number next to each point according to which ones you intend to make first, second and so forth.

Provide analysis and fact

Very few essay questions require merely factual descriptions of what the law is; you will almost always be required to analyse the factual content in some way, usually highlighting any problems or gaps in the law, and suggesting possible reforms. If a question asks you to analyse whether consumers are adequately protected by the law when they buy goods, you should not write everything you know about consumer protection and finish with one sentence saying consumers are or are not adequately protected. Instead you should select your relevant material and your whole answer should be targeted at answering whether the protection is adequate, by, for example, pointing out any gaps or problems in it, and highlighting changes which have improved protection.

Where a question uses the word 'critically', as in 'critically describe' or 'critically evaluate', the examiners are merely drawing your attention to the fact that your approach should be analytical and not merely descriptive; you are not obliged to criticize every provision you describe. Having said that, even if you do not agree with particular criticisms which you have read, you should still discuss them and say why you do not think they are valid; there is very little mileage in an essay that simply describes the law and says it is perfectly satisfactory.

Structure

However good your material, you will only gain really high marks if you structure it well. Making a plan for each answer will help in this, and you should also try to learn your material in a logical order – this will make it easier to remember as well. The exact construction of your essay will obviously depend on the question, but you should aim to have an introduction, then the main discussion, and a conclusion. Where a question is divided into two or more parts, you should reflect that structure in your answer.

A word about conclusions: it is not good enough just to repeat the question, turning it into a statement, for the conclusion. So, for example, if the question is 'Are the rules on offer and acceptance satisfactory?', a conclusion which simply states that the rules are or are not satisfactory will gain you very little credit. Your conclusion will often summarize the arguments that you have developed during the course of your essay.

Problem questions

In problem questions, the exam paper will describe an imaginary situation, and then ask what the legal implications of the facts are – usually by asking you to advise one of the parties involved.

Read the question thoroughly

The first priority is to read the question thoroughly, at least a couple of times. Never start writing until you have done this, as you may well get halfway through and discover that what is said at the end makes half of what you have written irrelevant – or at worst, that the question raises issues you have no knowledge of at all.

Answer the question asked

This means paying close attention to the words printed immediately after the situation is described. If a question asks you to advise one or other of the parties, make sure you advise the right one – the realization as you discuss the exam with your friends afterwards that you have advised the wrong party and thus rendered most of your answer irrelevant is not an experience you will enjoy. Similarly, if a question asks about possible remedies, simply discussing whether there has been a breach of contract will not be enough – you need to say what the innocent party can claim as a result.

Spot the issues

In answering a problem question in an examination, you will often be short of time. One of the skills of doing well is spotting which issues are particularly relevant to the facts of the problem and spending most time on those, while skimming over more quickly those matters which are not really an issue on the facts, but which you clearly need to mention.

Apply the law to the facts

What a problem question requires you to do is to spot the issues raised by the situation, and to consider the law as it applies to those facts. It is not enough simply to describe the law without applying it to the facts. So in a question raising issues of offer and acceptance, for example, it is not enough to say what constitutes an offer and what makes an acceptance.

You need to say whether, in the light of those rules, there has been an offer and acceptance in the situation described in the problem.

Do not start your answer by copying out all the facts, or keep referring to them at great length. This is a complete waste of time, and will gain you no marks.

Unlike essay questions, problem questions are not usually seeking a critical analysis of the law. If you have time, it may be worth making the point that a particular area of the law you are discussing is problematic, and briefly stating why, but if you are addressing all the issues raised in the problem you are unlikely to have much time for this. What the examiner is looking for is essentially an understanding of the law and an ability to apply it to the particular facts given.

Use authority

As always, you must back up your points with authority from case or statute law.

Structure

The introduction and conclusion are much less important for problem questions than for essay questions. Your introduction can be limited to pointing out the issues raised by the question, or, where you are asked to 'advise' a person mentioned in the problem, what outcome that person will be looking for. You can also say in what order you intend to deal with the issues. It is not always necessary to write a conclusion, but you may want to summarize what you have said, highlighting whether, as a result, you think the party you have advised has a strong case or not.

There is no set order in which the main part of the answer must be discussed. Sometimes it will be appropriate to deal with the problem chronologically, in which case it will usually be a matter of looking at the question line by line, while in other cases it may be appropriate to group particular issues together. If the question is broken down into clear parts – a, b, c and so on – the answer can be broken down into the same parts; whether this is the case varies with different examining boards.

Whichever order you choose, try to deal with one issue at a time. Jumping backwards and forwards gives the impression that you have not thought about your answer. If you work through your material in a structured way, you are also less likely to leave anything out.

Glossary

Acceptance of an offer means unconditional agreement to all the terms of that offer. Acceptance will often be oral or in writing, but in some cases an offeree may accept an offer by doing something (such as delivering goods in response to an offer to buy). The courts will only interpret conduct as indicating acceptance where it seems reasonable to infer that the offeree acted with the intention of accepting the offer.

Accord and satisfaction occur where one party's obligations under a contract change and consideration is provided in return for the other party's agreement to the change. The agreement is called 'accord' and the provision of consideration for it is called 'satisfaction', thus the arrangement is called 'accord and satisfaction'.

Agent. A person authorized to act on behalf of another who is known as the principal. The principal will be bound by any contract the agent makes, so long as the agent is acting within the authority granted by the principal or apparently granted by the principal.

Bilateral contract. This is where each party takes on an obligation, usually by promising the other something (for example, where A promises to sell something and B promises to buy it). It can be distinguished from a unilateral contract (discussed below).

Breach of contract. A contract is said to be breached when one party performs defectively, differently from the agreement, or not at all (actual breach), or indicates in advance that he or she will not be performing as agreed (anticipatory breach).

Caveat emptor (Latin for 'Let the buyer beware'). It is a traditional rule that a purchaser is required to ask questions about important matters if necessary – the seller is not usually expected to volunteer information which may put the buyer off.

Chartered corporation. A corporation set up by Royal Charter, which means that its powers are officially granted by the Crown. Examples are some charities, and some universities and other educational institutions.

Common mistake is where both parties to a contract make the same mistake (for example, if A buys a painting from B, which both parties believe is a Constable, but which is in fact a fake, they have made a common or shared mistake).

Condition. A term in a contract which is an important one, in the sense that a breach of it would have very significant consequences for the innocent party, will usually be regarded by the courts as a condition. Where a condition is breached, the innocent party is entitled to regard the contract as repudiated, and so need not render any further performance, and may also be able to sue for damages.

Consideration is something that must be provided by each of the parties in order to make a binding contract. Put simply, this means that there must be some kind of exchange between the parties. If, for example, A says that she will give B her car, and B simply agrees to have it, A has voluntarily made her a promise (called a gratuitous promise) which B cannot enforce if A changes her mind. If, however, A promises to hand over her car to B and B promises to pay A a sum of money in return, they have each provided consideration.

Contra proferentem **rule**. This means that where the words, for example of an exemption clause, are ambiguous, they will be interpreted against the party relying on them.

Contract. In law this means a legally binding agreement, written or unwritten. In order to be legally binding, the agreement has to satisfy certain requirements (see Chapters 1–6) but, with few exceptions, being in writing is not one of these requirements.

Corporation. A corporation is a legal entity (usually a group of people) which is treated by law as having a separate identity from the person or persons who constitute it.

Cross-purposes mistake. This occurs where each party to the contract has a different view of the situation – for example, where A thinks he is buying B's Rolls-Royce when in fact it is his Daimler that is for sale.

Economic duress occurs where one party is forced into a contract due to economic pressure, which is much more than the ordinary pressure of the market. To constitute economic duress there must be compulsion of the will to the extent that the party under threat has no practical alternative but to comply and the pressure used is regarded by the law as illegitimate.

Exclusion clause. A clause which seeks to exclude all liability for certain breaches of contract (for example, the terms often imposed by holiday companies which exclude liability for holiday problems caused by events beyond the company's control, such as war).

Exemption clause. This is a term commonly used to cover both limitation clauses (see below) and exclusion clauses (see above).

Freedom of contract. This doctrine promotes the idea that, since parties are the best judge of their own interest, they should be allowed to make the bargain that suits them without interference from the courts.

Gratuitous promise. A promise for which no consideration is given in return.

Implied terms. Terms which are not expressly stated in a contract but which the courts will 'read in'.

Indemnity clause. Provides that one party will reimburse (indemnify) the other in the event of any loss arising from the contract.

Innominate terms. These are terms which can be broken with either important or trivial consequences, depending on the nature of the breach.

Laches (delay). The court will often refuse relief to a claimant who it considers has, in all the circumstances of the case, been guilty of unreasonable delay in seeking relief.

Legal tender. The following are regarded as legal tender for the purpose of paying a debt: Bank of England notes for any amount, silver coins up to the value of £5, and copper up to the value of 20p.

Limitation clause. This is one whereby a party to a contract seeks to limit his or her liability for particular breaches.

Liquidated claim. This is one for a fixed amount, for example a sum of money lent or the agreed price of goods or services supplied.

Liquidated damages. This term can be used where a contract specifies the amount of damages to be paid in the event of breach, and this amount represents a genuine attempt to work out what the loss in the event of such a breach would be.

Minor. A person under the age of 18.

Misrepresentation. If one party has been induced to enter into a contract by a statement made by the other party, and that statement is in fact untrue, the contract is voidable and the innocent party may also claim damages. For a misrepresentation to be actionable, it has to fulfil three requirements: it must (1) be untrue; (2) be a statement of fact, not mere opinion; and (3) have induced the innocent party to enter the contract.

Mistake. See **Common mistake; Cross-purposes mistake**.

Non est factum (Latin for 'This is not my deed'). Where a person signs a document believing it to be something totally different from what it actually is, the common law remedy of *non est factum* may make the contract void.

Novation is an act whereby, with the consent of all the parties, a new contract is substituted for an existing contract and the latter is discharged. Usually it takes the form of the introduction of a new party to the contract and the discharge of a person who was a party to the old contract. For example, if A owes B £100 under one contract and C owes A £100 under another, novation will occur if C agrees to pay B £100 if she will release A from her debt to B. The first two contracts are destroyed and a new one is created.

Offer. A communication is treated as an offer if it indicates the terms on which the offeror is prepared to make a contract and gives a clear indication that the offeror intends to be bound by those terms if they are accepted by the offeree.

Parol evidence rule. Under this rule, where there is a written contract, extrinsic (parol) evidence cannot usually change the express terms laid down in that document.

Privity of contract. This doctrine specifies that only the parties to a contract incur rights and obligations under it – so a person who is not a party to the contract (called a third party) can neither sue nor be sued on the contract. There are a series of exceptions to this rule.

Quantum meruit. (Latin for 'As much as is deserved'). Where a price has not been specified in a contract between the parties but work has been done or goods supplied under it, an action called a *quantum meruit* is available under which the claimant can claim a reasonable price for the performance rendered.

Registered company. A company registered under the Companies Act 1985.

Representation. This is a statement which may have encouraged one party to make a contract but is not itself part of that contract.

Severable contract. A contract is said to be severable where payment becomes due at various stages of performance rather than in one lump sum when performance is complete.

Severance. In some cases it is possible to divide the illegal part of a contract from the rest, and enforce the provisions which are not affected by the illegality (this is called severance).

Specialty contract. An agreement by deed.

Statutory corporation. A corporation created for particular purposes by an Act of Parliament, for example the Independent Broadcasting Authority.

Subject to contract. Use of these words in an agreement is usually (though not always) taken to mean that the parties do not intend to be legally bound until formal contracts are exchanged.

Terms of the contract describe the duties and obligations which each party assumes under the agreement.

Uberrimae fidei (Latin for 'of Utmost good faith'). This is essential to the validity of certain contracts between persons bearing a particular relationship to one another (for example insurer and insured). Failure to disclose a matter regarding which utmost good faith is required allows the innocent party to rescind the contract.

Ultra vires (Latin for 'Outside the powers'). A contract, for example, which is outside a company's range of activities is said to be *ultra vires*.

Unilateral contracts arise where only one party assumes an obligation, for example W will pay a £100 reward to anyone who finds his dog. Here W is obliged to pay a reward to anyone who finds his dog but nobody is obliged to do so.

Unliquidated claim. Where the amount of claim is uncertain it is said to be unliquidated.

Void contract. Where a contract is declared void, the effect is that there never was a contract in the first place, so neither party can enforce the agreement.

Voidable contract is one where an innocent party can choose whether or not to be bound by it.

Warranty. This describes a contractual term which can be broken without highly important consequences. If a warranty is breached, the innocent party can sue for damages but is not entitled to terminate the contract.

Index

acceptance, 18–39, 300
  auctions, 31–2
  battle of the forms, 20–1
  communication of, 24, 26–8, 30,
    39–40
  conduct, 18–19, 25, 30
  counter-offers, 20
  damages, 36, 40
  domestic arrangements, 52
  electronic communications, 30
  fax, by, 28
  implied by the court, 30–1
  instantaneous communications, by,
    26, 27–8
  intention to create legal relations,
    52
  methods, specified, 22–4
  negotiations, 20–1
  offer, 9, 20–2, 115–16
  oral, 30
  part performance, 22
  postal rule, 23–8, 30, 231
  sale of goods contracts, 312
  sale of land, 37, 38
  silence, 19–20, 23, 25, 302
  standard forms, 20–1
  telemessages, 26
  telexes, 25, 27–8, 39–40
  tenders, 32–4
  unconditional, 20, 21
  unilateral contracts, 20, 25
  unsolicited goods, 322
accord and satisfaction, 256
account of profits, 281–2
acknowledgement of claims, 295
advance payments, 245–6, 261
advertisements
  auctions, 31
  commercial agreements, 49
  express terms, 116

invitation to treat, 11–13
  mere puffs, 49
  offer, 10, 18, 40–1, 115–16
  sale of goods contracts, 326
  tenders, 32
agency, 218–20
agreed sum, action for an, 282
apprenticeships, 55, 61–2
assignment, 220
auctions, 31–2

bargaining power, inequality of
  duress, 207–8, 209
  exemption clauses, 125, 128, 130
  fairness, 4–5
  standard forms, 328
  undue influence, 207–8, 209
  unfair contract terms, 135–6, 328
battle of the forms, 20–1
bills of exchange, 70, 218
breach, 249–55
  actual breach, 249–50
  affirmation or discharge, choice of,
    253–5
  anticipatory, 250
  conditions, 110–11, 114, 231, 252,
    261, 303–4
  damages, 249–51, 254–5, 262–82,
    298, 303
  exemption clauses, 125
  fundamental, 125
  innominate terms, 112–13, 252–3,
    303–4
  mitigation, 254–5
  repudiation, 251–2, 253–4
  sale of goods contracts, 312–13
  warranties, 111, 114, 231, 252,
    303–4
building contracts, 222–3, 227–8, 286–7,
  293

cancellation, 324
capacity, 53–62
chance, loss of a, 278–9
chartered corporations, 60
cheques, 221
children *see* minors
citation of authorities, 331–2
codes of practice, 325
collateral contracts, 101, 224–5, 229–30
collective bargaining agreements, 51
commercial agreements
　advertising, 49
　collective bargaining agreements, 51
　damages, 264
　ex gratia payments, 50–1
　honour clauses, 49–50
　intention to create legal relations,
　　48–61
　mental distress, damages for, 264
　mere puffs, 49
　subject to contract, 50
competition, 185–6
composition agreements, 78
conditional gifts, 85–6
conditions
　breach, 110–11, 114, 231, 252, 261,
　　303–4
　charterparties, 111
　sale of goods contracts, 111
　subsequent, 257
　termination, agreements on, 257
consent, 5–6
consideration, 66–92
　bills of exchange, 70
　conditional gifts, 85–6
　deeds, agreements by, 63, 85
　definition, 66–73
　detriment, 67–8
　economic value, of, 71
　executed, 68
　executory, 68
　existing duties, performance of,
　　73–80, 89, 90
　failure of, 283–5, 309
　forbearance, 72–3
　freedom of contract, 70–1
　future of, 88–9
　intention to create legal relations,
　　51–2

moral obligations, 86
offers open, promises to keep, 89
part payment, 87, 89
past, 68–70, 89, 91–2
peppercorn principle, 86–7
performance,
　complete, 68
　existing duties, of, 73–80
practical benefits, 74, 75–6, 90, 91
problems with, 86–7
promises, 90–1
　gratuitous, 66, 89
　offers open, to keep, 89
　sue, not to, 72–3
　written, 89
promisees, 67
promisors, 67–8
promissory estoppel, 80–5, 88–9
reform, 89
restitution, 283–5
sale of goods contracts, 309
sue, promise not to, 72–3
sufficient, 70–1
termination, agreements on, 256
third parties, 68, 73
unilateral contracts, 89
waiver, 80, 88–9
constructive trusts, 225–6
consumer protection, 305–30 *see also*
　　manufacturers' liability, sale of
　　goods contracts
cancellation, 324
care and skill, 315, 330
codes of practice, 325
consumer credit, 323
consumers, definition of, 327
cooling off, 324
criminal offences, 320–2, 327
EC law, 325
exemption clauses, 127–30
fair trading, 321
freedom of contract, 328
guarantees, 326
hire contracts, 316
hire purchase, 323–4
implied terms, 109, 315–16, 325–6,
　330
prices, 316, 322
property, passing of, 316

reform, 324–7
remedies, 316, 326
repairs or replacements, 326
safety, 321
standard forms, 328
supply of services, 315–16, 330
time, 315
trade descriptions, 321–2
unfair contract terms, 132–3, 327
unsolicited goods, 322–3
works and materials, contracts for,
   315
contents of contracts, 93–141 *see also*
   terms
contra proferentem rule, 123–5, 141
contributory negligence, 320
cooling off period, 324
corporations, 60
corruption in public life, encouraging,
   189–90
criminal offences, 313, 320–2, 327
cure, cost of, 277–8
custom, 44, 100–1, 110

damages
   acceptance, 36, 40
   account of profits, 281–2
   agreed sum, action for an, 282
   amenity, loss of, 266–7
   auctions, 32
   bad bargain rule, 275
   breach, 249–51, 254–5, 262–82, 298,
      303
   building contracts, 293
   calculation of, 156–8, 161, 273–82,
      300–1, 303
   causation, 267–8
   chance, loss of a, 278–9
   commercial agreements, 264
   cure, cost of, 277–8
   employment contracts, 264
   exemption clauses, 117, 119–20,
      139–40
   expectation loss, 273–6, 303
   holidays, 264–6
   illegality, 193, 196
   indemnities and, 154
   limitation on, 267–73
   liquidated, 293, 294

manufacturers' liability, 319
market price rule, 276–7
mental distress, 264, 266, 267, 298,
   299
misrepresentation, 156–61, 260–1
mitigation, 272–3, 276, 298, 303
negligence, 279
non-pecuniary loss, 263, 303
offer, 36
opportunity, loss of an, 278–9
pecuniary loss, 263, 303
penalty clauses, 293–4
performance, 238, 258–9
physical inconvenience, mental
   distress caused by, 267
pleasure, relaxation and peace of
   mind, whole or part of contract
   is for, 264–7
privity of contract, 221–3, 231
profits, loss of, 298
profits made by the defendant, 280–2
promissory estoppel, 85
reliance loss, 274–5
remoteness, 157–8, 268–72, 298
rescission, 158–9
restitution, 297
sale of goods contracts, 312
sale of land, 34–5, 300–1
specific performance, 288–9
tax, 279–80
tenders, 34
third parties, 217, 221–3, 231
warranties, 111
deceit, 57, 58, 150
deeds, 63, 85
defective products *see* manufacturers'
   liability
descriptions, 309–10, 330
discharge of contracts, 235–62 *see also*
   breach, frustration, performance,
   termination
display, goods on, 12–13
domestic arrangements, 46–8, 52
drunkenness, 58–9
duress, 197–200
   bargaining power, inequality of,
      207–8, 209
   economic, 197–8, 200
   inducement, 199

industrial disputes, 200
pressure, 197–200, 210
protests, 200
threats, 199–200
voidable contracts, 197, 199

EC law
consumer protection, 325
electronic commerce, 64–5
guarantees, 317
manufacturers' liability, 317, 319, 320
unfair contract terms, 117, 132
economic duress, 197–8, 200
economic loss, 318
electronic communications, 30, 63–5
employment contracts, 3
collective bargaining agreements, 51
damages, 264
dismissal, 5
fairness, 5
implied terms, 109
mental distress, damages for, 264
minors, 54–5, 61–2
performance, 237
restraints of trade, 183–5
specific performance, 289, 292
territorial restrictions, 184–5
trust and confidence, 109
enemies, trading with the, 189
entire agreement clauses, 101–2, 235–9
essay questions, answering, 333–5
estoppel see promissory estoppel
European Union see EC law
ex gratia payments, 50–1
examination questions, answering,
331–6
exemption clauses
bargaining power, inequality of, 125,
128, 130
business, dealing in the course of a,
127–8
common law controls, 118–27
consumers, dealing as, 127–30
contra proferentem rule, 123–5, 141
course of dealing, incorporation by a
previous, 122–3, 130
damages, 117, 119–20, 139–40
exclusion clauses, 117
fundamental breach, 125

guarantees of consumer goods, 129
hire purchase contracts, implied
terms in, 129–30
implied terms, 129–30, 139
inconsistent oral promises, 126
incorporation, 118–23, 139
indemnity clauses, 129
interpretation, 123–5, 141
misrepresentation, 118, 126, 130, 159
negligence, 123–6, 128, 131, 141
non-performance, 129
notice,
form of, 120
incorporation by reasonable,
118–20, 140–1, 327, 329
time of, 119–20
occupiers' liability, 128
privity of contract, 126–7
reasonableness, 128, 130–2, 138, 141
sale of goods contracts, implied terms
in, 129–30
small print, 118, 140–1
standard terms, 129
statutory controls, 127–32
third parties, no protection for,
126–7, 224–5
ticket cases, 118–20, 140–1
unfair contract terms, 117–32, 138
unusual or onerous clauses, 120–1
existing duties, performance of
additional benefits, 74, 75–6, 90
composition agreements, 78
consideration, 73–80, 89, 90
contractual duties, existing, 75–8, 90
debts, contractual duties to pay, 76–7,
78
detriment, 79
disputed claims, 78
goods or services, contractual duties
to supply, 75–6
instalments, 77
part payment, 76–7
penalty clauses, 75–6
Pinnel's case, rule in, 76–8, 87
public duties, 73–4
public policy, 73–4
third parties, 78–80, 90
unliquidated claims, 78
expenses, 247, 259, 261

express terms, 95–105, 116
  advertisements, 116
  collateral contracts, 101
  construction, rules of, 102–5
  entire agreement clauses, 101–2
  oral statements, 95–9, 102
  parol evidence rule, 99–101
  redundancy, 103–4
  representations, 97–8
  written, 97–102

fairness, 4–5 *see also* unfair contract
    terms
family homes, sureties and, 202–8
fiduciaries, 147, 201–2, 208, 210, 260
fitness for purpose, 311–12, 326
forbearance, 72–3
formalities, 63–5, 256–7
formation of contracts, 7–92 *see also*
    acceptance, consideration, offer
  capacity, 53–62
  certainty, 42–5
  deeds, 63
  electronic commerce, 64–5
  electronic communications, 63
  electronic signatures, 63, 65
  e-mail, 64–5
  formalities, 63–5
  guarantees, 64
  illegality, 182
  intention to create legal relations,
    46–52, 115
  Internet, 64–5
  invitations to treat, 10–14, 115
  leases, contracts made by deeds for, 63
  oral contracts, 63
  sale of land, 63–4
  time for, 30
  writing, 63–4
fraud
  misrepresentation, 150–1, 154, 157–8,
    160, 181, 261
  mistake, 174–6, 178–9
freedom of contract, 4, 70–1, 328
frustration, 240–9
  advance payments, 245–6, 261
  common law, 245–6
  contractual provision for, 244
  delay, 241–2

expenses, 247, 259, 261
foreseen and unforeseen events, 244
hardship, 241–2
implied terms, 248
impossibility, 240–2, 258–9, 261
just solution theory, 249
legal consequences of, 245–8
limits to, 243–4
money, obligations to pay, 245–6
onerous or more expensive
    performance, 241–2, 257–8
personal performance, 241, 261
pointless, performance made, 242–3
restitution, 284
self-induced, 244–5
specific goods, perishing of, 248
supervening illegality, 242, 244
time of frustrating event, 243
valuable benefit, obtaining a, 247–8

gazumping, 38
guarantees
  consumer protection, 326
  EC law, 317
  family homes, 202–8
  formation of contracts, 64
  manufacturers' liability, 317, 326
  minors, 57
  unfair contract terms, 317
  writing, 64

hardship, 241–2, 289, 290
hire contracts, 316
hire purchase, 15, 42, 129–30, 175–6,
    323–4
holidays, 221–2, 226, 231, 264–6
honour clauses, 49–50
husband and wife, agreements between,
    46–7

illegality, 182–96
  administration of justice, prejudicial
    to, 189
  competition, 185–6
  complexity, 194
  corruption in public life, tending to
    encourage, 189–90
  damages, 193, 196
  enemies, trading with, 189

formation, at time of, 182
injustice, 194
legal rules, violation of, 183–7
legislation, breach of, 185–7
marriage, prejudicial to status of, 188–9
ousting the jurisdiction of the court, 189
performance, 182, 191–3
public policy, 187–90
quantum meruit, 193
recovery of property, 191
reform, 195
restitution, 284
restraints of trade, 183–5, 195–6
restrictive trade agreements, 185–6
safety, contracts, prejudicial to, 189
severance, 193
sexual immorality, promoting, 188
solus agreements, 184
territorial restrictions, 184–5
tying, 185
uncertainty, 194
wagering contracts, 186–7
illiteracy, 59
implied terms, 105–10, 116
business efficacy test, 105–7
certainty, 43
consumer contracts, 109, 315–16, 325–6, 330
custom, implied by, 110
employment contracts, 109
exemption clauses, 129–30, 139
fact, implied in, 105–8
frustration, 248
hire contracts, 316
hire purchase, 129–30
interest on debts, 109
law, implied in, 108–9
officious bystander test, 105, 107
parol evidence rule, 100
redundancy, 109
sale of goods contracts, 129–30, 300, 308–13, 325–7
services, contracts for, 315–16
statute, by, 43
subjectivity, 107–8
trade usage, by, 110
indemnities, 129, 154–6, 160, 260

industrial disputes, 200
injunctions, 291–2, 295–6
innominate terms, 112–13, 252–3, 303–4
insurance contracts, 145–6, 217
intention to create legal relations
acceptance, 52
commercial agreements, 48–61
consideration, 51–2
domestic arrangements, 46–8, 52
formation of contracts, 46–52, 115
husband and wife, agreements between, 46–7
importance of, 51–2
maintenance agreements, 46–7
offer, 52
parent and child, agreements between, 47–8
social agreements, 48
interest on debts, 109
Internet, 64–5
invitations to treat, 10–14, 299–300, 302
advertisements, 11–13
auctions, 31
bilateral contracts, advertisements for, 12–13
display, goods on, 12–13
formation of contracts, 10–14, 115
negotiations, 11
prices marked on goods, 12–13
rewards, 11
self-service, 12–13
tickets for transport, 13–14
timetables, 13–14

laches, 295–6
laissez-faire, 3, 4
latent damage, 294–5
leases, 63, 81–2, 92, 99, 101, 290
legal relations *see* intention to create legal relations

maintenance agreements, 46–7
manufacturers' liability, 316–20
contributory negligence, 320
damage, definition of, 319
damages, 319
defences, 320

development risks defence, 320
EC law, 317, 319, 320
economic loss, 318
guarantees, 317, 326
negligence, 317–18
producers, 319
strict liability, 319, 320
unfair contract terms, 138
marriage, prejudicial to the status of,
    188–9
mental distress, damages for, 264, 266,
    267, 298, 299
mental incapacity
drunkenness, 58–9
illiteracy, 59
language, 59
mental illness, 58–9
minors, 57–8
necessaries, 59
time limits, 295
void contracts, 59
voidable contracts, 58
mere puffs, 49
minors
apprenticeships, 55, 61–2
binding contracts, 53–5
capacity, 53–8, 61–2
deceit, 57, 58
employment contracts of, 54–5,
    61–2
guarantees, 57
mental incapacity, 57–8
necessaries, 53–4, 56, 62, 287
parents and children, agreements
    between, 47–8
partnerships, 56
quantum meruit, 287
reform, 58
remedies against, 56–7
restitution, 56–7
service, contracts of, 54–5, 62
specific performance, 57
time limits, 295
tortious liability, 57
trading contracts, 55, 62
very young children, 57–8
voidable contracts at common law, 56,
    62
misleading prices, 322

misrepresentation, 145–61
affirmation, 155–6
constructive knowledge, 149–50
damages, 156–61, 260–1
    measure of, 156–8, 161
    remoteness of, 157–8
    rescission or, 158–9
deceit, 150
definition, 145–50
destruction of subject matter, 155
exemption clauses, 118, 126, 130, 159
facts, statements of, 147–8, 210, 260
fiduciary relationships, 147
fraudulent, 150–1, 154, 157–8, 160,
    181, 261
indemnity payments, 154–6, 160, 260
inducement, 149–50, 156, 159–60
innocent, 153, 156, 261
law, statements of, 148
mistake, 174–5, 179–81
negligence, 150–3, 158, 160, 261
negligent misstatements, 150–1
opinions, 147–8, 260
oral statements, 95–6
partial relevation, 146–7
prospectuses, 149
rehabilitation of offenders, 146
remedies, 153–61
rescission, 153–6, 158–9, 161, 181
restitution, impossibility of, 155
sales talk, 148
silence, 146
statute, under, 151–2
subsequent falsity, 146
terms and, 159
third party rights, 155
types of, 150–3
untrue statements, 145–7
utmost good faith, 145–6
voidable contracts, 146, 179, 181, 260
mistake, 161–81
common, 165–70, 180
consent, 162, 163, 170
criticism, 178–80
cross-purposes, 170–6
documents, relating to, 176–8
equity, in, 169–70, 176
fact, of, 163–5
fraud, 174–6, 178–9

fundamental, 167–70
hire purchase, 175–6
identity, 172–6, 180–1, 288
inducement, 163, 171
innocent purchasers of dishonestly
    obtained goods, 174–6, 179–80
law, of, 163–5
misrepresentation, 174–5, 179, 181
mutual, 170
non est factum, 176–7, 210
overpayments, 164–5
preceding the contract, 163
quality, 168
quantum meruit, 288
rectification, 177–8
reform, 178–80
rescission, 175
sale of goods, 166
subject matter, existence of the,
    165–7
terms, unilateral mistake over, 171
title, as to, 167
unilateral, 170–6, 178, 180–1
void contracts, 162, 166–7, 169,
    170–1, 179–81, 288
voidable contracts, 162, 169, 179–80
moral obligations, 86

necessaries, 53–4, 56, 59, 62, 287
negligence
    contributory, 320
    damages, 279
    exemption clauses, 123–6, 128, 131,
        141
    manufacturers' liability, 317–18, 320
    misrepresentation, 150–3, 158, 160,
        261
    negligent misstatements, 150–1
    unfair contract terms, 124–5
non est factum, 176–7, 210
novation, 221, 257

occupiers' liability, 128
offer *see also* invitations to treat
    acceptance, 9, 115–16
    advertisements, 10, 18, 40–1, 115–16
    'all or nothing' approach, 38–9
    auctions, 31–2
    bilateral contracts, 9, 41

conduct, implied from, 10, 30
consideration, 89
counter-offers, 15, 20
cross, 29–30
damages, 36
death of offerors or offerees, 16
definition, 41
domestic arrangements, 52
duration of, 14–18, 300
hire purchase, 15
ignorance of, 28–9
implied by the court, 30–1
importance of, 36–7
information, requests for, 15–16, 302
intention to create legal relations, 52
lapse, 14
length of time, reasonable, 14
objectivity, 39
open, keeping, 89
oral, 30
performance, withdrawal following
    substantial, 37–8
postal rule, 17
preconditions, failure of, 14–15
public at large, to, 10
questions, answering, 39–41
rejection, 15
revocation,
    communication of, 16–18
    specific periods, for, 38
    unilateral offers, of, 37–8
rewards, 29, 40–1
sale of land, 34–5, 37, 38
tenders, 32–4
unilateral, 21–2, 37–8
unilateral contracts, 9, 10, 18, 41, 329
withdrawal, 16–18
opinions, 147–8, 260
oral statements
    collateral contracts, 101
    importance of, 96
    inducements, strength of, 98–9
    knowledge and skill, special, 96–7
    misrepresentation, 95–6
    negotiations, 95–6
    representations, 95–6, 102
    timing of, 97
origins of contract law, 2–3
ousting the jurisdiction of the court, 189

parents and children, agreements
   between, 47–8
parol evidence rule, 99–101
partnerships, 56
penalty clauses, 75–6, 293–4
peppercorn principle, 86–8
performance, 235–40 *see also* existing
   duties, performance of
   acceptance, 22
   anticipation of a contract, in, 283
   complete, 68
   consideration, 68, 73–80
   damages, 238, 258–9
   delay, 238–9, 304
   employment contracts, 237
   entire performance rule, 235–9
   essence, time of the, 238–9, 304
   illegality, 182, 191–3
   offer, withdrawal following substantial,
      37–8
   partial, 22, 237, 287
   prevention of, by other party, 237–8,
      287
   quantum meruit, 237–8, 287
   rejection, 238
   restitution, 283
   severable contracts, 237
   substantial, 37–8, 236, 304
   time, breach of terms concerning,
      238–9, 261, 304
   vicarious, 239–40
postal rule, 23–8, 30, 231
price, 12–13, 43, 44, 316, 322
privity of contract, 211–31
   arguments against, 228–30
   arguments for, 226–8
   building contracts, 222–3, 227–8
   damages, 221–3, 231
   exemption clauses, 126–7
   floodgates arguments, 227–8
   free will, 226, 229
   intention of the parties, 229
   international approach, 230
   irrationality of, 228–9
   legal complexity, 230
   litigation, extended, 228
   package holidays, 221–2, 226, 231
   promises, enforcement of gratuitous,
      227

reciprocal rights, lack of, 226
reform, 213–14, 230
reliance, justifiable, 229–30
restriction of contracting party's
   rights, 226–7
unjust enrichment, 229
variation of third party rights, 228
problem questions, answering, 335–6
product liability *see* manufacturers'
   liability
profits, loss of, 298
promises *see also* promissory estoppel
   binding, 1–2
   consideration, 66–8, 72–3, 89–91
   gratuitous, 1, 66, 89, 227
   offers open, to keep, 89
   privity of contract, 227
   sue, not to, 72–3
   written, 89
promissory estoppel
   consideration, 80–5, 88–9
   damages, 85
   enforcement of strict legal rights,
      inequity of, 83–4, 87
   future rights, destruction of, 84
   leases, 81–2, 92
   new rights, no creation of, 84–5, 88
   pre-existing contractual relationships,
      82, 90
   promises, existence of, 82
   reliance, 82–3, 90, 92
   tax, payment by instalments of, 83–4
   waiver, 85
prospectuses, 149

quality
   certainty, 45
   merchantable, 310–12
   mistake, 168
   sale of goods contracts, 109, 310–12,
      330
   satisfactory, 109, 310–12, 330
quantum meruit, 193, 237–8, 283, 286–8

rectification, 99, 177–8
redundancy, 103–4, 109
registered companies, 60
rehabilitation of offenders, 146
rejection, 15, 238, 301, 312–13

remedies *see also* damages, specific
    performance
  agreed by the parties, 293–4
  agreed sum, action for an, 282
  consumer protection, 316, 326
  equitable, 288–92
  extinction of, 294–7
  injunctions, 291–2, 295–6
  interests protected, 296–7
  minors, 56–7
  misrepresentation, 153–61
  practicalities, 297
  problems with, 296–7
  quantum meruit, 286–8
  restitution, 283–5, 297
  time limits, 294–6, 297
repairs or replacement, 326
repudiation, 112, 251–2, 253–4, 282
rescission, 153–6, 158–9, 161, 181
reserve, auctions without, 31–2
restitution, 56–7, 155, 283–5, 297
restraint of trade, 183–5, 195–6
restrictive covenants, 217–18, 226
restrictive trade agreements, 185–6
rewards, 11, 29, 40–1

sale of goods contracts, 308–14
  acceptance, 312
  advertising, 326
  breach, 312–13
  bulk goods, 314
  burden of proof, change in, 326
  business, in the course of a, 308–10
  conditions, 111
  consideration, total failure of, 309
  damages, 312
  descriptions, 309–10, 330
  display, goods on, 12–13
  examination of goods, 310, 313
  exclusion clauses, 129–30, 313, 327
  fitness for purpose, 311–12, 326
  implied terms, 129–30, 300, 308–13,
    325–7
  installation, incorrect, 326
  merchantable quality, 310–12
  mistake, 166
  passing of ownership, 313–14
  rejection, 312–13
  remedies, 312–13, 327

samples, 312, 327
satisfactory quality, 109, 310–12, 330
self-service, 12–13
title, 111, 309
unfair contract terms, 313, 327, 330
warranties, 111
sale of land
  acceptance, 37, 38
  damages, 34–5, 300–1
  exchange of contracts, 35–6
  formation of contracts, 63–4
  gazumping, 38
  inquiries, 35–6
  offers, 34–5, 37, 38
  problems with, 37–9
  rejection, 301
  restrictive covenants, 217–18, 226
  subject to contract, 35
  termination, agreements on, 256–7
  writing, 62–4
samples, 312, 327
self-service, 12–13
set-off, 217
settlements, agents by, 219
severance, 193, 237
sexual immorality, promoting, 188
silence, 19–20, 23, 25, 146, 302
social agreements, 48
solus agreements, 184
specific performance, 288–92
  damages, inadequacy of, 288–9
  employment contracts, 289, 292
  hardship to the defendant, 289,
    290
  injunctions, 292
  leases, 290
  mutuality, principle of, 291
  minors, 57
  personal service contracts, 289, 292
  third parties, 217
  time limits, 295–6
  unfair contracts, 289
  unjust enrichment, 288–9
  unsuitable for, contracts, 289–91
standard forms, 20–1, 129, 135–6,
  328
statutory corporations, 60
subject to contract, 35, 50
sue, promises not to, 72–3

supply of goods or services, 75–6,
    315–16, 330
sureties, family homes and, 202–8

tax, 83–4, 279–80
tenders, 32–4
termination, agreements on, 255–7
  accord and satisfaction, 256
  conditions subsequent, 257
  consideration, 256
  formalities, 256–7
  novation, 257
  sale of land, 256–7
terms *see also* express terms, implied
    terms, unfair contract terms
  certainty, 44–5
  conditions, breach of, 110–11, 114,
    231
  importance of, relative, 110–11
  innominate terms, 111–14
    breach of, 112–13
    uncertainty of, 113–14
  misrepresentation, 159
  mistake, 171
  repudiation, 112
  warranties, breach of, 111, 114, 231
third parties, 211–31 *see also* privity of
    contract
  agency, 218–20
  assignment, 220
  benefit, contract purports to confer a,
    215–16
  bills of exchange, 218
  cheques, 221
  collateral contracts, 224–5, 229–30
  consideration, 68, 73
  constructive trusts, 225–6
  damages, 217, 221–3, 231
  defences, 217
  enforcement, 217
  exceptions, 218–55
  exclusion clauses, 126–7, 224–5
  existing duties, performance of,
    78–80, 90
  express provisions in contract, 215
  identification of, 216
  insurance, 217
  misrepresentation, 155
  negotiability, 221

novation, 221
restrictive covenants, 217–18, 226
set-off, 217
specific performance, 217
statutory rights, 215–18
undue influence, 203–7
variations, consent to, 216
threats, 199–200
tickets, 13–14, 118–20, 140–1
time limits, 294–6, 297
  essence, of the, 238–9, 304
  performance, 238–9, 261, 304
  mental incapacity, 295
  specific performance, 295–6
trade descriptions, 321–2
trade usage, 110
tying, 185

ultra vires, 60
undue influence, 200–10
  actual, 200–1, 208, 259
  bargaining power, inequality of,
    207–8, 209
  constructive notice, 204–6
  family homes, sureties and, 202–8
  fiduciary relationship, 201–2, 208,
    210, 260
  independent legal advice, 205–7
  inquiry, placed on, 204–5
  manifest disadvantage, 201–3, 208,
    260
  presumed, 201–2, 208, 209–10,
    259–60
  sureties, family homes and, 202–8
  third parties, 203–7
  threats, 200
unfair contract terms, 4, 117–41
  bargaining power, inequality of,
    135–6, 328
  consumers, 132–3, 138, 141, 327
  core terms, 133–4
  criminal offences, 313
  dangerous goods, 138
  definition, 134–5
  EC law, 117, 132
  enforcement, 135–8
  exemption clauses, 117–32, 138
  good faith, 134–5
  guarantees, 317

indicative list of terms, 134
negligence, 124–5
product liability, 138
reasonableness, 128, 130–2, 138,
   141
sale of goods contracts, 313, 327,
   330
standard contracts, 135–6, 328
Unfair Contracts Terms Unit, 136–7
unilateral contracts
   acceptance, 20, 25
   consideration, 89
   mistake, 170–6, 178, 180–1
   offer, 9, 10, 18, 41, 329
   tenders, 33
unjust enrichment, 228–9, 229
unsolicited goods, 322–3
utmost good faith, 145–6

vitiating factors *see* duress, illegality,
   misrepresentation, mistake,
   undue influence

wagering contracts, 186–7
waiver, 80, 85, 88–9
warranties, 111, 114, 231, 252, 303–4
works and materials, contracts for, 315
writing
   consideration, 89
   express terms, 97–102
   formation of contracts, 63–4
   guarantees, 64
   partial, 99–100
   promises, 89
   sale of land, 62–4

young people *see* minors